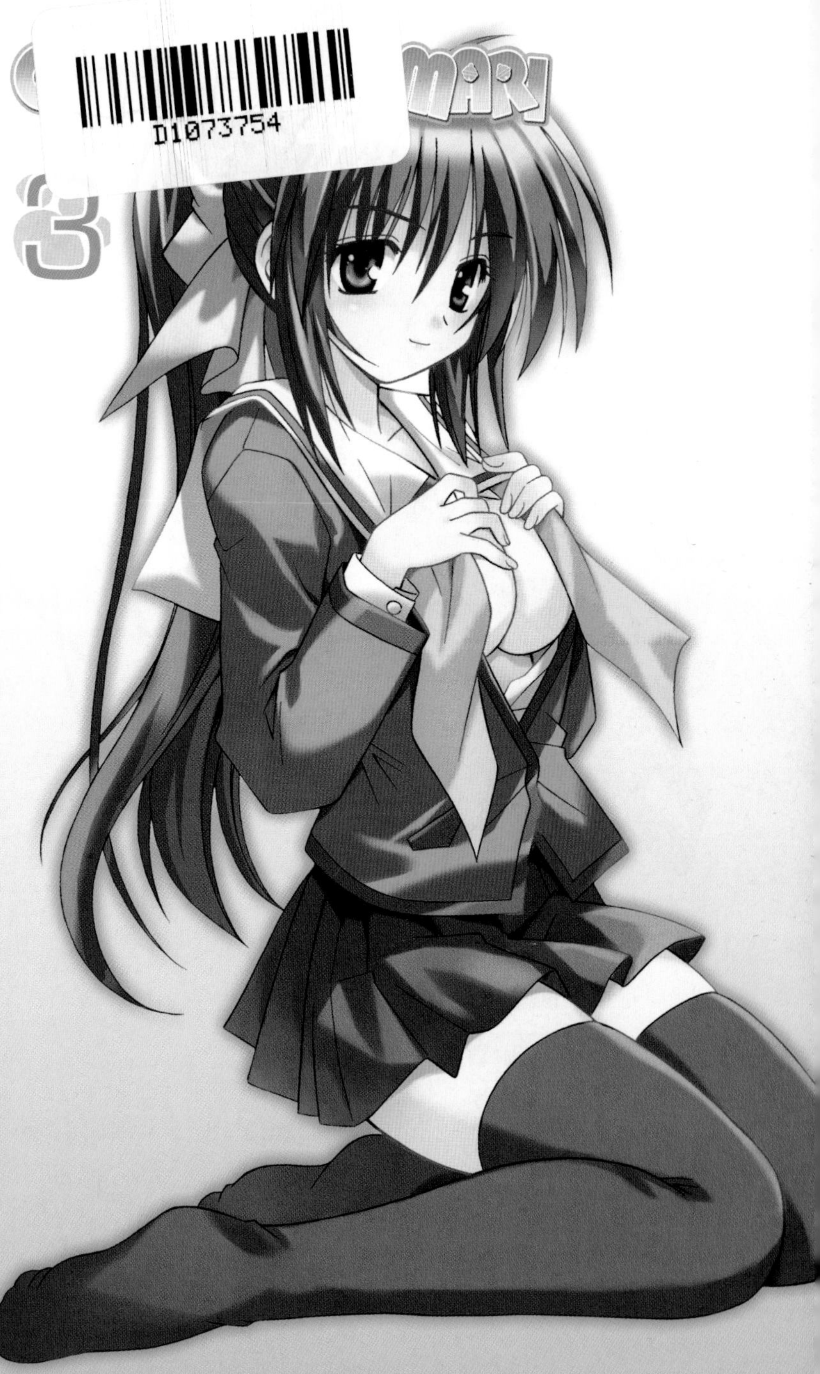
3

CONTENTS

MENAGERIE 13 THE CAT OF MEMORY & SILENCE P 005

MENAGERIE 14 CALM HEART OF THE HARRIED CAT P 033

MENAGERIE 15 THE BOASTFUL COUNTER CAT P 057

MENAGERIE 16 KISS X CAT X <KISS> P 081

MENAGERIE 17 THE CAT'S FEELINGS AND THE WITCH'S MELANCHOLY P 109

MENAGERIE 18 AND SO THE CAT FACES OFF P 133

BONUS COMICS P 158

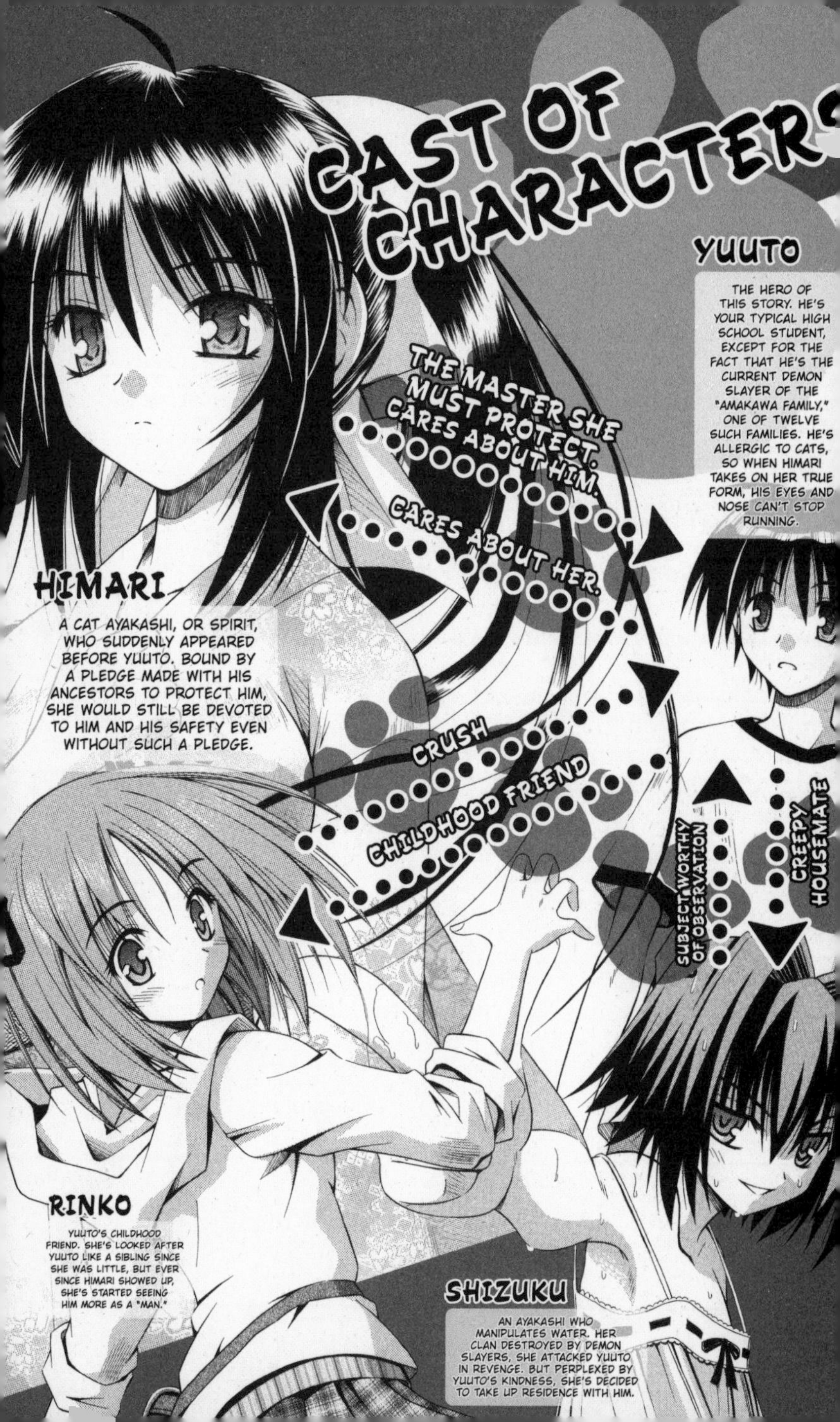
CAST OF CHARACTERS
YUUTO
THE HERO OF THIS STORY. HE'S YOUR TYPICAL HIGH SCHOOL STUDENT, EXCEPT FOR THE FACT THAT HE'S THE CURRENT DEMON SLAYER OF THE "AMAKAWA FAMILY," ONE OF TWELVE SUCH FAMILIES. HE'S ALLERGIC TO CATS, SO WHEN HIMARI TAKES ON HER TRUE FORM, HIS EYES AND NOSE CAN'T STOP RUNNING.
THE MASTER SHE MUST PROTECT. CARES ABOUT HIM.
CARES ABOUT HER.
HIMARI
A CAT AYAKASHI, OR SPIRIT, WHO SUDDENLY APPEARED BEFORE YUUTO. BOUND BY A PLEDGE MADE WITH HIS ANCESTORS TO PROTECT HIM, SHE WOULD STILL BE DEVOTED TO HIM AND HIS SAFETY EVEN WITHOUT SUCH A PLEDGE.
CRUSH
CHILDHOOD FRIEND
CREEPY HOUSEMATE
SUBJECT WORTHY OF OBSERVATION
RINKO
YUUTO'S CHILDHOOD FRIEND. SHE'S LOOKED AFTER YUUTO LIKE A SIBLING SINCE SHE WAS LITTLE, BUT EVER SINCE HIMARI SHOWED UP, SHE'S STARTED SEEING HIM MORE AS A "MAN."
SHIZUKU
AN AYAKASHI WHO MANIPULATES WATER. HER CLAN DESTROYED BY DEMON SLAYERS, SHE ATTACKED YUUTO IN REVENGE. BUT PERPLEXED BY YUUTO'S KINDNESS, SHE'S DECIDED TO TAKE UP RESIDENCE WITH HIM.

❀THE❀STORY❀SO❀FAR❀

"I'M GOING TO PROTECT MY MASTER!"

SO PROCLAIMS THE CAT AYAKASHI, HIMARI, TO YUUTO AMAKAWA, A HIGH SCHOOL STUDENT WITH SEVERE ALLERGIES TO CATS, WHEN SHE SUDDENLY APPEARS BEFORE HIM.

SHE'S BEEN GIVEN THE DUTY OF PROTECTING YUUTO, THANKS TO A PLEDGE MADE LONG AGO. BUT YUUTO ALSO HAS TO DEAL WITH HIS NEIGHBOR AND CHILDHOOD FRIEND, RINKO, AS WELL AS THE AYAKASHI SHIZUKU, WHO WAS SWAYED BY YUUTO'S KINDNESS AND DECIDED TO LIVE WITH HIM. WITH ALL THESE GIRLS IN HIS LIFE, HIS DAYS QUICKLY BECOME OFF-THE-WALL AND FULL OF FUN, WITH NO END OF SUR-PRISES. HOWEVER, HIMARI HAS ONE MAJOR BONE TO PICK—

"FORGETTING UTTERLY AND COMPLETELY THE MEMORIES OF HIS YOUTH AND THOSE THAT HE SHARED WITH ME, AND SHOWING NO INDICATION OF RECALLING THEM ANY TIME SOON IS SOME-THING I SIMPLY CANNOT TOLERATE!!"

GROWING IMPATIENT, HIMARI BRINGS YUUTO TO NOIHARA, WHERE HE WAS BORN AND RAISED.

BUT WHAT AWAITS THEM IS AN AYAKASHI DUO WITH A PLAN TO WIPE OUT ALL DEMON SLAYERS!

HIMARI IS IN OVER HER HEAD WHEN SHE'S PULLED INTO A TWO-ON-ONE BATTLE, SO YUUTO THROWS HIMSELF IN TO SAVE HER...ONLY TO END UP TAKING AN ATTACK SQUARE IN THE BACK.

SEEING THE HURT AND UNCONSCIOUS YUUTO, HIMARI LOSES HER MIND AND GOES ON A RAMPAGE.

"DIE. DIE. DIE!!"

HIMARI SWINGS HER BLADE ABOUT IN A FRENZY, READY TO KILL THE OFFENDING AYAKASHI.

BUT THE DEMON-SLAYER BLOOD THAT WAS ASLEEP IN YUUTO UNTIL THAT POINT SUDDENLY AWAKENS, AND HE STOPS HER BLADE COLD.

AFTER HIMARI'S BATTLE WITH THE AYAKASHI ENDS IN A DRAW AND WITH ALL PARTIES INJURED...

"I DON'T WANT HIMARI TO BECOME SOMEONE WHO ENJOYS FIGHTING."

GIVING THE UNCONSCIOUS HIMARI A SHOULDER TO LEAN ON, YUUTO MAKES THIS EARNEST WISH...

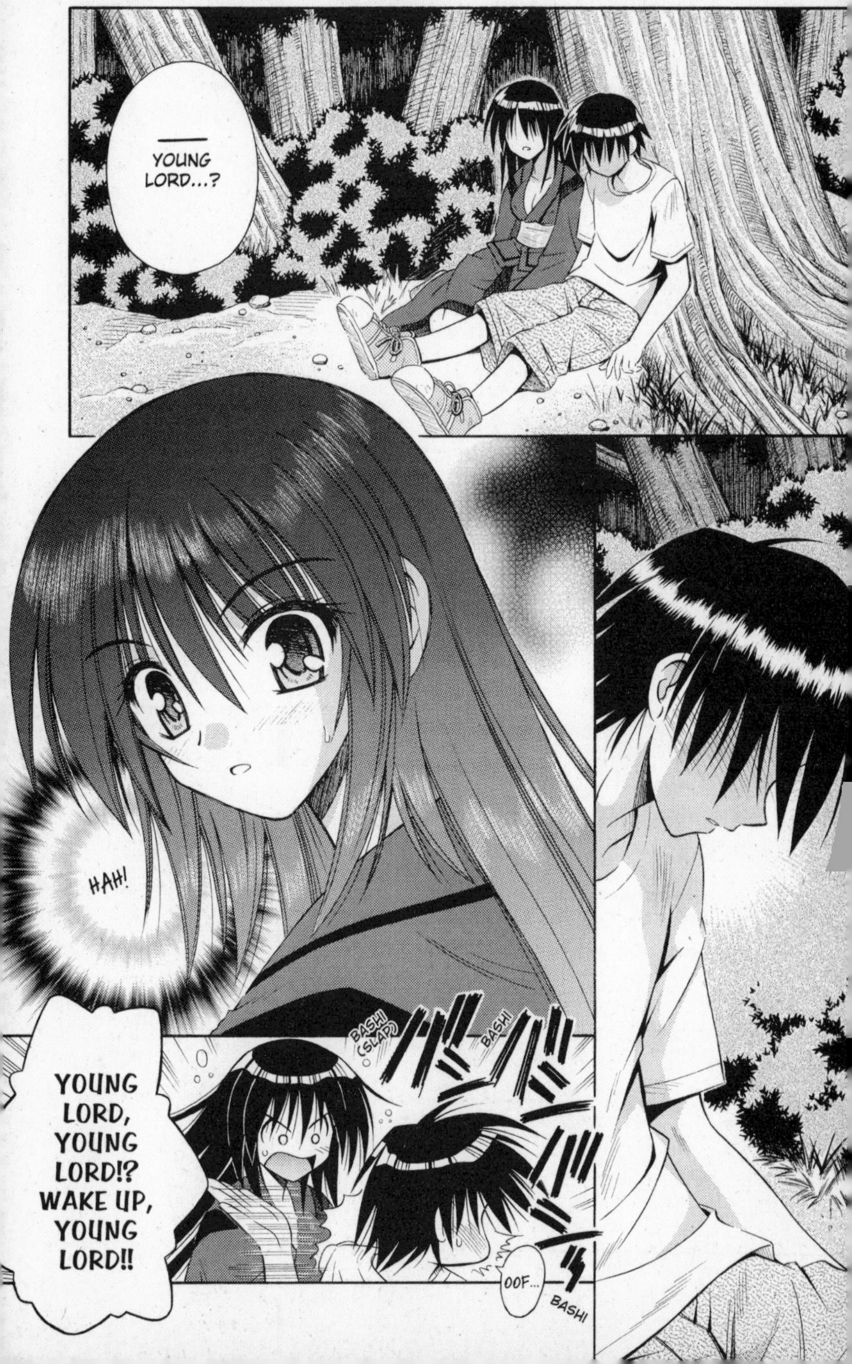
YOUNG LORD...?
HAH!
BASHI
BASHI (SLAP)
YOUNG LORD, YOUNG LORD!? WAKE UP, YOUNG LORD!!
OOF...
BASHI

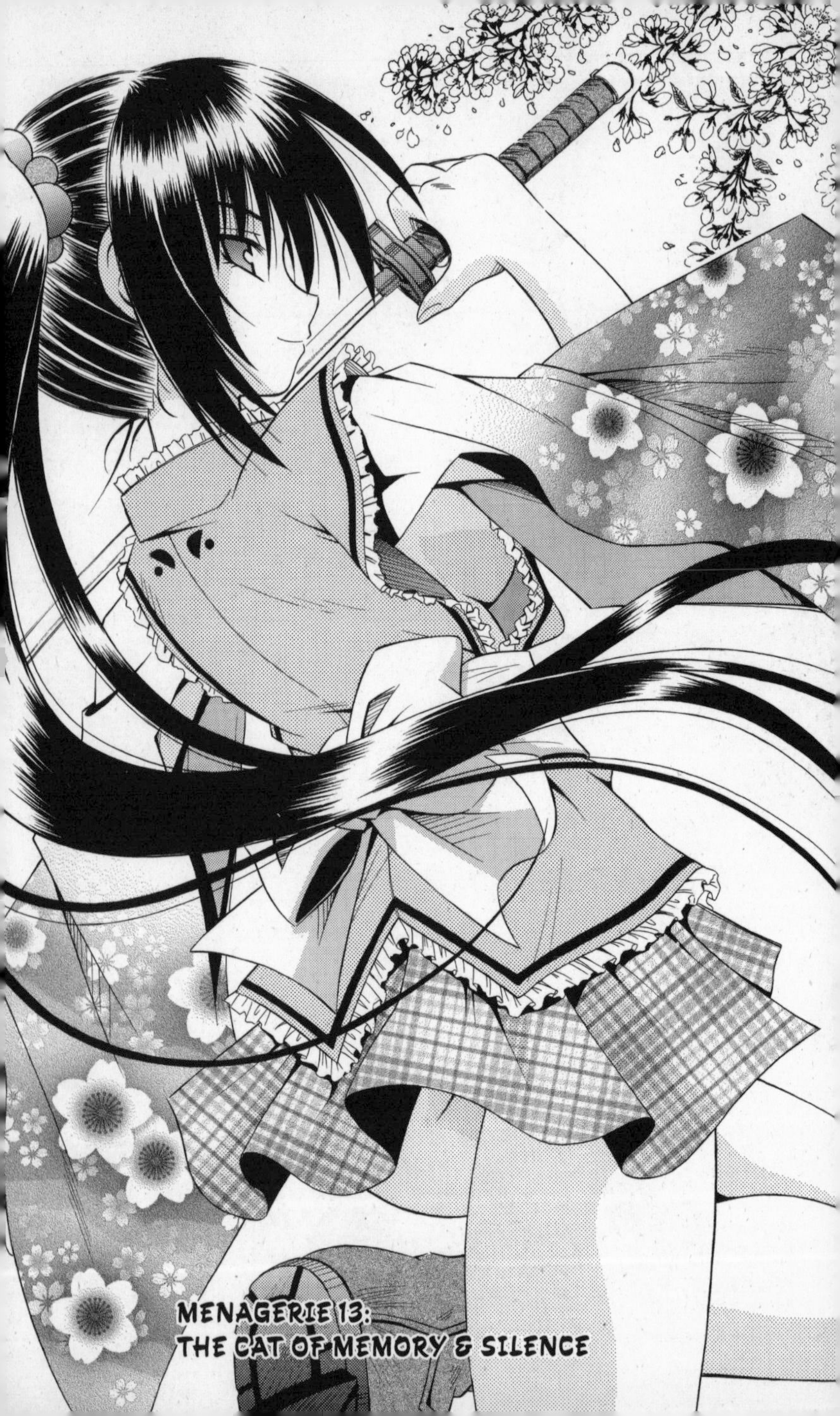

MENAGERIE 13: THE CAT OF MEMORY & SILENCE

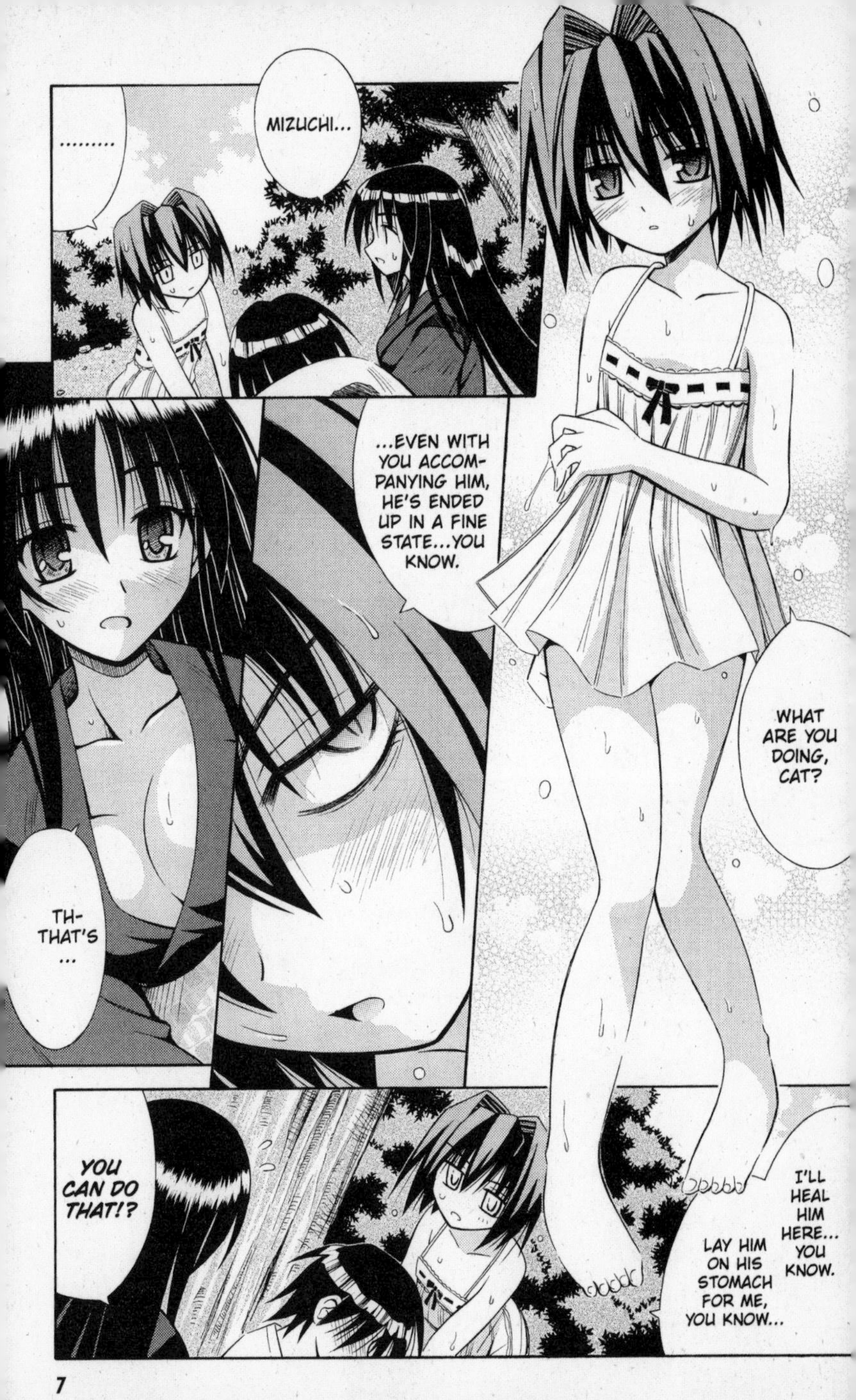

MIZUCHI...
....
...EVEN WITH YOU ACCOMPANYING HIM, HE'S ENDED UP IN A FINE STATE...YOU KNOW.
WHAT ARE YOU DOING, CAT?
TH-THAT'S ...
I'LL HEAL HIM HERE... YOU KNOW.
LAY HIM ON HIS STOMACH FOR ME, YOU KNOW...
YOU CAN DO THAT!?

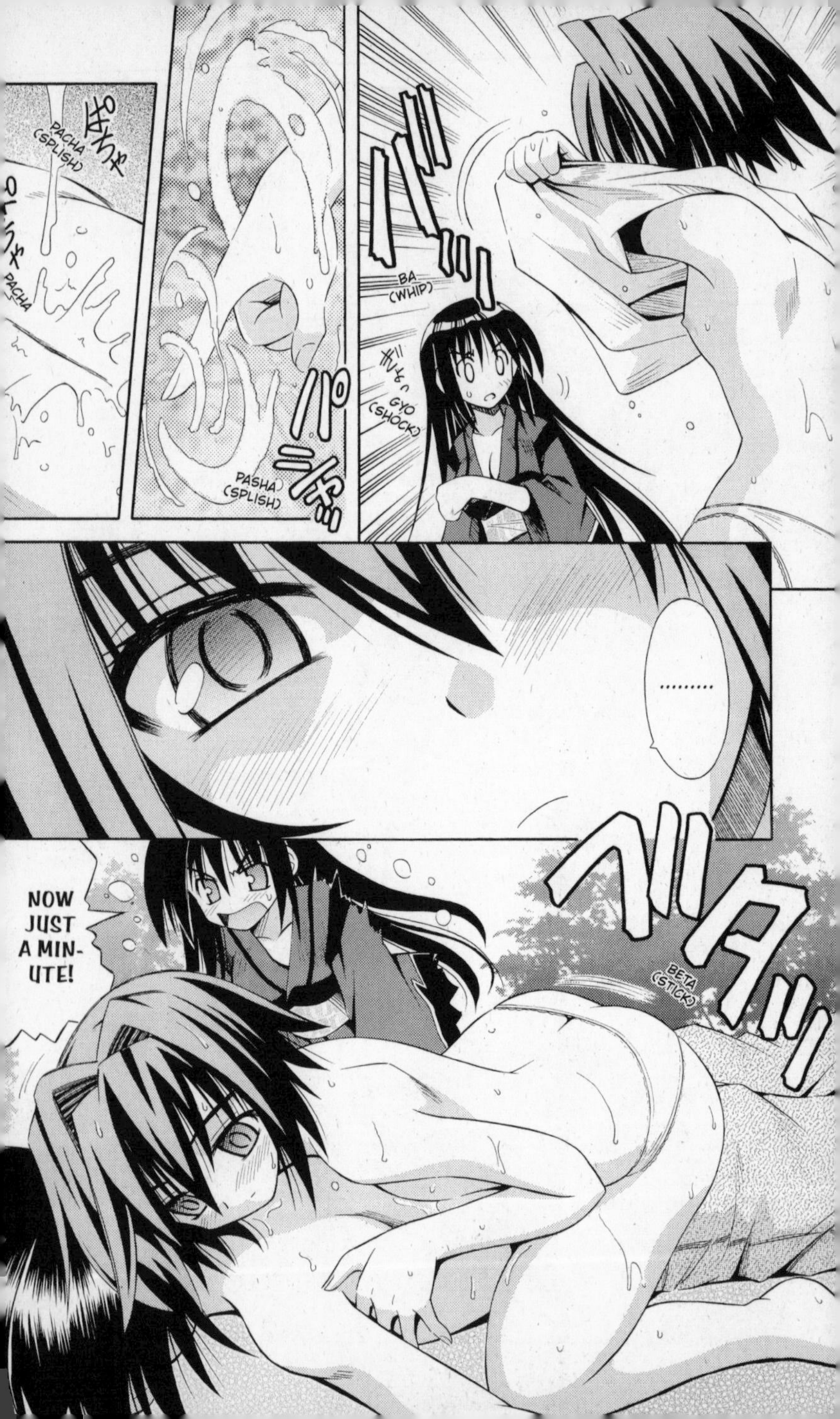
BA (WHIP)
GYO (SHOCK)
PASHA (SPLISH)
PACHA (SPLISH)
PACHA
....
NOW JUST A MIN-UTE!
BETA (STICK)

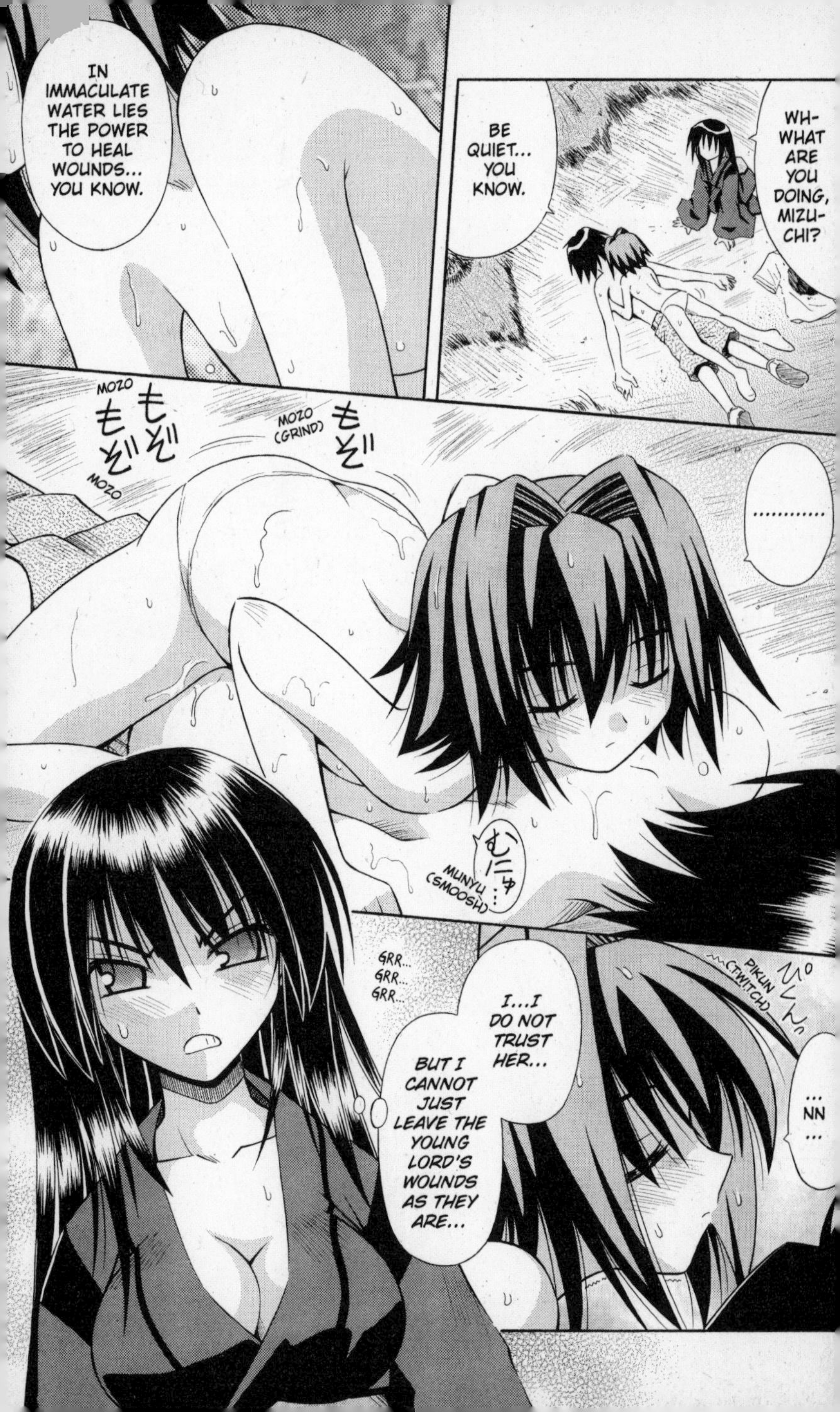
WH-WHAT ARE YOU DOING, MIZU-CHI?
BE QUIET... YOU KNOW.
IN IMMACULATE WATER LIES THE POWER TO HEAL WOUNDS... YOU KNOW.
....
もぞ
MOZO (GRIND)
もぞもぞ
MOZO
MOZO
むにゅ…
MUNYU (SMOOSH)
ぴくん
PIKUN (TWITCH)
...NN...
I...I DO NOT TRUST HER...
BUT I CANNOT JUST LEAVE THE YOUNG LORD'S WOUNDS AS THEY ARE...
GRR... GRR... GRR...

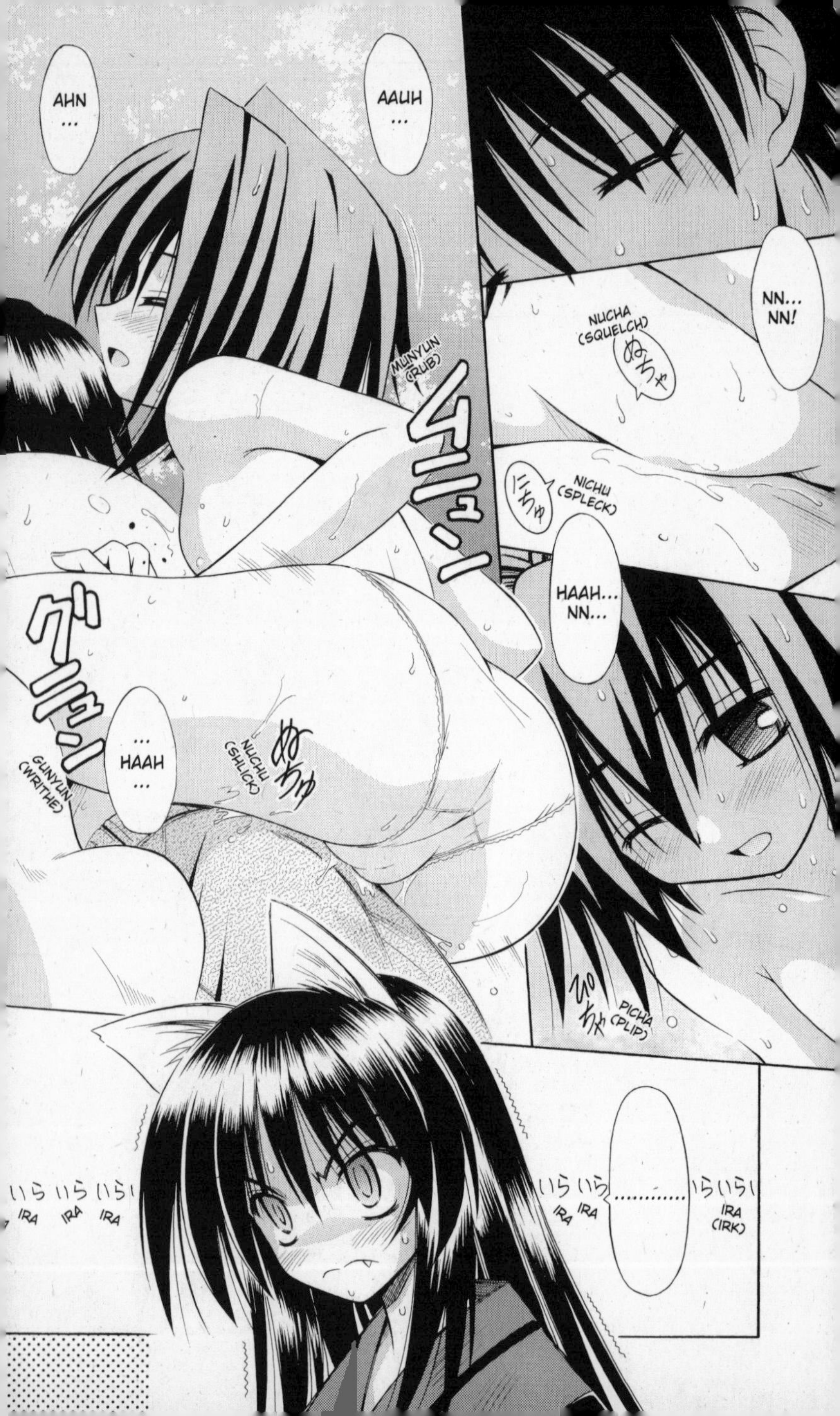

NN... NN!
ぬちゃ
NUCHA (SQUELCH)
にちゅ
NICHU (SPLECK)
HAAH... NN...
ぴちゃ
PICHA (PLIP)
AAUH ...
AHN ...
ムニュン
MUNYUN (RUB)
ぬちゅ
NUCHU (SHLICK)
... HAAH ...
グニュン
GUNYUN (WRITHE)
いらいら
IRA (IRK)
....
いら いら
IRA IRA
いら いら いら
IRA IRA IRA

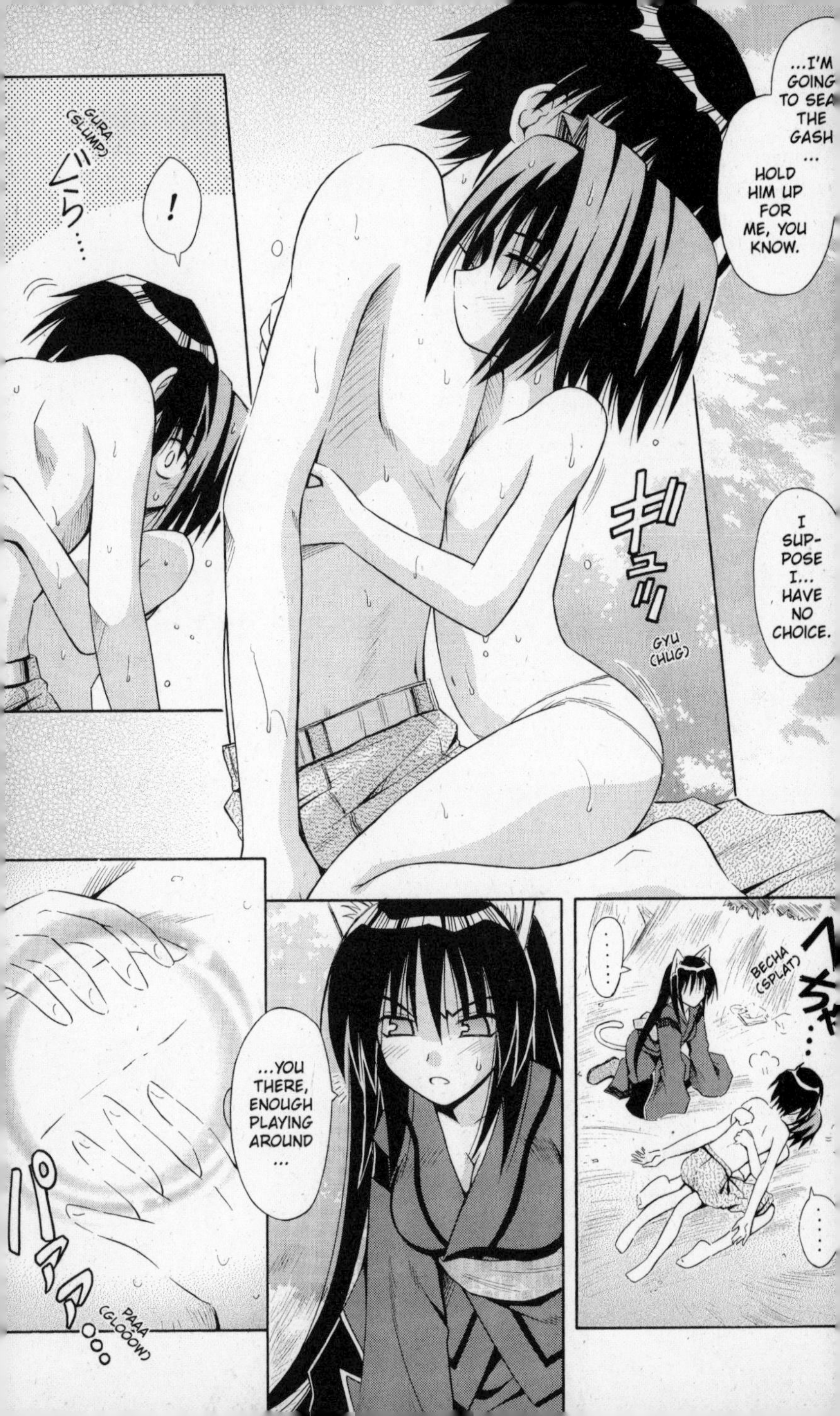
...I'M GOING TO SEA THE GASH ... HOLD HIM UP FOR ME, YOU KNOW.
ギュッ
GYU (HUG)
I SUP-POSE I... HAVE NO CHOICE.
GURA (SLUMP)
ぐら...
!
......
べちゃ...
BECHA (SPLAT)
......
...YOU THERE, ENOUGH PLAYING AROUND ...
パァーー
PAAA (GLOOOW)
ooo

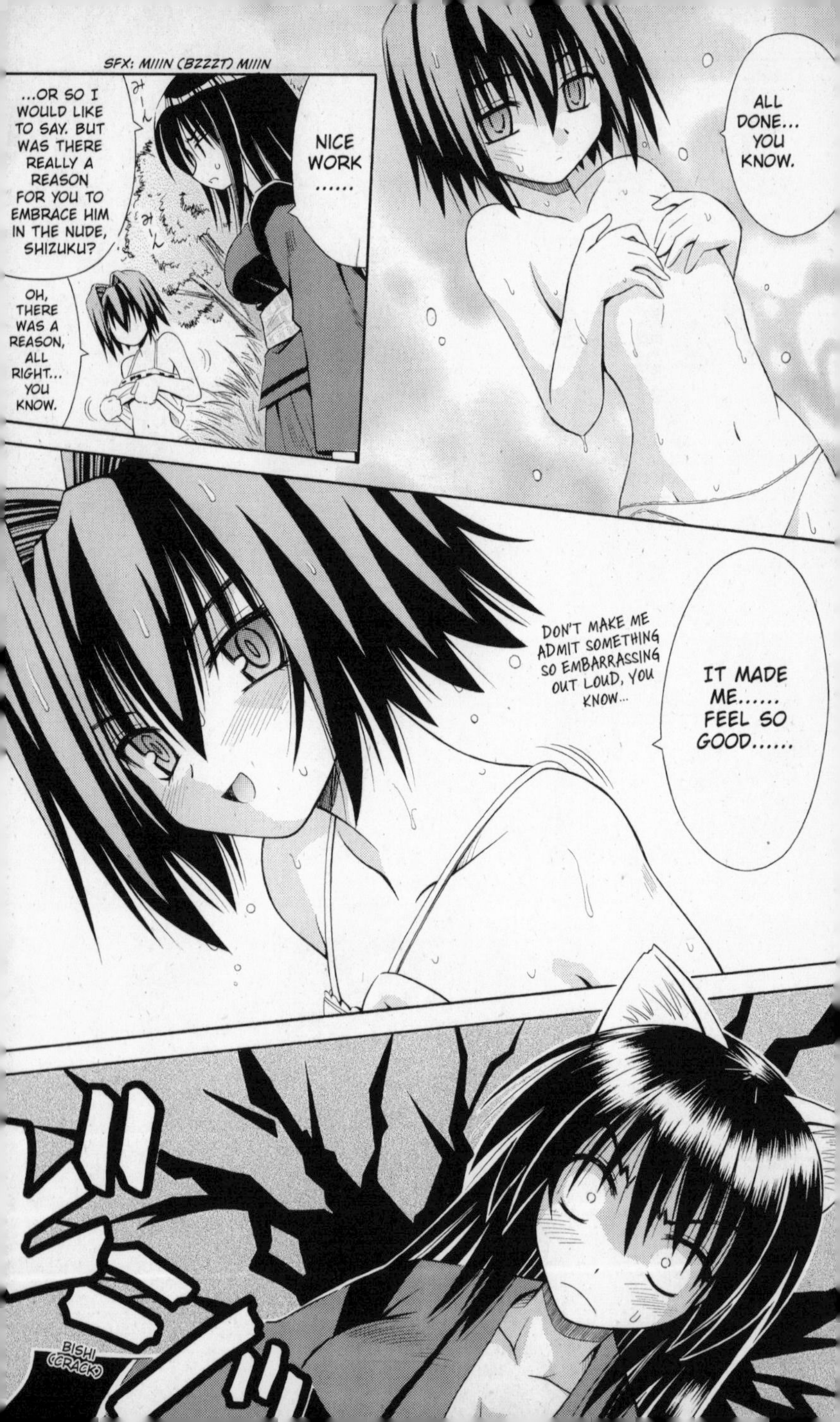
ALL DONE... YOU KNOW.
SFX: MIIIN (BZZZT) MIIIN
みーん
NICE WORK ......
...OR SO I WOULD LIKE TO SAY. BUT WAS THERE REALLY A REASON FOR YOU TO EMBRACE HIM IN THE NUDE, SHIZUKU?
OH, THERE WAS A REASON, ALL RIGHT... YOU KNOW.
IT MADE ME...... FEEL SO GOOD......
DON'T MAKE ME ADMIT SOMETHING SO EMBARRASSING OUT LOUD, YOU KNOW...
BISHI (CRACK)

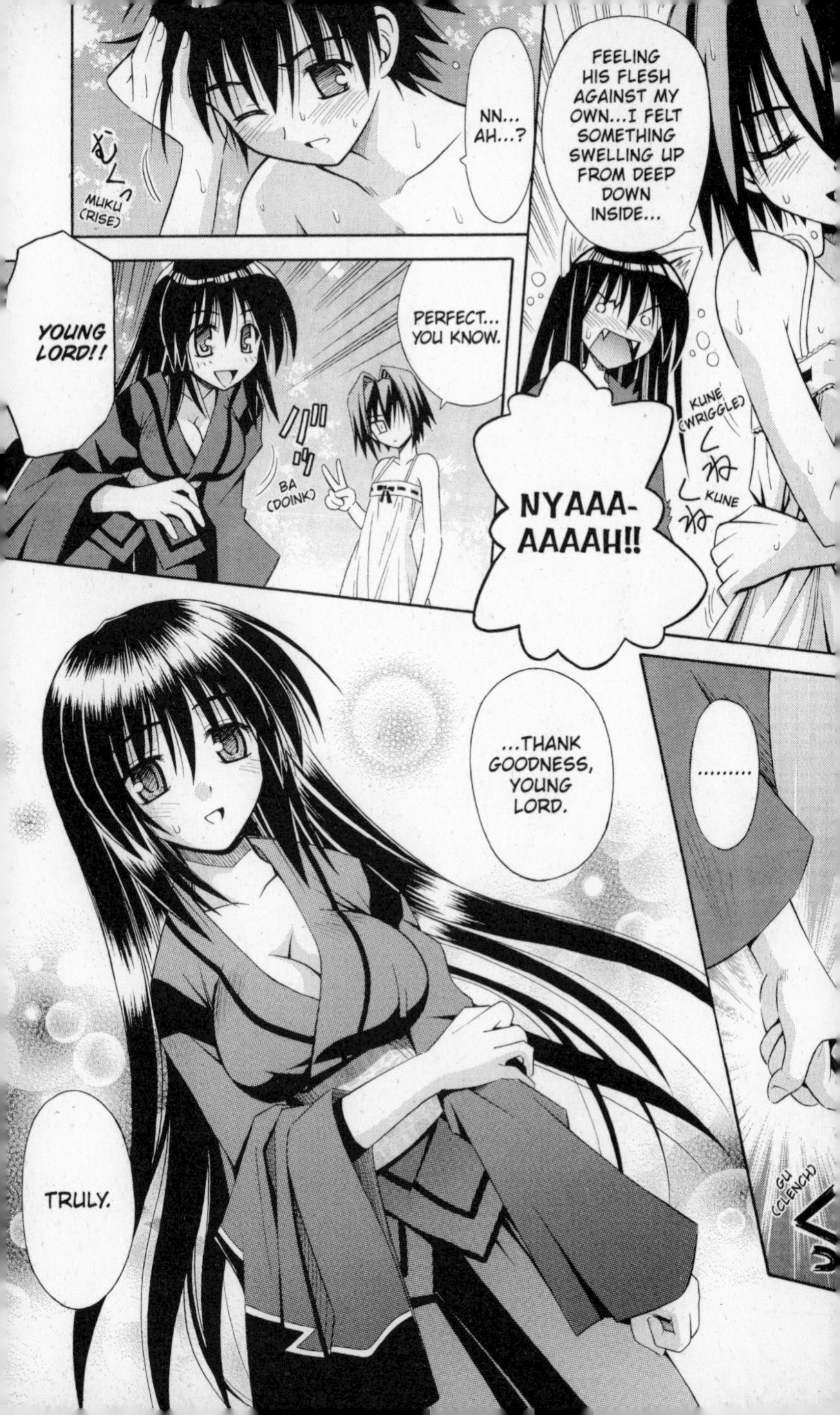
FEELING HIS FLESH AGAINST MY OWN...I FELT SOMETHING SWELLING UP FROM DEEP DOWN INSIDE...
KUNE (WRIGGLE) KUNE
NYAAA-AAAAH!!
NN... AH...?
MUKU (RISE)
PERFECT... YOU KNOW.
YOUNG LORD!!
BA (DOINK)
....
GU (CLENCH)
...THANK GOODNESS, YOUNG LORD.
TRULY.

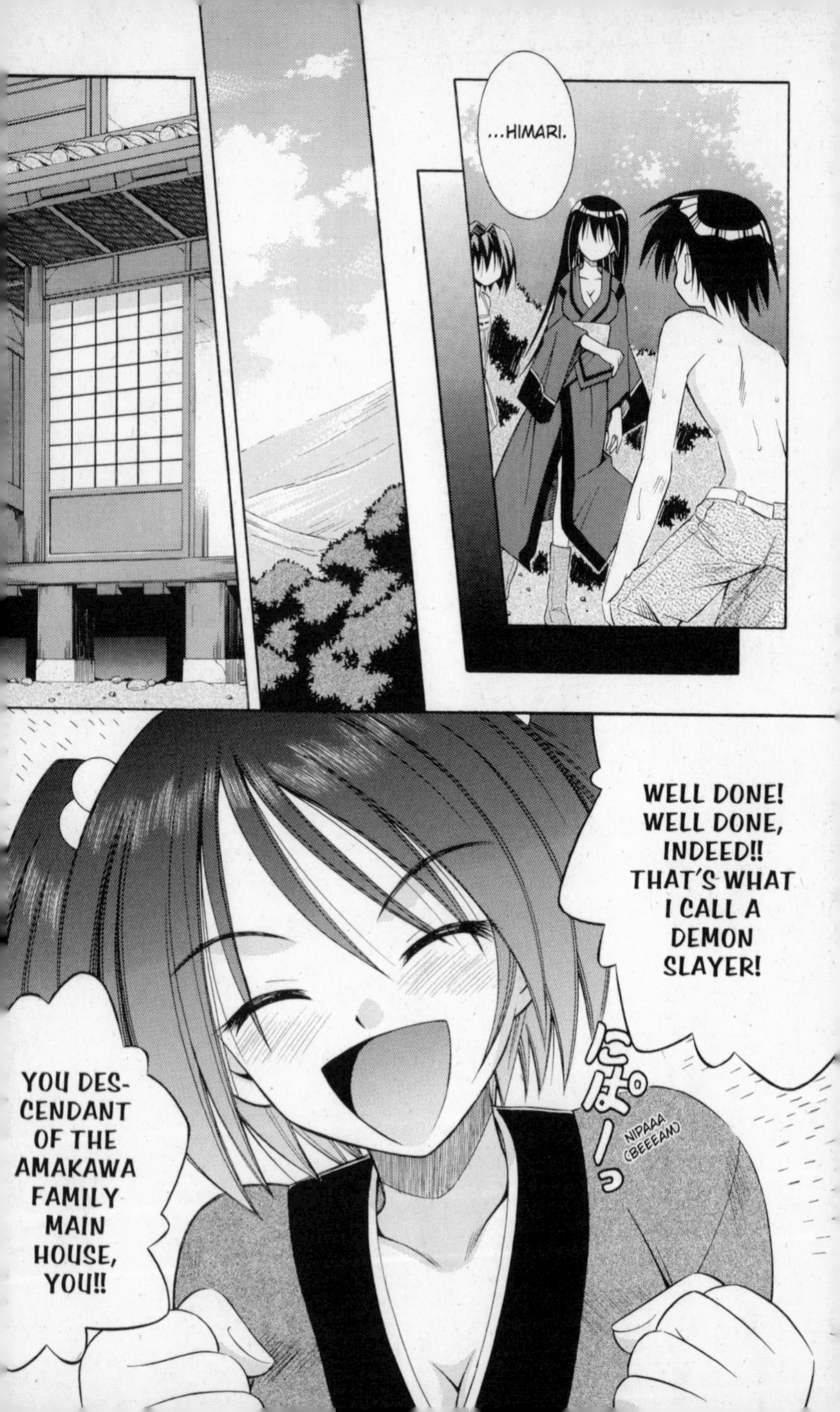
...HIMARI.
WELL DONE! WELL DONE, INDEED!! THAT'S WHAT I CALL A DEMON SLAYER!
にぱーっ
NIPAAA (BEEEAM)
YOU DES-CENDANT OF THE AMAKAWA FAMILY MAIN HOUSE, YOU!!

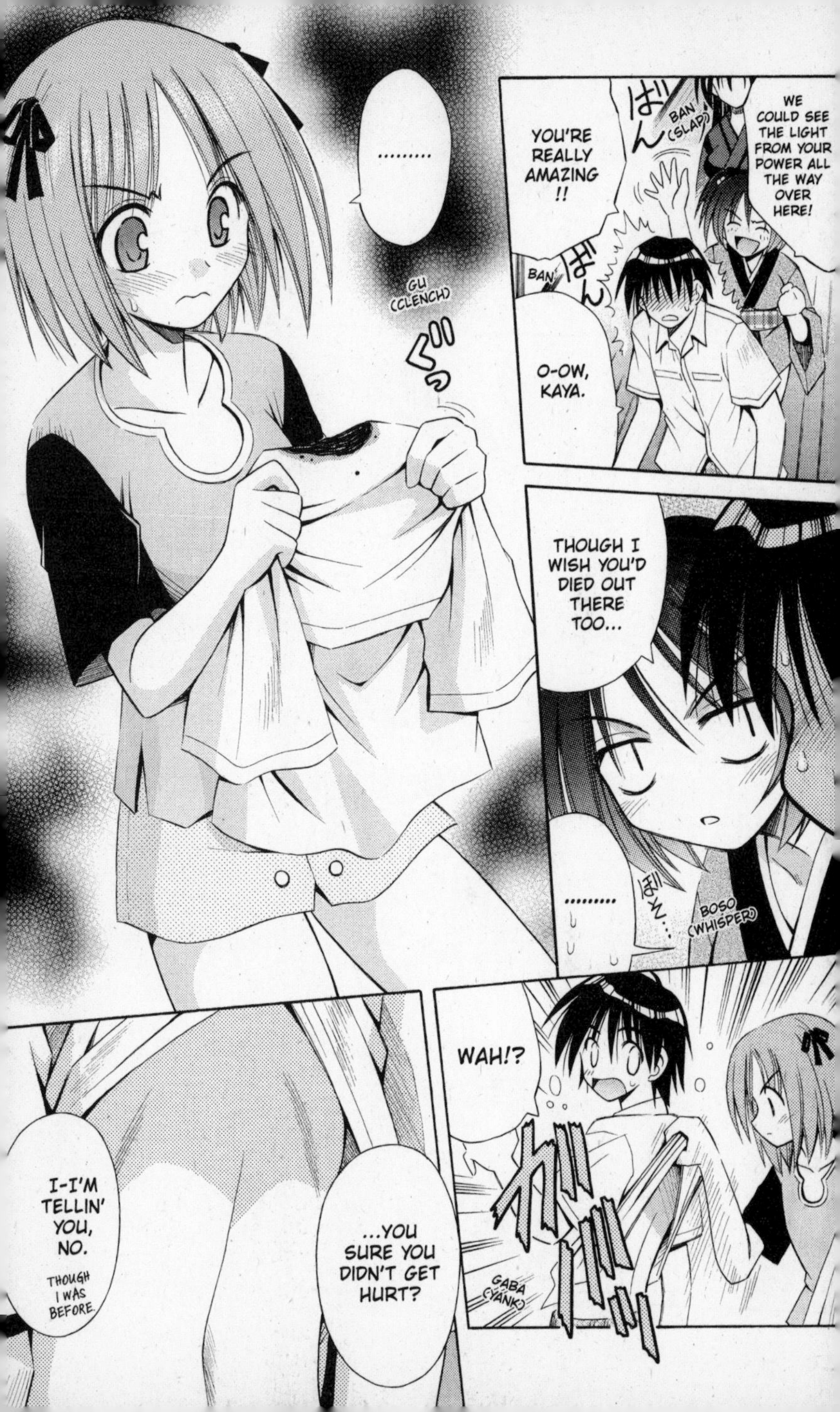

WE COULD SEE THE LIGHT FROM YOUR POWER ALL THE WAY OVER HERE!
ばん
BAN (SLAP)
YOU'RE REALLY AMAZING !!
BAN
O-OW, KAYA.
THOUGH I WISH YOU'D DIED OUT THERE TOO...
BOSO (WHISPER)
....
....
GU (CLENCH)
ぐっ
WAH!?
GABA (YANK)
...YOU SURE YOU DIDN'T GET HURT?
I-I'M TELLIN' YOU, NO.
THOUGH I WAS BEFORE.

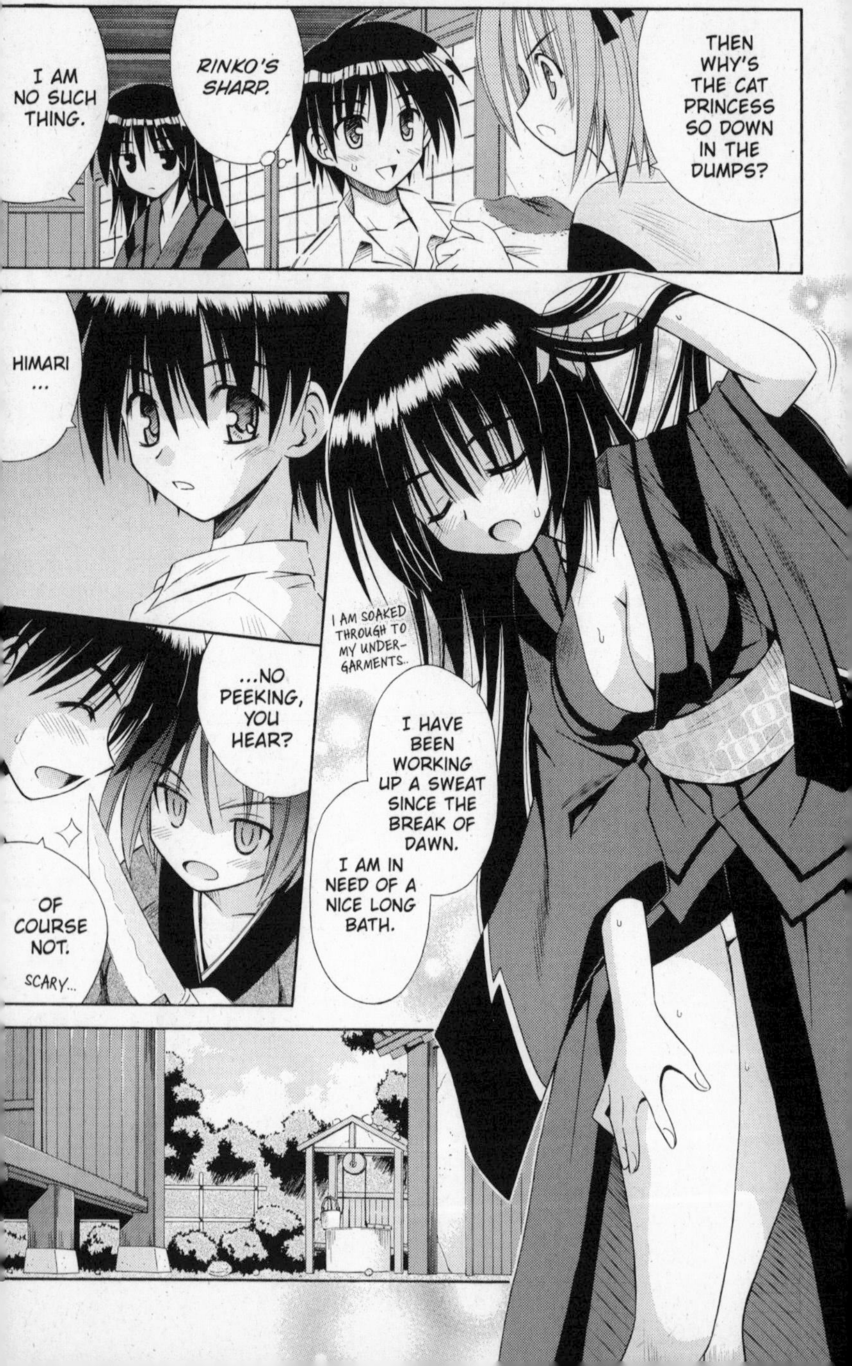
THEN WHY'S THE CAT PRINCESS SO DOWN IN THE DUMPS?
RINKO'S SHARP.
I AM NO SUCH THING.
I AM SOAKED THROUGH TO MY UNDER-GARMENTS..
I HAVE BEEN WORKING UP A SWEAT SINCE THE BREAK OF DAWN.
I AM IN NEED OF A NICE LONG BATH.
HIMARI ...
...NO PEEKING, YOU HEAR?
OF COURSE NOT.
SCARY...

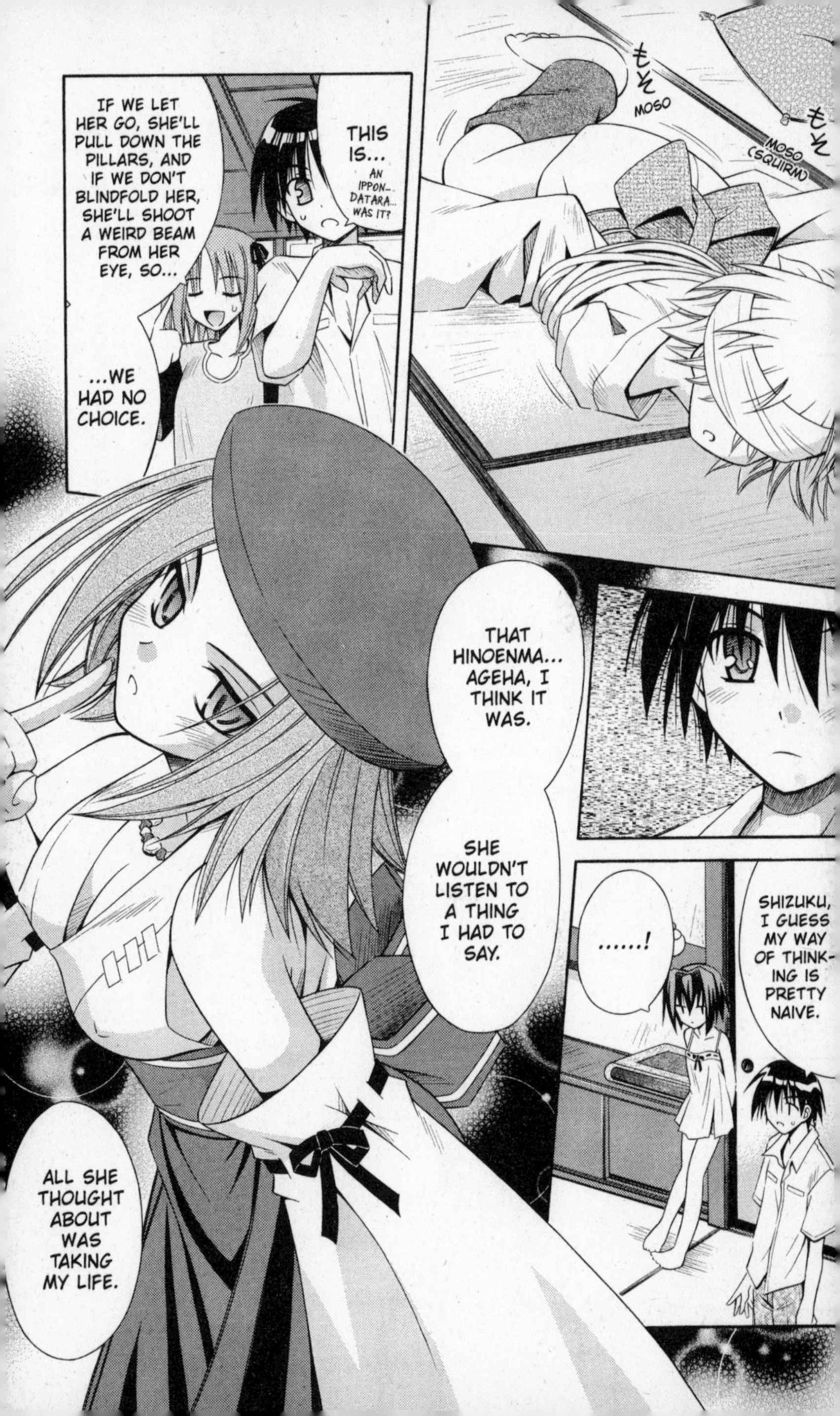
もそ
MOSO
もそ
MOSO (SQUIRM)
THIS IS...
AN IPPON-DATARA... WAS IT?
IF WE LET HER GO, SHE'LL PULL DOWN THE PILLARS, AND IF WE DON'T BLINDFOLD HER, SHE'LL SHOOT A WEIRD BEAM FROM HER EYE, SO...
...WE HAD NO CHOICE.
SHIZUKU, I GUESS MY WAY OF THINK-ING IS PRETTY NAIVE.
......!
THAT HINOENMA... AGEHA, I THINK IT WAS.
SHE WOULDN'T LISTEN TO A THING I HAD TO SAY.
ALL SHE THOUGHT ABOUT WAS TAKING MY LIFE.

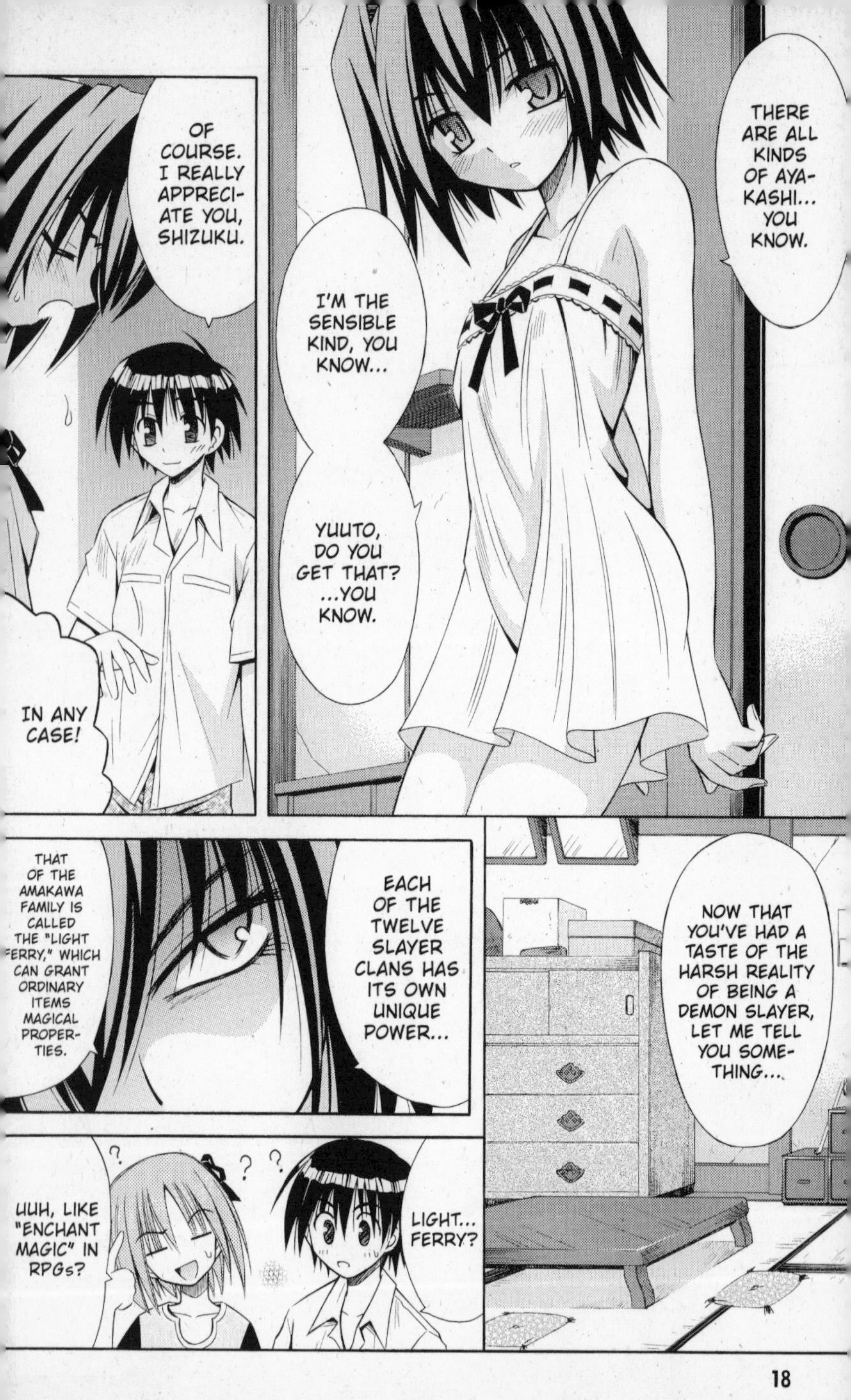
THERE ARE ALL KINDS OF AYA-KASHI... YOU KNOW.
I'M THE SENSIBLE KIND, YOU KNOW...
YUUTO, DO YOU GET THAT? ...YOU KNOW.
OF COURSE. I REALLY APPRECI-ATE YOU, SHIZUKU.
IN ANY CASE!
NOW THAT YOU'VE HAD A TASTE OF THE HARSH REALITY OF BEING A DEMON SLAYER, LET ME TELL YOU SOME-THING...
EACH OF THE TWELVE SLAYER CLANS HAS ITS OWN UNIQUE POWER...
THAT OF THE AMAKAWA FAMILY IS CALLED THE "LIGHT FERRY," WHICH CAN GRANT ORDINARY ITEMS MAGICAL PROPER-TIES.
LIGHT... FERRY?
UUH, LIKE "ENCHANT MAGIC" IN RPGs?

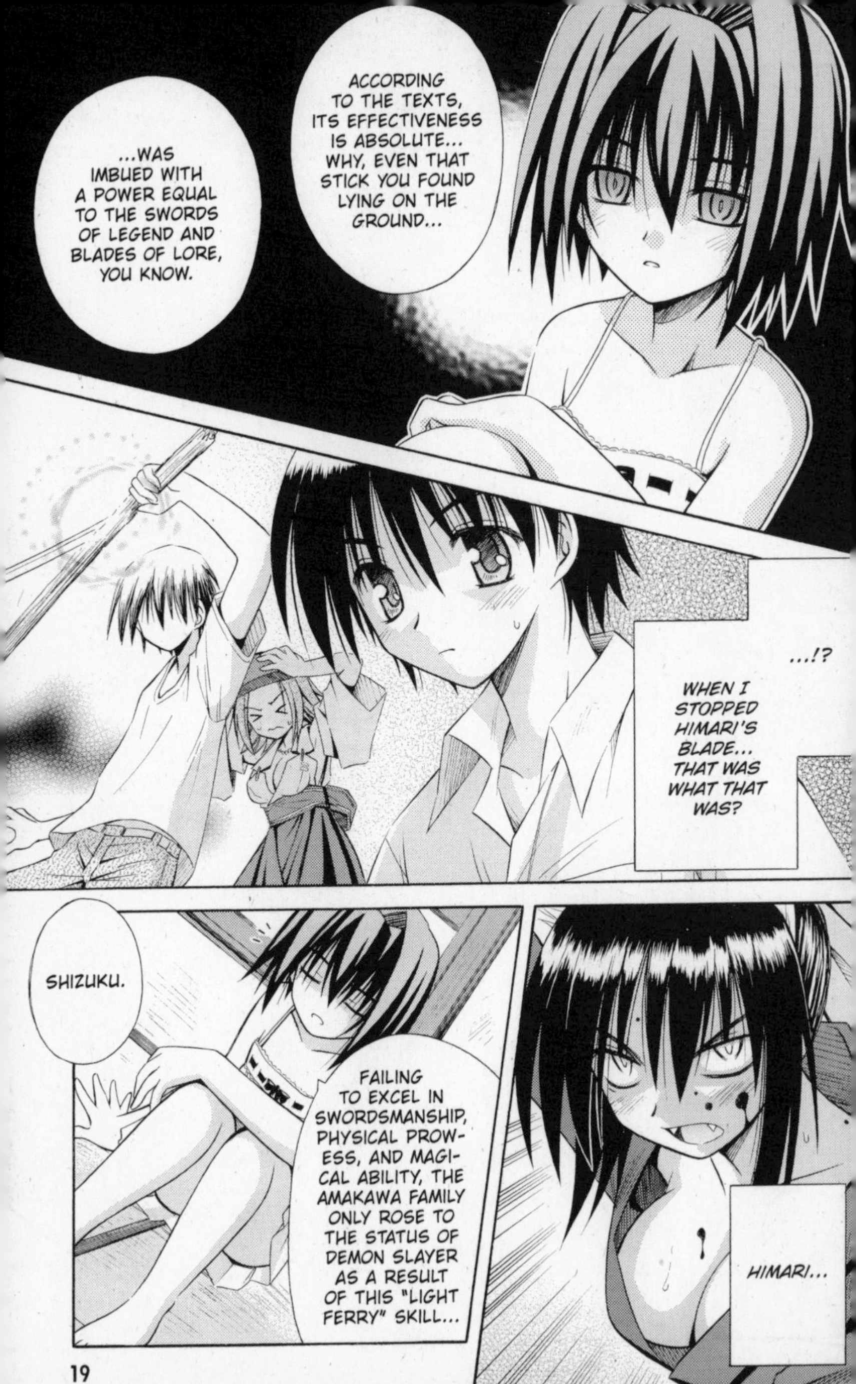
ACCORDING TO THE TEXTS, ITS EFFECTIVENESS IS ABSOLUTE... WHY, EVEN THAT STICK YOU FOUND LYING ON THE GROUND...
...WAS IMBUED WITH A POWER EQUAL TO THE SWORDS OF LEGEND AND BLADES OF LORE, YOU KNOW.
...!?
WHEN I STOPPED HIMARI'S BLADE... THAT WAS WHAT THAT WAS?
HIMARI...
SHIZUKU.
FAILING TO EXCEL IN SWORDSMANSHIP, PHYSICAL PROW-ESS, AND MAGI-CAL ABILITY, THE AMAKAWA FAMILY ONLY ROSE TO THE STATUS OF DEMON SLAYER AS A RESULT OF THIS "LIGHT FERRY" SKILL...

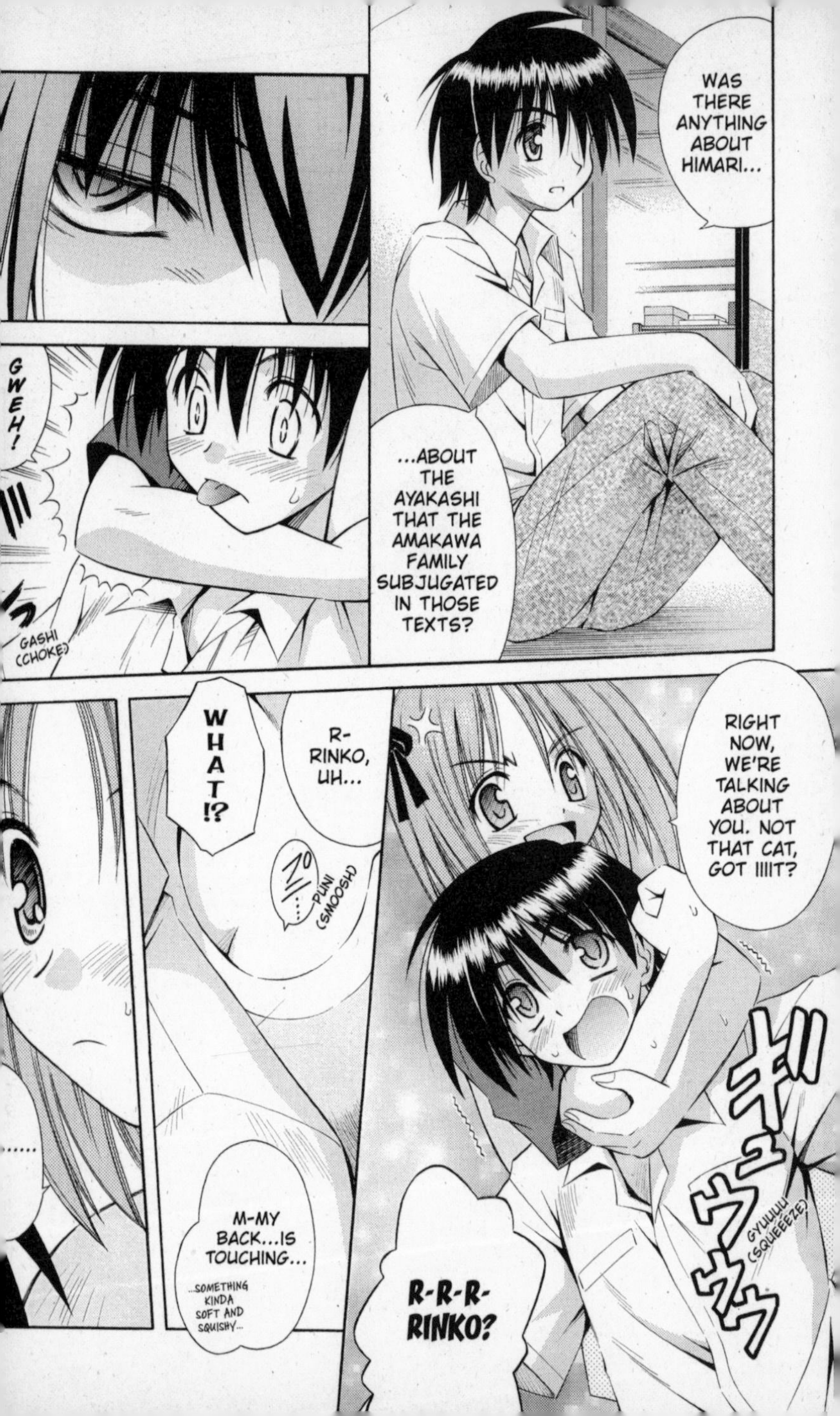
WAS THERE ANYTHING ABOUT HIMARI...
...ABOUT THE AYAKASHI THAT THE AMAKAWA FAMILY SUBJUGATED IN THOSE TEXTS?
GWEH!
GASHI (CHOKE)
RIGHT NOW, WE'RE TALKING ABOUT YOU. NOT THAT CAT, GOT IIIIT?
GYUUUU (SQUEEEZE)
R-R-R-RINKO?
R-RINKO, UH...
WHAT!?
PUNI (SMOOSH)
M-MY BACK...IS TOUCHING...
...SOMETHING KINDA SOFT AND SQUISHY...
......

SFX: GUNYUUU (SMOOOOSH)

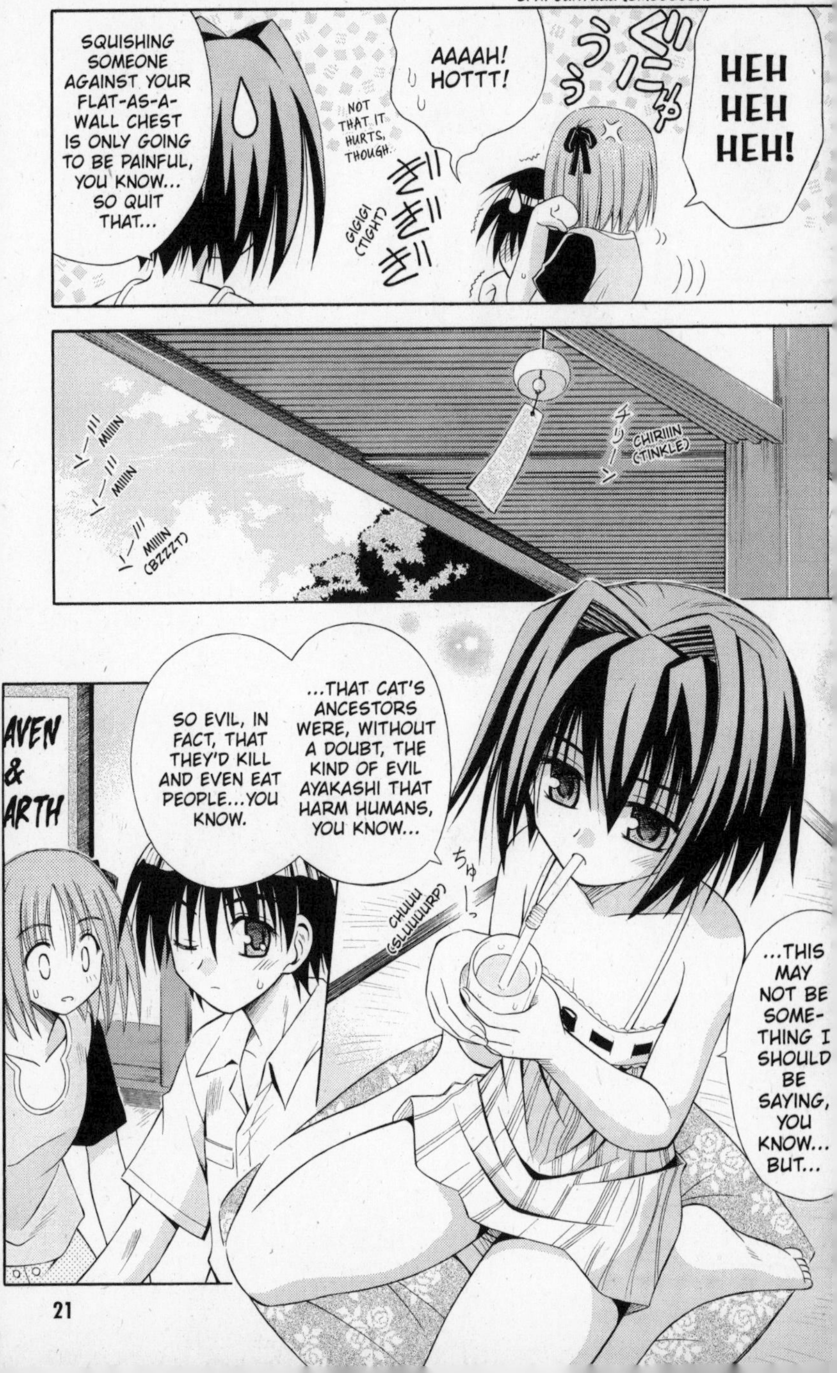

HEH HEH HEH!
AAAAH! HOTTT!
NOT THAT IT HURTS, THOUGH.
GIGIGI (TIGHT)
SQUISHING SOMEONE AGAINST YOUR FLAT-AS-A-WALL CHEST IS ONLY GOING TO BE PAINFUL, YOU KNOW... SO QUIT THAT...
CHIRIIIN (TINKLE)
MIIIN
MIIIN
MIIIN (BZZZT)
...THIS MAY NOT BE SOME-THING I SHOULD BE SAYING, YOU KNOW... BUT...
CHUUU (SLUUUURP)
...THAT CAT'S ANCESTORS WERE, WITHOUT A DOUBT, THE KIND OF EVIL AYAKASHI THAT HARM HUMANS, YOU KNOW...
SO EVIL, IN FACT, THAT THEY'D KILL AND EVEN EAT PEOPLE...YOU KNOW.
AVEN & ARTH

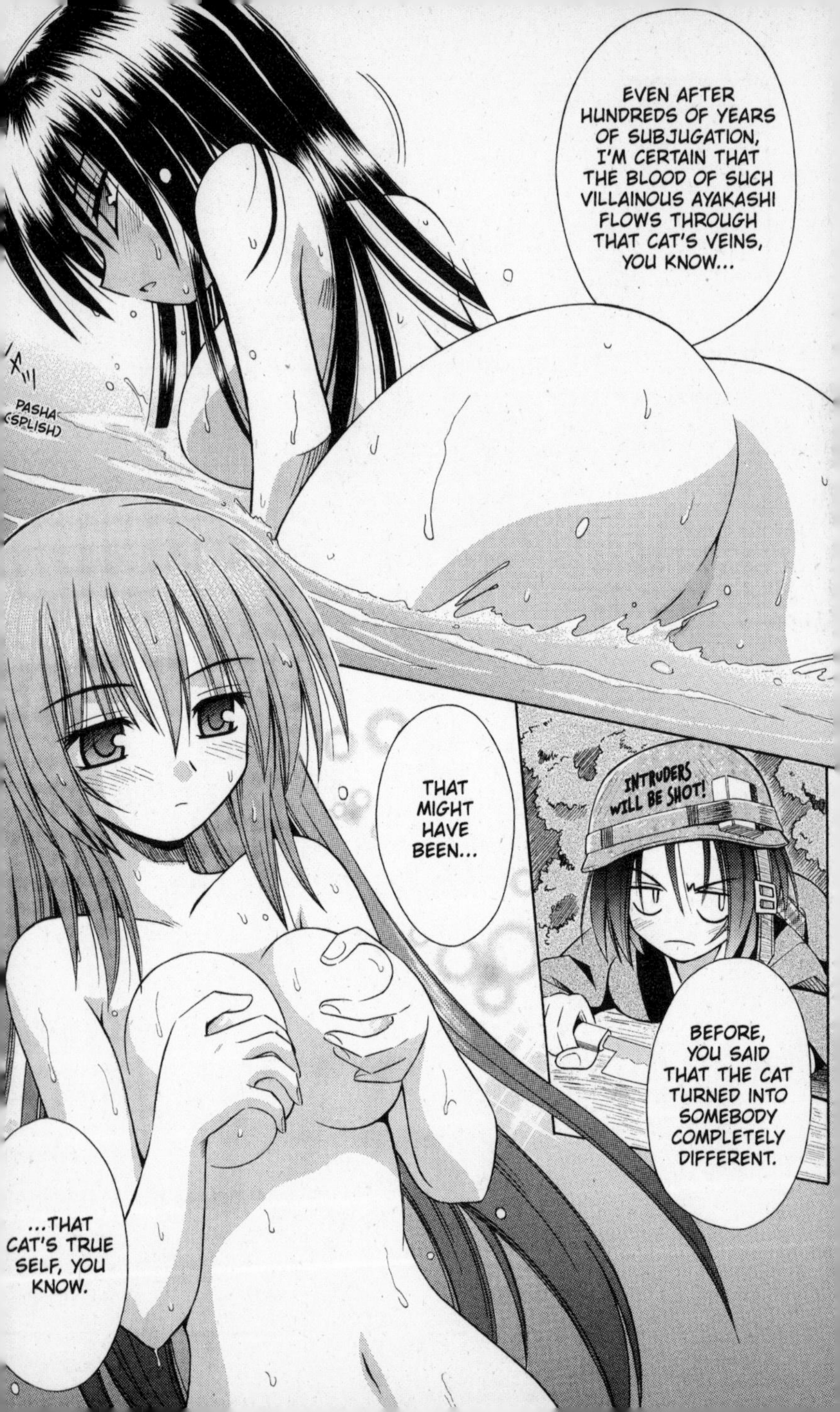
EVEN AFTER HUNDREDS OF YEARS OF SUBJUGATION, I'M CERTAIN THAT THE BLOOD OF SUCH VILLAINOUS AYAKASHI FLOWS THROUGH THAT CAT'S VEINS, YOU KNOW...
PASHA (SPLISH)
INTRUDERS WILL BE SHOT!
BEFORE, YOU SAID THAT THE CAT TURNED INTO SOMEBODY COMPLETELY DIFFERENT.
THAT MIGHT HAVE BEEN...
...THAT CAT'S TRUE SELF, YOU KNOW.

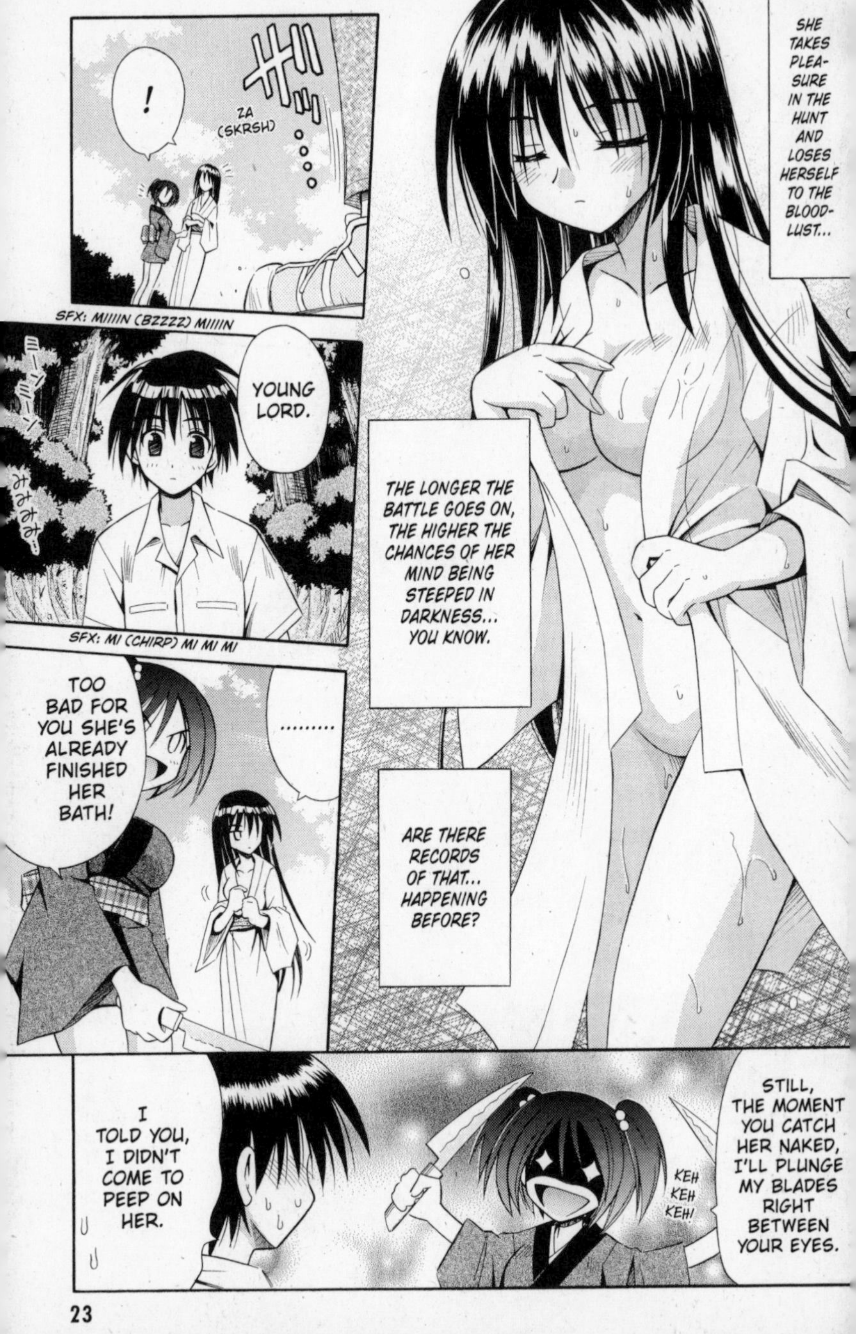
SHE TAKES PLEASURE IN THE HUNT AND LOSES HERSELF TO THE BLOODLUST...
THE LONGER THE BATTLE GOES ON, THE HIGHER THE CHANCES OF HER MIND BEING STEEPED IN DARKNESS... YOU KNOW.
ARE THERE RECORDS OF THAT... HAPPENING BEFORE?
ZA (SKRSH)
!
SFX: MIIIN (BZZZZ) MIIIN
ミーンミーン
YOUNG LORD.
みみみみ…
SFX: MI (CHIRP) MI MI MI
....
TOO BAD FOR YOU SHE'S ALREADY FINISHED HER BATH!
STILL, THE MOMENT YOU CATCH HER NAKED, I'LL PLUNGE MY BLADES RIGHT BETWEEN YOUR EYES.
KEH KEH KEH!
I TOLD YOU, I DIDN'T COME TO PEEP ON HER.

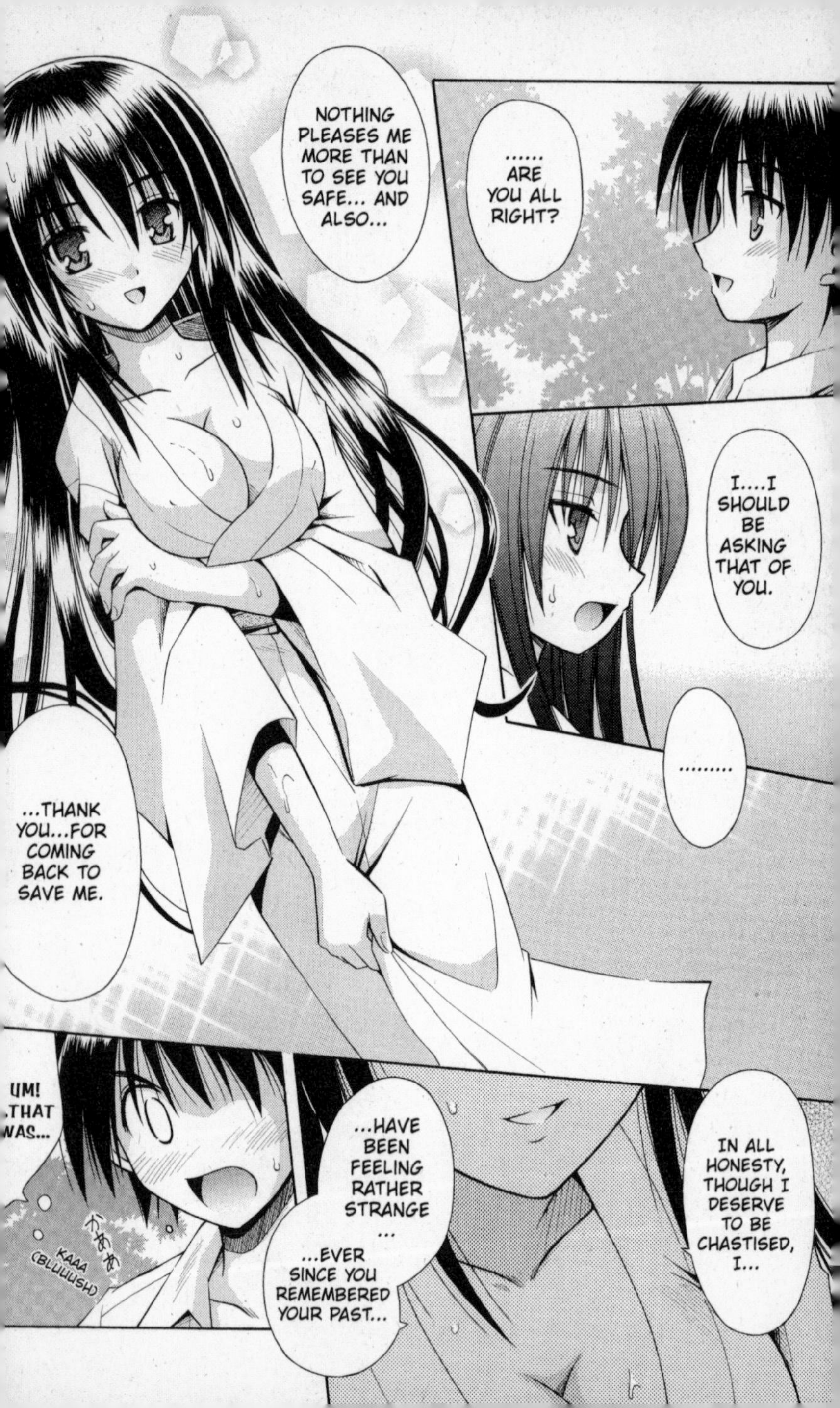

......
ARE YOU ALL RIGHT?
I....I SHOULD BE ASKING THAT OF YOU.
....
NOTHING PLEASES ME MORE THAN TO SEE YOU SAFE... AND ALSO...
...THANK YOU...FOR COMING BACK TO SAVE ME.
IN ALL HONESTY, THOUGH I DESERVE TO BE CHASTISED, I...
...HAVE BEEN FEELING RATHER STRANGE ...
...EVER SINCE YOU REMEMBERED YOUR PAST...
UM! .THAT WAS...
KAAA (BLUUUSH)

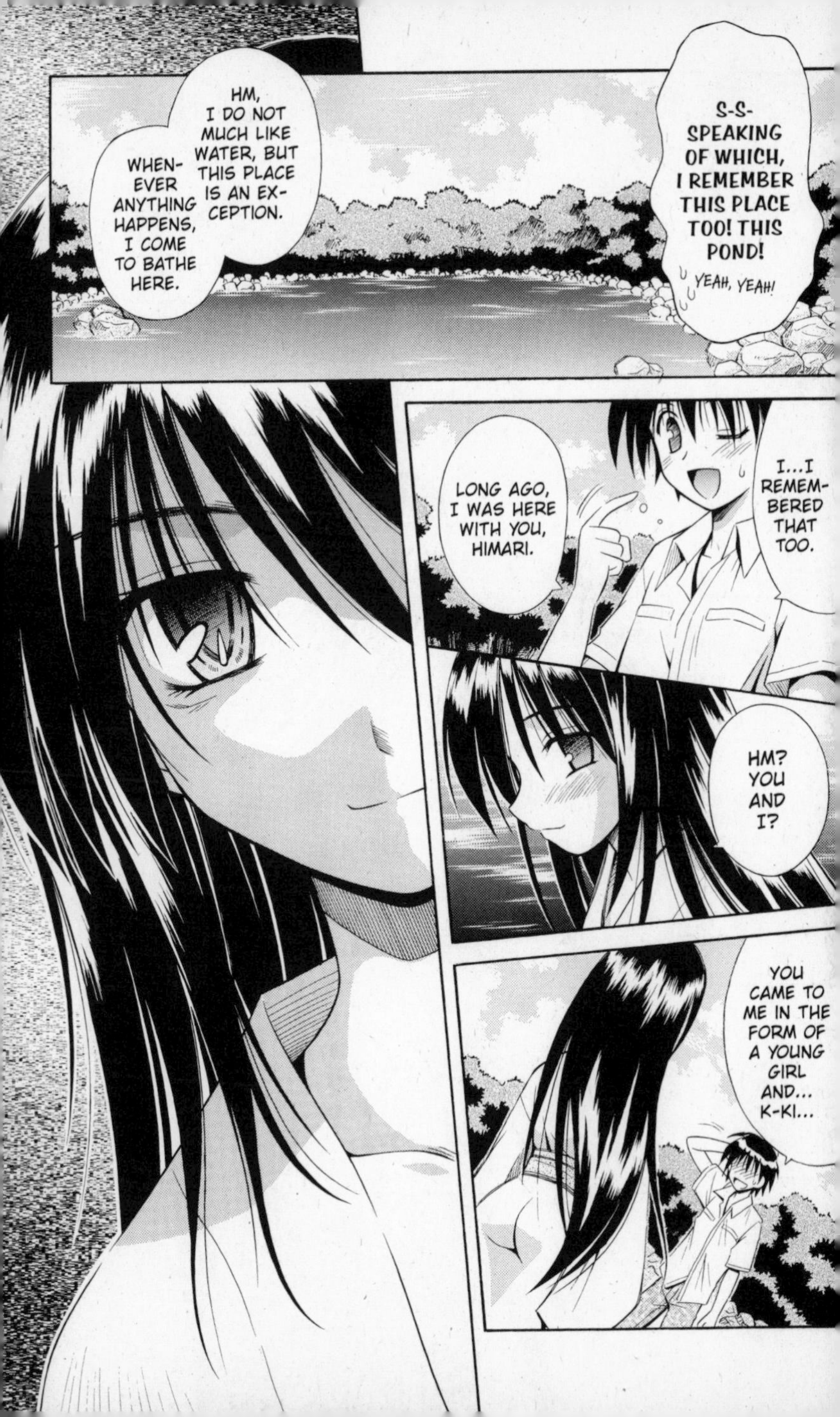
S-S-SPEAKING OF WHICH, I REMEMBER THIS PLACE TOO! THIS POND!
YEAH, YEAH!
HM, I DO NOT MUCH LIKE WATER, BUT THIS PLACE IS AN EXCEPTION.
WHENEVER ANYTHING HAPPENS, I COME TO BATHE HERE.
I...I REMEMBERED THAT TOO.
LONG AGO, I WAS HERE WITH YOU, HIMARI.
HM? YOU AND I?
YOU CAME TO ME IN THE FORM OF A YOUNG GIRL AND... K-KI...

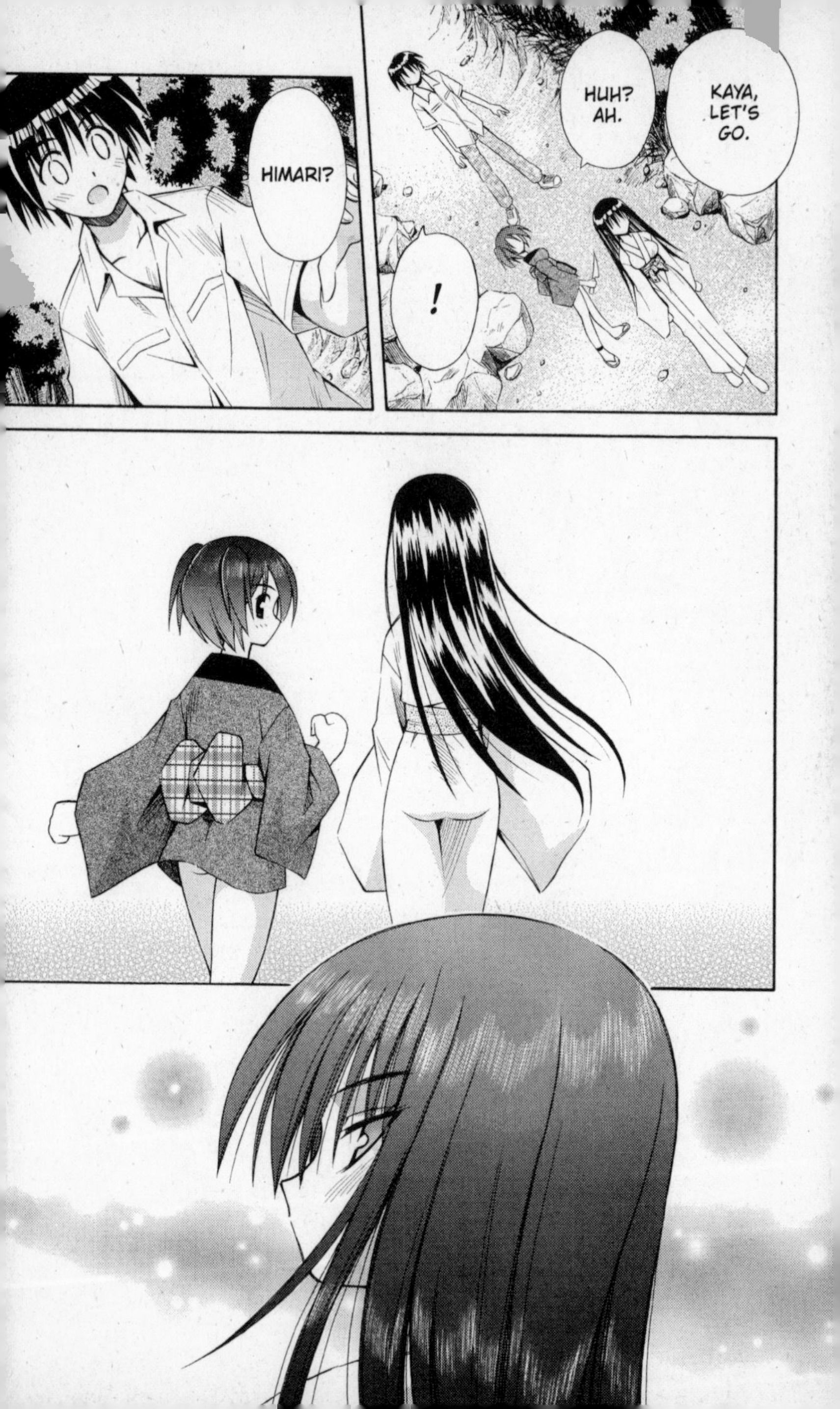
KAYA, LET'S GO.
HUH? AH.
!
HIMARI?

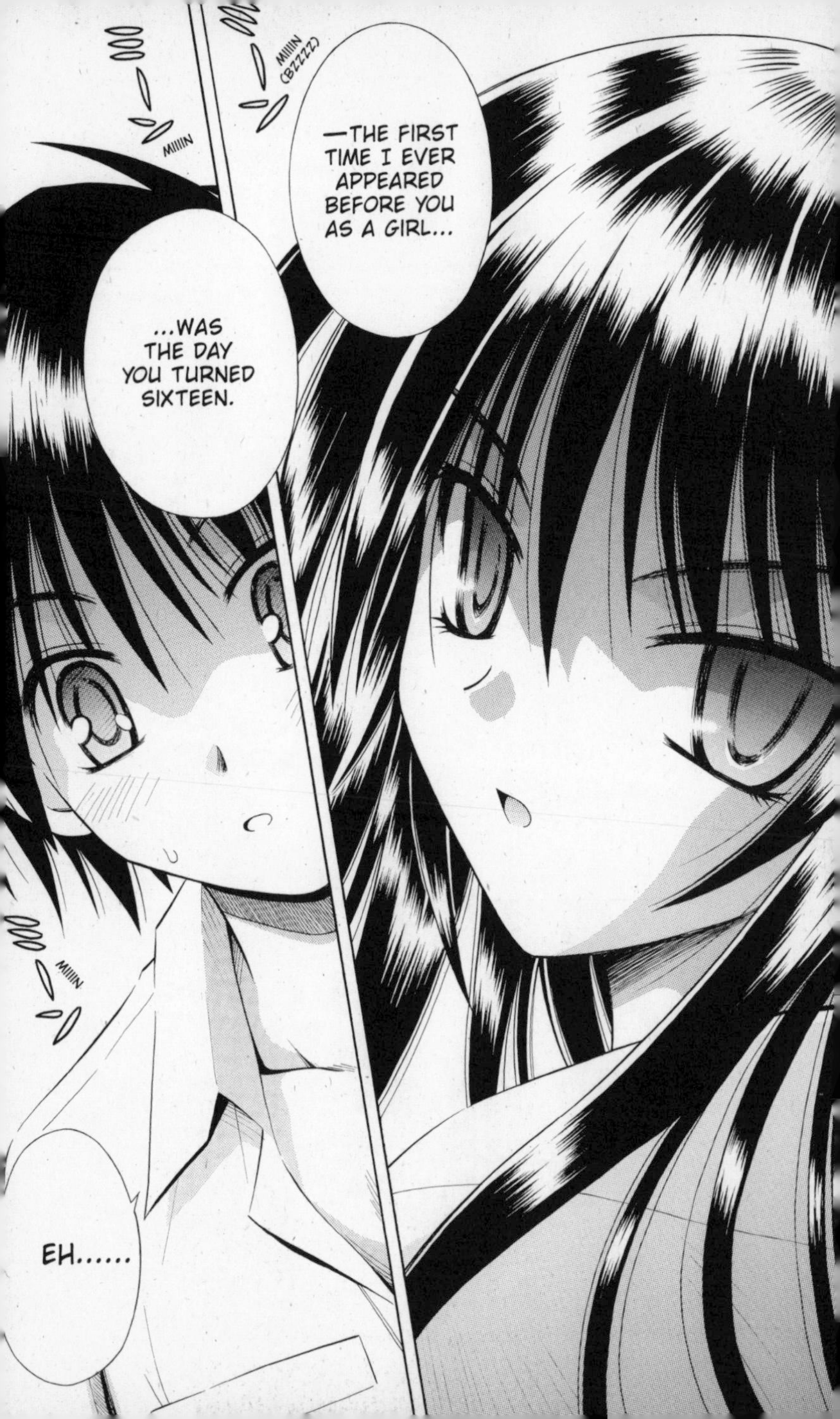
MIIIN (BZZZZ)
—THE FIRST TIME I EVER APPEARED BEFORE YOU AS A GIRL...
MIIIN
...WAS THE DAY YOU TURNED SIXTEEN.
MIIIN
EH......

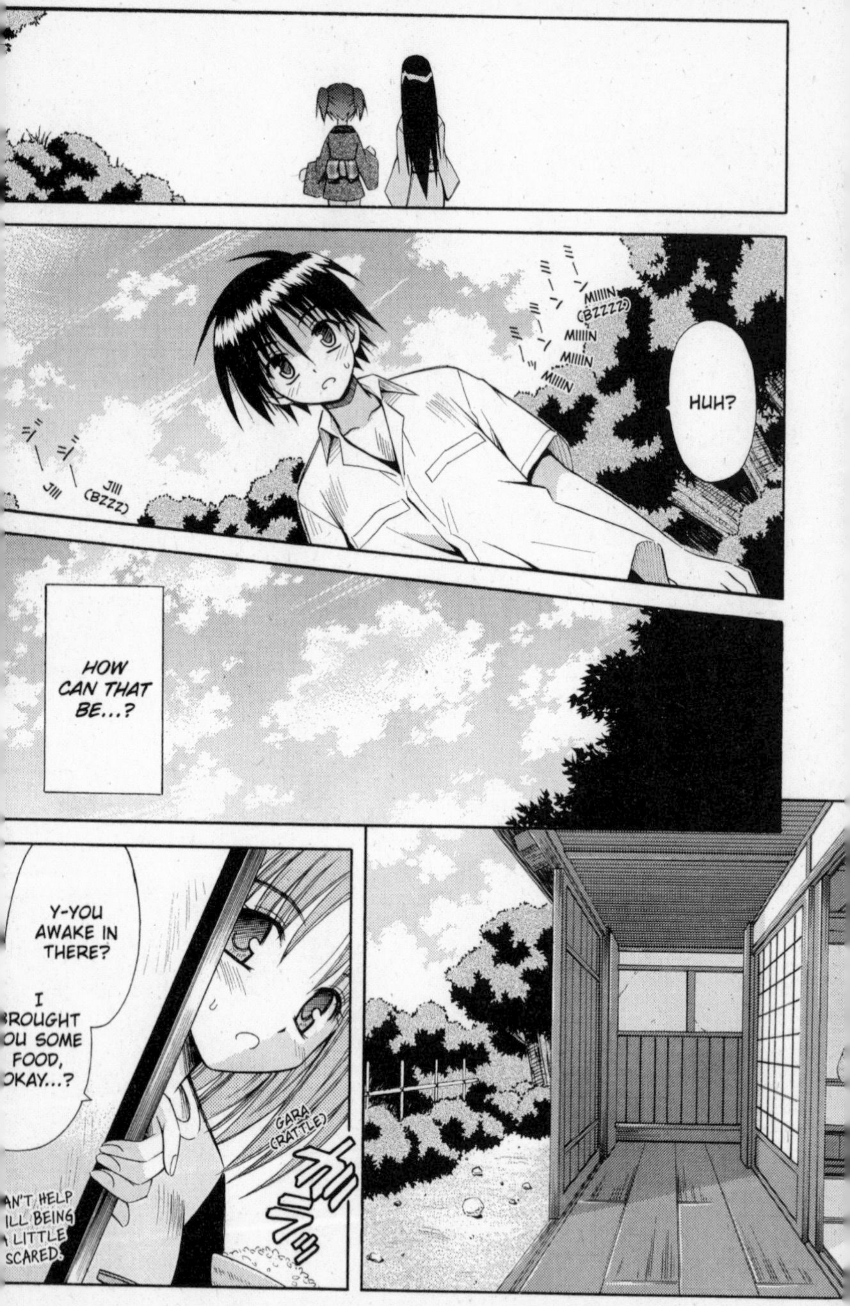

HUH?
MIIIIN (BZZZZ) MIIIN MIIIIN MIIIIN
JIII JIII (BZZZ)
HOW CAN THAT BE...?
Y-YOU AWAKE IN THERE?
I BROUGHT OU SOME FOOD, OKAY...?
GARA (RATTLE)
AN'T HELP ILL BEING LITTLE SCARED.

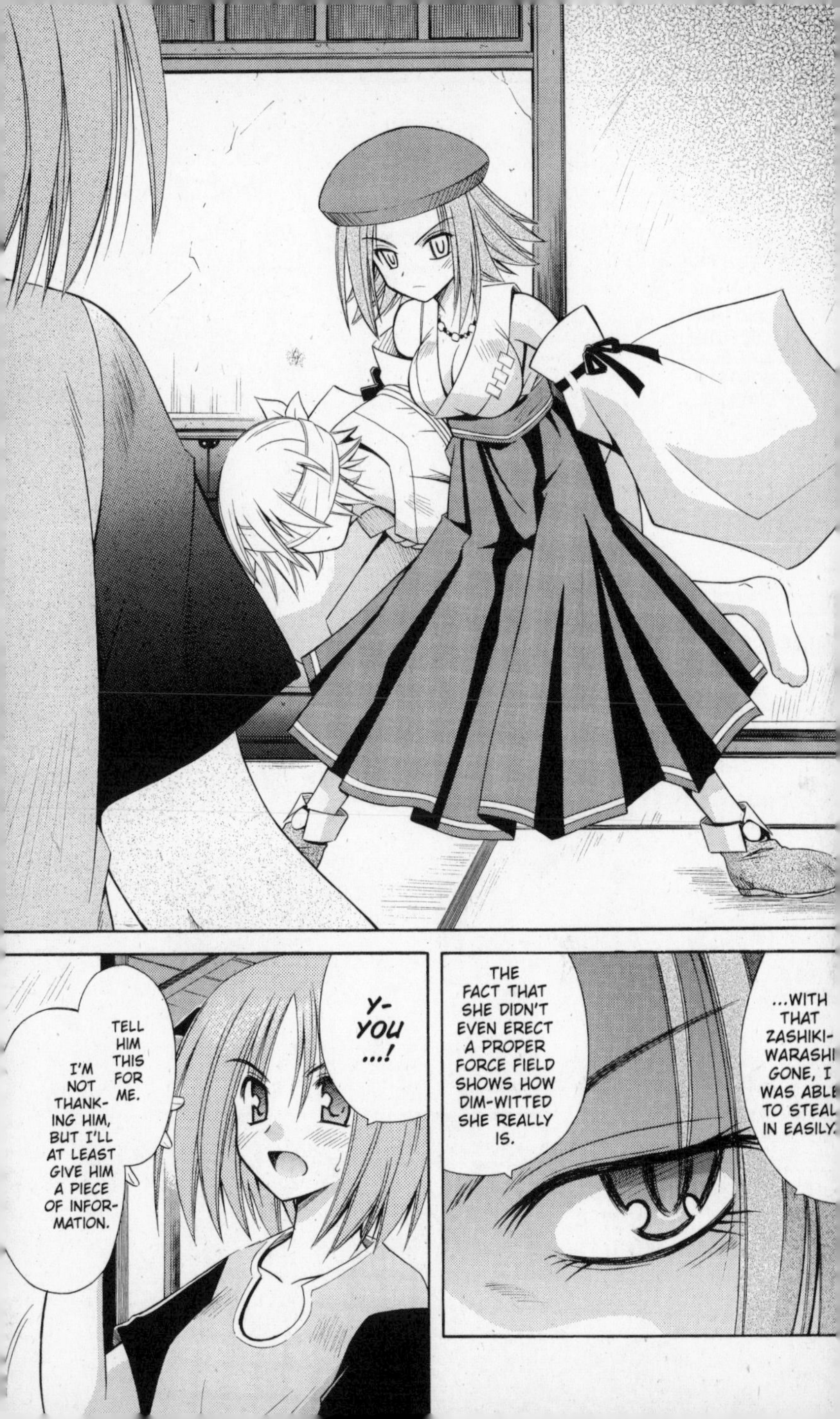
...WITH THAT ZASHIKI-WARASHI GONE, I WAS ABLE TO STEAL IN EASILY.
THE FACT THAT SHE DIDN'T EVEN ERECT A PROPER FORCE FIELD SHOWS HOW DIM-WITTED SHE REALLY IS.
Y-YOU ...!
TELL HIM THIS FOR ME.
I'M NOT THANKING HIM, BUT I'LL AT LEAST GIVE HIM A PIECE OF INFORMATION.

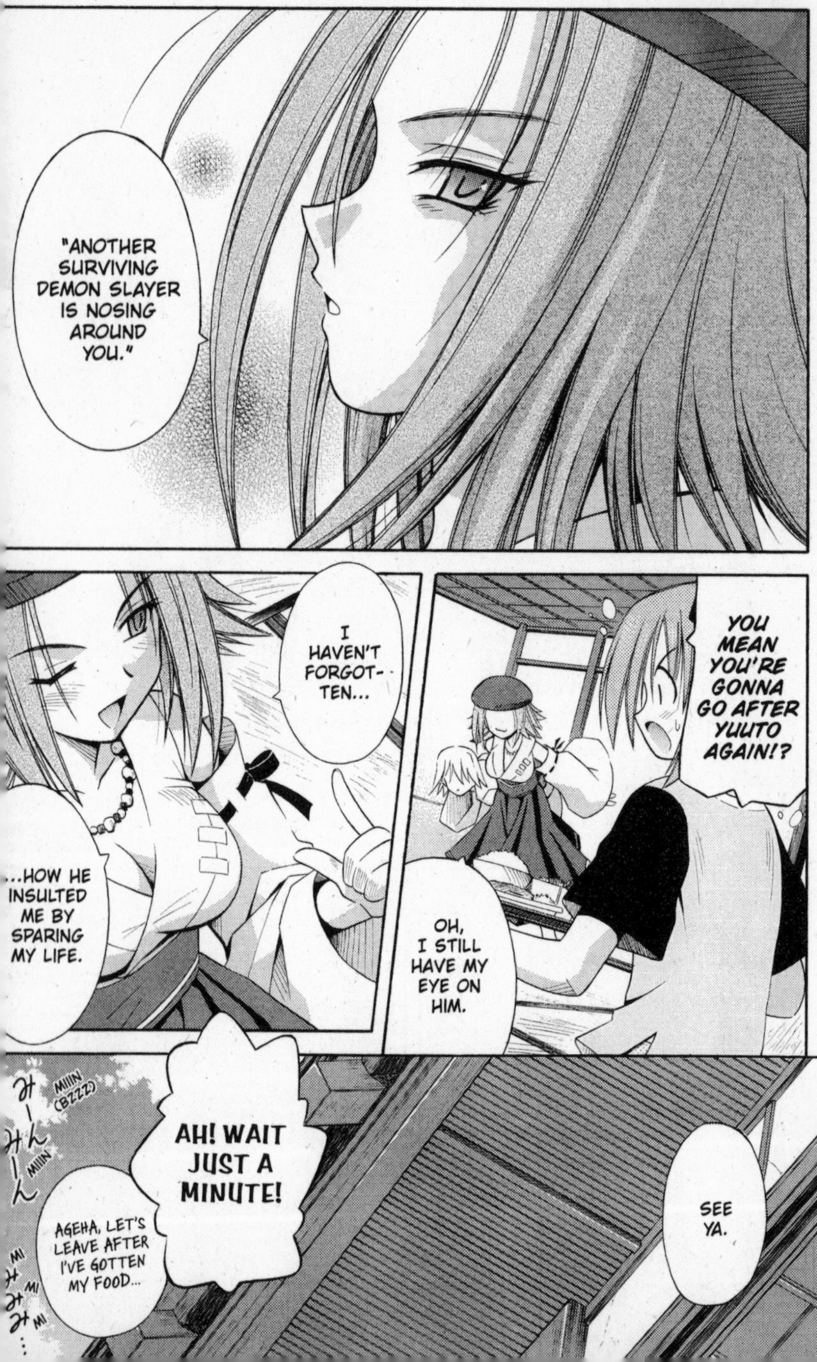
"ANOTHER SURVIVING DEMON SLAYER IS NOSING AROUND YOU."
YOU MEAN YOU'RE GONNA GO AFTER YUUTO AGAIN!?
OH, I STILL HAVE MY EYE ON HIM.
I HAVEN'T FORGOT-TEN...
...HOW HE INSULTED ME BY SPARING MY LIFE.
SEE YA.
AH! WAIT JUST A MINUTE!
AGEHA, LET'S LEAVE AFTER I'VE GOTTEN MY FOOD...
みーん MIIN (BZZZ)
みーん MIIN
みみみ… MI MI MI

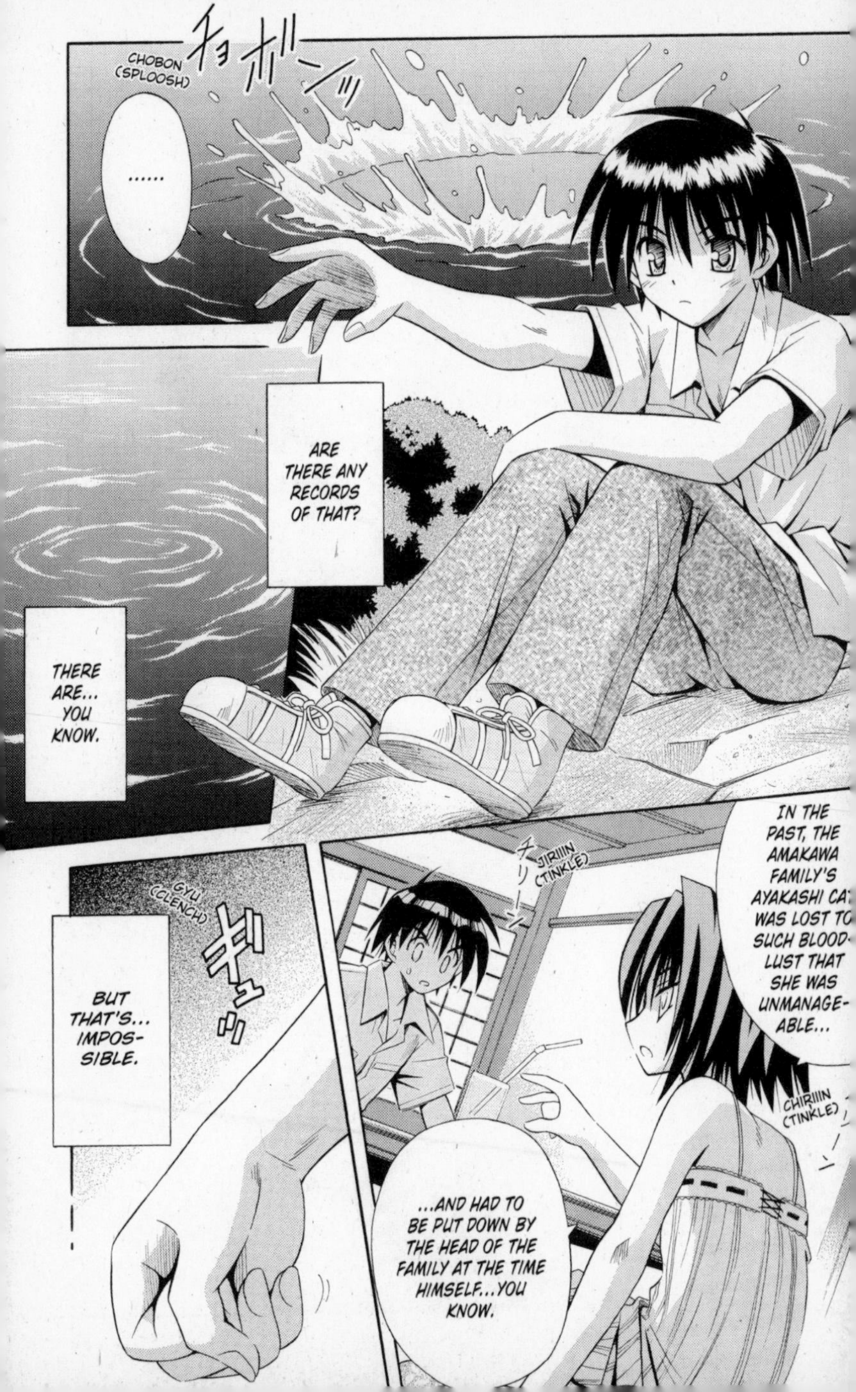

CHOBON (SPLOOSH)
......
ARE THERE ANY RECORDS OF THAT?
THERE ARE... YOU KNOW.
IN THE PAST, THE AMAKAWA FAMILY'S AYAKASHI CAT WAS LOST TO SUCH BLOOD-LUST THAT SHE WAS UNMANAGE-ABLE...
JIRIIIN (TINKLE)
CHIRIIIN (TINKLE)
...AND HAD TO BE PUT DOWN BY THE HEAD OF THE FAMILY AT THE TIME HIMSELF...YOU KNOW.
GYU (CLENCH)
BUT THAT'S... IMPOS-SIBLE.

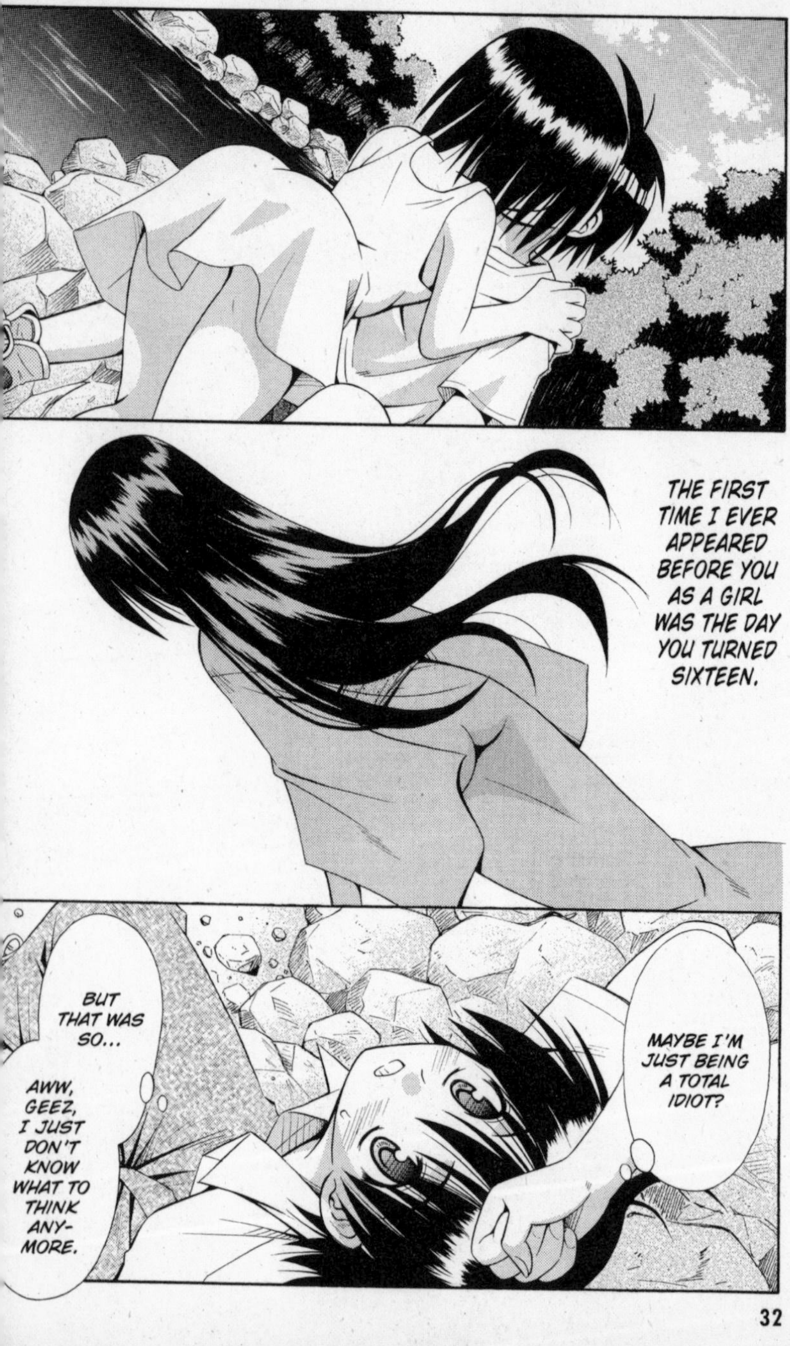
THE FIRST TIME I EVER APPEARED BEFORE YOU AS A GIRL WAS THE DAY YOU TURNED SIXTEEN.
MAYBE I'M JUST BEING A TOTAL IDIOT?
BUT THAT WAS SO...
AWW, GEEZ, I JUST DON'T KNOW WHAT TO THINK ANY-MORE.

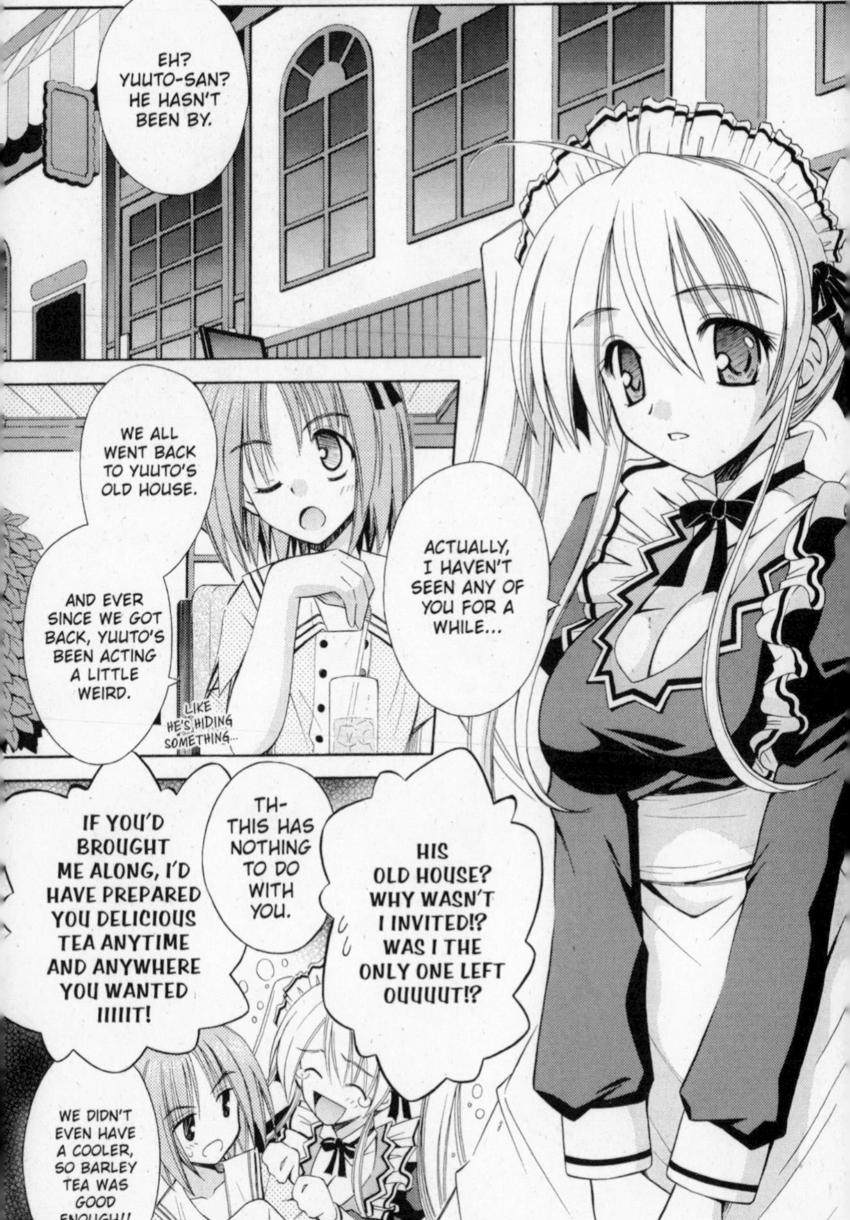
ACTUALLY, I HAVEN'T SEEN ANY OF YOU FOR A WHILE...
EH? YUUTO-SAN? HE HASN'T BEEN BY.
WE ALL WENT BACK TO YUUTO'S OLD HOUSE.
AND EVER SINCE WE GOT BACK, YUUTO'S BEEN ACTING A LITTLE WEIRD.
LIKE HE'S HIDING SOMETHING...
HIS OLD HOUSE? WHY WASN'T I INVITED!? WAS I THE ONLY ONE LEFT OUUUUT!?
TH- THIS HAS NOTHING TO DO WITH YOU.
IF YOU'D BROUGHT ME ALONG, I'D HAVE PREPARED YOU DELICIOUS TEA ANYTIME AND ANYWHERE YOU WANTED IIIIIT!
WE DIDN'T EVEN HAVE A COOLER, SO BARLEY TEA WAS GOOD ENOUGH!!

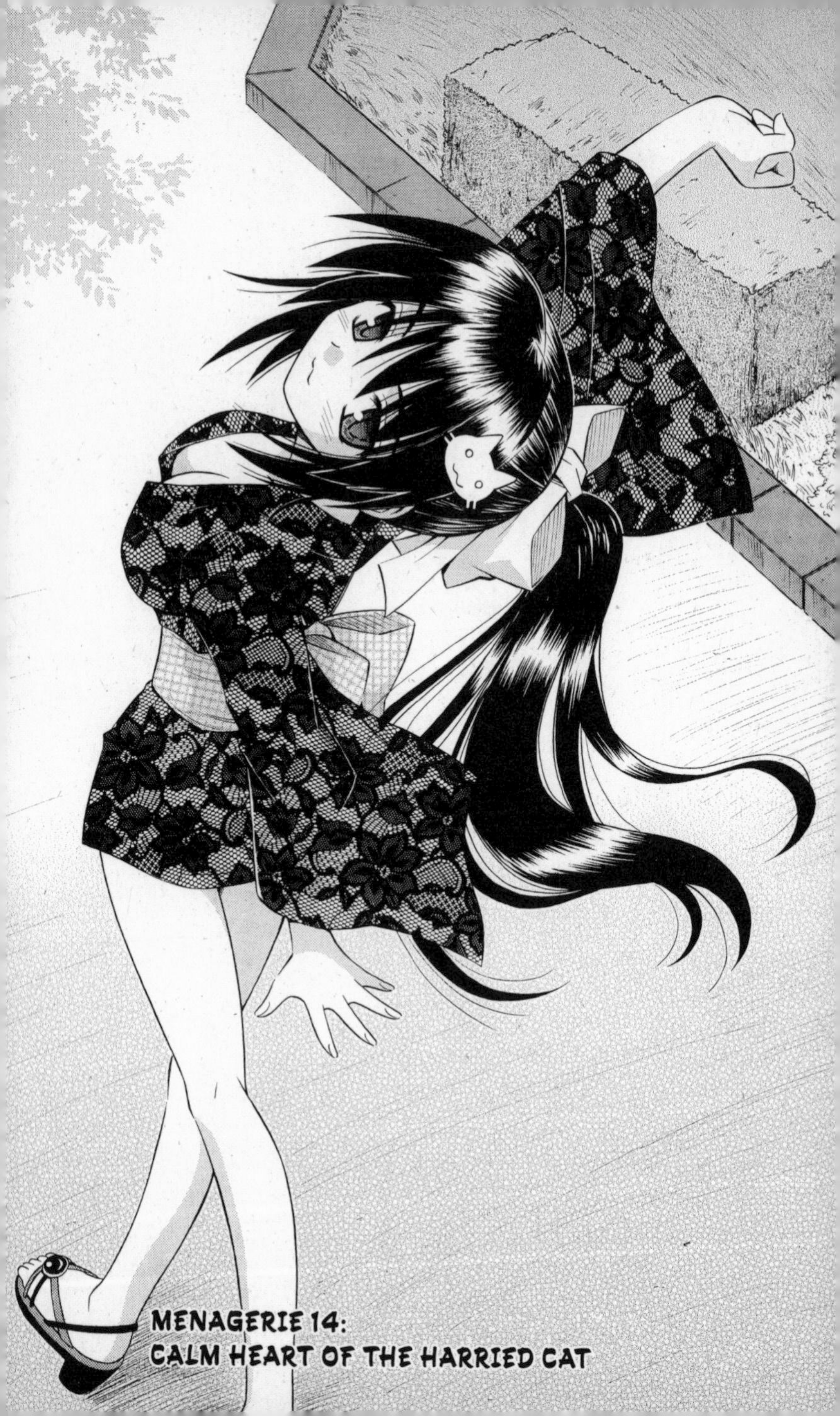

MENAGERIE 14:
CALM HEART OF THE HARRIED CAT

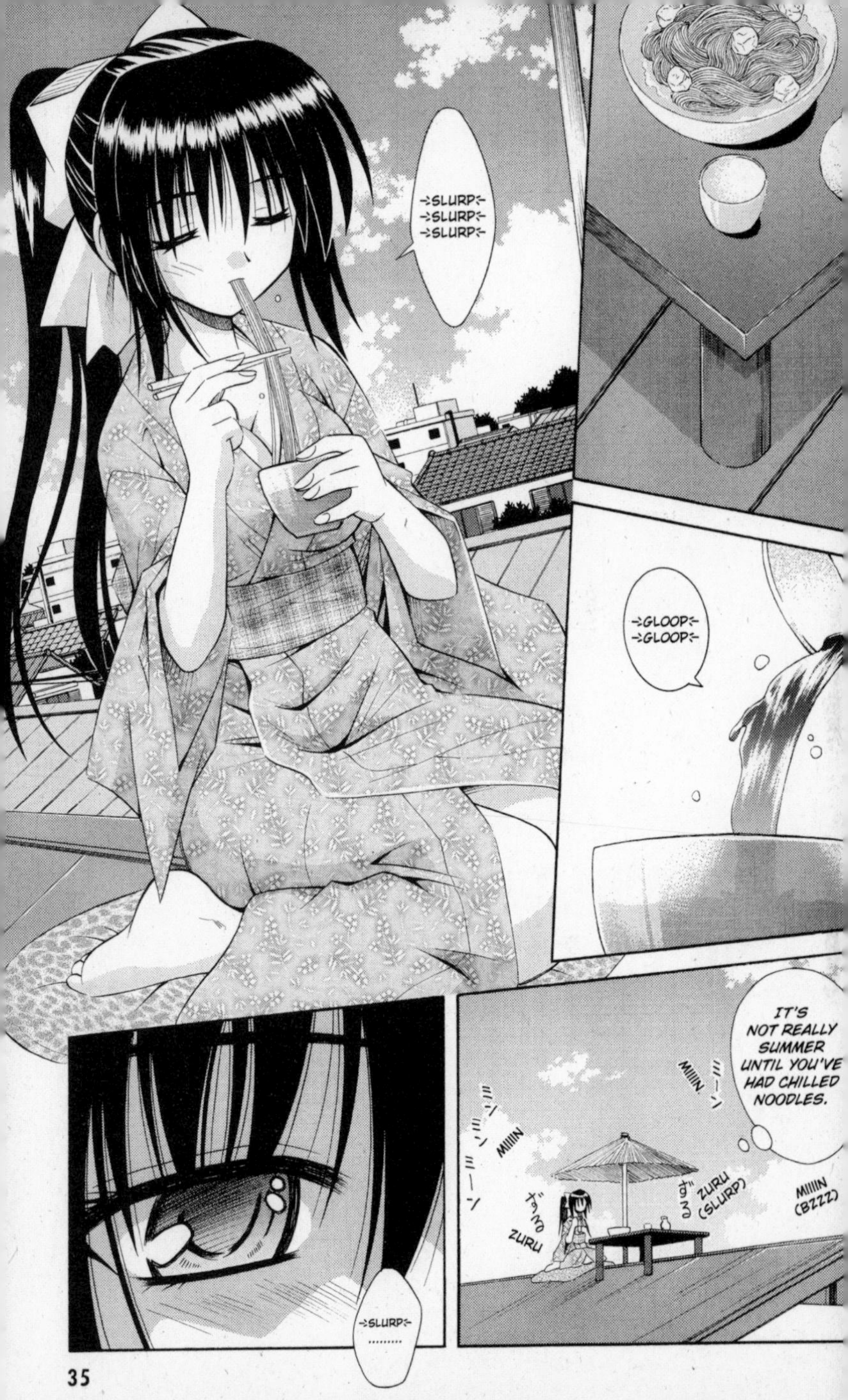

~GLOOP~
~GLOOP~
~SLURP~
~SLURP~
~SLURP~
IT'S NOT REALLY SUMMER UNTIL YOU'VE HAD CHILLED NOODLES.
ミーン
MIIIN
MIIIN (BZZZ)
ずる
ZURU (SLURP)
ZURU
ミーン ミーン
MIIIN
ミーン
~SLURP~
....

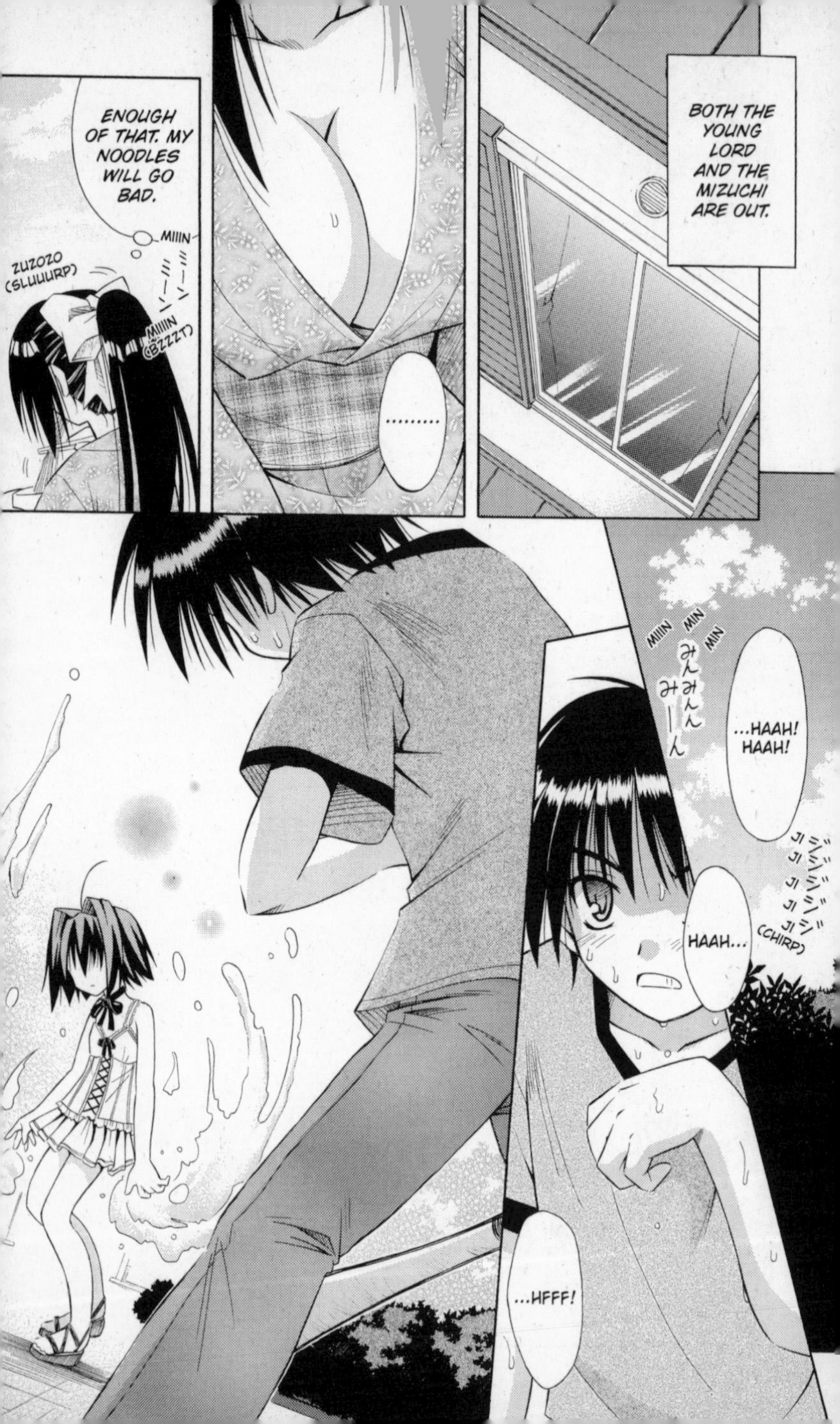
BOTH THE YOUNG LORD AND THE MIZUCHI ARE OUT.
....
ENOUGH OF THAT. MY NOODLES WILL GO BAD.
MIIIN
ZUZOZO (SLUUURP)
MIIIN (BZZZT)
MIIIN MIN MIN
みんみんみーん
...HAAH! HAAH!
JI JI JI JI JI (CHIRP)
ジジジジジ
HAAH...
...HFFF!

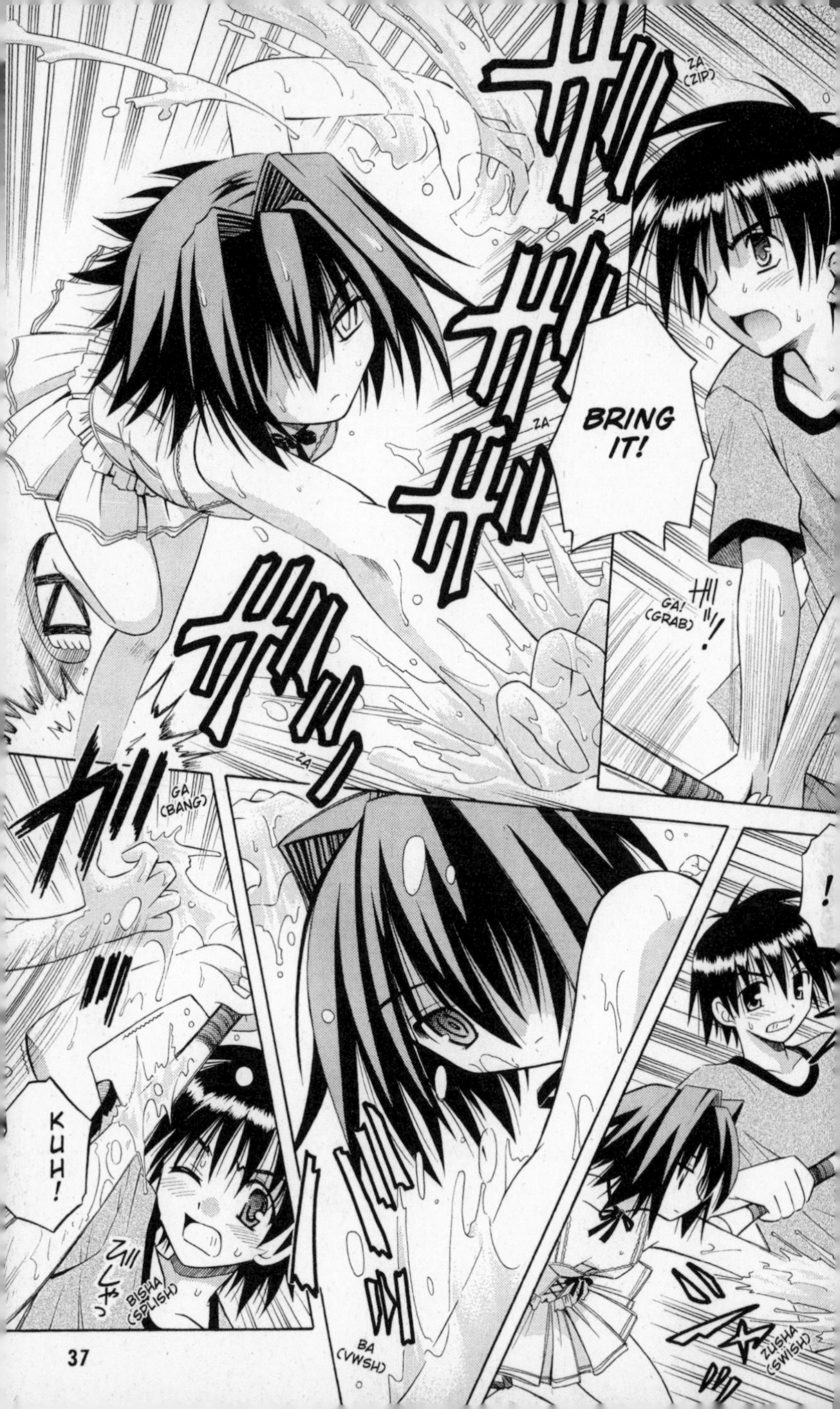
ZA (ZIP)
ZA
ZA
BRING IT!
GA! (GRAB)
ZA
GA (BANG)
!
ZUSHA (SWISH)
BA (VWSH)
KUH!
BISHA (SPLISH)

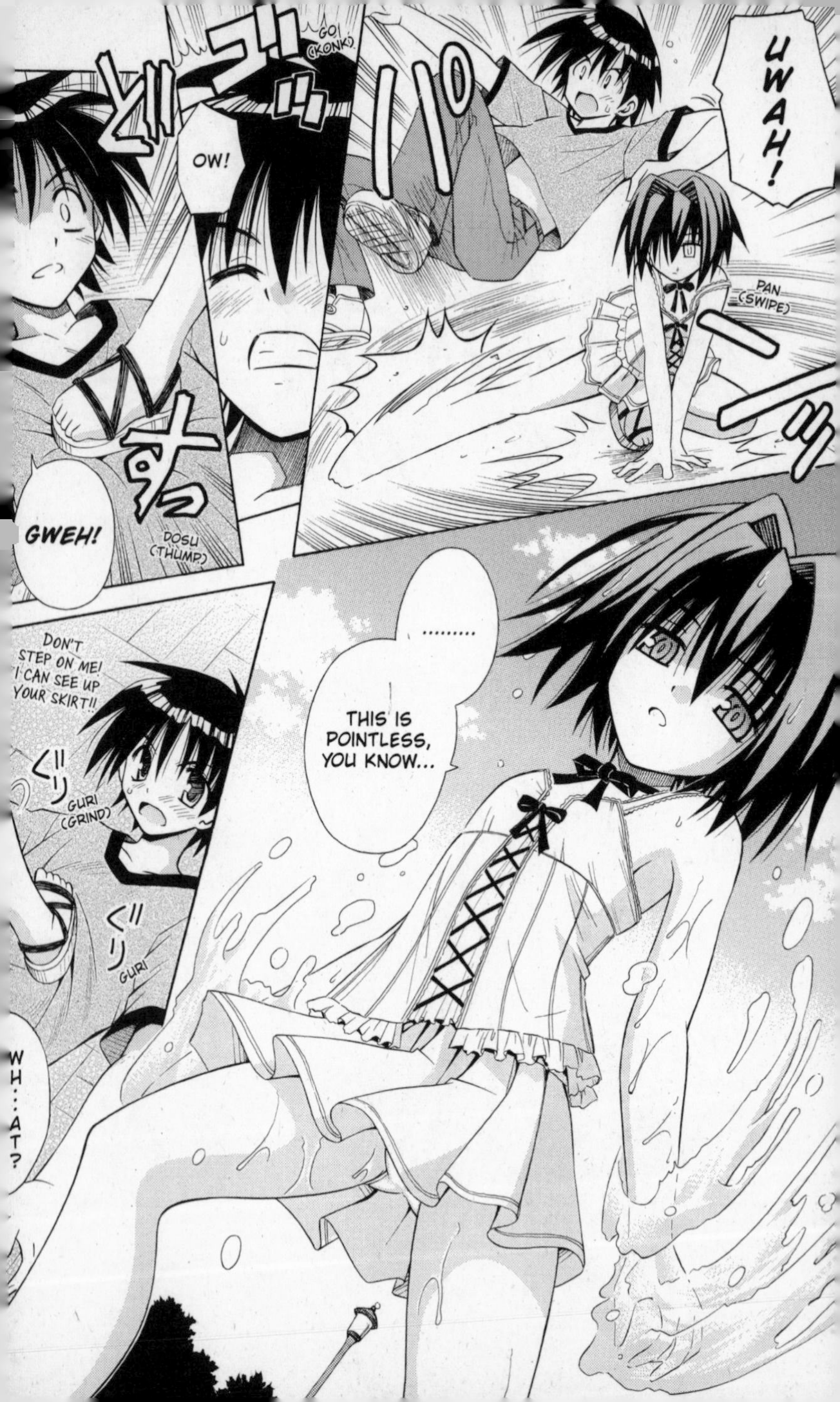

UWAH!
PAN (SWIPE)
GO! (KONK)
OW!
GWEH!
DOSU (THUMP)
....
THIS IS POINTLESS, YOU KNOW...
DON'T STEP ON ME! I CAN SEE UP YOUR SKIRT!!
GURI (GRIND)
GURI
WH...AT?

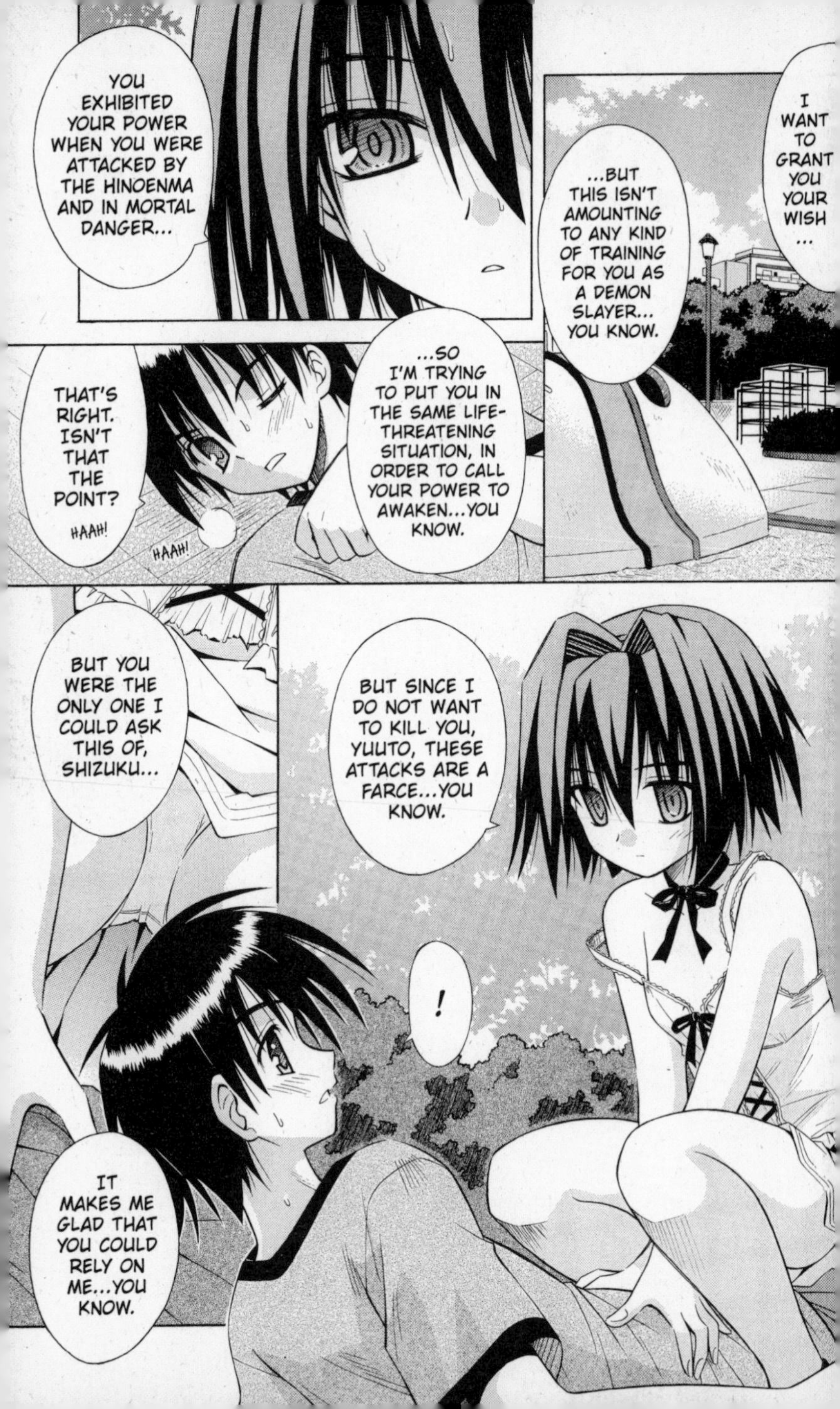
I WANT TO GRANT YOU YOUR WISH...
...BUT THIS ISN'T AMOUNTING TO ANY KIND OF TRAINING FOR YOU AS A DEMON SLAYER... YOU KNOW.
YOU EXHIBITED YOUR POWER WHEN YOU WERE ATTACKED BY THE HINOENMA AND IN MORTAL DANGER...
...SO I'M TRYING TO PUT YOU IN THE SAME LIFE-THREATENING SITUATION, IN ORDER TO CALL YOUR POWER TO AWAKEN...YOU KNOW.
THAT'S RIGHT. ISN'T THAT THE POINT?
HAAH!
HAAH!
BUT SINCE I DO NOT WANT TO KILL YOU, YUUTO, THESE ATTACKS ARE A FARCE...YOU KNOW.
BUT YOU WERE THE ONLY ONE I COULD ASK THIS OF, SHIZUKU...
!
IT MAKES ME GLAD THAT YOU COULD RELY ON ME...YOU KNOW.

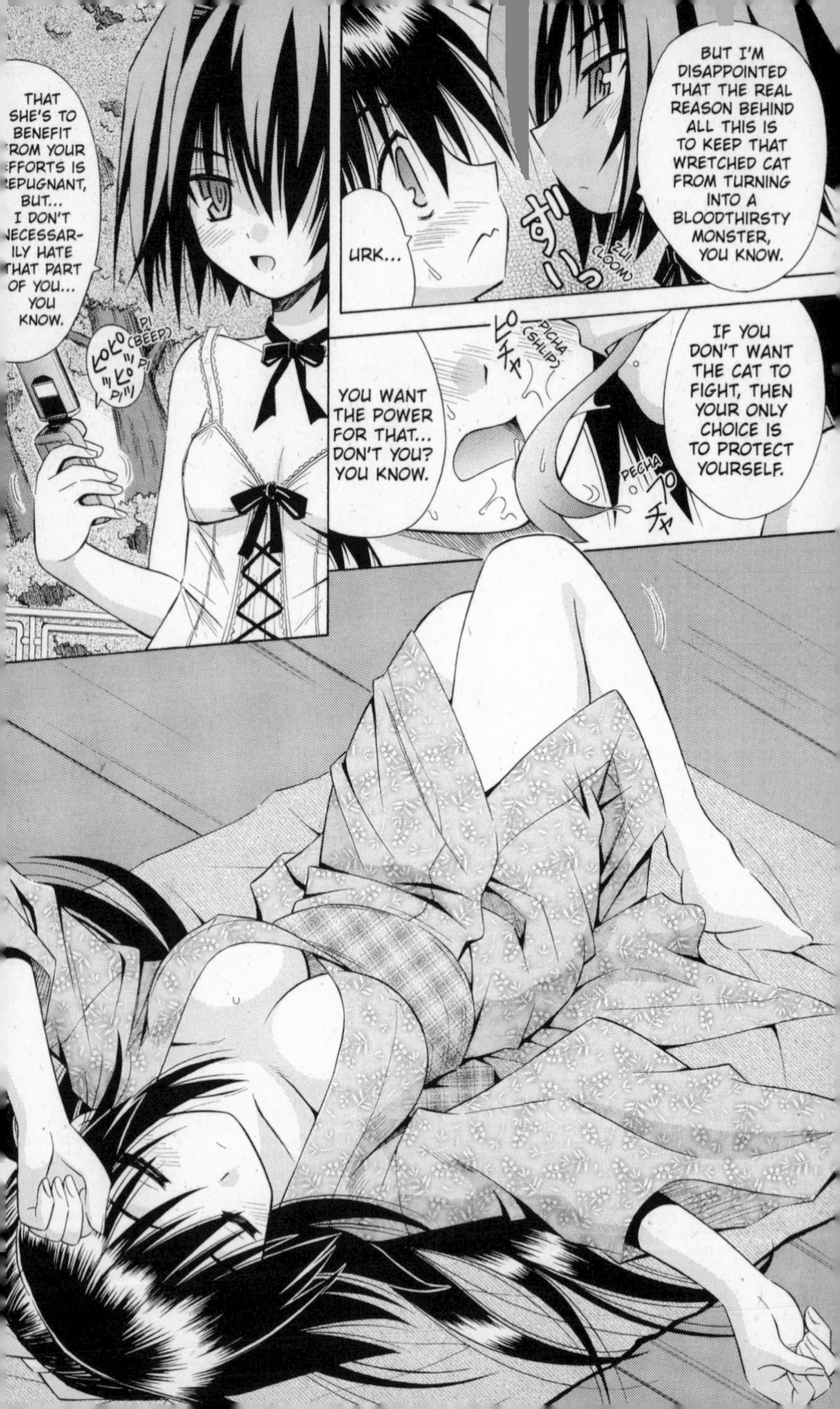
BUT I'M DISAPPOINTED THAT THE REAL REASON BEHIND ALL THIS IS TO KEEP THAT WRETCHED CAT FROM TURNING INTO A BLOODTHIRSTY MONSTER, YOU KNOW.
ZUI (LOOM)
URK...
IF YOU DON'T WANT THE CAT TO FIGHT, THEN YOUR ONLY CHOICE IS TO PROTECT YOURSELF.
PECHA
PICHA (SHLIP)
YOU WANT THE POWER FOR THAT... DON'T YOU? YOU KNOW.
THAT SHE'S TO BENEFIT ROM YOUR FFORTS IS EPUGNANT, BUT... I DON'T ECESSAR-ILY HATE HAT PART OF YOU... YOU KNOW.
PI (BEEP) PI PI

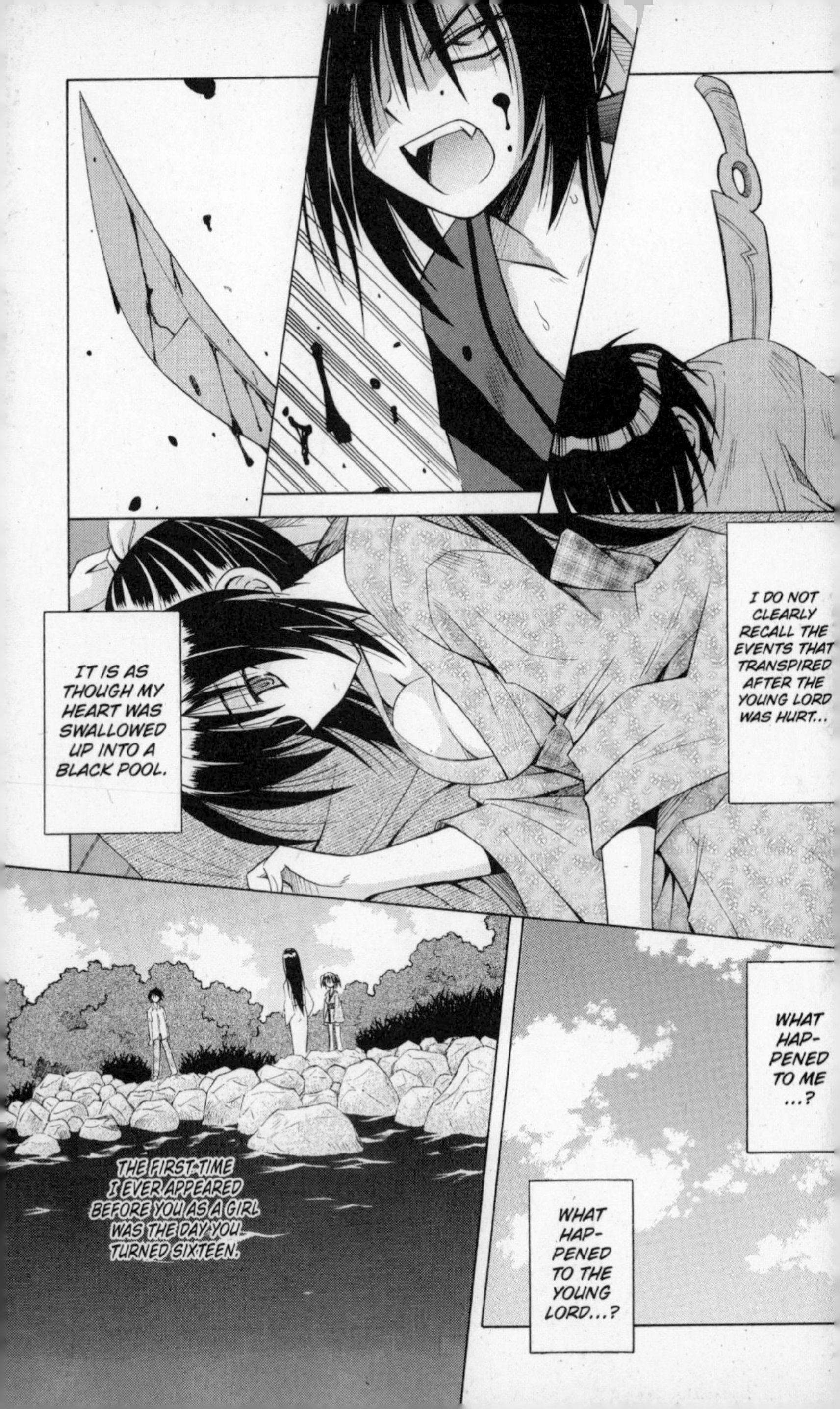
I DO NOT CLEARLY RECALL THE EVENTS THAT TRANSPIRED AFTER THE YOUNG LORD WAS HURT...
IT IS AS THOUGH MY HEART WAS SWALLOWED UP INTO A BLACK POOL.
WHAT HAP-PENED TO ME ...?
WHAT HAP-PENED TO THE YOUNG LORD...?
THE FIRST TIME I EVER APPEARED BEFORE YOU AS A GIRL WAS THE DAY YOU TURNED SIXTEEN.

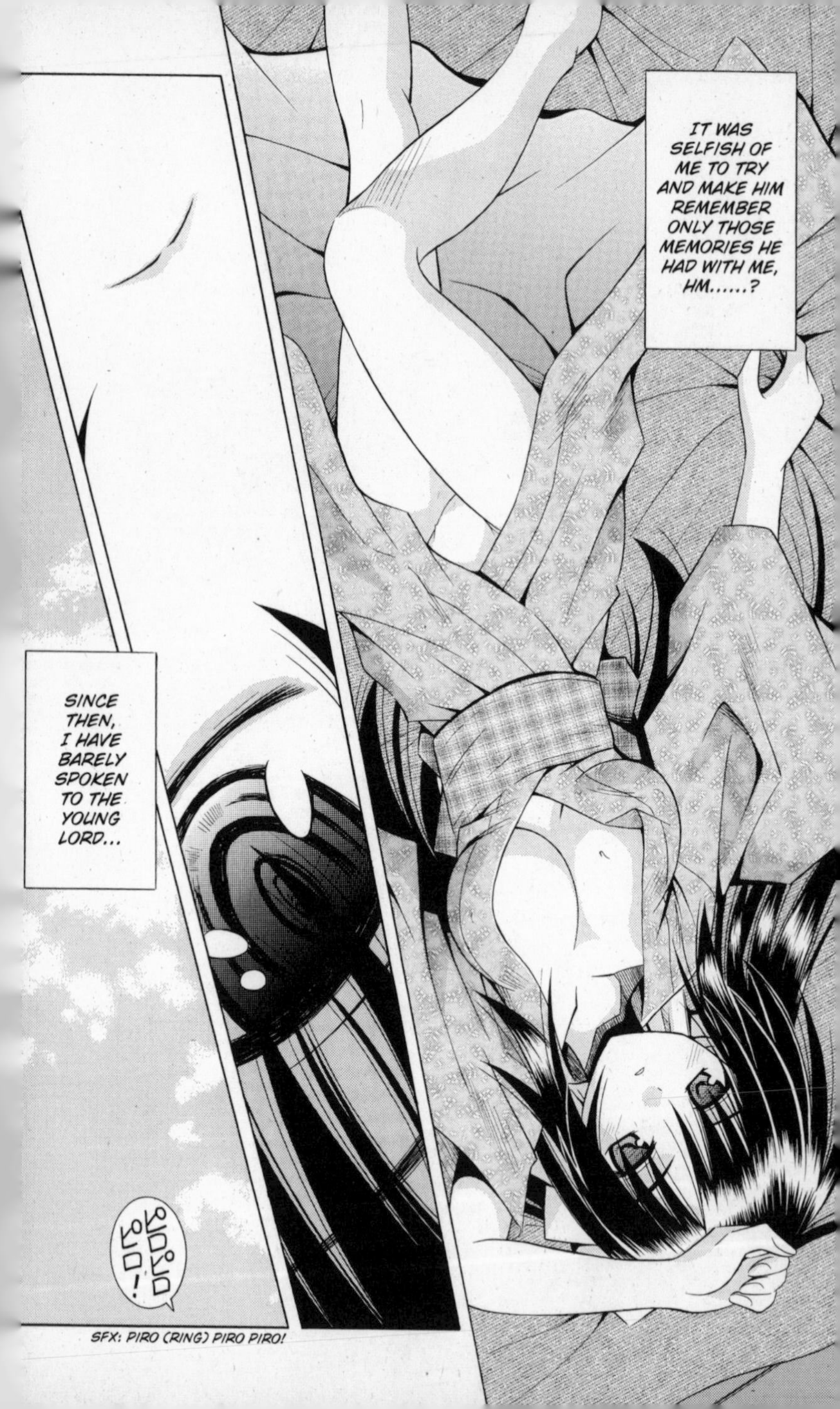
IT WAS SELFISH OF ME TO TRY AND MAKE HIM REMEMBER ONLY THOSE MEMORIES HE HAD WITH ME, HM......?
SINCE THEN, I HAVE BARELY SPOKEN TO THE YOUNG LORD...
ピロピロピロ!

SFX: PIRO (RING) PIRO PIRO!

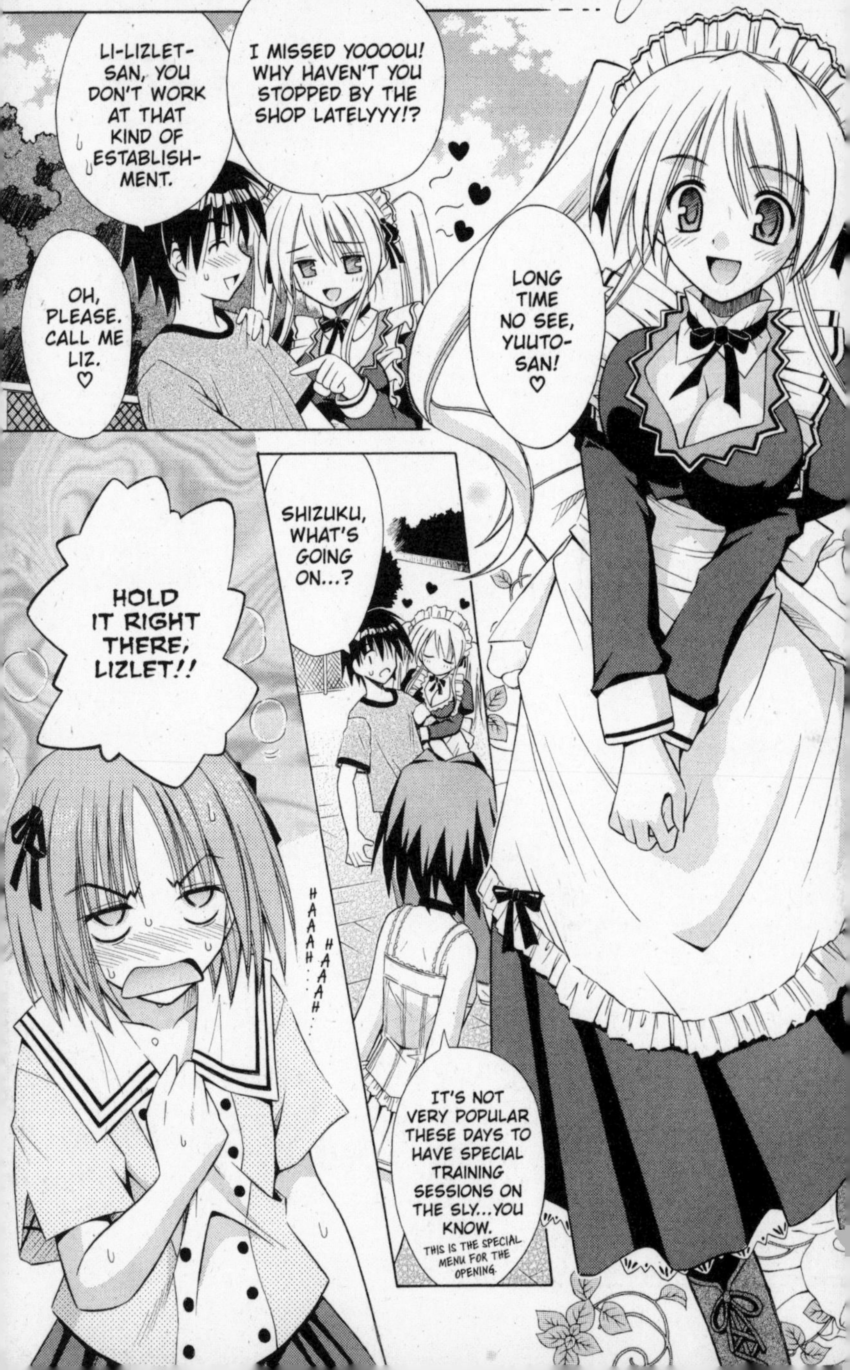
LONG TIME NO SEE, YUUTO-SAN! ♡
IT'S NOT VERY POPULAR THESE DAYS TO HAVE SPECIAL TRAINING SESSIONS ON THE SLY...YOU KNOW.
THIS IS THE SPECIAL MENU FOR THE OPENING.
I MISSED YOOOOU! WHY HAVEN'T YOU STOPPED BY THE SHOP LATELYYY!?
LI-LIZLET-SAN, YOU DON'T WORK AT THAT KIND OF ESTABLISH-MENT.
OH, PLEASE. CALL ME LIZ. ♡
SHIZUKU, WHAT'S GOING ON...?
HAAAAH... HAAAAH...
HOLD IT RIGHT THERE, LIZLET!!

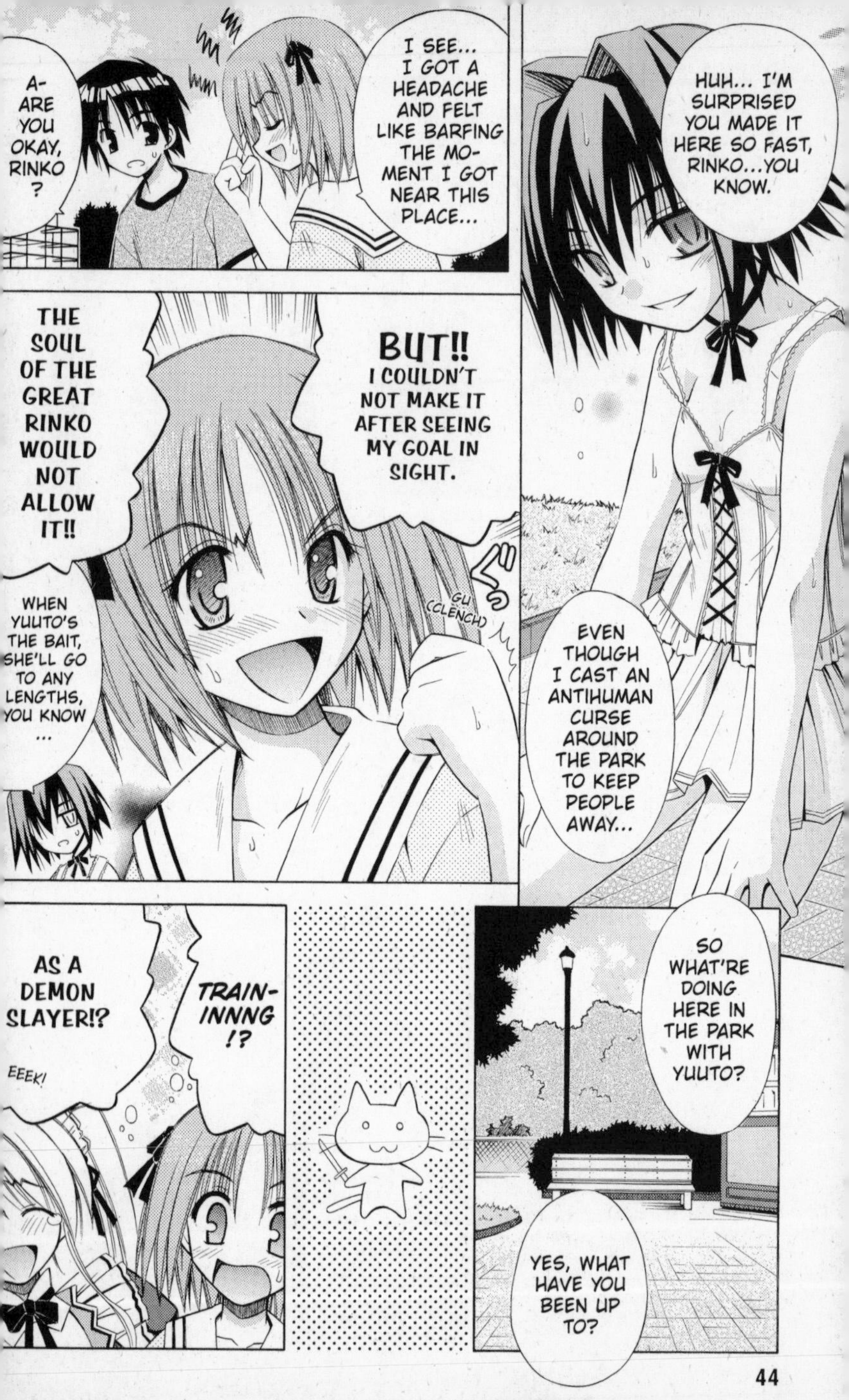
HUH... I'M SURPRISED YOU MADE IT HERE SO FAST, RINKO...YOU KNOW.
EVEN THOUGH I CAST AN ANTIHUMAN CURSE AROUND THE PARK TO KEEP PEOPLE AWAY...
I SEE... I GOT A HEADACHE AND FELT LIKE BARFING THE MO-MENT I GOT NEAR THIS PLACE...
A-ARE YOU OKAY, RINKO?
BUT!! I COULDN'T NOT MAKE IT AFTER SEEING MY GOAL IN SIGHT.
THE SOUL OF THE GREAT RINKO WOULD NOT ALLOW IT!!
GU (CLENCH)
WHEN YUUTO'S THE BAIT, SHE'LL GO TO ANY LENGTHS, YOU KNOW...
SO WHAT'RE DOING HERE IN THE PARK WITH YUUTO?
YES, WHAT HAVE YOU BEEN UP TO?
TRAIN-INNNG!?
AS A DEMON SLAYER!?
EEEK!

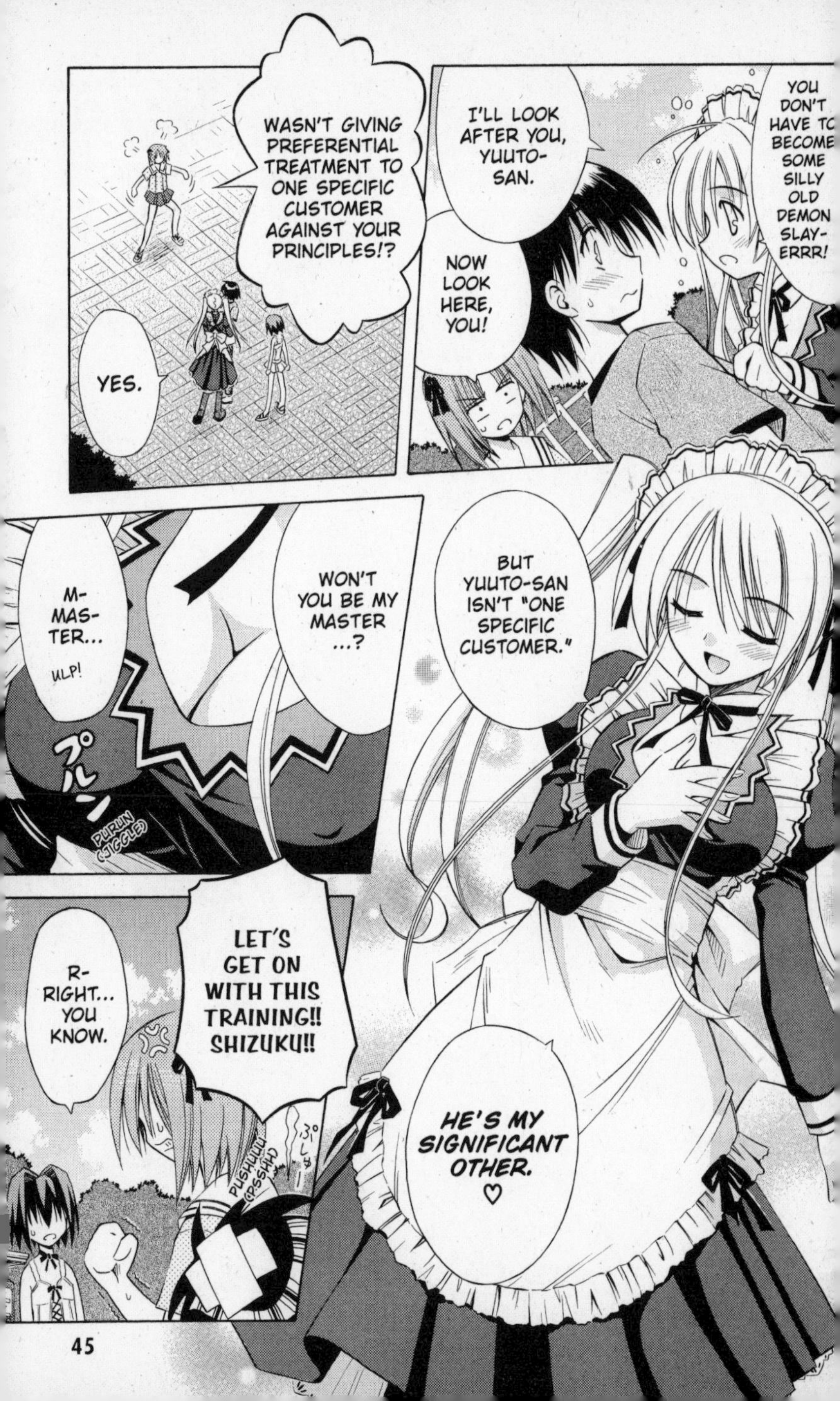
YOU DON'T HAVE TO BECOME SOME SILLY OLD DEMON SLAY-ERRR!
I'LL LOOK AFTER YOU, YUUTO-SAN.
NOW LOOK HERE, YOU!
WASN'T GIVING PREFERENTIAL TREATMENT TO ONE SPECIFIC CUSTOMER AGAINST YOUR PRINCIPLES!?
YES.
BUT YUUTO-SAN ISN'T "ONE SPECIFIC CUSTOMER."
HE'S MY SIGNIFICANT OTHER. ♡
WON'T YOU BE MY MASTER ...?
M-MASTER...
ULP!
プルン
PURUN (JIGGLE)
LET'S GET ON WITH THIS TRAINING!! SHIZUKU!!
ぷしゅ～
PUSHUUU (PSSHH)
R-RIGHT... YOU KNOW.

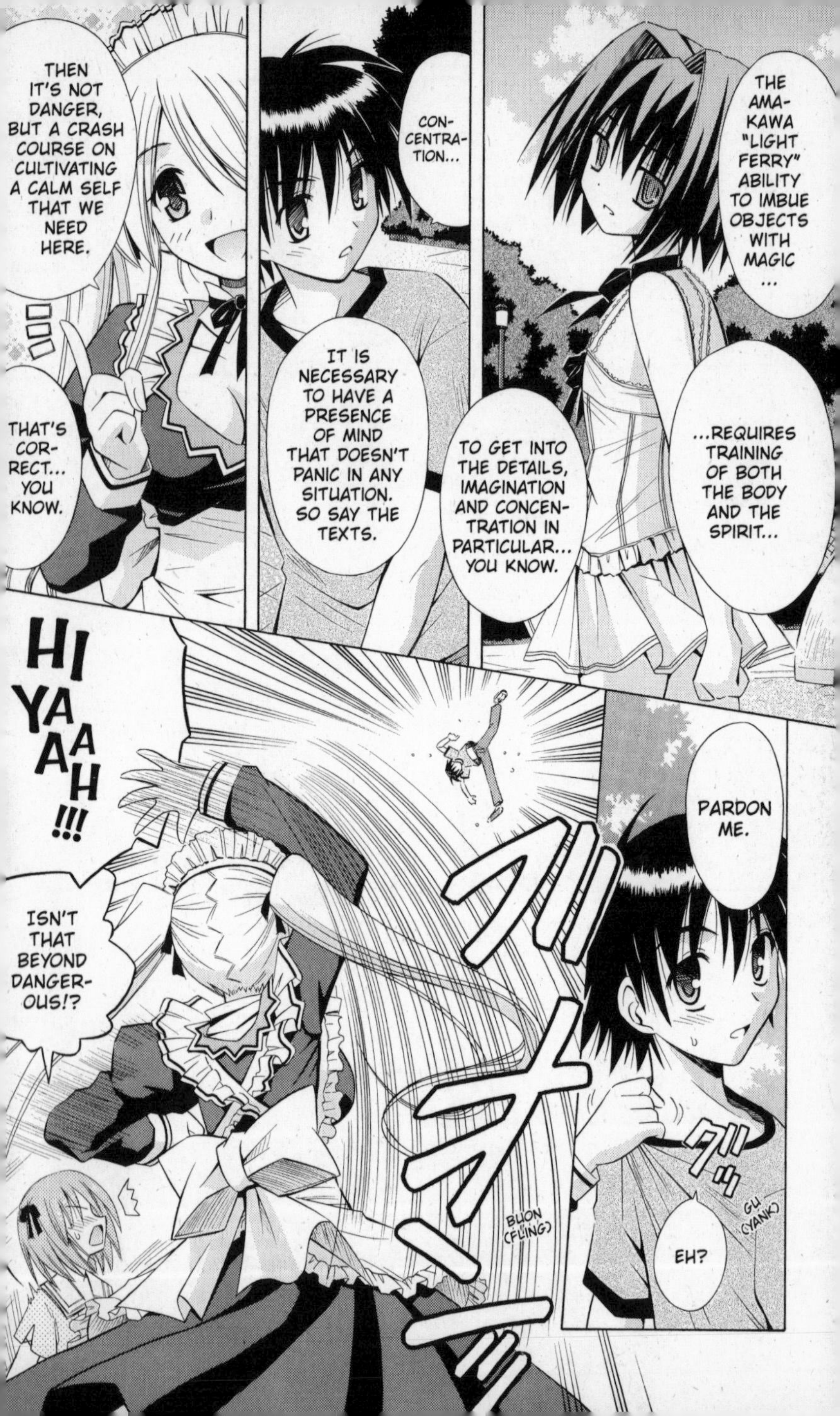
THE AMAKAWA "LIGHT FERRY" ABILITY TO IMBUE OBJECTS WITH MAGIC ...
...REQUIRES TRAINING OF BOTH THE BODY AND THE SPIRIT...
TO GET INTO THE DETAILS, IMAGINATION AND CONCENTRATION IN PARTICULAR... YOU KNOW.
CONCENTRATION...
IT IS NECESSARY TO HAVE A PRESENCE OF MIND THAT DOESN'T PANIC IN ANY SITUATION. SO SAY THE TEXTS.
THEN IT'S NOT DANGER, BUT A CRASH COURSE ON CULTIVATING A CALM SELF THAT WE NEED HERE.
THAT'S CORRECT... YOU KNOW.
PARDON ME.
GU (YANK)
EH?
BUON (FLING)
HIYAAAH!!!
ISN'T THAT BEYOND DANGEROUS!?

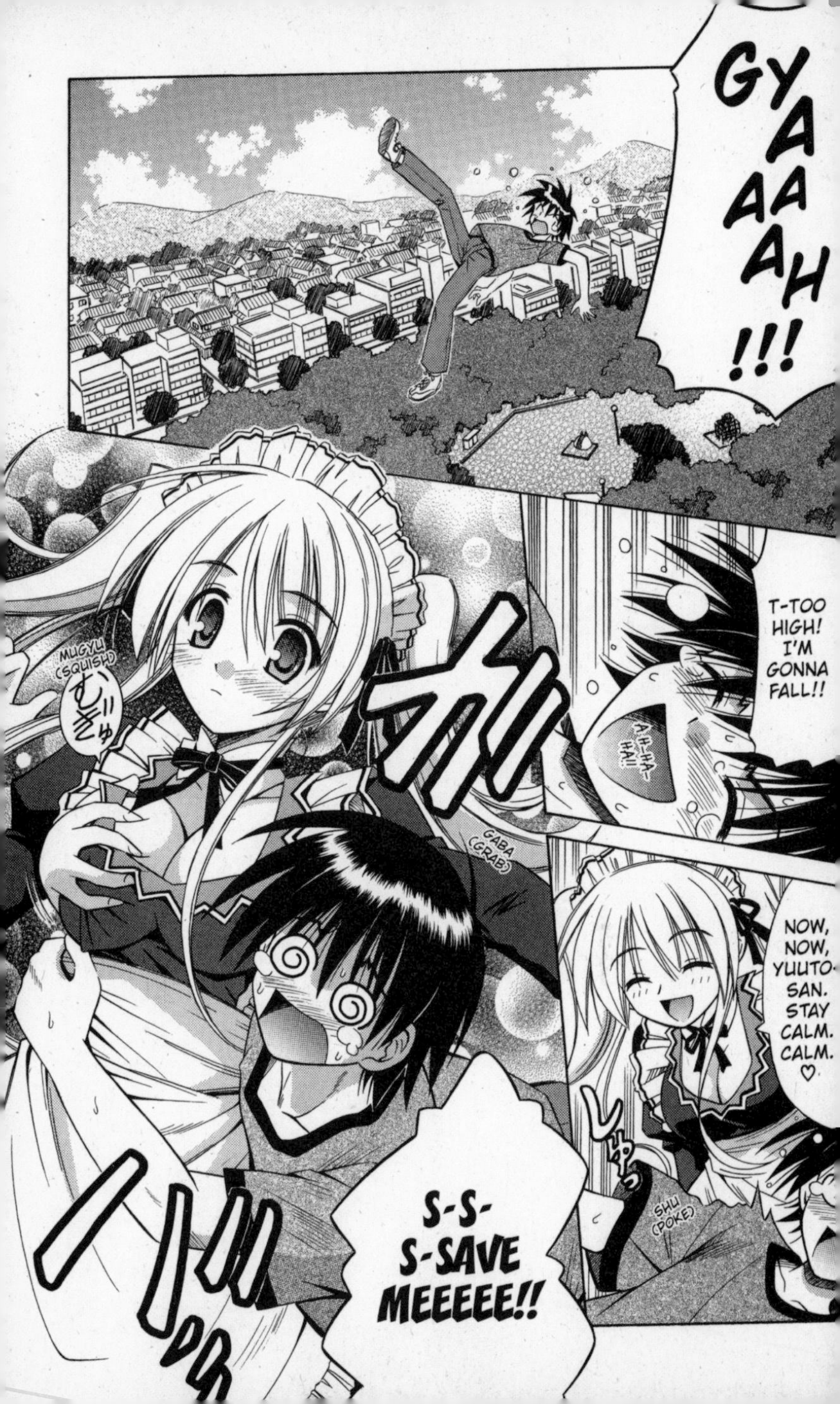

GYAAAAH!!!
T-TOO HIGH! I'M GONNA FALL!!
A-HA-HA!!
MUGYU (SQUISH)
GABA (GRAB)
NOW, NOW, YUUTO-SAN. STAY CALM. CALM. ♡
SHU (POKE)
S-S-S-SAVE MEEEEE!!

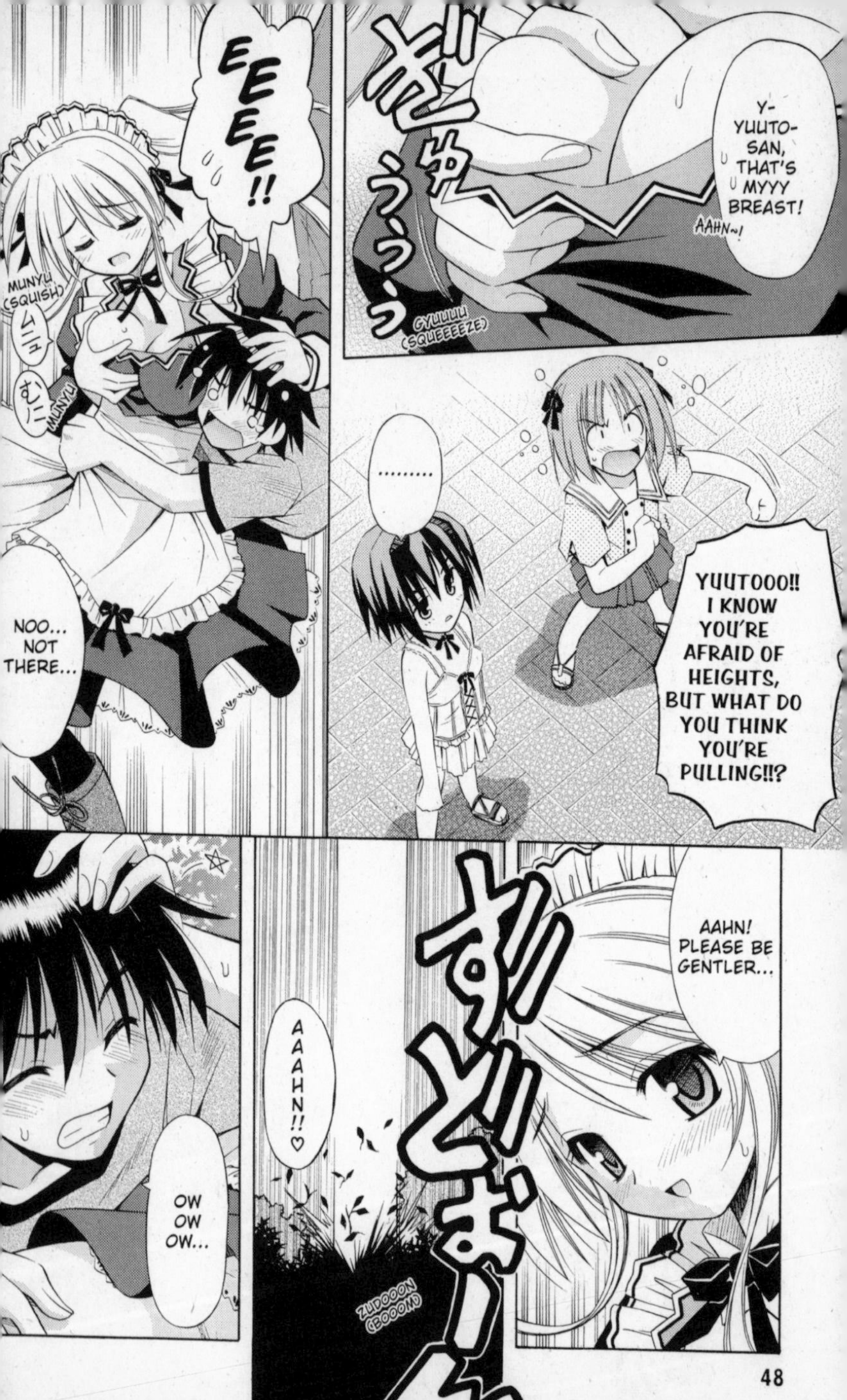

ぎゅううっ
Y-YUUTO-SAN, THAT'S MYYY BREAST!
AAHN~!
GYUUUU (SQUEEEEZE)
YUUTOOO!! I KNOW YOU'RE AFRAID OF HEIGHTS, BUT WHAT DO YOU THINK YOU'RE PULLING!!?
....
EEEE!!
MUNYU (SQUISH)
ムニュ
むに
MUNYU
NOO... NOT THERE...
AAHN! PLEASE BE GENTLER...
ずどぉ
ZUDOOON (BOOOM)
AAAAHN!!♡
OW OW OW...

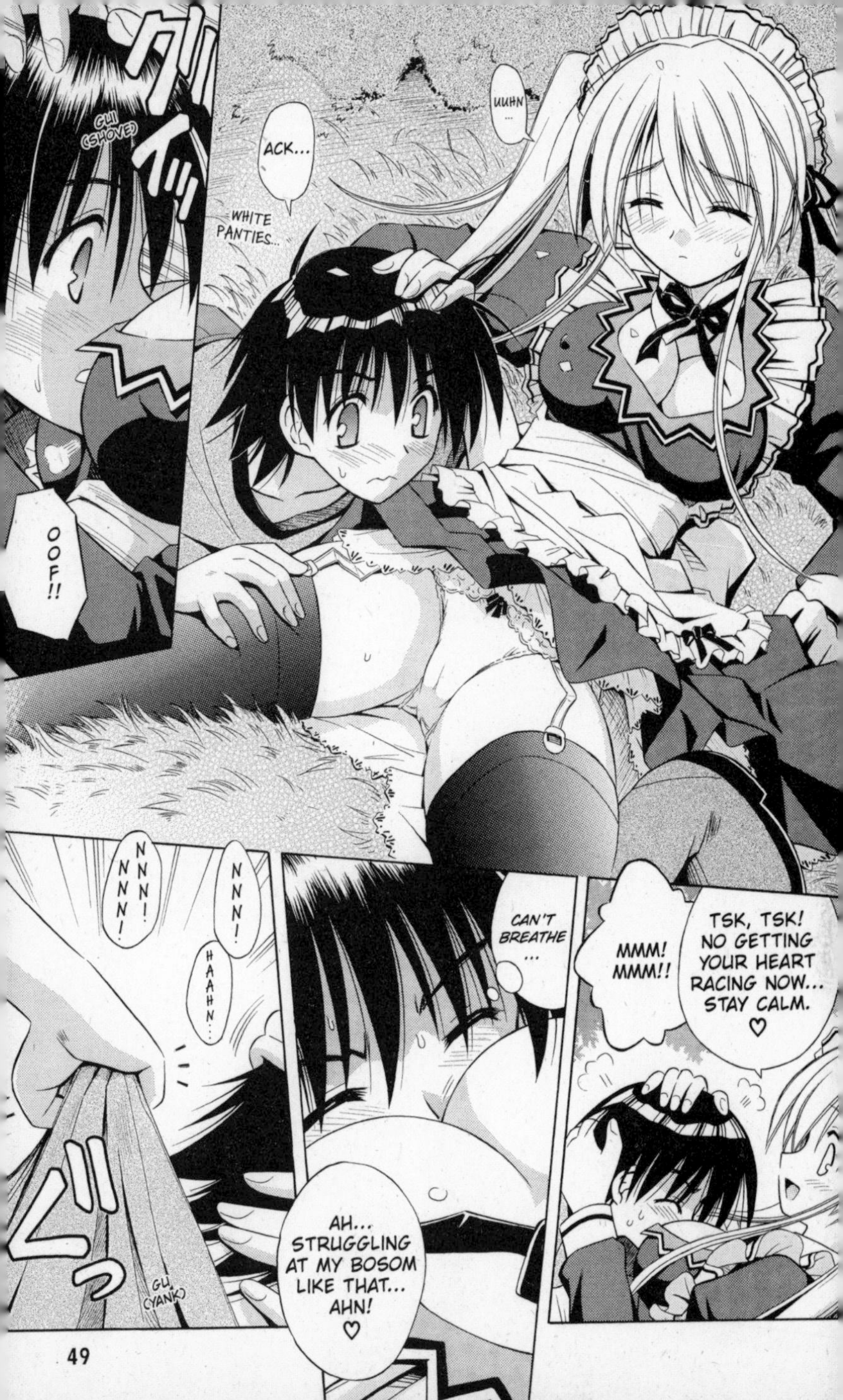
UUHN ...
ACK...
WHITE PANTIES...
GUI (SHOVE)
OOF!!
TSK, TSK! NO GETTING YOUR HEART RACING NOW... STAY CALM. ♡
MMM! MMM!!
CAN'T BREATHE ...
AH... STRUGGLING AT MY BOSOM LIKE THAT... AHN! ♡
NNN!
NNN! NNN!
HAAAHN...
GU (YANK)

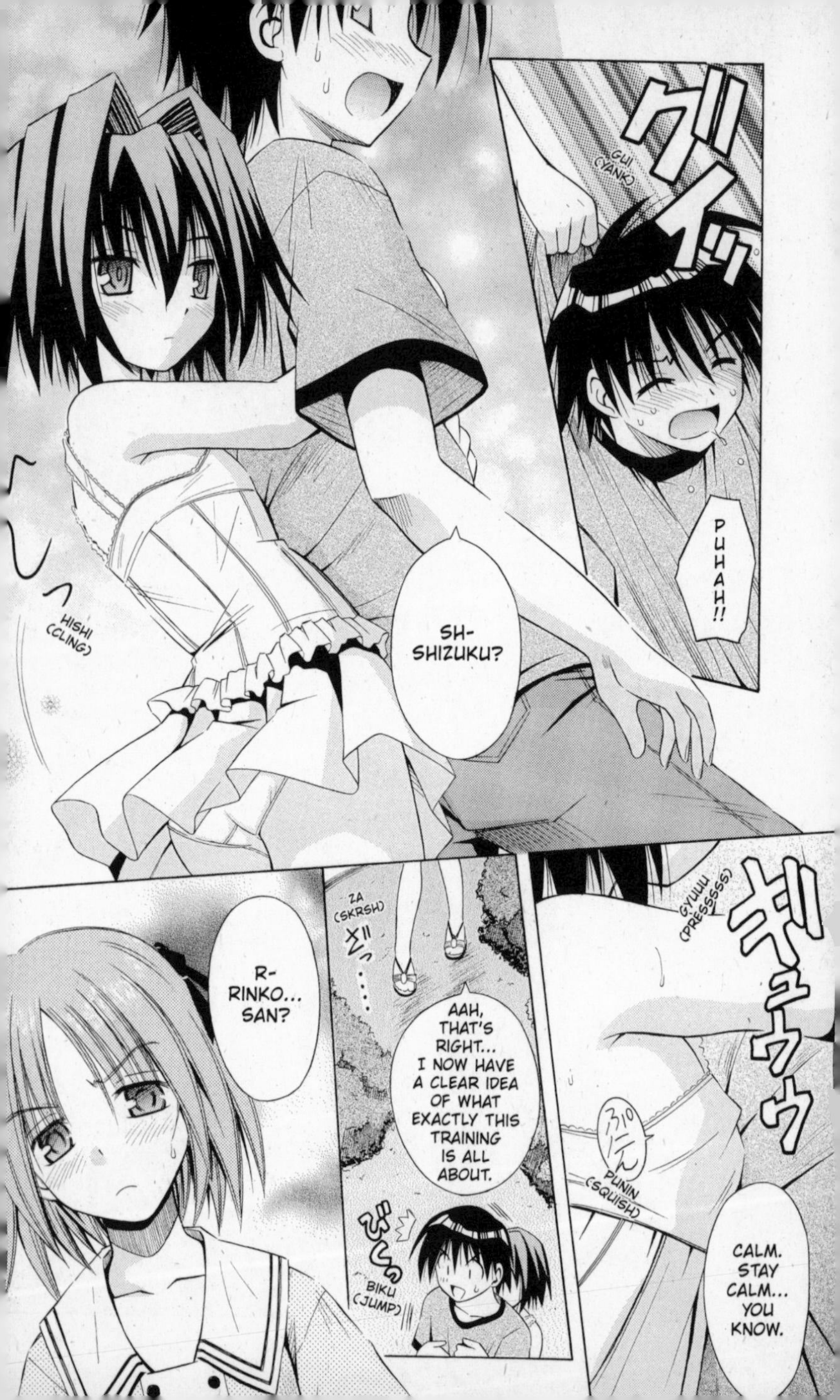
GUI (YANK)
PUHAH!!
SH-SHIZUKU?
HISHI (CLING)
GYUUU (PRESSSSS)
PUNIN (SQUISH)
CALM. STAY CALM... YOU KNOW.
ZA (SKRSH)
AAH, THAT'S RIGHT... I NOW HAVE A CLEAR IDEA OF WHAT EXACTLY THIS TRAINING IS ALL ABOUT.
BIKU (JUMP)
R-RINKO... SAN?

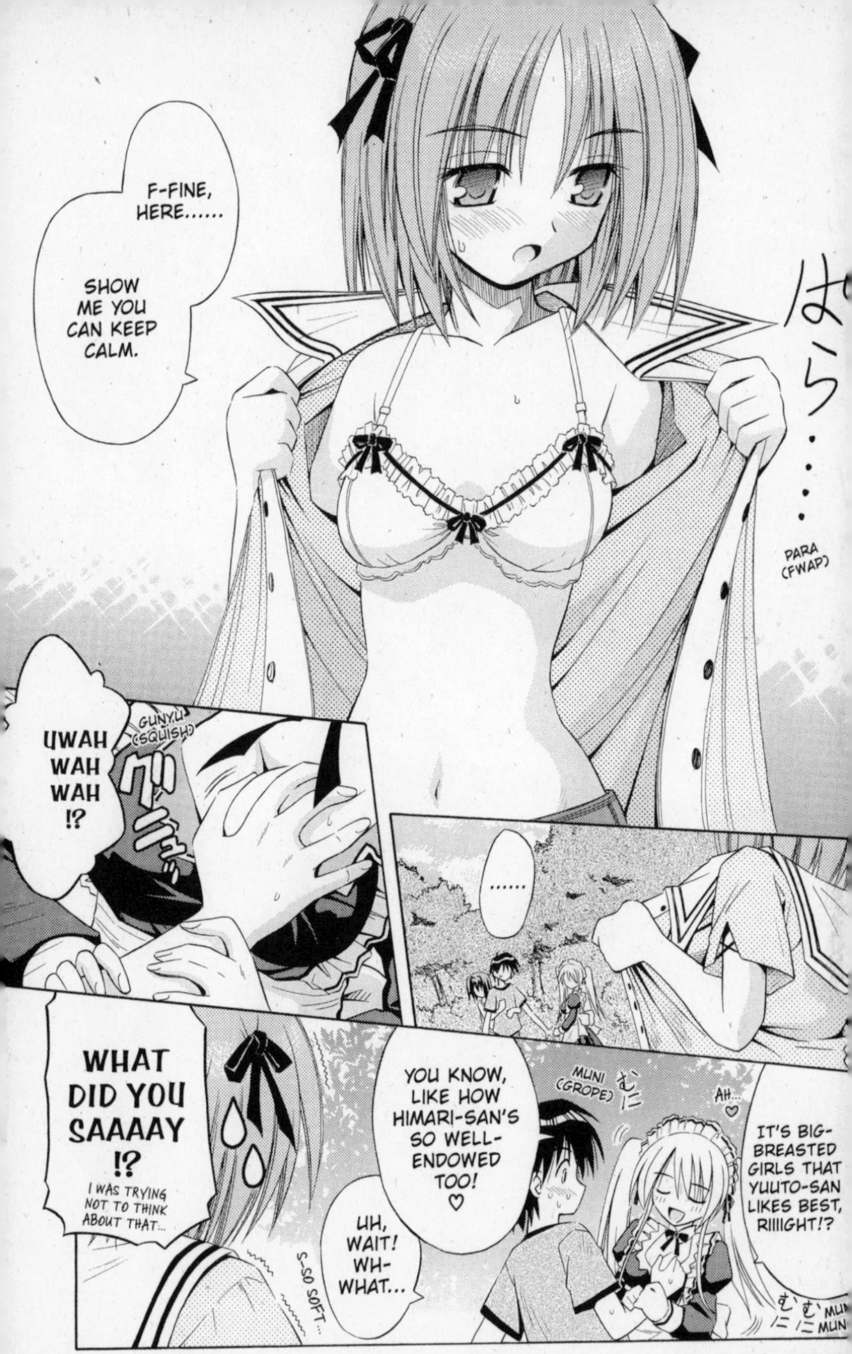
F-FINE, HERE......
SHOW ME YOU CAN KEEP CALM.
はら・・・
PARA (FWAP)
......
UWAH WAH WAH !?
GUNYU (SQUISH)
IT'S BIG-BREASTED GIRLS THAT YUUTO-SAN LIKES BEST, RIIIGHT!?
AH...♡
MUNI (GROPE)
むに
YOU KNOW, LIKE HOW HIMARI-SAN'S SO WELL-ENDOWED TOO! ♡
UH, WAIT! WH-WHAT...
S-SO SOFT...
むにむに
WHAT DID YOU SAAAAY !?
I WAS TRYING NOT TO THINK ABOUT THAT...

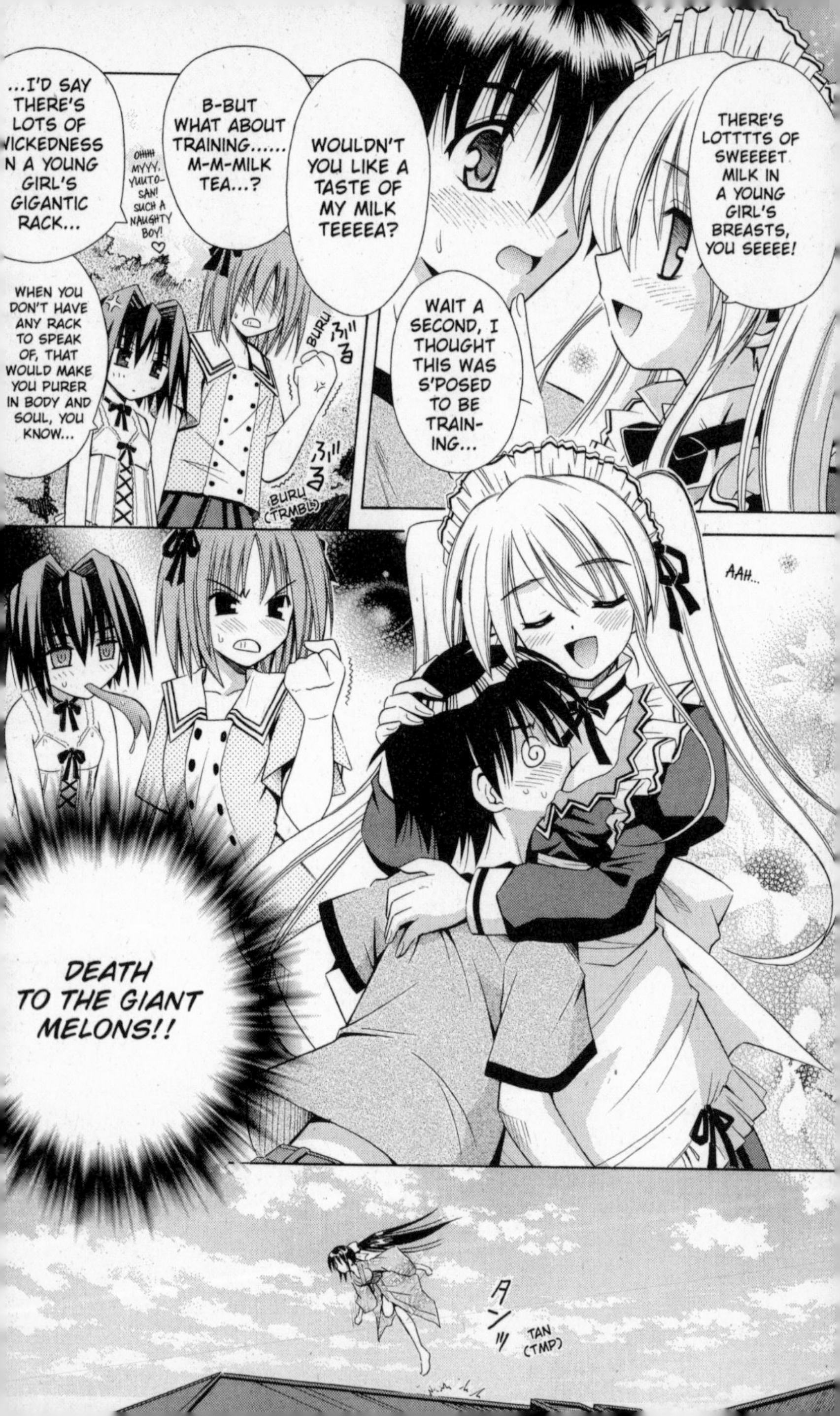

THERE'S LOTTTTS OF SWEEEET MILK IN A YOUNG GIRL'S BREASTS, YOU SEEEE!
WOULDN'T YOU LIKE A TASTE OF MY MILK TEEEEA?
WAIT A SECOND, I THOUGHT THIS WAS S'POSED TO BE TRAINING...
B-BUT WHAT ABOUT TRAINING...... M-M-MILK TEA...?
OHHH MYYY, YUUTO-SAN! SUCH A NAUGHTY BOY! ♡
...I'D SAY THERE'S LOTS OF VICKEDNESS N A YOUNG GIRL'S GIGANTIC RACK...
BURU
WHEN YOU DON'T HAVE ANY RACK TO SPEAK OF, THAT WOULD MAKE YOU PURER IN BODY AND SOUL, YOU KNOW...
BURU (TRMBL)
AAH...
DEATH TO THE GIANT MELONS!!
TAN (TMP)

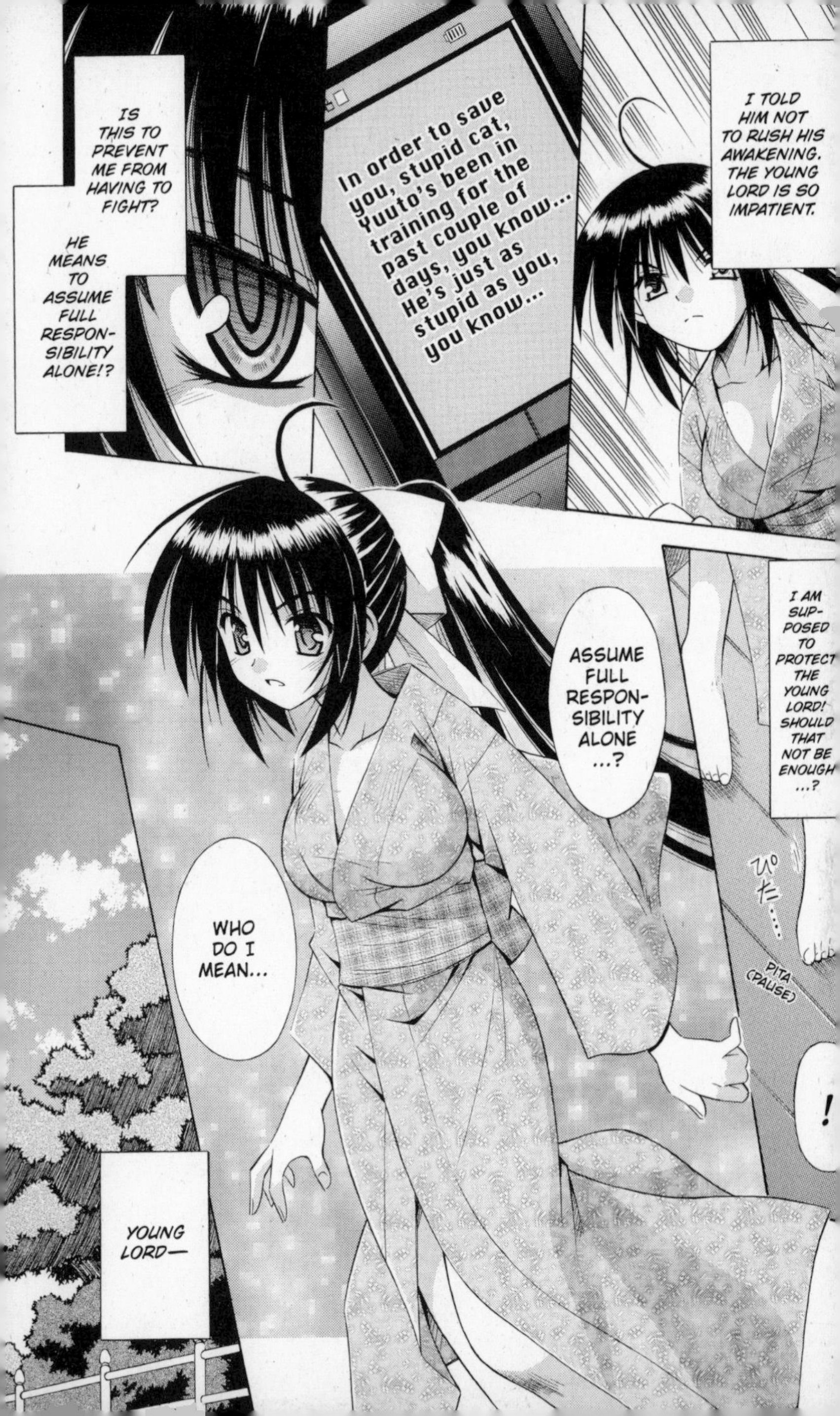
I TOLD HIM NOT TO RUSH HIS AWAKENING. THE YOUNG LORD IS SO IMPATIENT.
In order to save you, stupid cat, Yuuto's been in training for the past couple of days, you know... He's just as stupid as you, you know...
IS THIS TO PREVENT ME FROM HAVING TO FIGHT?
HE MEANS TO ASSUME FULL RESPON-SIBILITY ALONE!?
I AM SUP-POSED TO PROTECT THE YOUNG LORD! SHOULD THAT NOT BE ENOUGH ...?
ぴた…
PITA (PAUSE)
!
ASSUME FULL RESPON-SIBILITY ALONE ...?
WHO DO I MEAN...
YOUNG LORD—

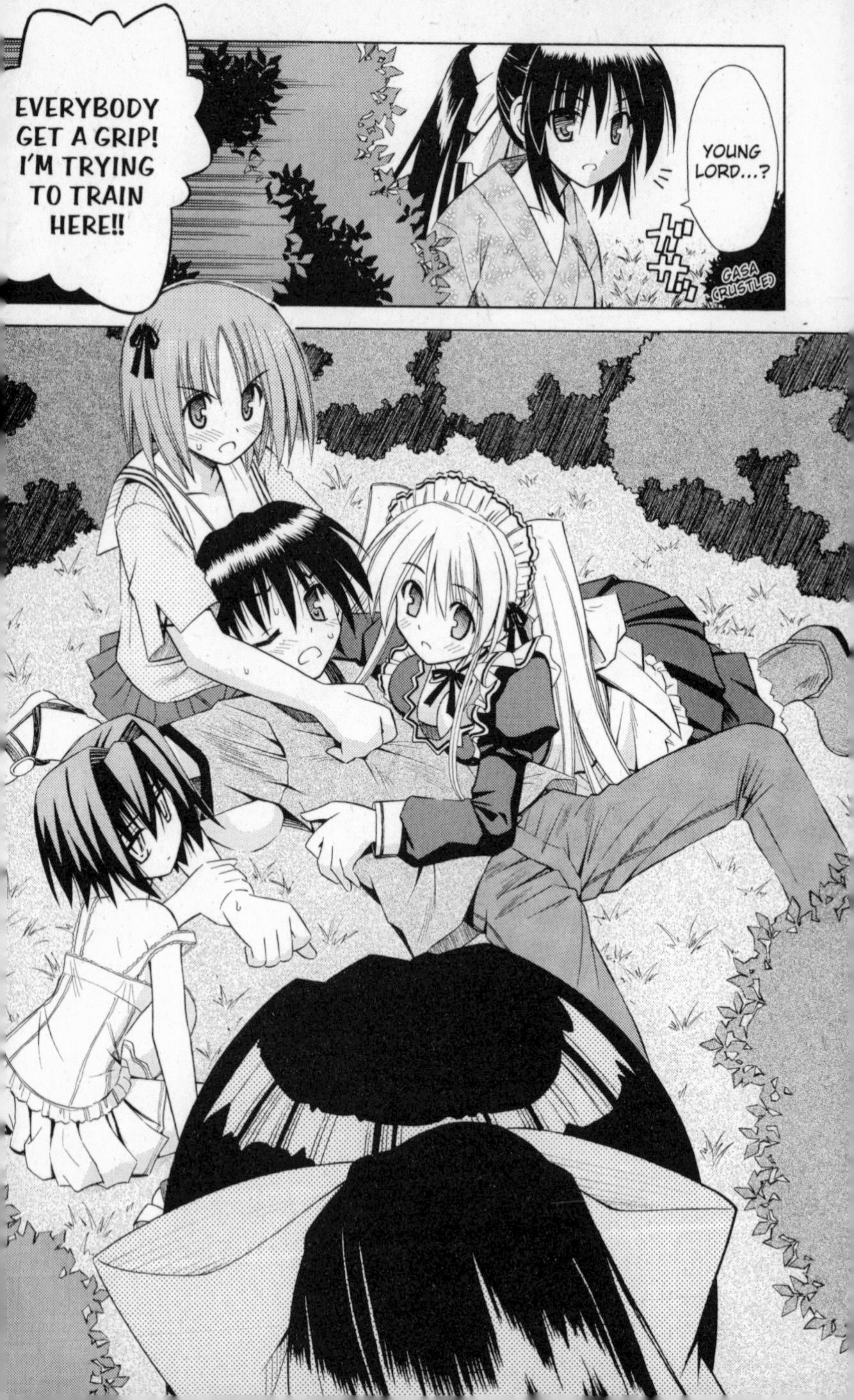
YOUNG LORD...?
GASA (RUSTLE)
EVERYBODY GET A GRIP! I'M TRYING TO TRAIN HERE!!

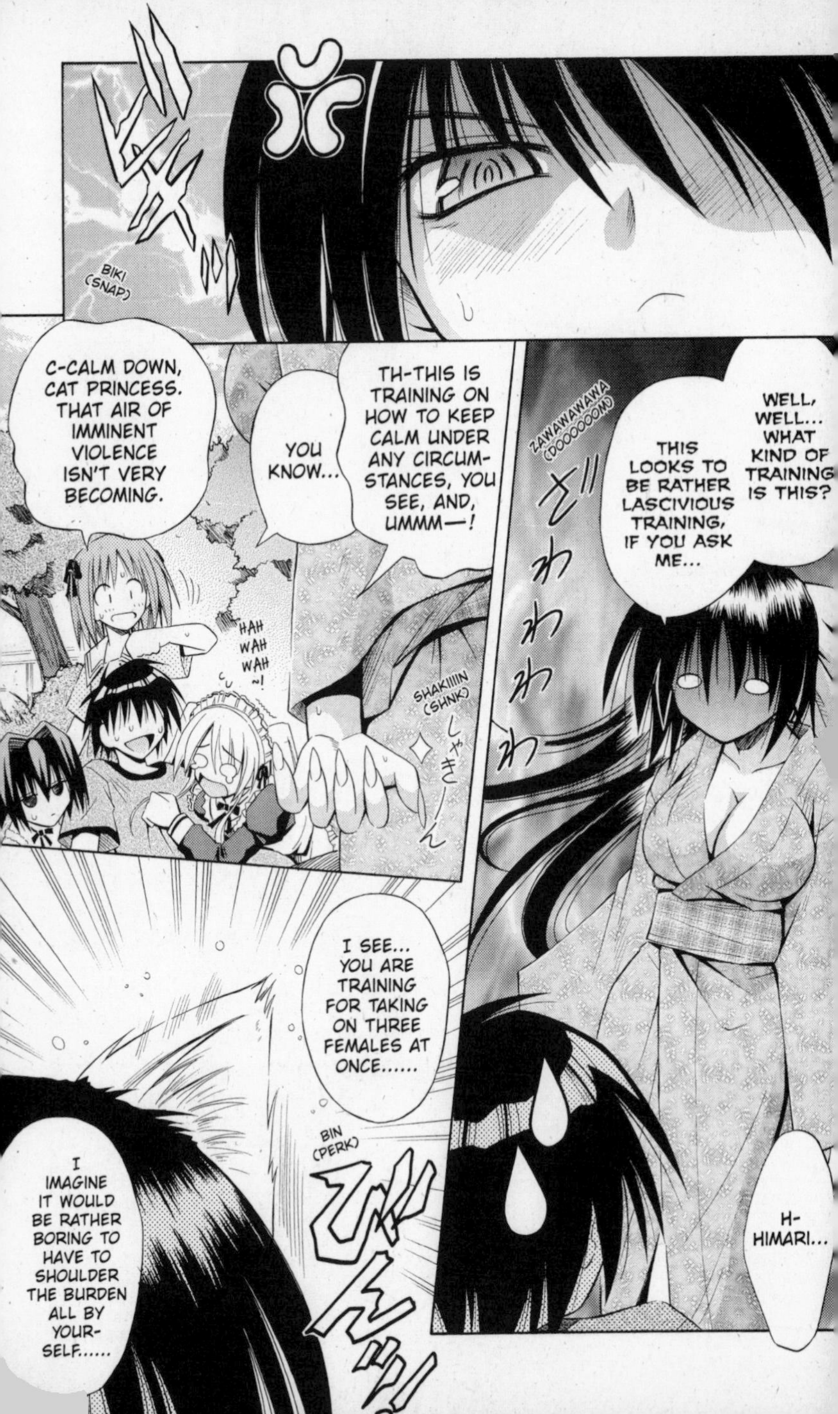
BIKI (SNAP)
WELL, WELL... WHAT KIND OF TRAINING IS THIS?
ZAWAWAWAWA (DOOOOOOOM)
THIS LOOKS TO BE RATHER LASCIVIOUS TRAINING, IF YOU ASK ME...
H-HIMARI...
TH-THIS IS TRAINING ON HOW TO KEEP CALM UNDER ANY CIRCUM-STANCES, YOU SEE, AND, UMMM—!
YOU KNOW...
C-CALM DOWN, CAT PRINCESS. THAT AIR OF IMMINENT VIOLENCE ISN'T VERY BECOMING.
HAH WAH WAH ~!
SHAKIIIIN (SHNK)
I SEE... YOU ARE TRAINING FOR TAKING ON THREE FEMALES AT ONCE......
BIN (PERK)
I IMAGINE IT WOULD BE RATHER BORING TO HAVE TO SHOULDER THE BURDEN ALL BY YOUR-SELF......

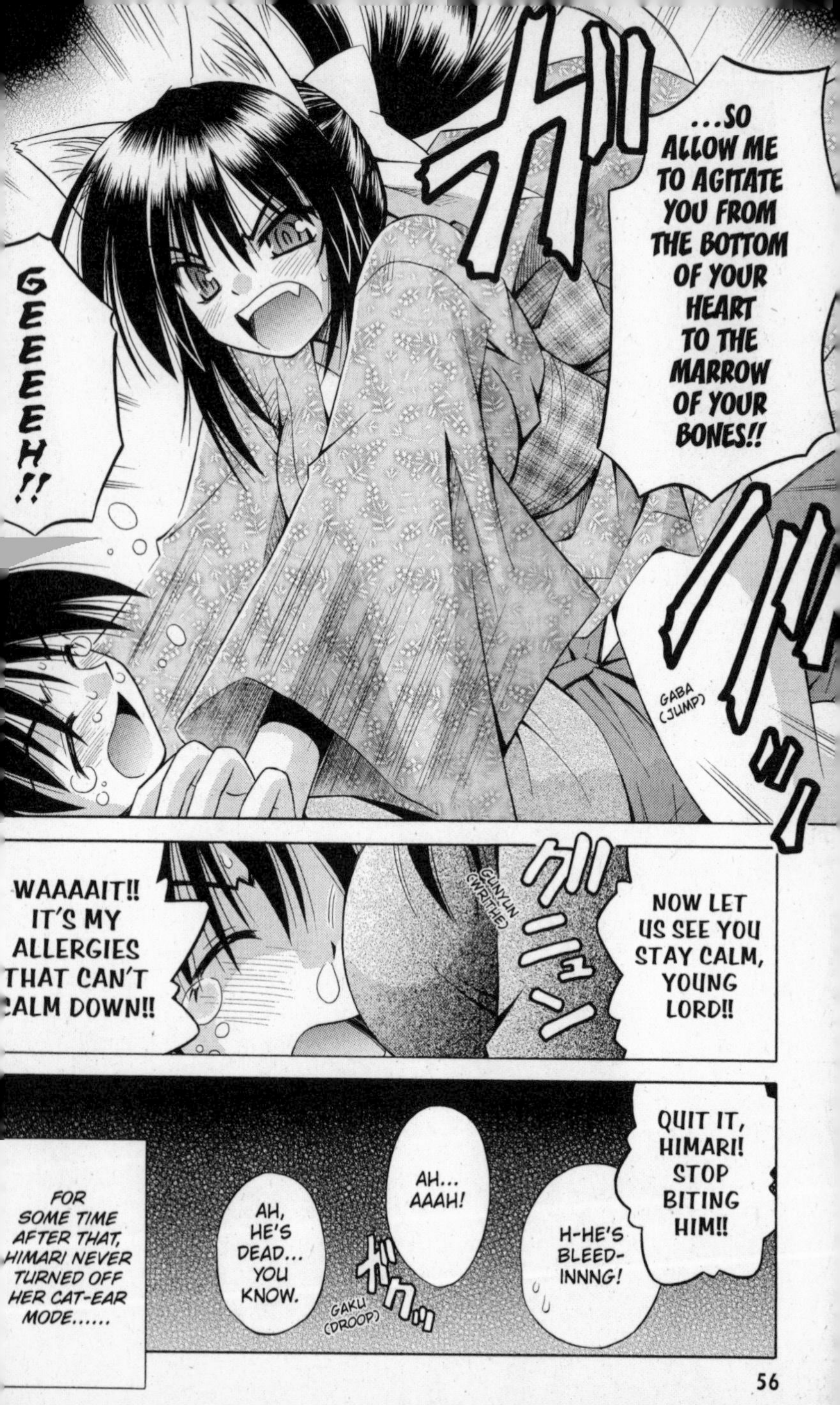
...SO ALLOW ME TO AGITATE YOU FROM THE BOTTOM OF YOUR HEART TO THE MARROW OF YOUR BONES!!
GEEEEEH!!
GABA (JUMP)
NOW LET US SEE YOU STAY CALM, YOUNG LORD!!
GUNYUN (WRITHE)
WAAAAIT!! IT'S MY ALLERGIES THAT CAN'T CALM DOWN!!
QUIT IT, HIMARI! STOP BITING HIM!!
H-HE'S BLEED-INNNG!
AH... AAAH!
AH, HE'S DEAD... YOU KNOW.
GAKU (DROOP)
FOR SOME TIME AFTER THAT, HIMARI NEVER TURNED OFF HER CAT-EAR MODE......

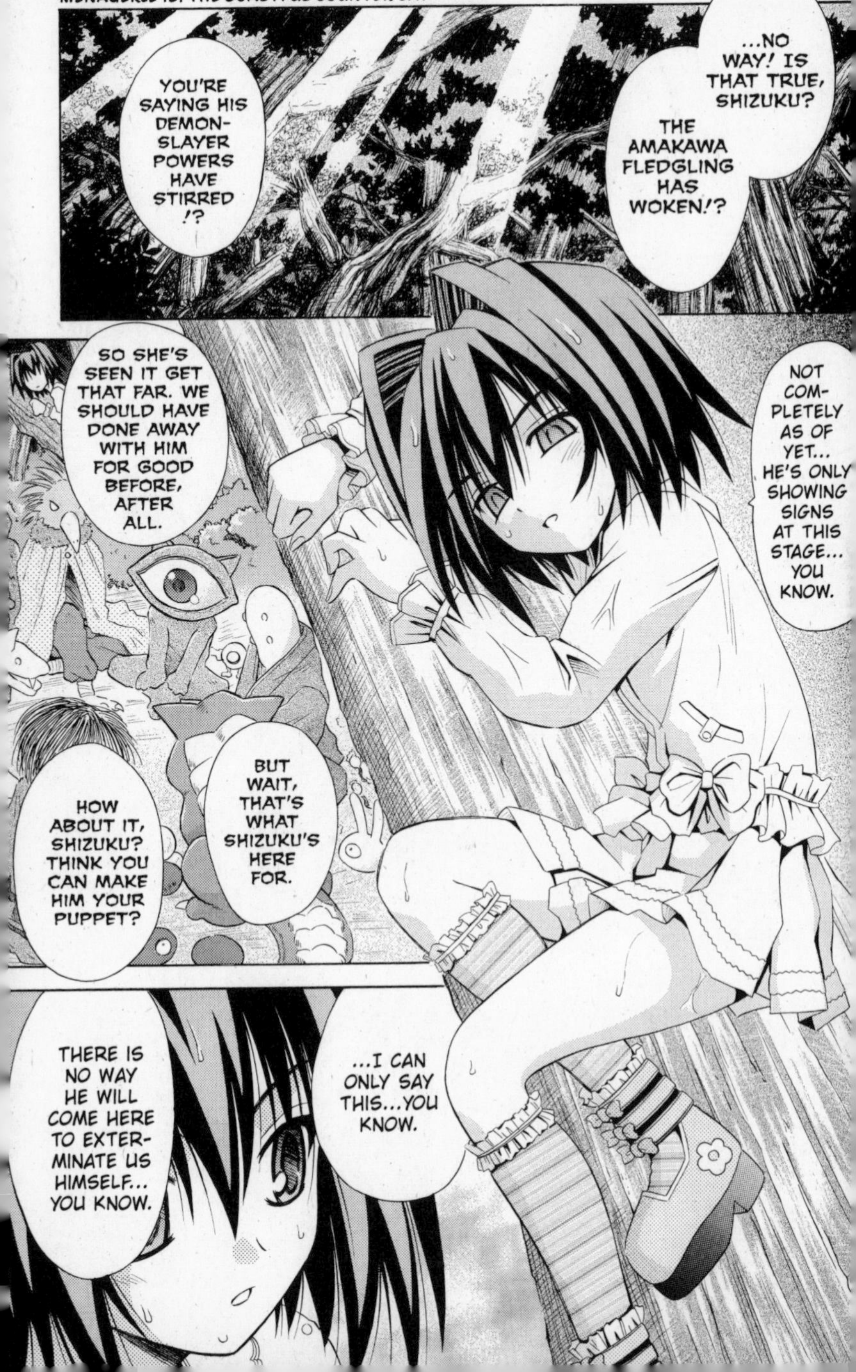
...NO WAY! IS THAT TRUE, SHIZUKU?
THE AMAKAWA FLEDGLING HAS WOKEN!?
YOU'RE SAYING HIS DEMON-SLAYER POWERS HAVE STIRRED!?
NOT COM-PLETELY AS OF YET... HE'S ONLY SHOWING SIGNS AT THIS STAGE... YOU KNOW.
SO SHE'S SEEN IT GET THAT FAR. WE SHOULD HAVE DONE AWAY WITH HIM FOR GOOD BEFORE, AFTER ALL.
BUT WAIT, THAT'S WHAT SHIZUKU'S HERE FOR.
HOW ABOUT IT, SHIZUKU? THINK YOU CAN MAKE HIM YOUR PUPPET?
...I CAN ONLY SAY THIS...YOU KNOW.
THERE IS NO WAY HE WILL COME HERE TO EXTER-MINATE US HIMSELF... YOU KNOW.

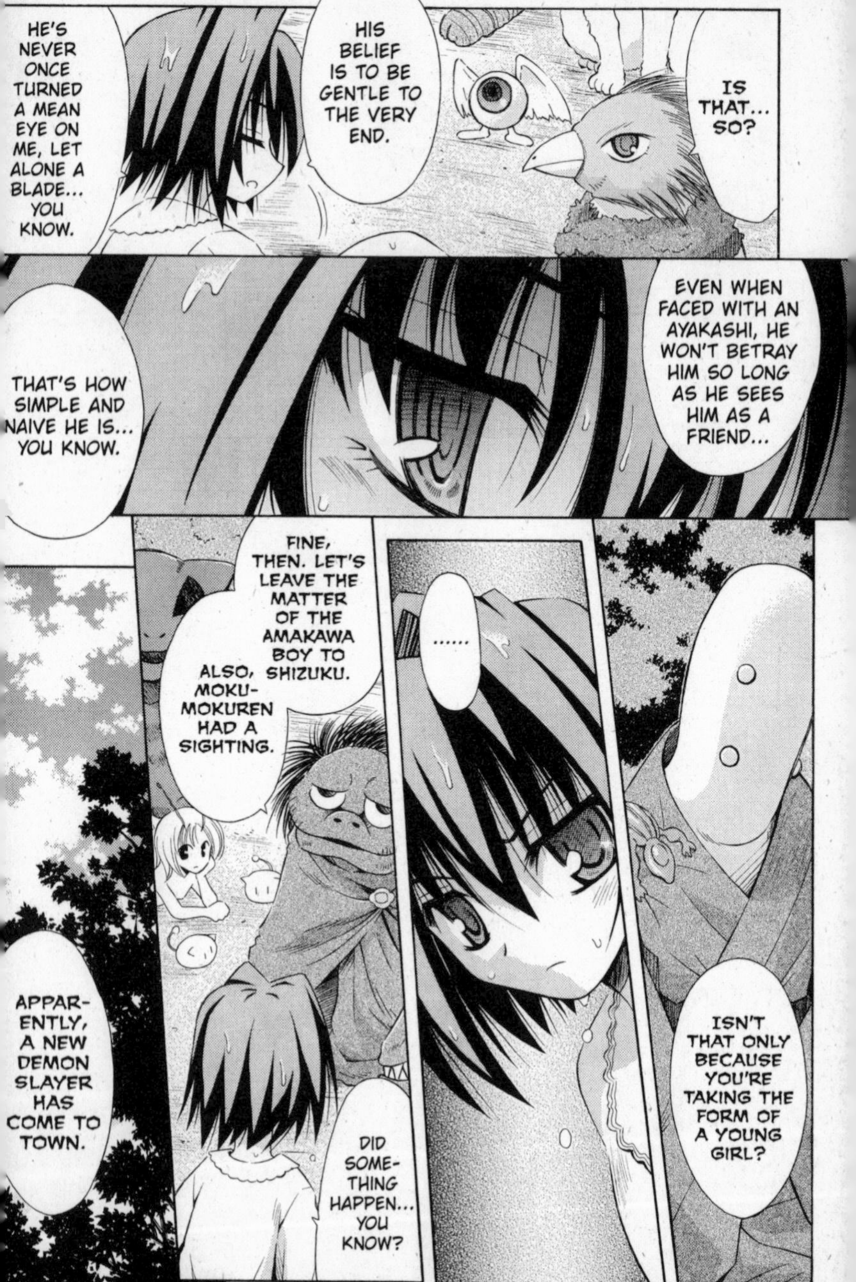
IS THAT... SO?
HIS BELIEF IS TO BE GENTLE TO THE VERY END.
HE'S NEVER ONCE TURNED A MEAN EYE ON ME, LET ALONE A BLADE... YOU KNOW.
EVEN WHEN FACED WITH AN AYAKASHI, HE WON'T BETRAY HIM SO LONG AS HE SEES HIM AS A FRIEND...
THAT'S HOW SIMPLE AND NAIVE HE IS... YOU KNOW.
......
ISN'T THAT ONLY BECAUSE YOU'RE TAKING THE FORM OF A YOUNG GIRL?
FINE, THEN. LET'S LEAVE THE MATTER OF THE AMAKAWA BOY TO SHIZUKU.
ALSO, MOKU-MOKUREN HAD A SIGHTING.
DID SOME-THING HAPPEN... YOU KNOW?
APPAR-ENTLY, A NEW DEMON SLAYER HAS COME TO TOWN.

NOTE: MOKUMOKUREN IS A JAPANESE SPIRIT THAT LIVES IN SLIDING PAPER DOORS.

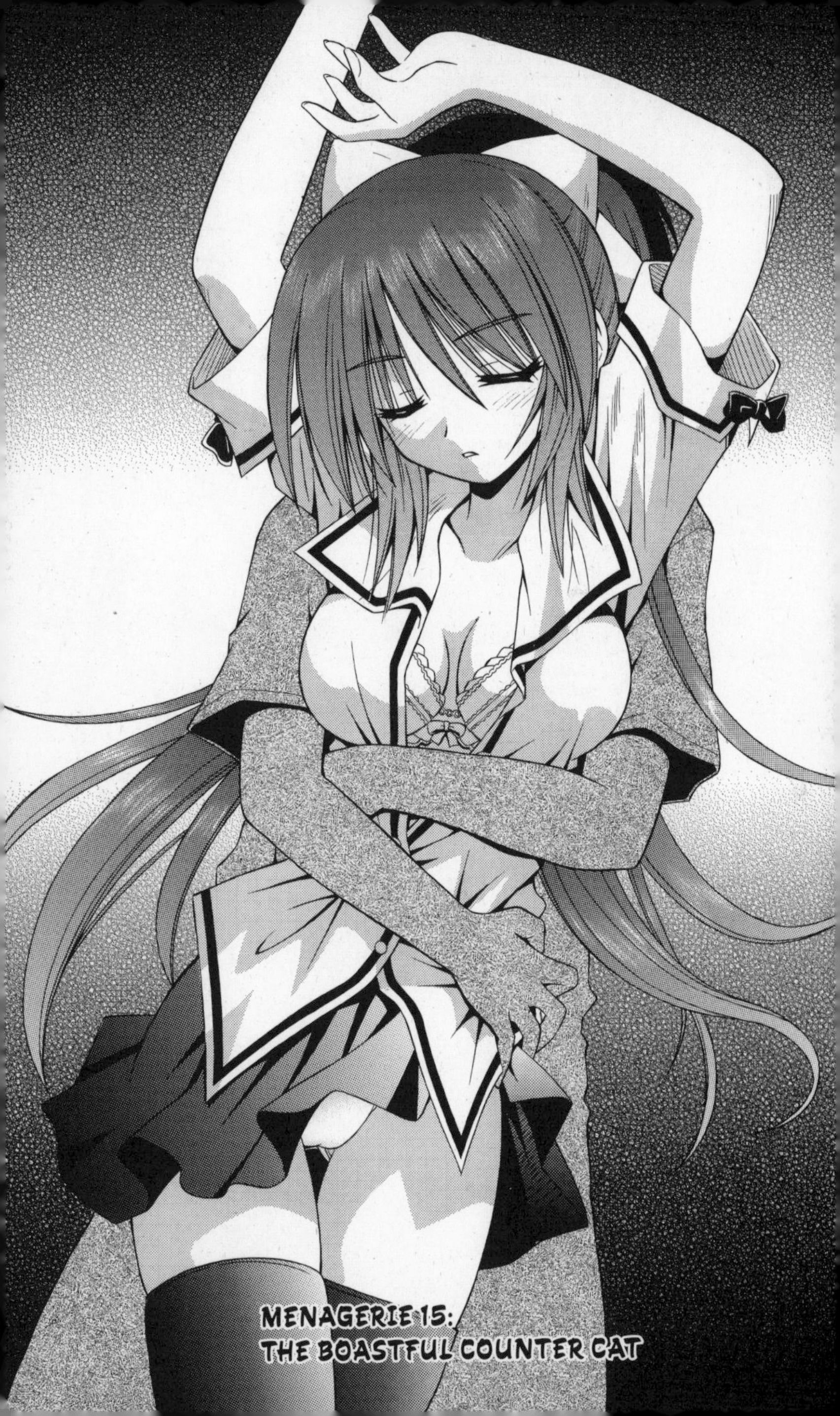
MENAGERIE 15:
THE BOASTFUL COUNTER CAT

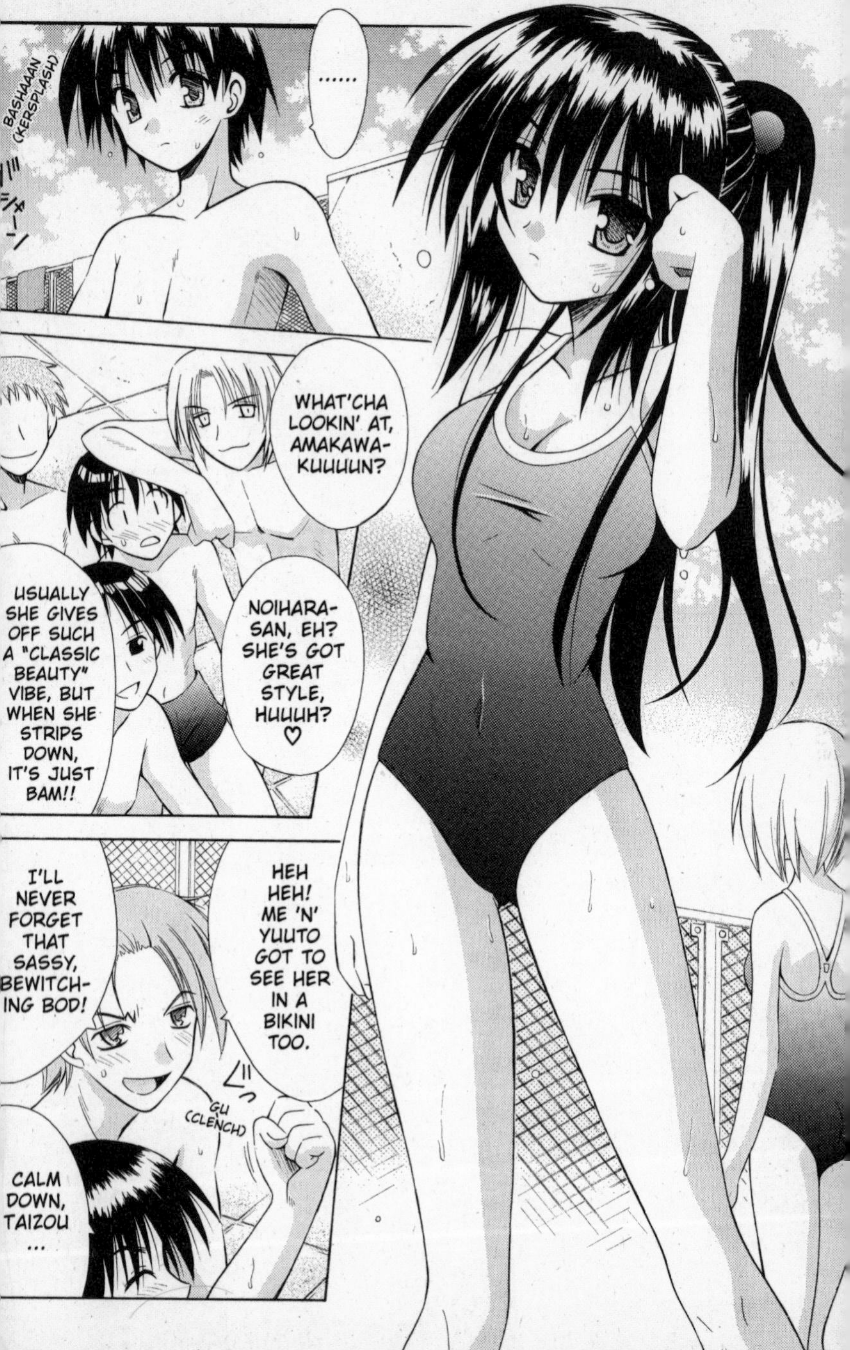

......
BASHAAAN (KERSPLASH)
WHAT'CHA LOOKIN' AT, AMAKAWA-KUUUUN?
NOIHARA-SAN, EH? SHE'S GOT GREAT STYLE, HUUUH? ♡
USUALLY SHE GIVES OFF SUCH A "CLASSIC BEAUTY" VIBE, BUT WHEN SHE STRIPS DOWN, IT'S JUST BAM!!
HEH HEH! ME 'N' YUUTO GOT TO SEE HER IN A BIKINI TOO.
GU (CLENCH)
I'LL NEVER FORGET THAT SASSY, BEWITCHING BOD!
CALM DOWN, TAIZOU ...

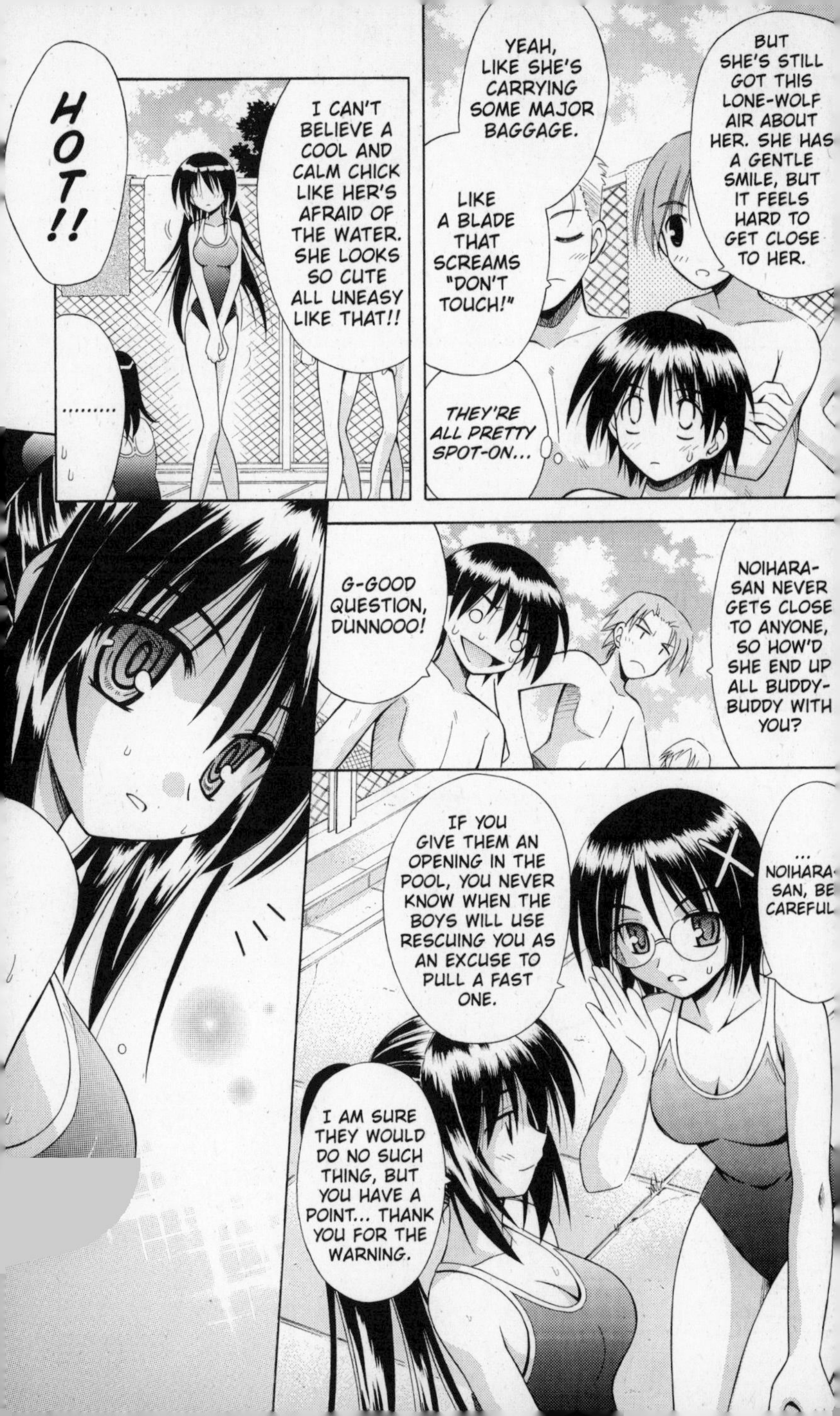
BUT SHE'S STILL GOT THIS LONE-WOLF AIR ABOUT HER. SHE HAS A GENTLE SMILE, BUT IT FEELS HARD TO GET CLOSE TO HER.
YEAH, LIKE SHE'S CARRYING SOME MAJOR BAGGAGE.
LIKE A BLADE THAT SCREAMS "DON'T TOUCH!"
THEY'RE ALL PRETTY SPOT-ON...
I CAN'T BELIEVE A COOL AND CALM CHICK LIKE HER'S AFRAID OF THE WATER. SHE LOOKS SO CUTE ALL UNEASY LIKE THAT!!
HOT!!
....
NOIHARA-SAN NEVER GETS CLOSE TO ANYONE, SO HOW'D SHE END UP ALL BUDDY-BUDDY WITH YOU?
G-GOOD QUESTION, DUNNOOO!
... NOIHARA-SAN, BE CAREFUL
IF YOU GIVE THEM AN OPENING IN THE POOL, YOU NEVER KNOW WHEN THE BOYS WILL USE RESCUING YOU AS AN EXCUSE TO PULL A FAST ONE.
I AM SURE THEY WOULD DO NO SUCH THING, BUT YOU HAVE A POINT... THANK YOU FOR THE WARNING.

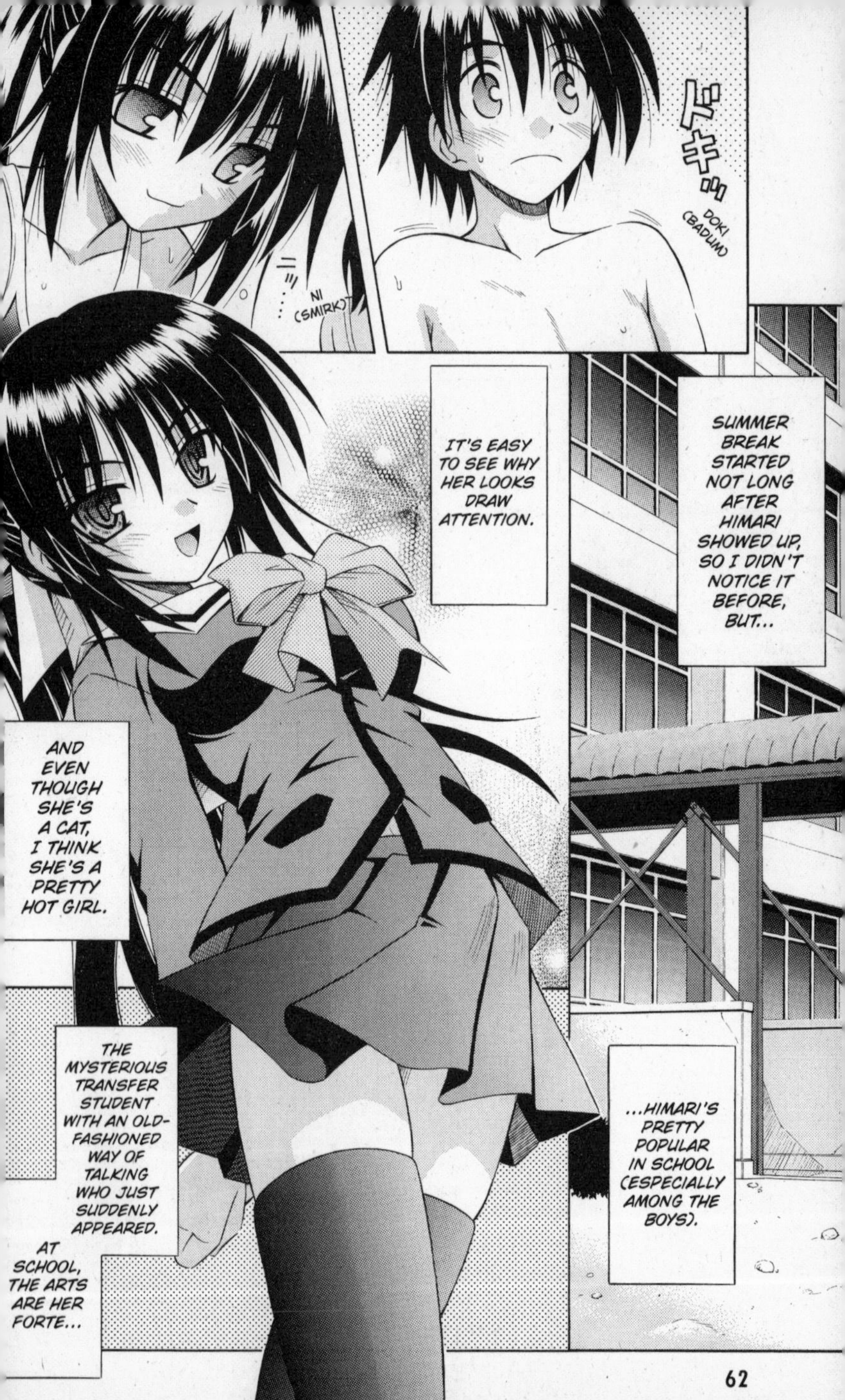
ドキッ
DOKI (BADUM)
ニッ…
NI (SMIRK)
SUMMER BREAK STARTED NOT LONG AFTER HIMARI SHOWED UP, SO I DIDN'T NOTICE IT BEFORE, BUT...
...HIMARI'S PRETTY POPULAR IN SCHOOL (ESPECIALLY AMONG THE BOYS).
IT'S EASY TO SEE WHY HER LOOKS DRAW ATTENTION.
AND EVEN THOUGH SHE'S A CAT, I THINK SHE'S A PRETTY HOT GIRL.
THE MYSTERIOUS TRANSFER STUDENT WITH AN OLD-FASHIONED WAY OF TALKING WHO JUST SUDDENLY APPEARED.
AT SCHOOL, THE ARTS ARE HER FORTE...

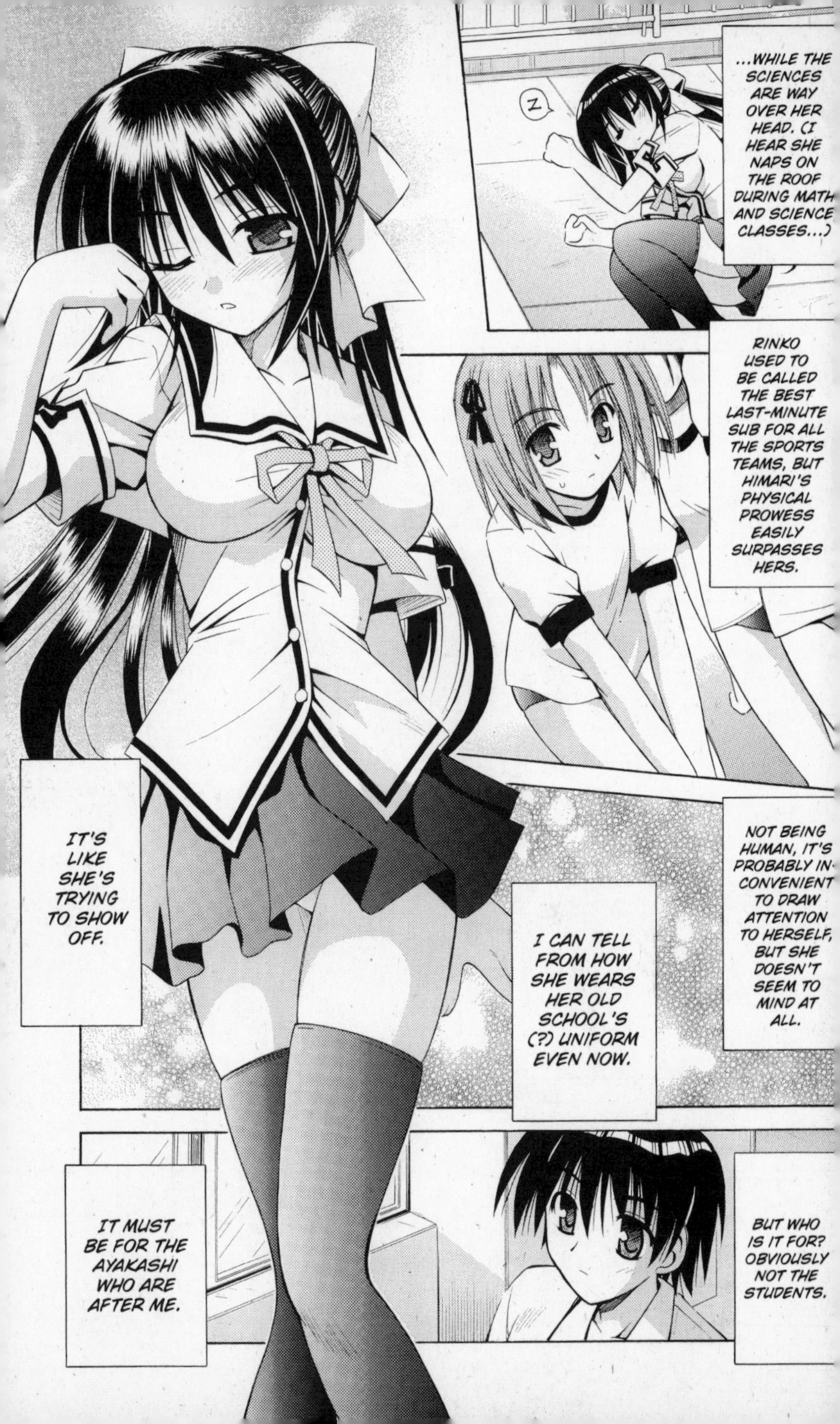
...WHILE THE SCIENCES ARE WAY OVER HER HEAD. (I HEAR SHE NAPS ON THE ROOF DURING MATH AND SCIENCE CLASSES...)
Z
RINKO USED TO BE CALLED THE BEST LAST-MINUTE SUB FOR ALL THE SPORTS TEAMS, BUT HIMARI'S PHYSICAL PROWESS EASILY SURPASSES HERS.
NOT BEING HUMAN, IT'S PROBABLY IN-CONVENIENT TO DRAW ATTENTION TO HERSELF, BUT SHE DOESN'T SEEM TO MIND AT ALL.
I CAN TELL FROM HOW SHE WEARS HER OLD SCHOOL'S (?) UNIFORM EVEN NOW.
IT'S LIKE SHE'S TRYING TO SHOW OFF.
BUT WHO IS IT FOR? OBVIOUSLY NOT THE STUDENTS.
IT MUST BE FOR THE AYAKASHI WHO ARE AFTER ME.

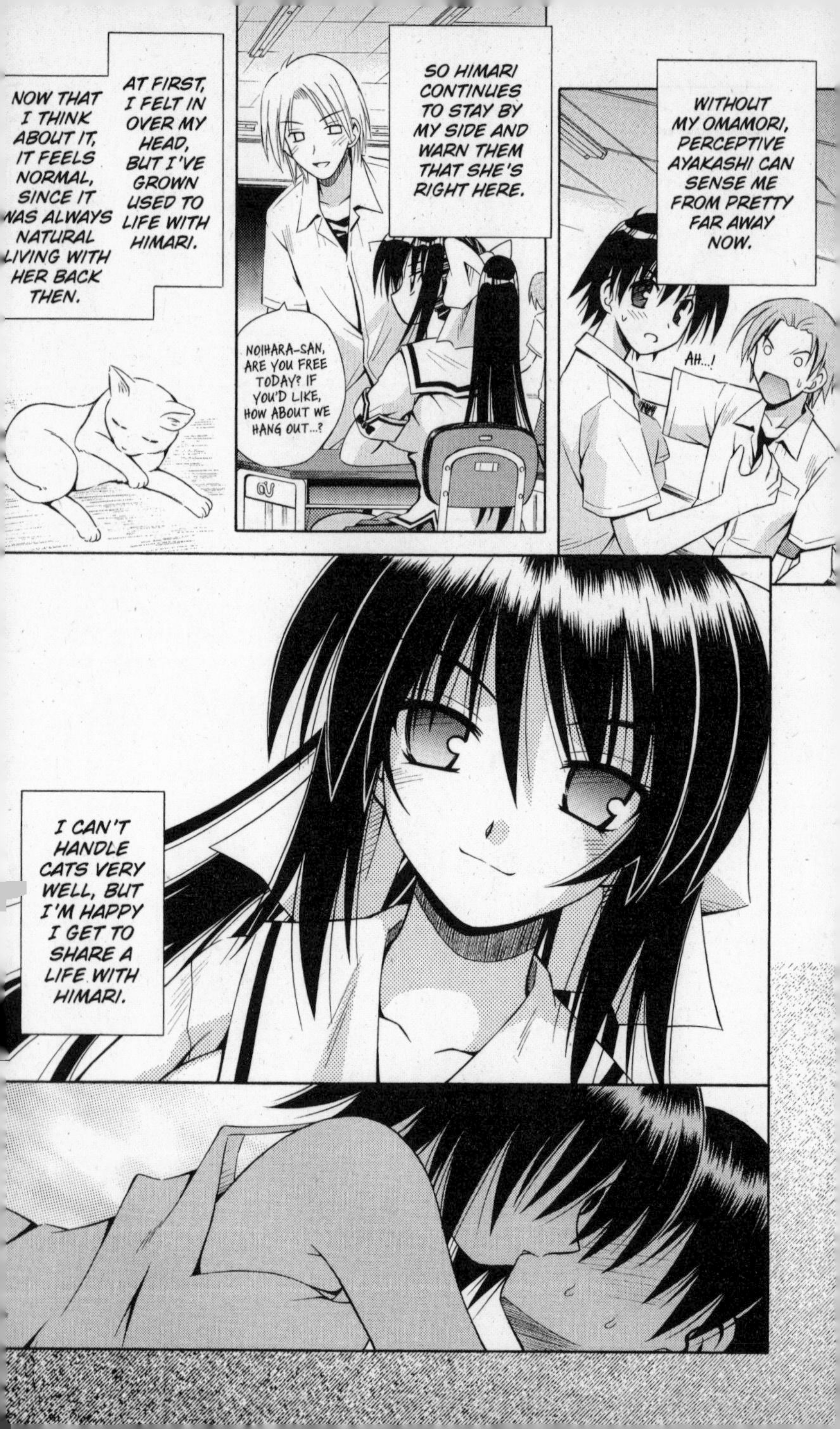
WITHOUT MY OMAMORI, PERCEPTIVE AYAKASHI CAN SENSE ME FROM PRETTY FAR AWAY NOW.
AH...!
SO HIMARI CONTINUES TO STAY BY MY SIDE AND WARN THEM THAT SHE'S RIGHT HERE.
NOIHARA-SAN, ARE YOU FREE TODAY? IF YOU'D LIKE, HOW ABOUT WE HANG OUT...?
AT FIRST, I FELT IN OVER MY HEAD, BUT I'VE GROWN USED TO LIFE WITH HIMARI.
NOW THAT I THINK ABOUT IT, IT FEELS NORMAL, SINCE IT WAS ALWAYS NATURAL LIVING WITH HER BACK THEN.
I CAN'T HANDLE CATS VERY WELL, BUT I'M HAPPY I GET TO SHARE A LIFE WITH HIMARI.

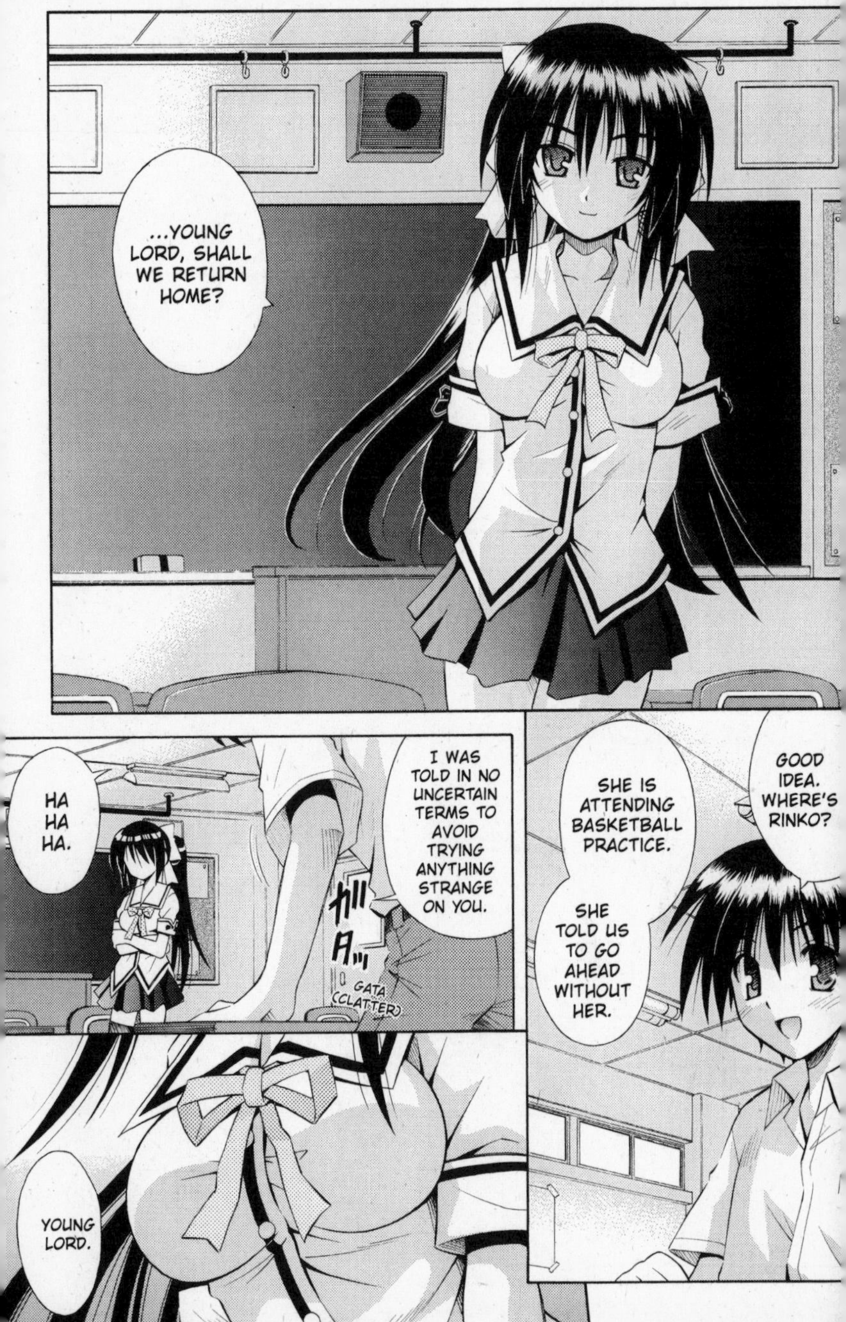
...YOUNG LORD, SHALL WE RETURN HOME?
GOOD IDEA. WHERE'S RINKO?
SHE IS ATTENDING BASKETBALL PRACTICE.
SHE TOLD US TO GO AHEAD WITHOUT HER.
I WAS TOLD IN NO UNCERTAIN TERMS TO AVOID TRYING ANYTHING STRANGE ON YOU.
GATA (CLATTER)
HA HA HA.
YOUNG LORD.

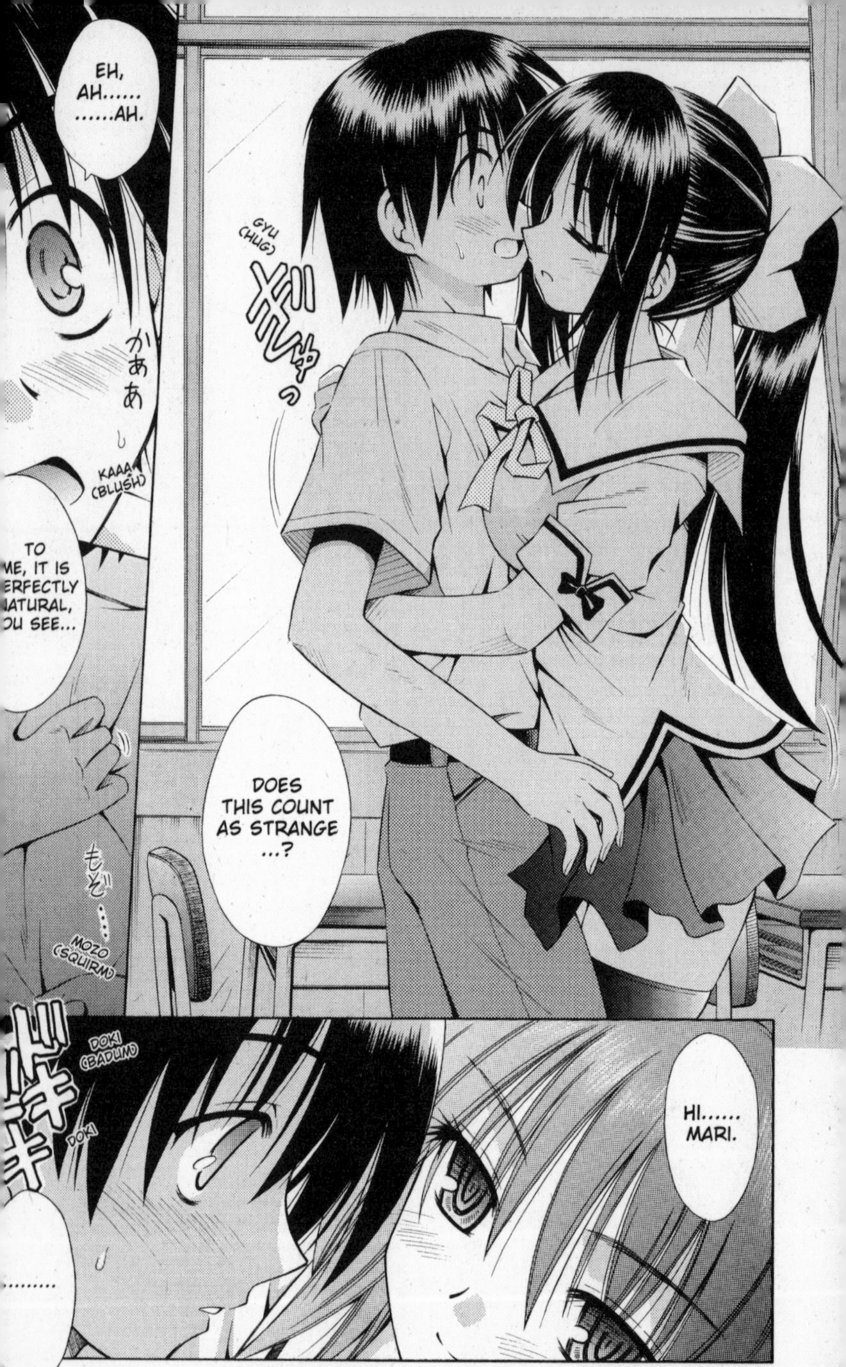

GYU (HUG)
DOES THIS COUNT AS STRANGE ...?
EH, AH...... ......AH.
かああ
KAAA (BLUSH)
TO ME, IT IS ERFECTLY NATURAL, OU SEE...
MOZO (SQUIRM)
HI...... MARI.
DOKI (BADUM)
DOKI
....

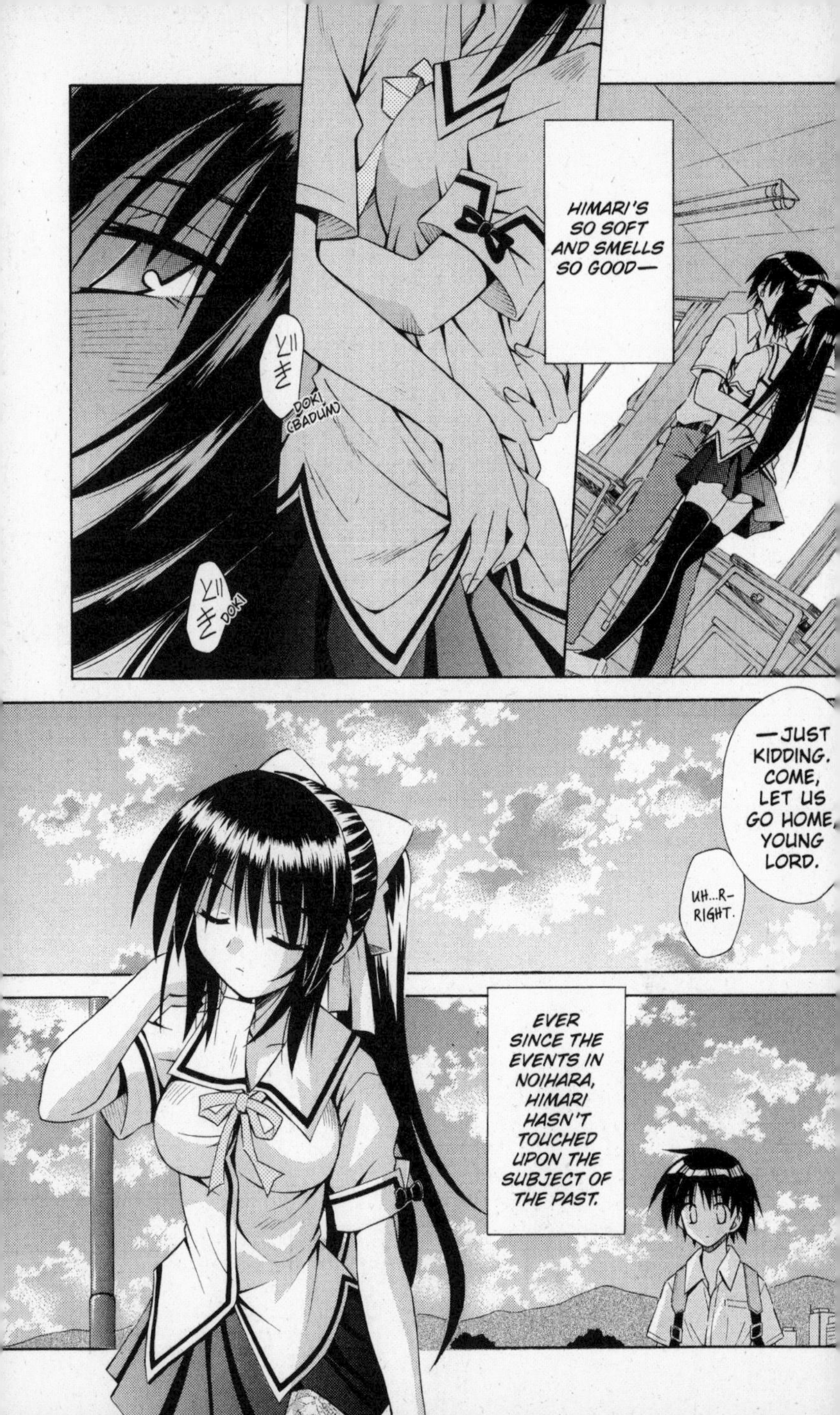
HIMARI'S SO SOFT AND SMELLS SO GOOD—
どき
DOKI (BADUMP)
どき
DOKI
—JUST KIDDING. COME, LET US GO HOME, YOUNG LORD.
UH...R-RIGHT.
EVER SINCE THE EVENTS IN NOIHARA, HIMARI HASN'T TOUCHED UPON THE SUBJECT OF THE PAST.

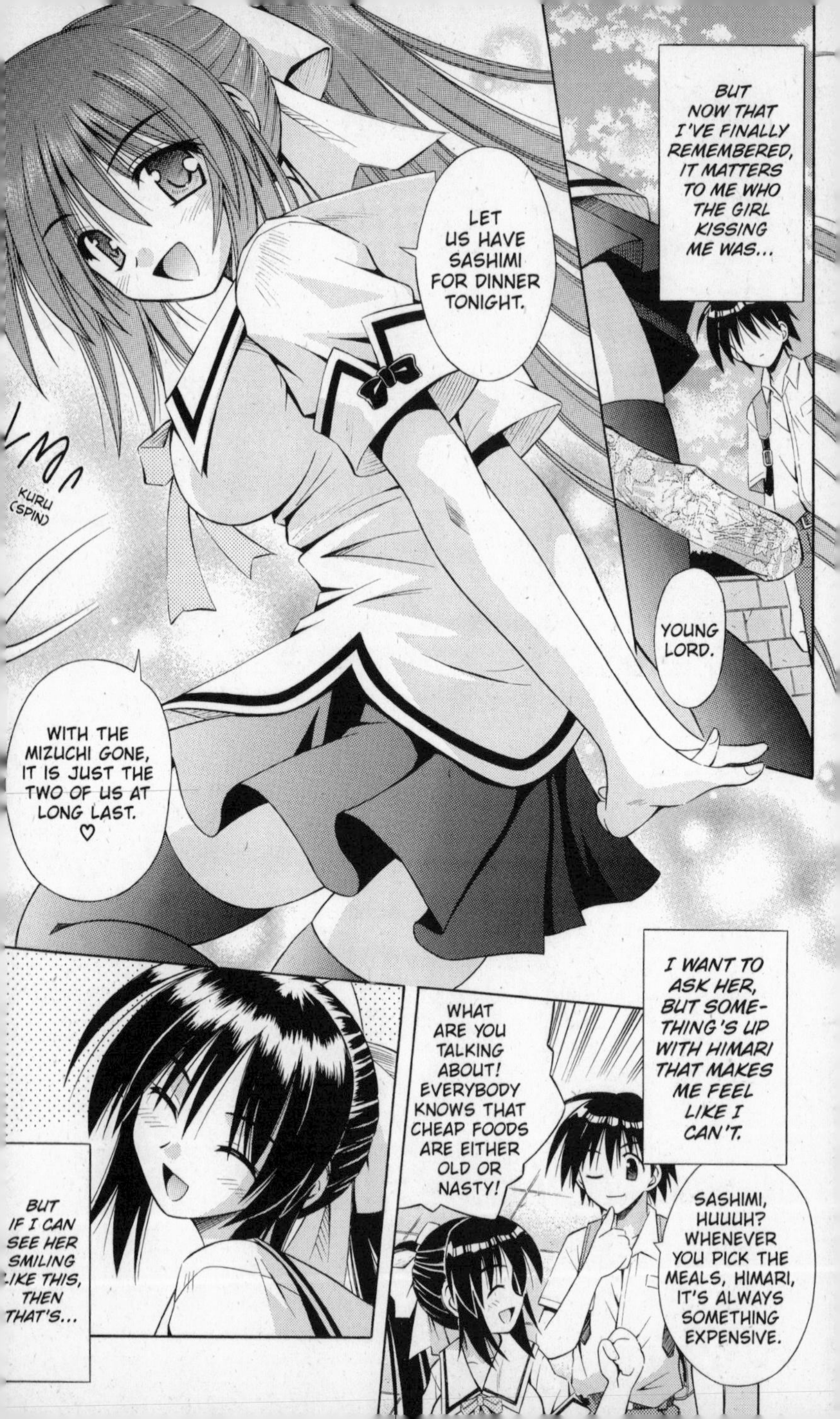
BUT NOW THAT I'VE FINALLY REMEMBERED, IT MATTERS TO ME WHO THE GIRL KISSING ME WAS...
YOUNG LORD.
LET US HAVE SASHIMI FOR DINNER TONIGHT.
KURU (SPIN)
WITH THE MIZUCHI GONE, IT IS JUST THE TWO OF US AT LONG LAST. ♡
I WANT TO ASK HER, BUT SOME-THING'S UP WITH HIMARI THAT MAKES ME FEEL LIKE I CAN'T.
SASHIMI, HUUUH? WHENEVER YOU PICK THE MEALS, HIMARI, IT'S ALWAYS SOMETHING EXPENSIVE.
WHAT ARE YOU TALKING ABOUT! EVERYBODY KNOWS THAT CHEAP FOODS ARE EITHER OLD OR NASTY!
BUT IF I CAN SEE HER SMILING LIKE THIS, THEN THAT'S...

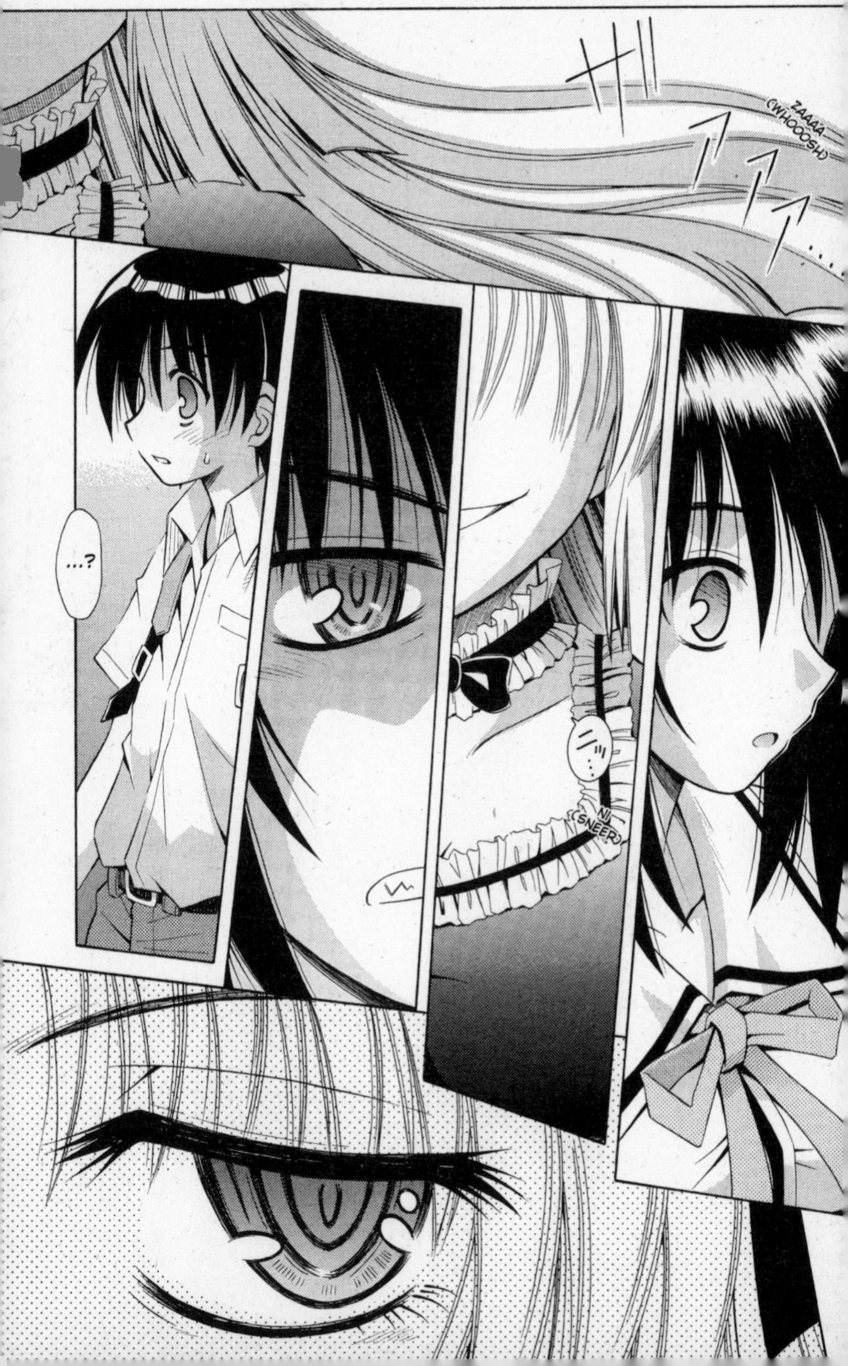
ZAAAA (WHOOOSH)
NI (SNEER)
...?

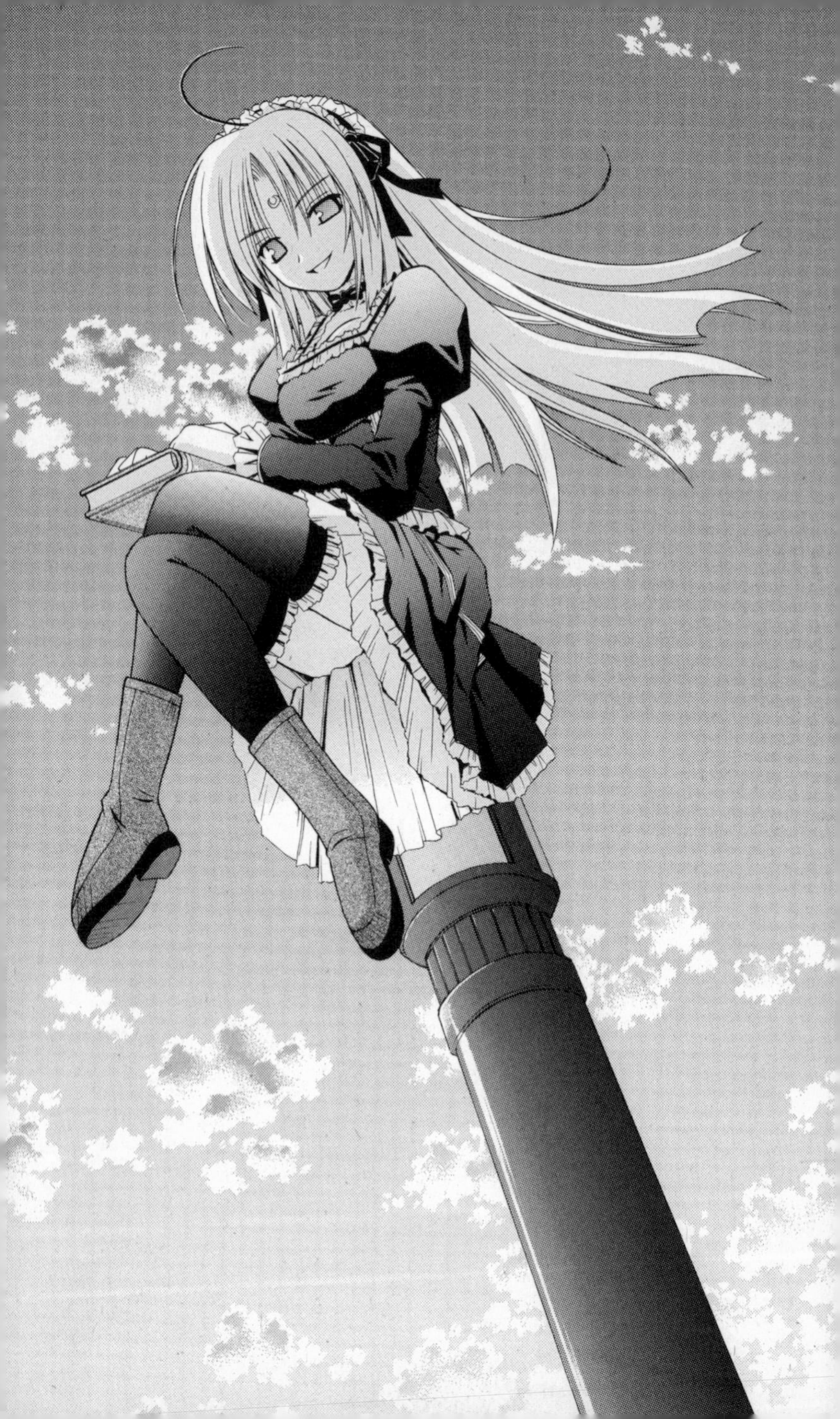

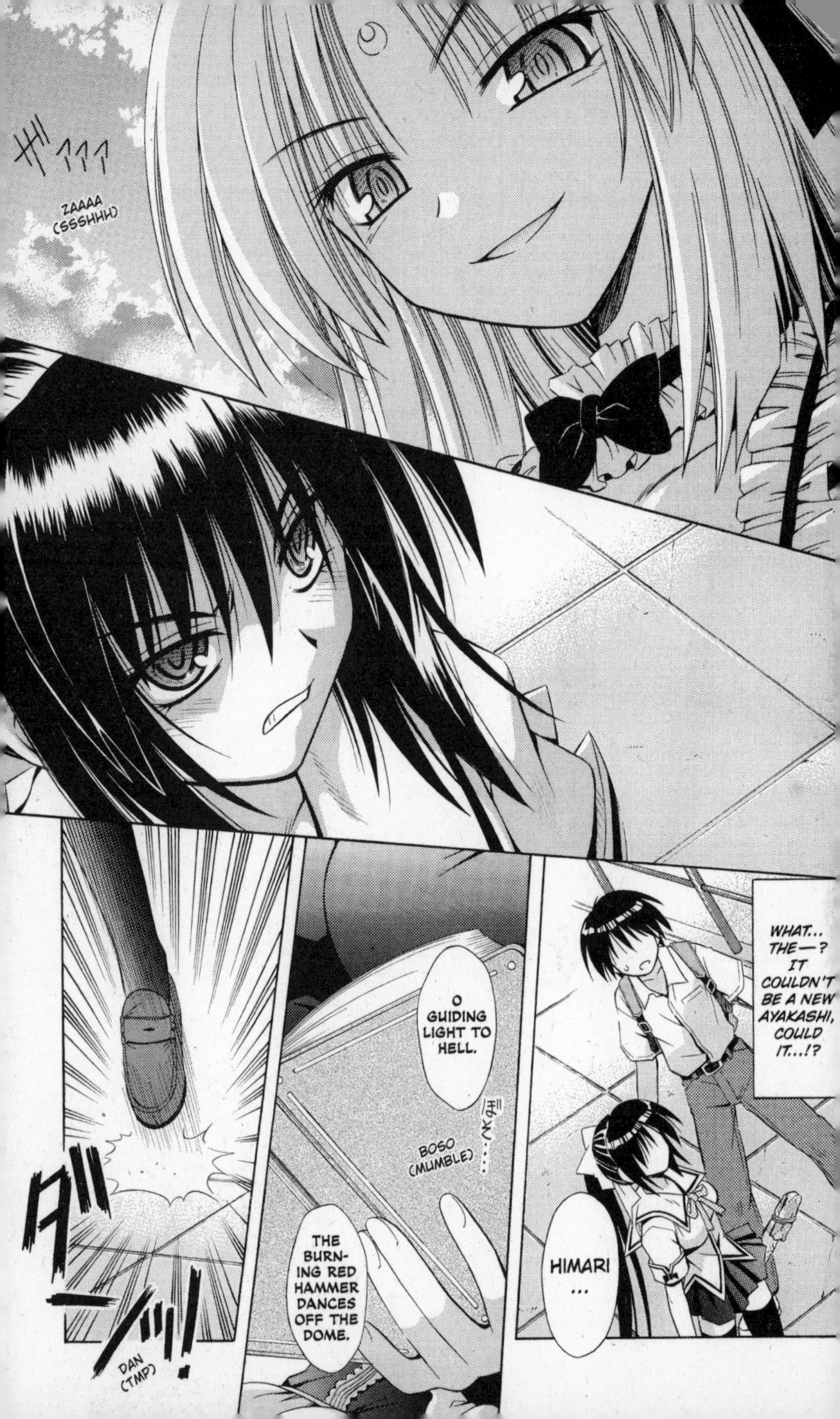
ザァァァ
ZAAAA (SSSHHH)
WHAT... THE—? IT COULDN'T BE A NEW AYAKASHI, COULD IT...!?
HIMARI ...
O GUIDING LIGHT TO HELL.
BOSO (MUMBLE)
THE BURNING RED HAMMER DANCES OFF THE DOME.
DAN (TMP)

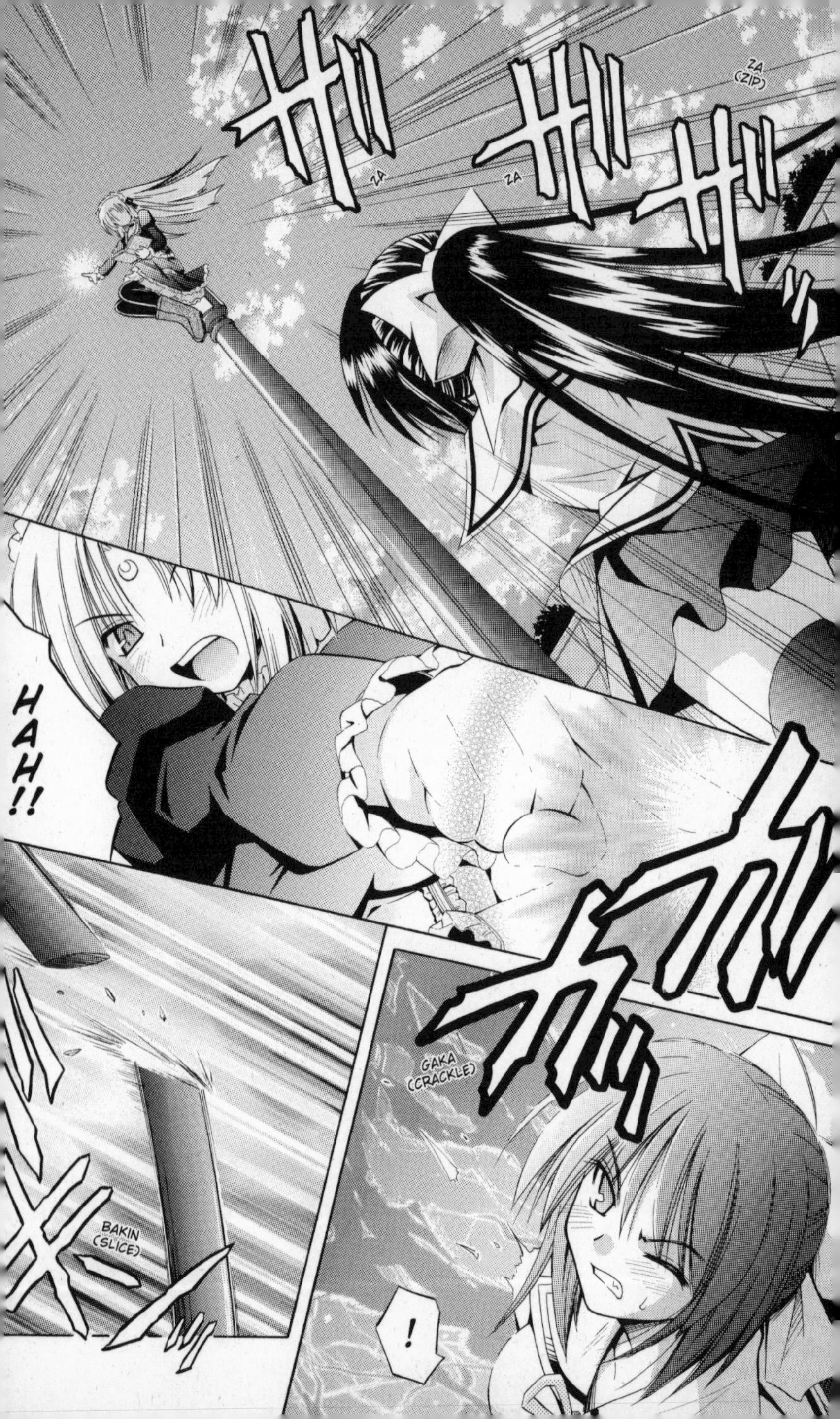
ZA (ZIP)
ZA
ZA
HAH!!
GAKA (CRACKLE)
!
BAKIN (SLICE)

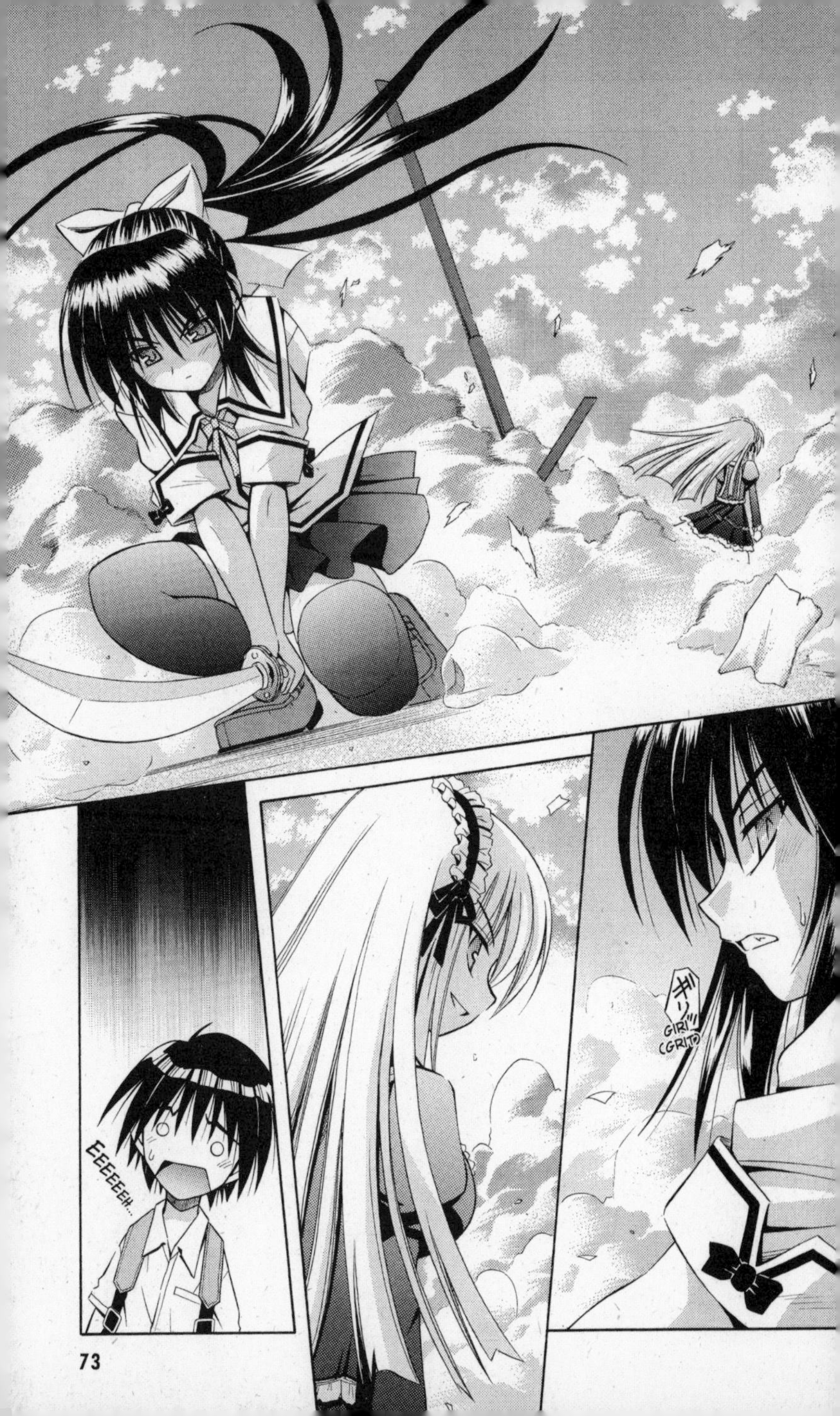
ギリッ
GIRI (GRIT)
EEEEEEH...

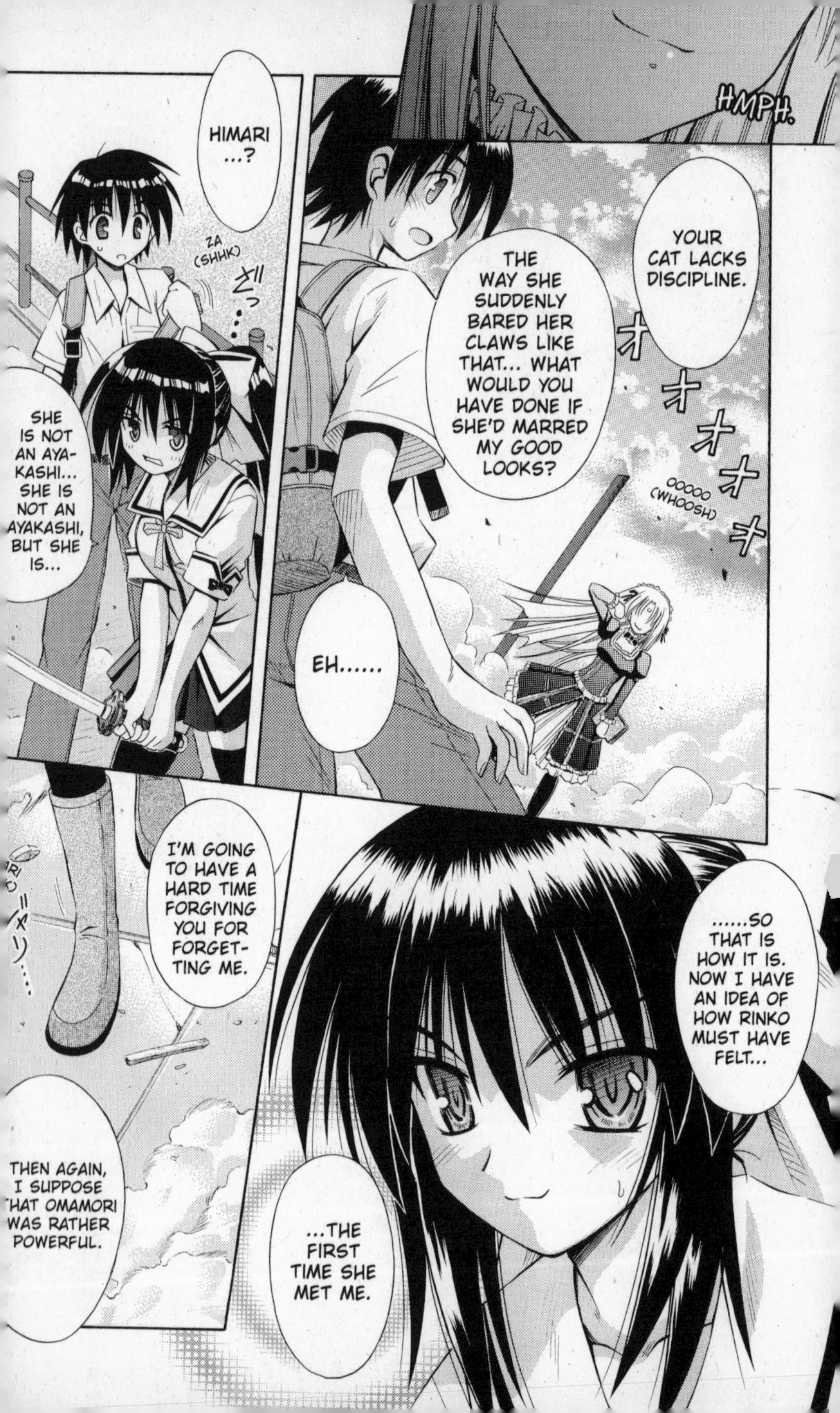
HMPH.
YOUR CAT LACKS DISCIPLINE.
THE WAY SHE SUDDENLY BARED HER CLAWS LIKE THAT... WHAT WOULD YOU HAVE DONE IF SHE'D MARRED MY GOOD LOOKS?
OOOOO (WHOOSH)
EH......
HIMARI ...?
ZA (SHHK)
SHE IS NOT AN AYA-KASHI... SHE IS NOT AN AYAKASHI, BUT SHE IS...
......SO THAT IS HOW IT IS. NOW I HAVE AN IDEA OF HOW RINKO MUST HAVE FELT...
I'M GOING TO HAVE A HARD TIME FORGIVING YOU FOR FORGET-TING ME.
...THE FIRST TIME SHE MET ME.
THEN AGAIN, I SUPPOSE THAT OMAMORI WAS RATHER POWERFUL.

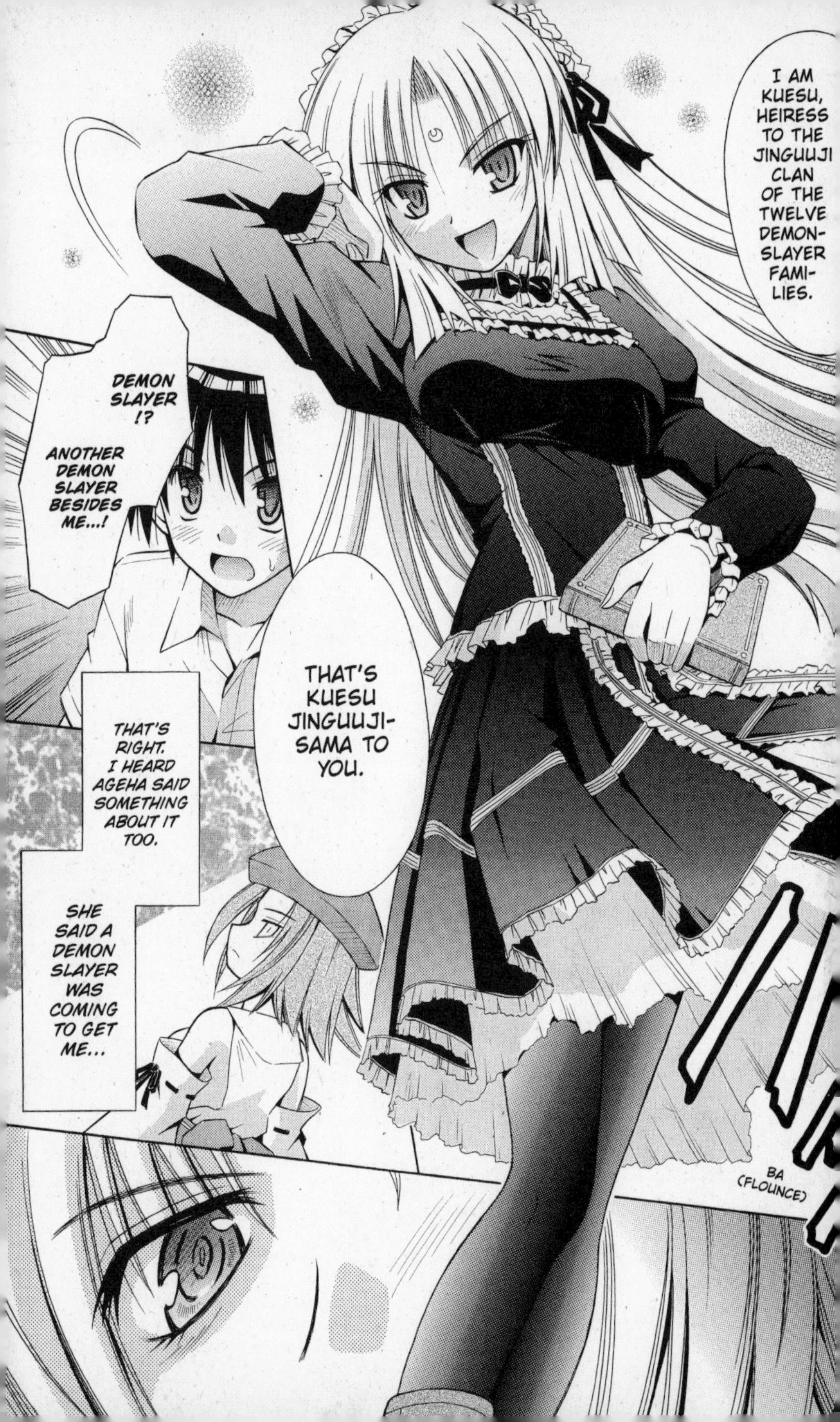
I AM KUESU, HEIRESS TO THE JINGUUJI CLAN OF THE TWELVE DEMON-SLAYER FAMILIES.
DEMON SLAYER !?
ANOTHER DEMON SLAYER BESIDES ME...!
THAT'S KUESU JINGUUJI-SAMA TO YOU.
THAT'S RIGHT. I HEARD AGEHA SAID SOMETHING ABOUT IT TOO.
SHE SAID A DEMON SLAYER WAS COMING TO GET ME...
BA (FLOUNCE)

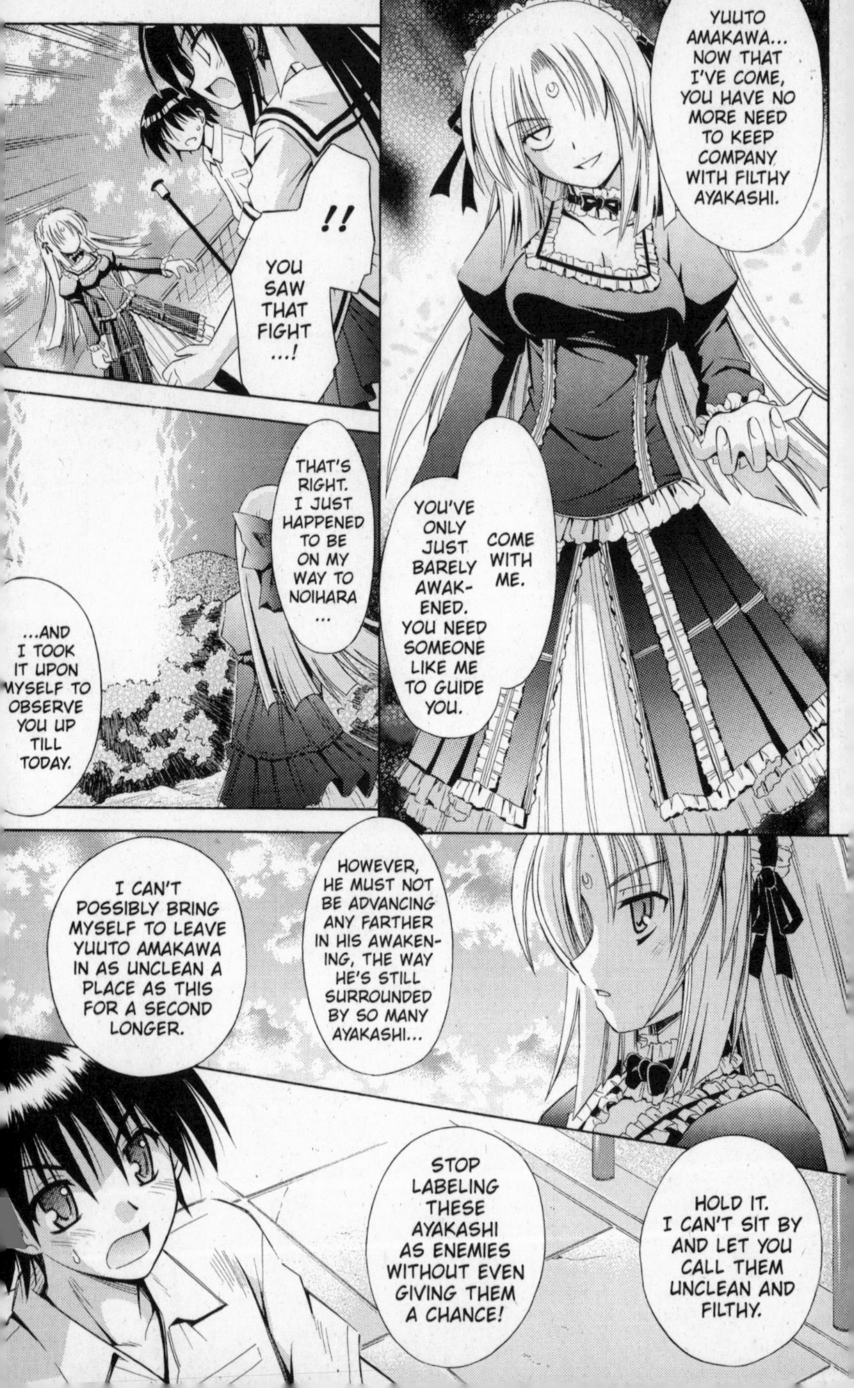
YUUTO AMAKAWA... NOW THAT I'VE COME, YOU HAVE NO MORE NEED TO KEEP COMPANY WITH FILTHY AYAKASHI.
COME WITH ME.
YOU'VE ONLY JUST BARELY AWAK-ENED. YOU NEED SOMEONE LIKE ME TO GUIDE YOU.
!!
YOU SAW THAT FIGHT ...!
THAT'S RIGHT. I JUST HAPPENED TO BE ON MY WAY TO NOIHARA ...
...AND I TOOK IT UPON MYSELF TO OBSERVE YOU UP TILL TODAY.
HOWEVER, HE MUST NOT BE ADVANCING ANY FARTHER IN HIS AWAKEN-ING, THE WAY HE'S STILL SURROUNDED BY SO MANY AYAKASHI...
I CAN'T POSSIBLY BRING MYSELF TO LEAVE YUUTO AMAKAWA IN AS UNCLEAN A PLACE AS THIS FOR A SECOND LONGER.
HOLD IT. I CAN'T SIT BY AND LET YOU CALL THEM UNCLEAN AND FILTHY.
STOP LABELING THESE AYAKASHI AS ENEMIES WITHOUT EVEN GIVING THEM A CHANCE!

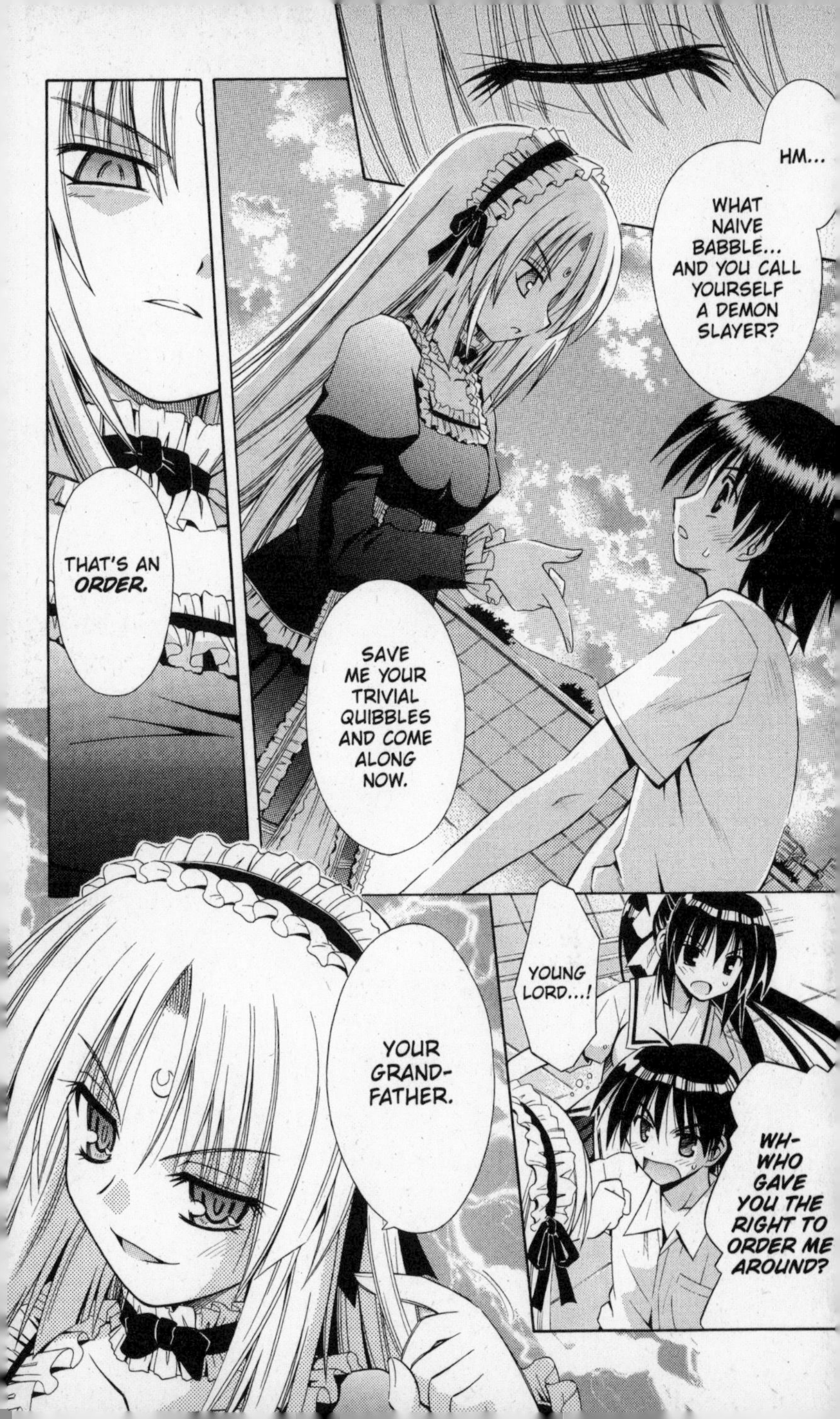

HM...
WHAT NAIVE BABBLE... AND YOU CALL YOURSELF A DEMON SLAYER?
SAVE ME YOUR TRIVIAL QUIBBLES AND COME ALONG NOW.
THAT'S AN ORDER.
YOUNG LORD...!
WH-WHO GAVE YOU THE RIGHT TO ORDER ME AROUND?
YOUR GRAND-FATHER.

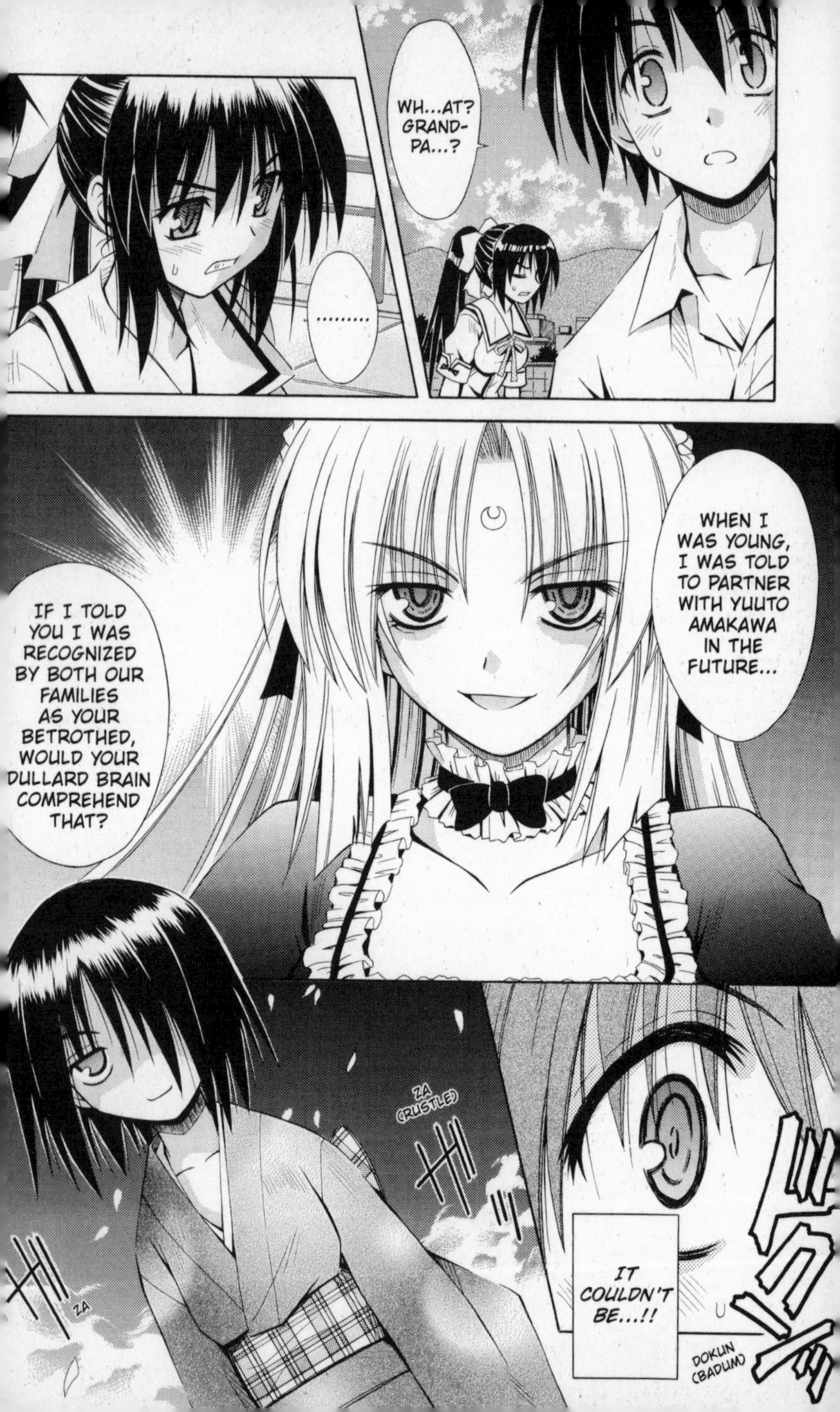
WH...AT? GRAND-PA...?
....
WHEN I WAS YOUNG, I WAS TOLD TO PARTNER WITH YUUTO AMAKAWA IN THE FUTURE...
IF I TOLD YOU I WAS RECOGNIZED BY BOTH OUR FAMILIES AS YOUR BETROTHED, WOULD YOUR DULLARD BRAIN COMPREHEND THAT?
IT COULDN'T BE...!!
DOKUN (BADUM)
ZA (RUSTLE)
ZA

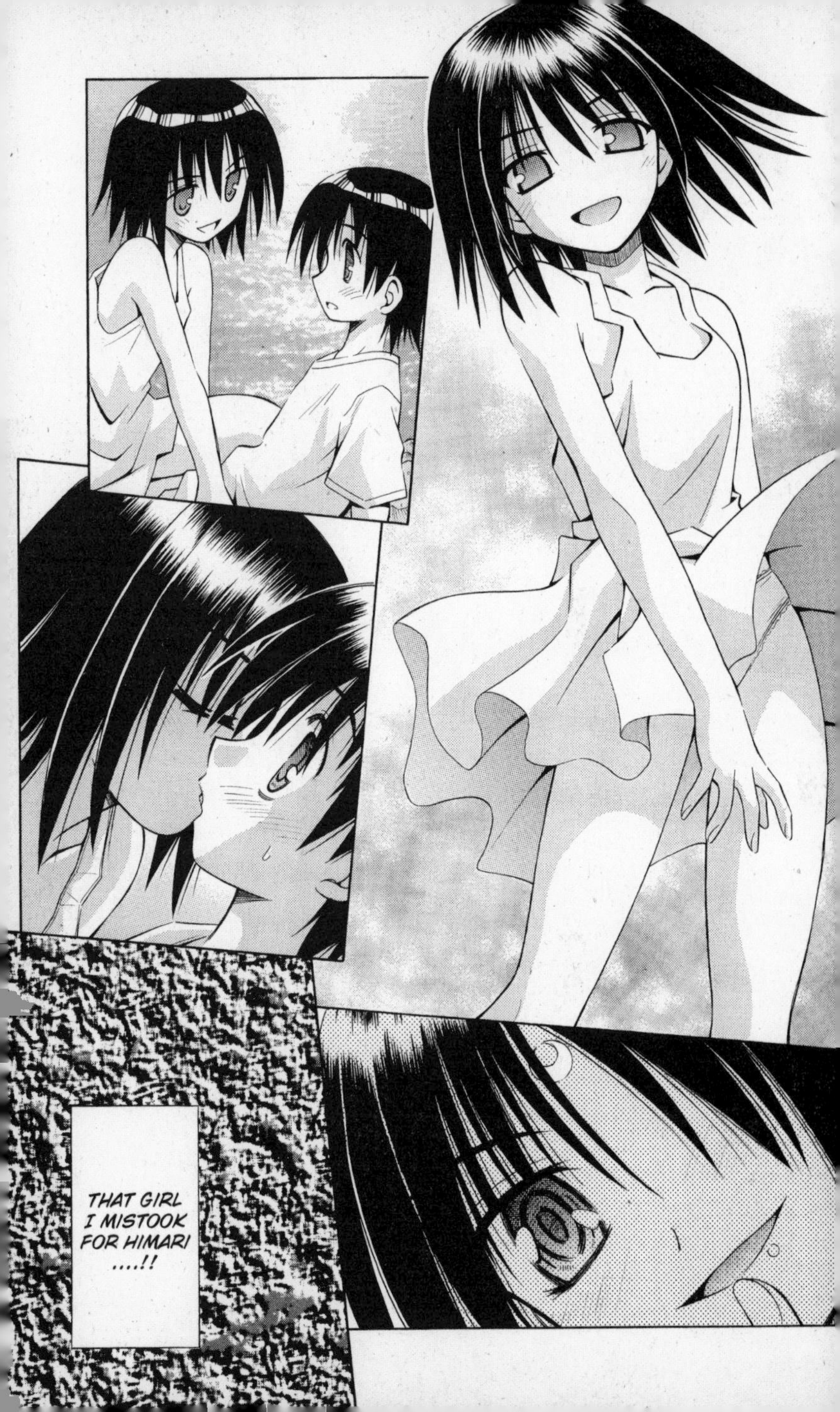
THAT GIRL I MISTOOK FOR HIMARI ....!!

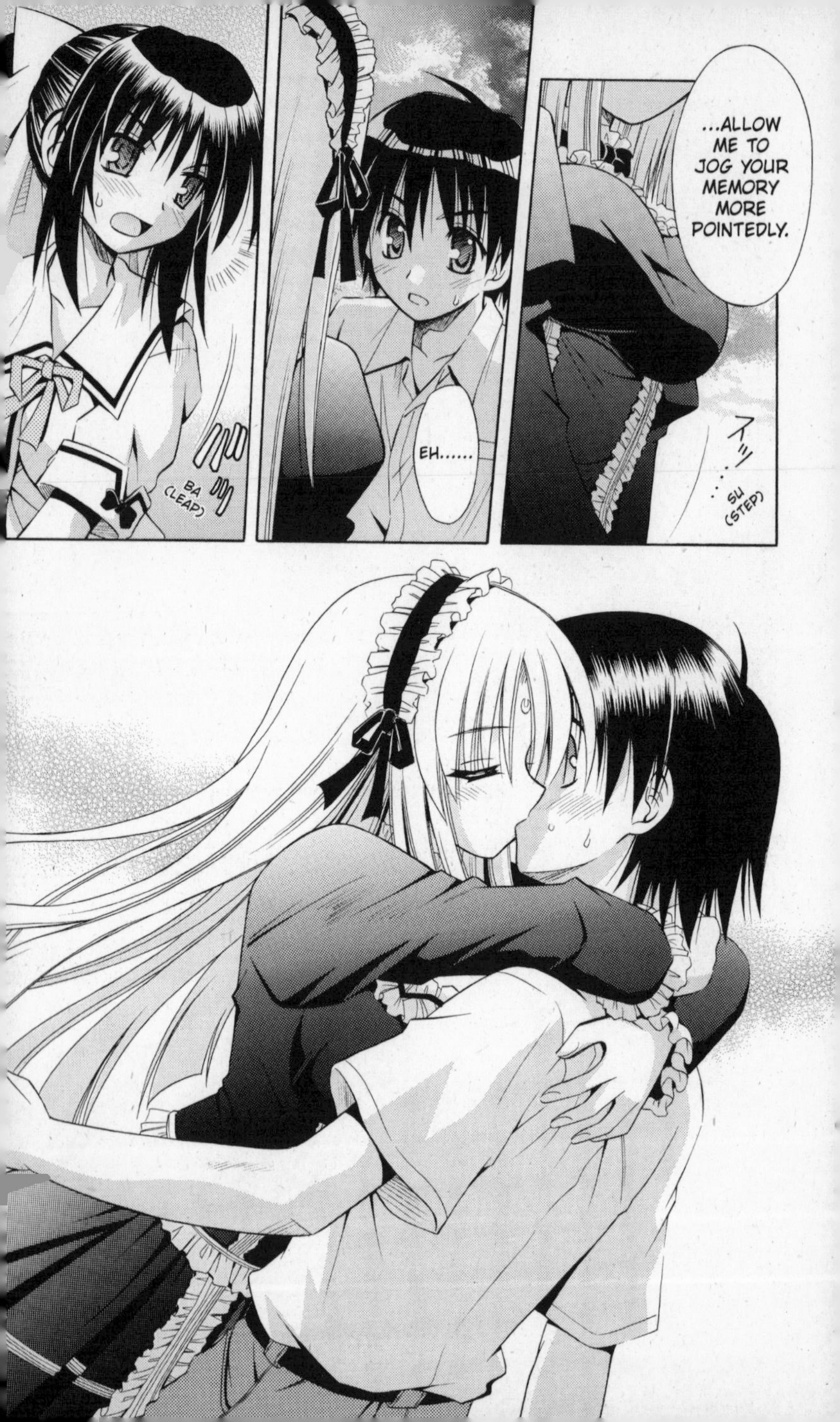
...ALLOW ME TO JOG YOUR MEMORY MORE POINTEDLY.
スッ
SU (STEP)
EH......
BA (LEAP)

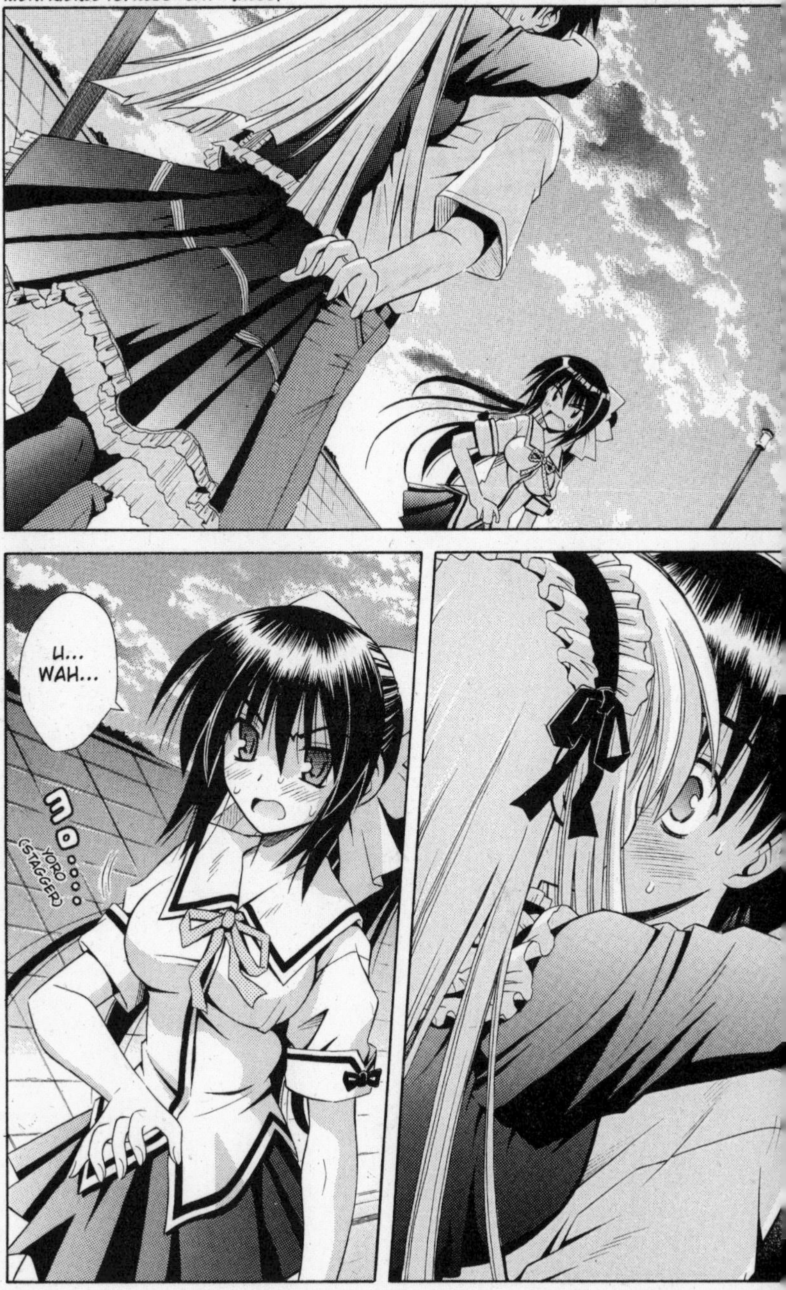
U... WAH...
YORO (STAGGER)

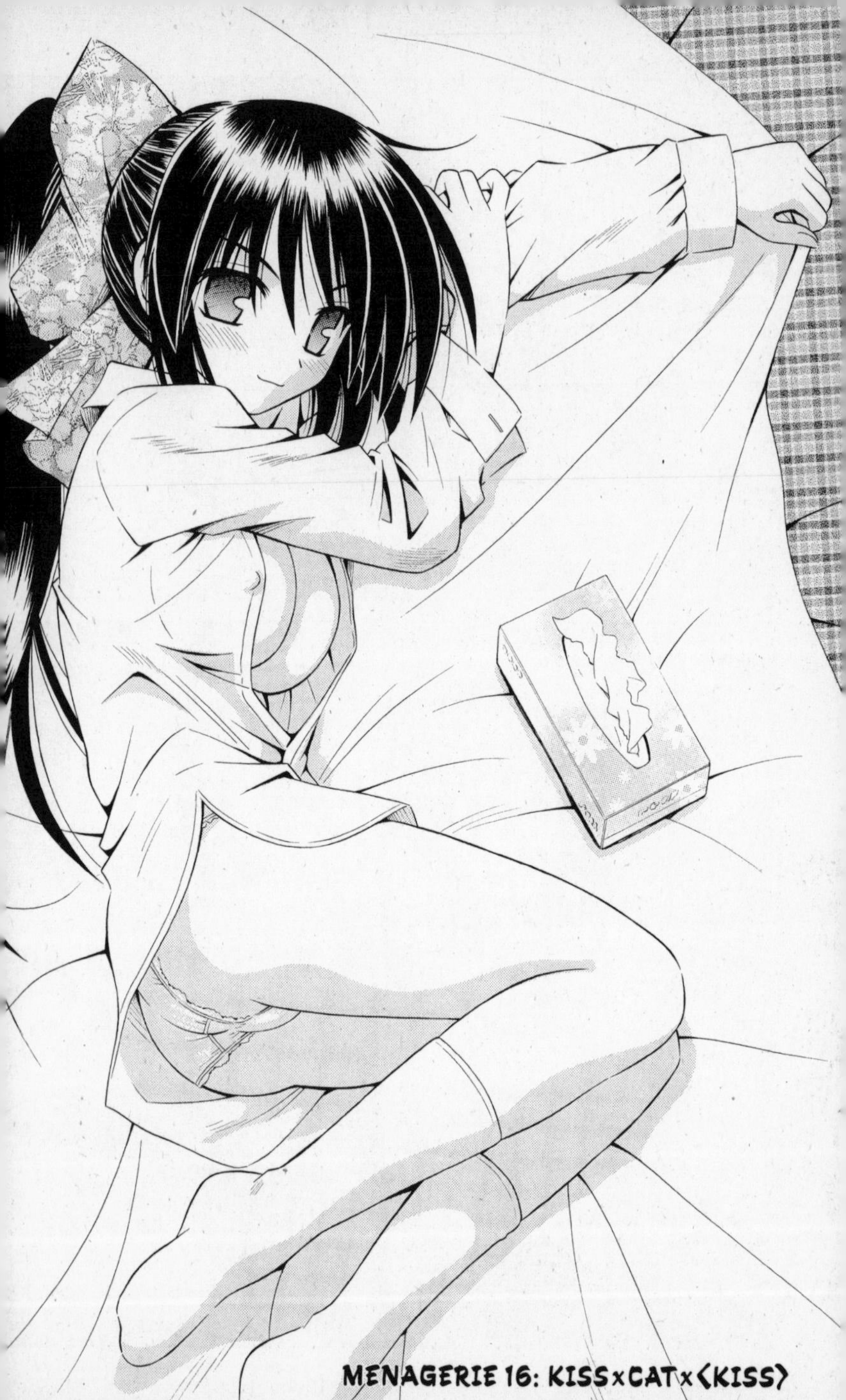

MENAGERIE 16: KISS x CAT x <KISS>

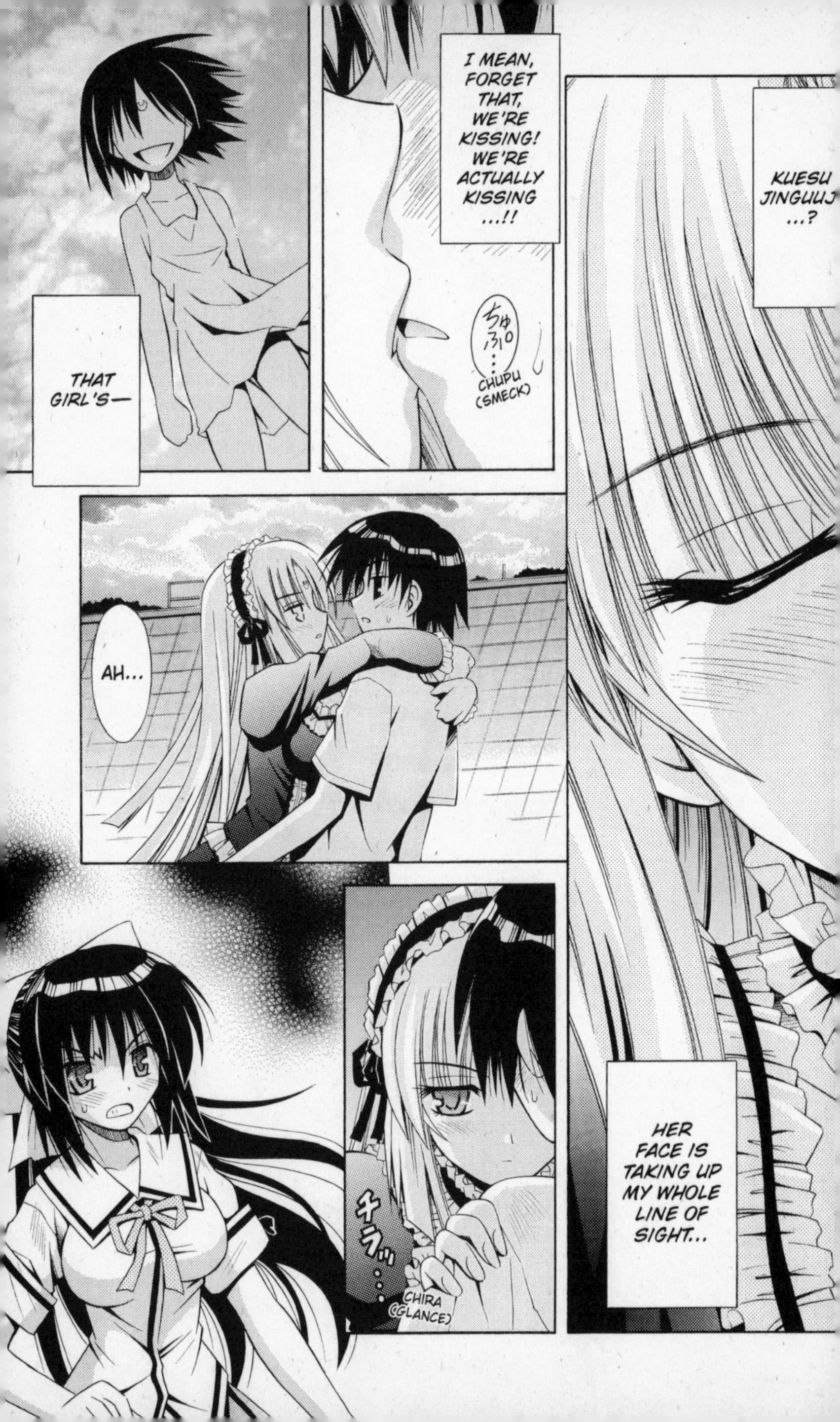

KUESU JINGUUJI ...?
HER FACE IS TAKING UP MY WHOLE LINE OF SIGHT...
I MEAN, FORGET THAT, WE'RE KISSING! WE'RE ACTUALLY KISSING ...!!
ちゅぷ…
CHUPU (SMECK)
THAT GIRL'S—
AH...
チラッ…
CHIRA (GLANCE)

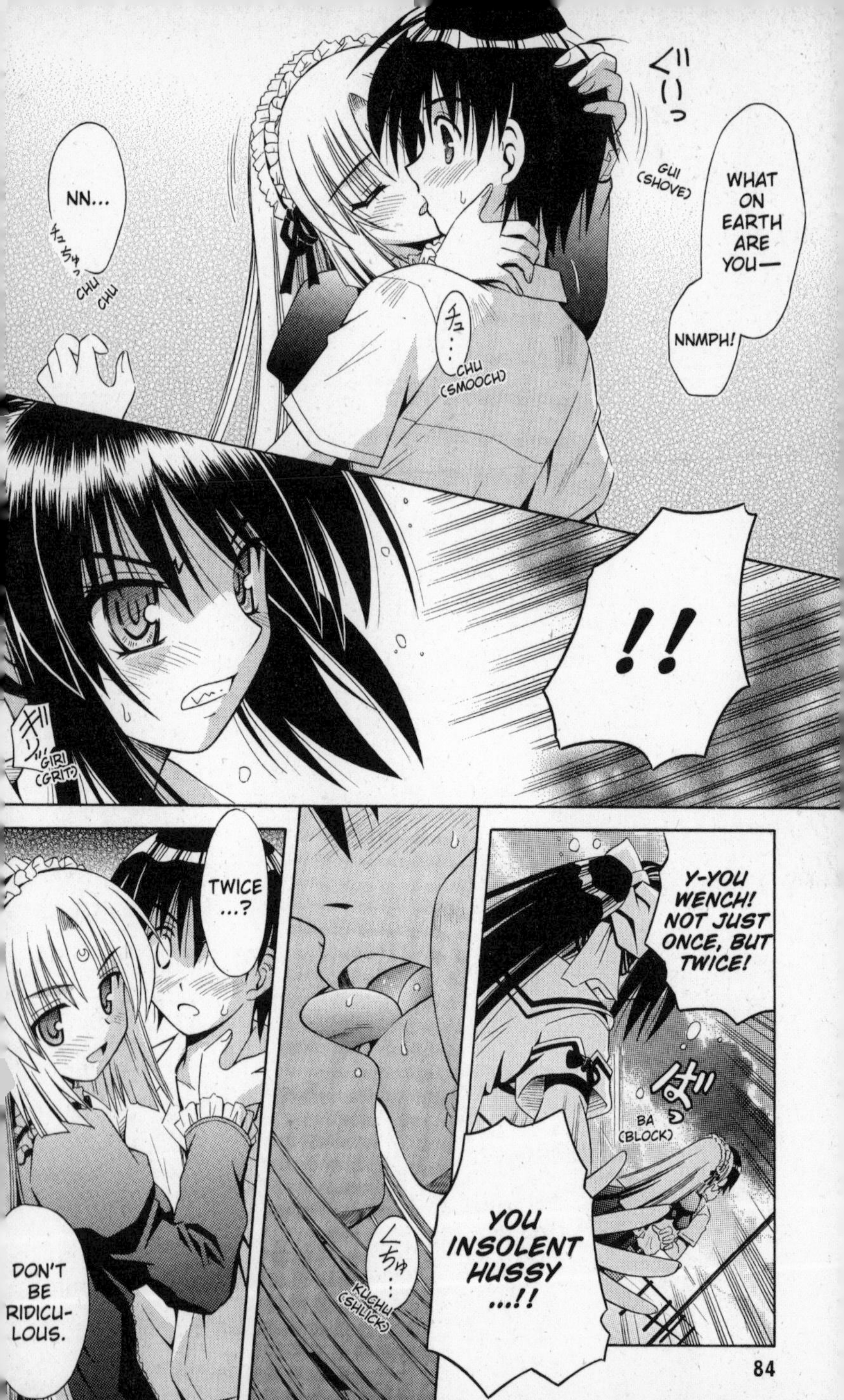

ぐいっ
GUI (SHOVE)
WHAT ON EARTH ARE YOU—
NNMPH!
チュ…
CHU (SMOOCH)
NN...
チュちゅっ
CHU CHU
!!
ギリ
GIRI (GRIT)
Y-YOU WENCH! NOT JUST ONCE, BUT TWICE!
ばっ
BA (BLOCK)
YOU INSOLENT HUSSY ...!!
くちゅ…
KUCHU (SHLICK)
TWICE ...?
DON'T BE RIDICU-LOUS.

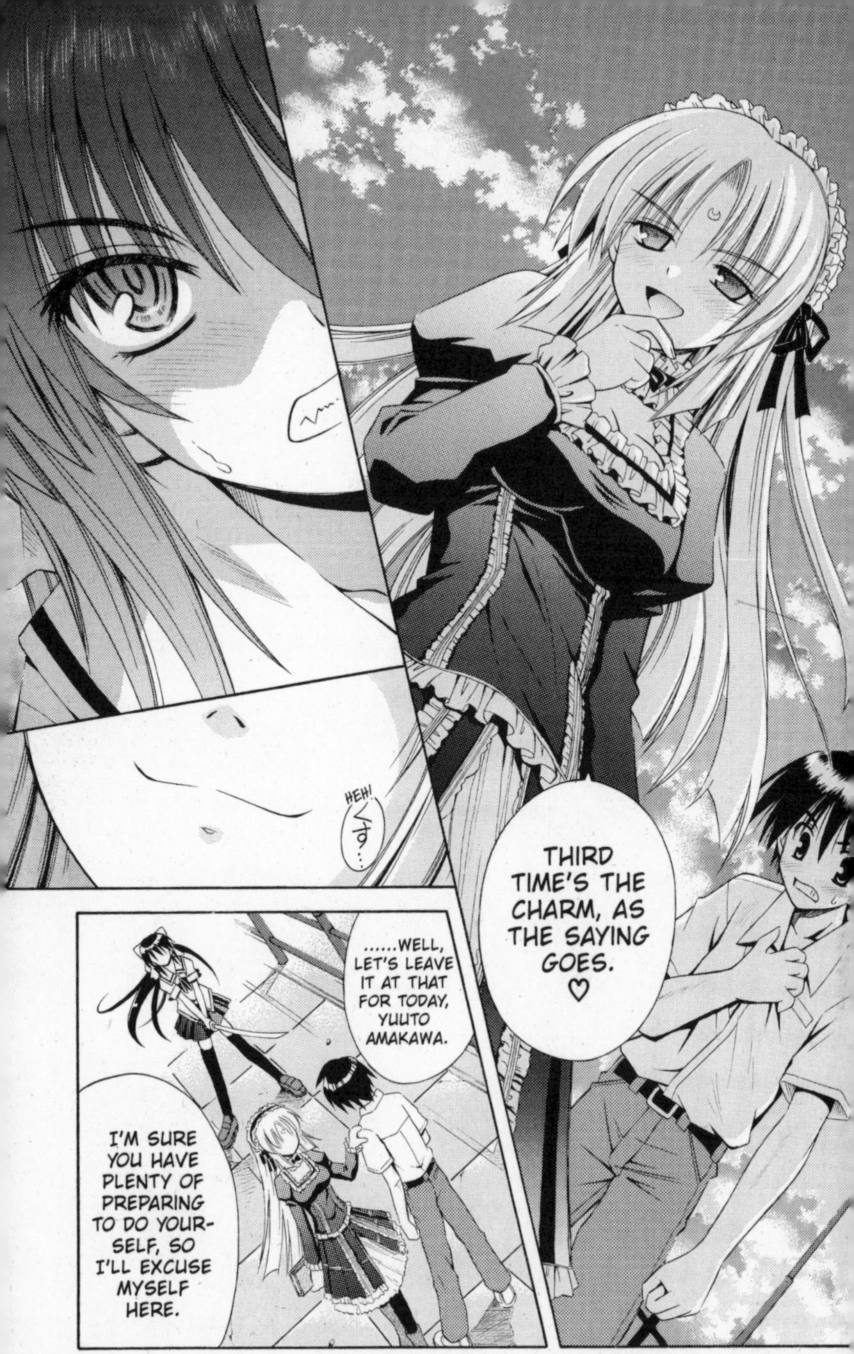
THIRD TIME'S THE CHARM, AS THE SAYING GOES. ♡
HEH! くす…
......WELL, LET'S LEAVE IT AT THAT FOR TODAY, YUUTO AMAKAWA.
I'M SURE YOU HAVE PLENTY OF PREPARING TO DO YOUR-SELF, SO I'LL EXCUSE MYSELF HERE.

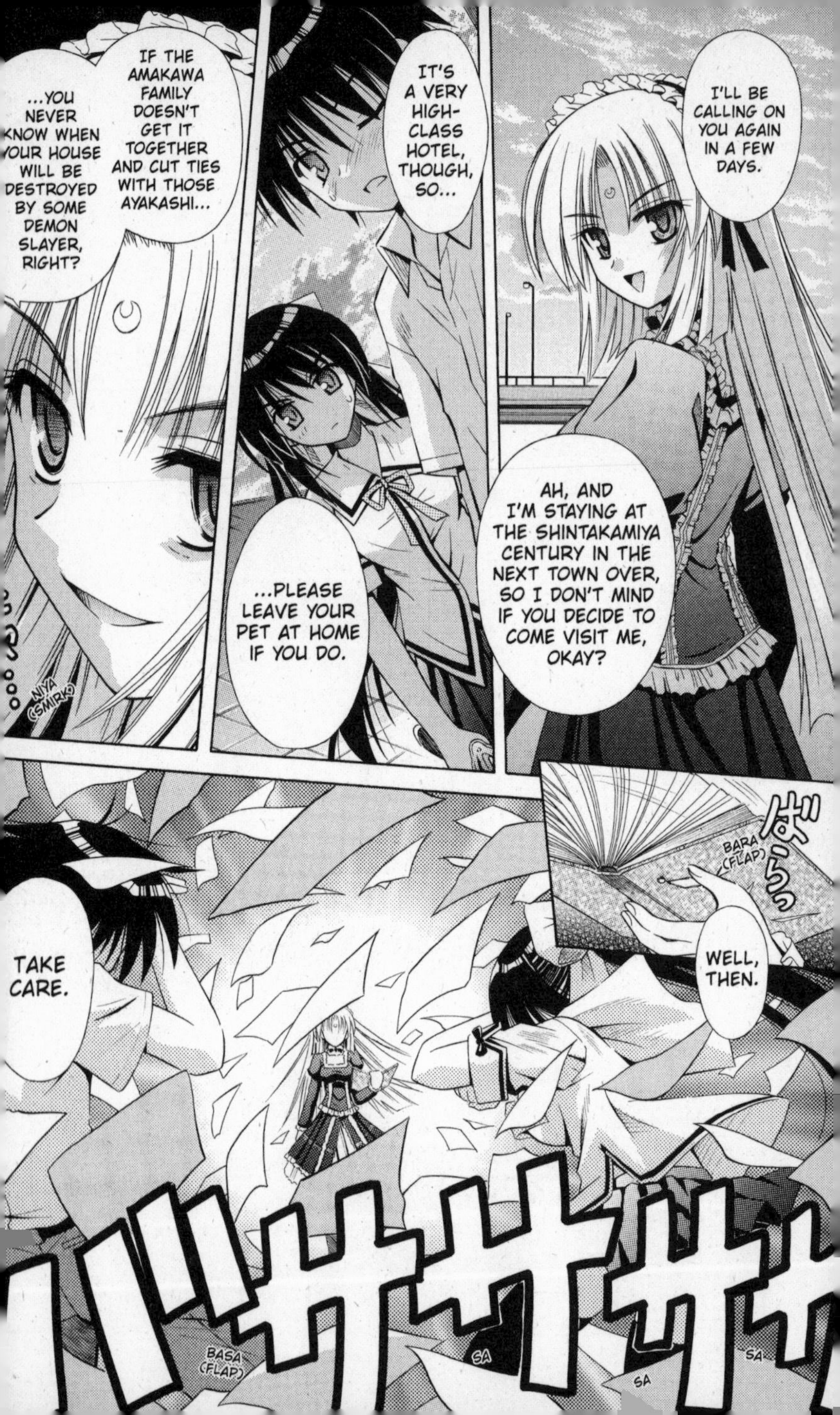

I'LL BE CALLING ON YOU AGAIN IN A FEW DAYS.
AH, AND I'M STAYING AT THE SHINTAKAMIYA CENTURY IN THE NEXT TOWN OVER, SO I DON'T MIND IF YOU DECIDE TO COME VISIT ME, OKAY?
IT'S A VERY HIGH-CLASS HOTEL, THOUGH, SO...
...PLEASE LEAVE YOUR PET AT HOME IF YOU DO.
IF THE AMAKAWA FAMILY DOESN'T GET IT TOGETHER AND CUT TIES WITH THOSE AYAKASHI...
...YOU NEVER KNOW WHEN YOUR HOUSE WILL BE DESTROYED BY SOME DEMON SLAYER, RIGHT?
NIYA (SMIRK)
ばらっ
BARA (FLAP)
WELL, THEN.
TAKE CARE.
BASA (FLAP)
SA
SA
SA

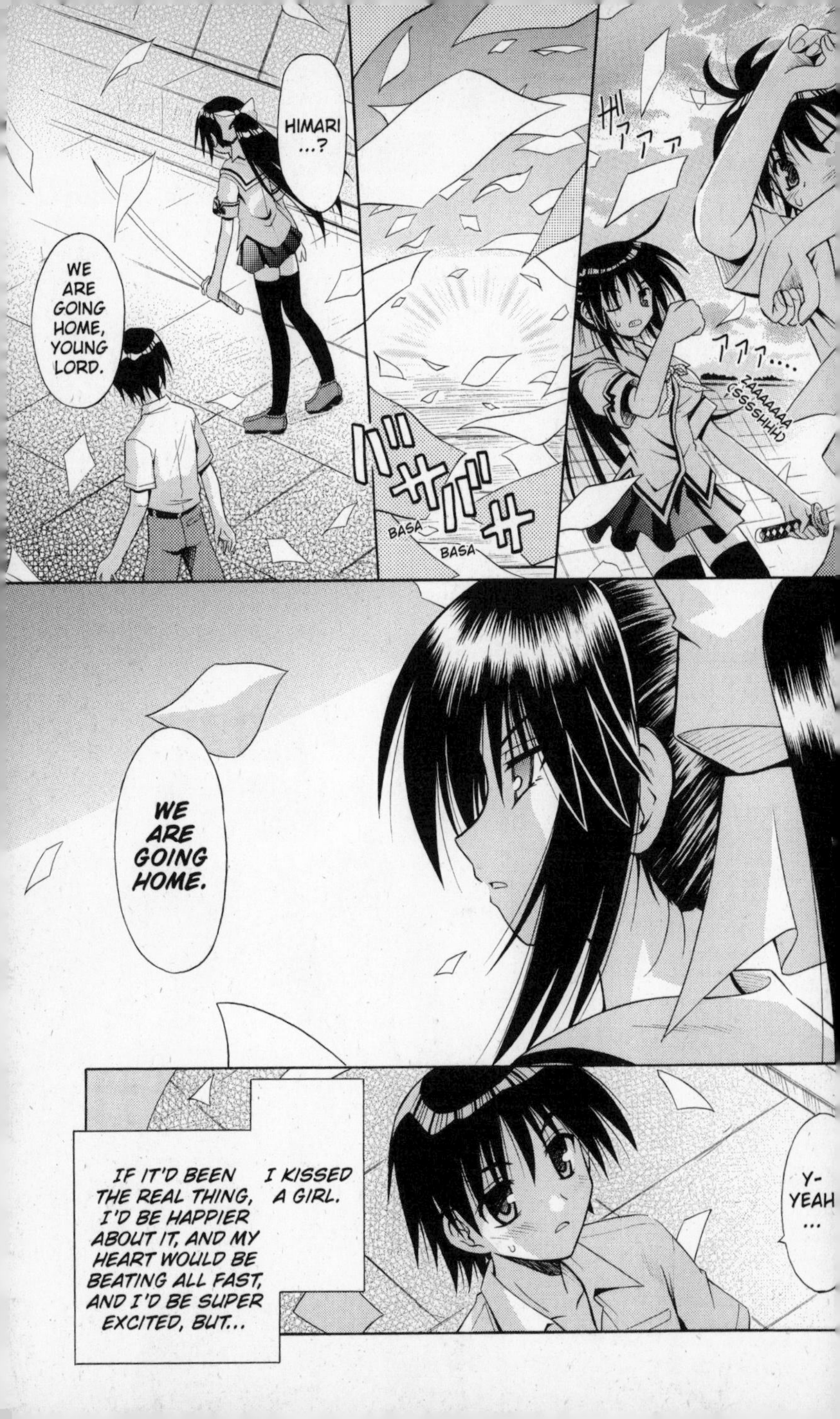

ザァァァ
ァァァ....
ZAAAAAAA
(SSSSHHH)
バサバサ
BASA
BASA
HIMARI ...?
WE ARE GOING HOME, YOUNG LORD.
WE ARE GOING HOME.
Y-YEAH ...
I KISSED A GIRL.
IF IT'D BEEN THE REAL THING, I'D BE HAPPIER ABOUT IT, AND MY HEART WOULD BE BEATING ALL FAST, AND I'D BE SUPER EXCITED, BUT...

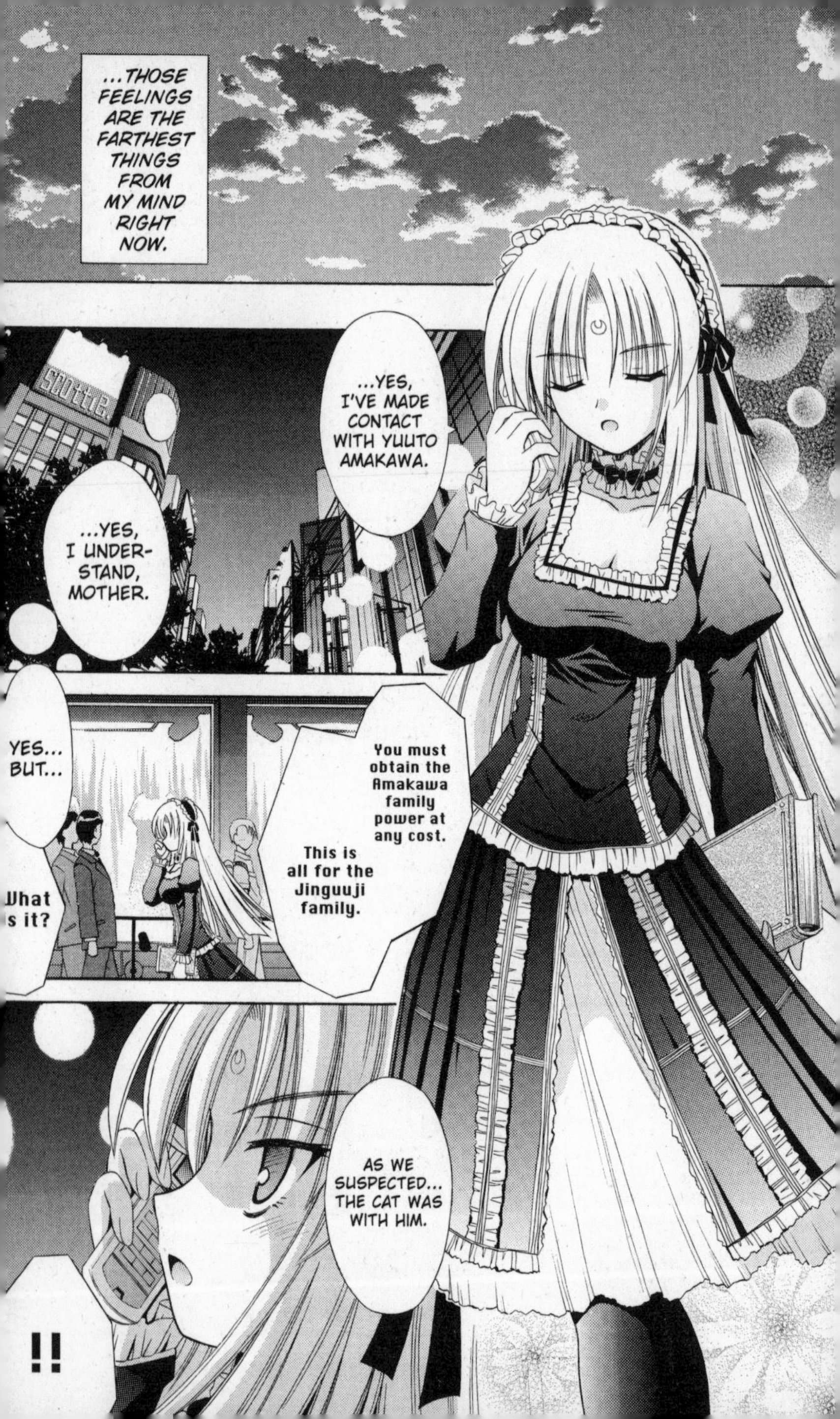
...THOSE FEELINGS ARE THE FARTHEST THINGS FROM MY MIND RIGHT NOW.
...YES, I'VE MADE CONTACT WITH YUUTO AMAKAWA.
...YES, I UNDER-STAND, MOTHER.
You must obtain the Amakawa family power at any cost.
This is all for the Jinguuji family.
YES... BUT...
What is it?
AS WE SUSPECTED... THE CAT WAS WITH HIM.
!!

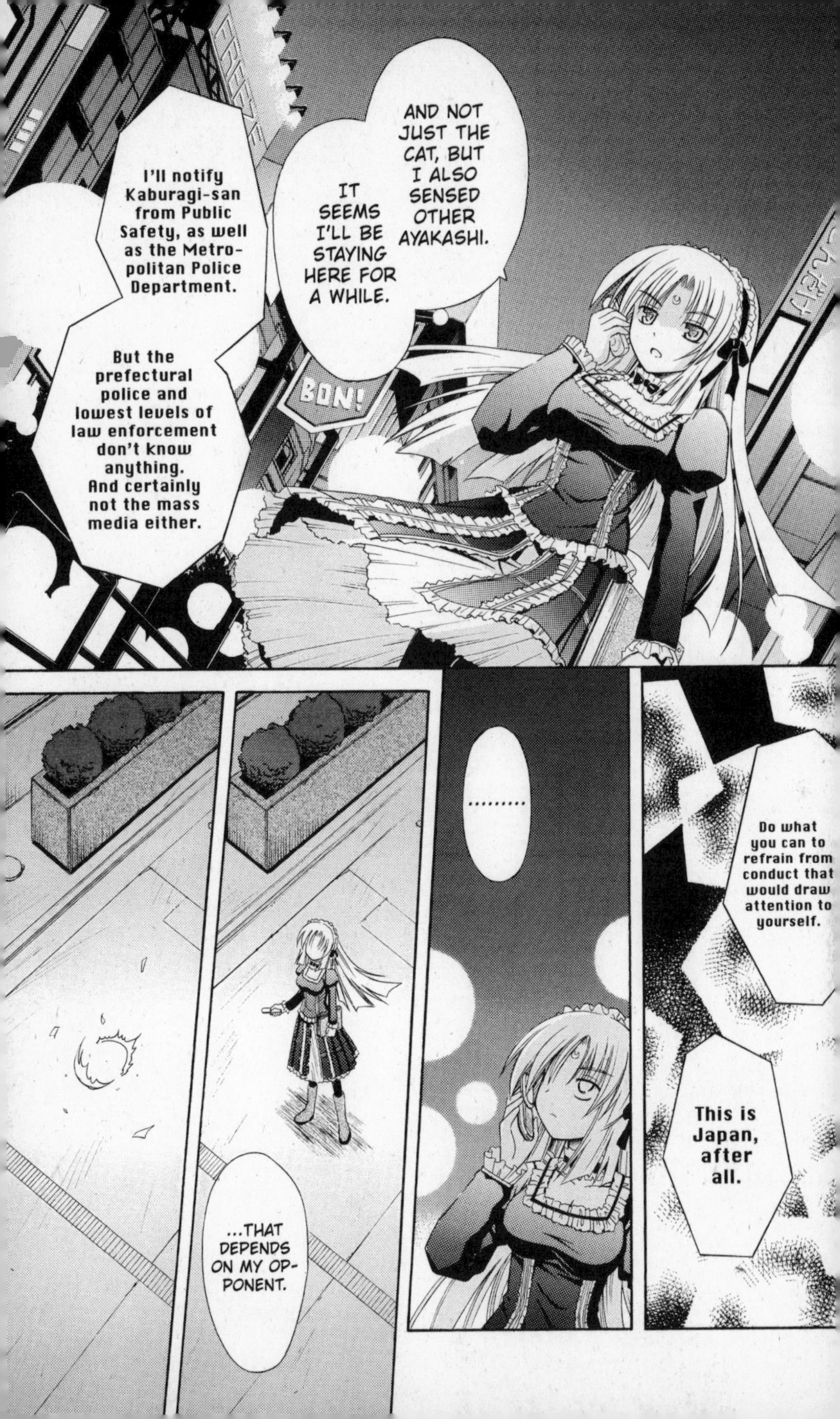
AND NOT JUST THE CAT, BUT I ALSO SENSED OTHER AYAKASHI.
IT SEEMS I'LL BE STAYING HERE FOR A WHILE.
BON!
I'll notify Kaburagi-san from Public Safety, as well as the Metro-politan Police Department.
But the prefectural police and lowest levels of law enforcement don't know anything. And certainly not the mass media either.
Do what you can to refrain from conduct that would draw attention to yourself.
This is Japan, after all.
....
...THAT DEPENDS ON MY OP-PONENT.

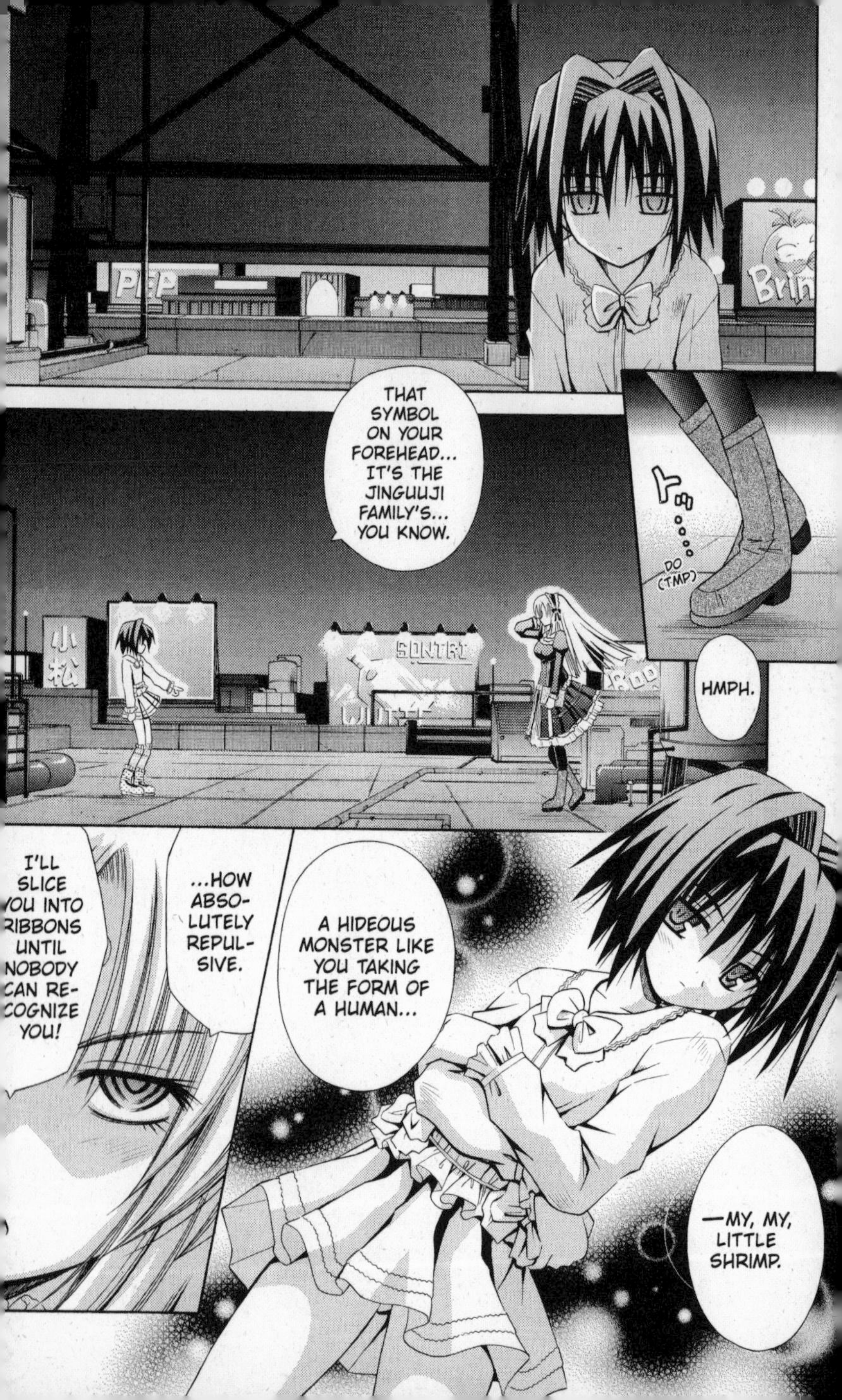
ドッ
DO (TMP)
THAT SYMBOL ON YOUR FOREHEAD... IT'S THE JINGUUJI FAMILY'S... YOU KNOW.
HMPH.
—MY, MY, LITTLE SHRIMP.
A HIDEOUS MONSTER LIKE YOU TAKING THE FORM OF A HUMAN...
...HOW ABSO-LUTELY REPUL-SIVE.
I'LL SLICE YOU INTO RIBBONS UNTIL NOBODY CAN RE-COGNIZE YOU!

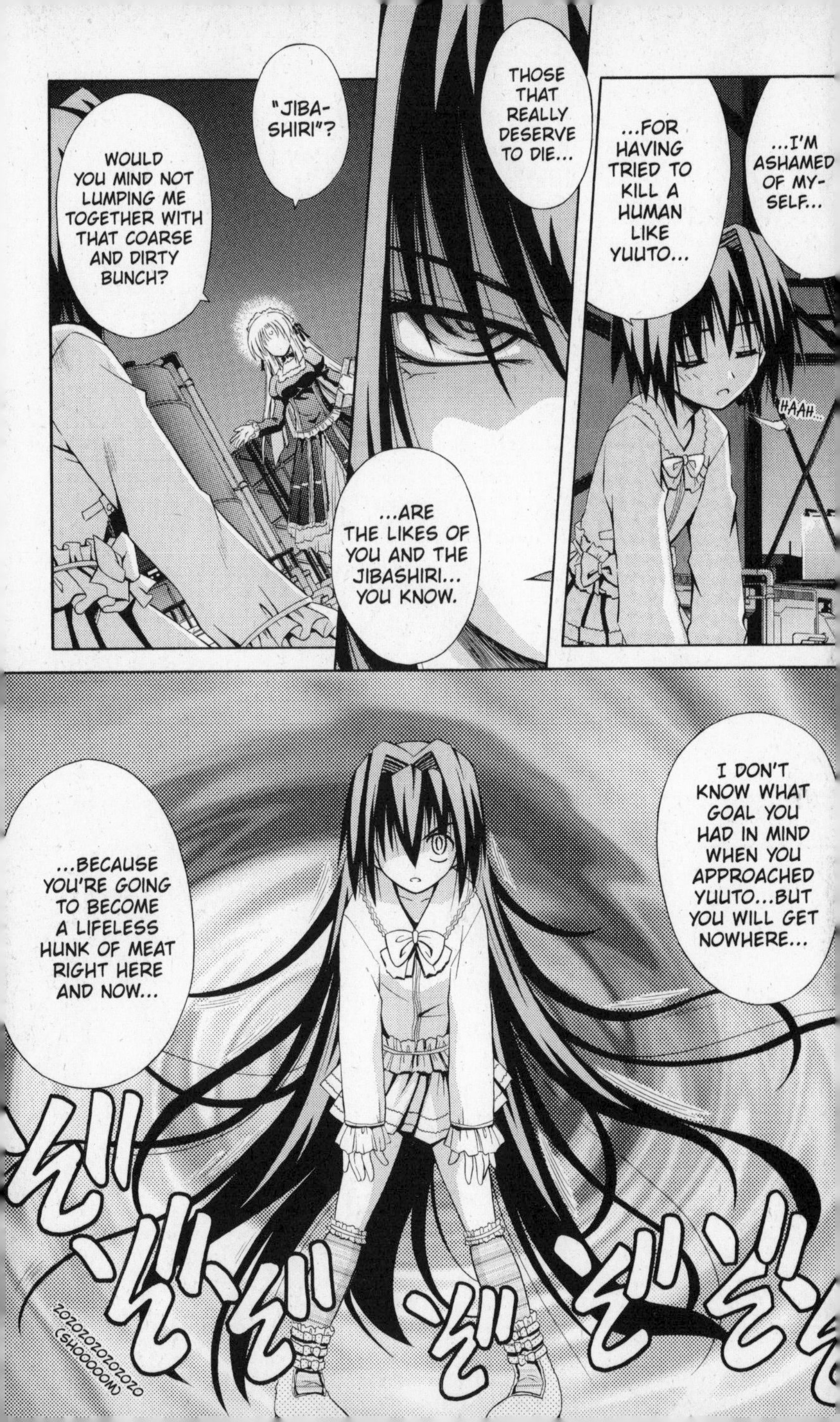
...I'M ASHAMED OF MY-SELF...
...FOR HAVING TRIED TO KILL A HUMAN LIKE YUUTO...
HAAH...
THOSE THAT REALLY DESERVE TO DIE...
...ARE THE LIKES OF YOU AND THE JIBASHIRI... YOU KNOW.
"JIBA-SHIRI"?
WOULD YOU MIND NOT LUMPING ME TOGETHER WITH THAT COARSE AND DIRTY BUNCH?
I DON'T KNOW WHAT GOAL YOU HAD IN MIND WHEN YOU APPROACHED YUUTO...BUT YOU WILL GET NOWHERE...
...BECAUSE YOU'RE GOING TO BECOME A LIFELESS HUNK OF MEAT RIGHT HERE AND NOW...
ZOZOZOZOZOZOZO (SHOOOOOM)

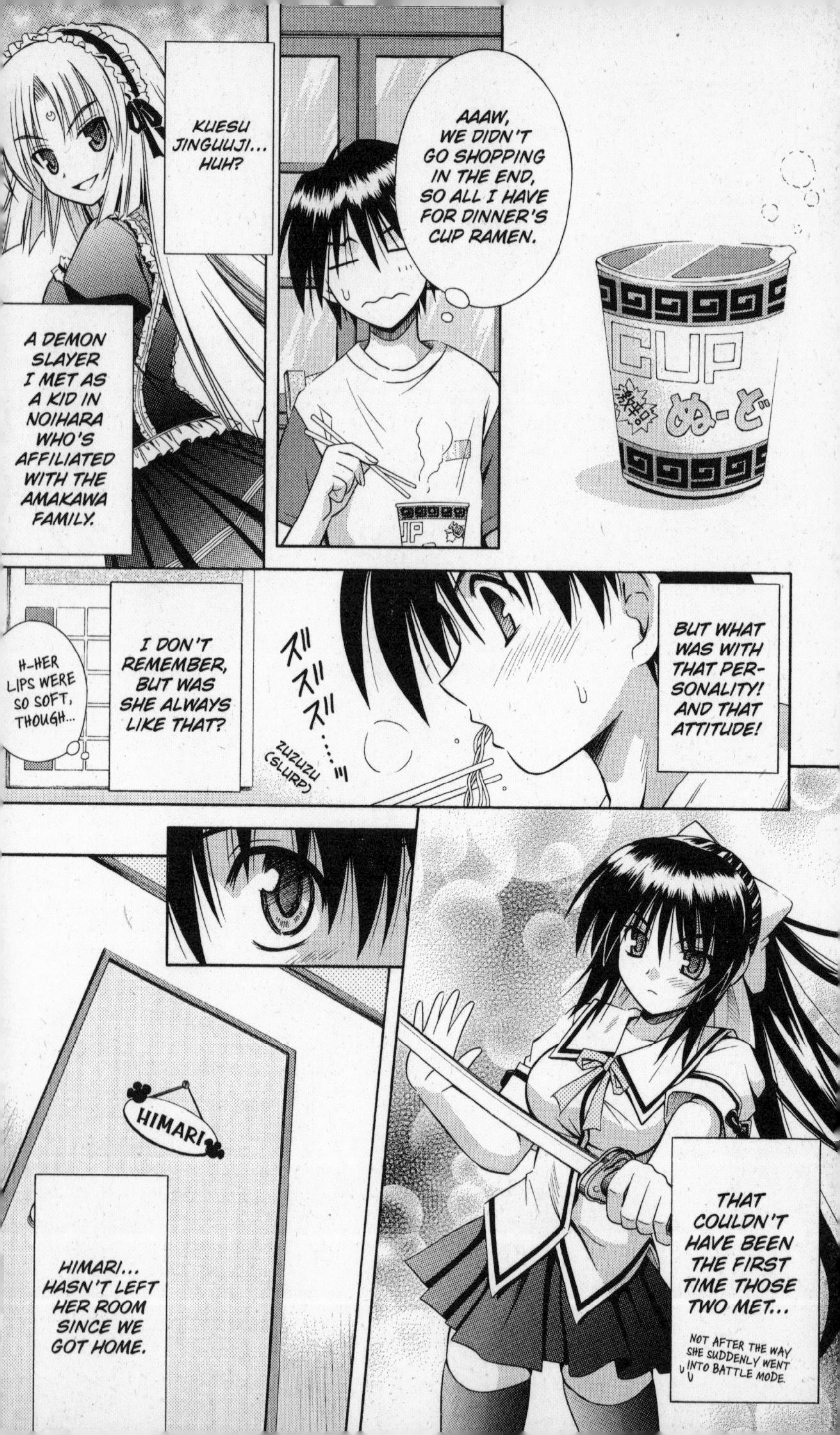
CUP
ぬーど
AAAW, WE DIDN'T GO SHOPPING IN THE END, SO ALL I HAVE FOR DINNER'S CUP RAMEN.
KUESU JINGUUJI... HUH?
A DEMON SLAYER I MET AS A KID IN NOIHARA WHO'S AFFILIATED WITH THE AMAKAWA FAMILY.
BUT WHAT WAS WITH THAT PER-SONALITY! AND THAT ATTITUDE!
ズズズ......ッ
ZUZUZU (SLURP)
I DON'T REMEMBER, BUT WAS SHE ALWAYS LIKE THAT?
H-HER LIPS WERE SO SOFT, THOUGH...
THAT COULDN'T HAVE BEEN THE FIRST TIME THOSE TWO MET...
NOT AFTER THE WAY SHE SUDDENLY WENT INTO BATTLE MODE.
HIMARI
HIMARI... HASN'T LEFT HER ROOM SINCE WE GOT HOME.

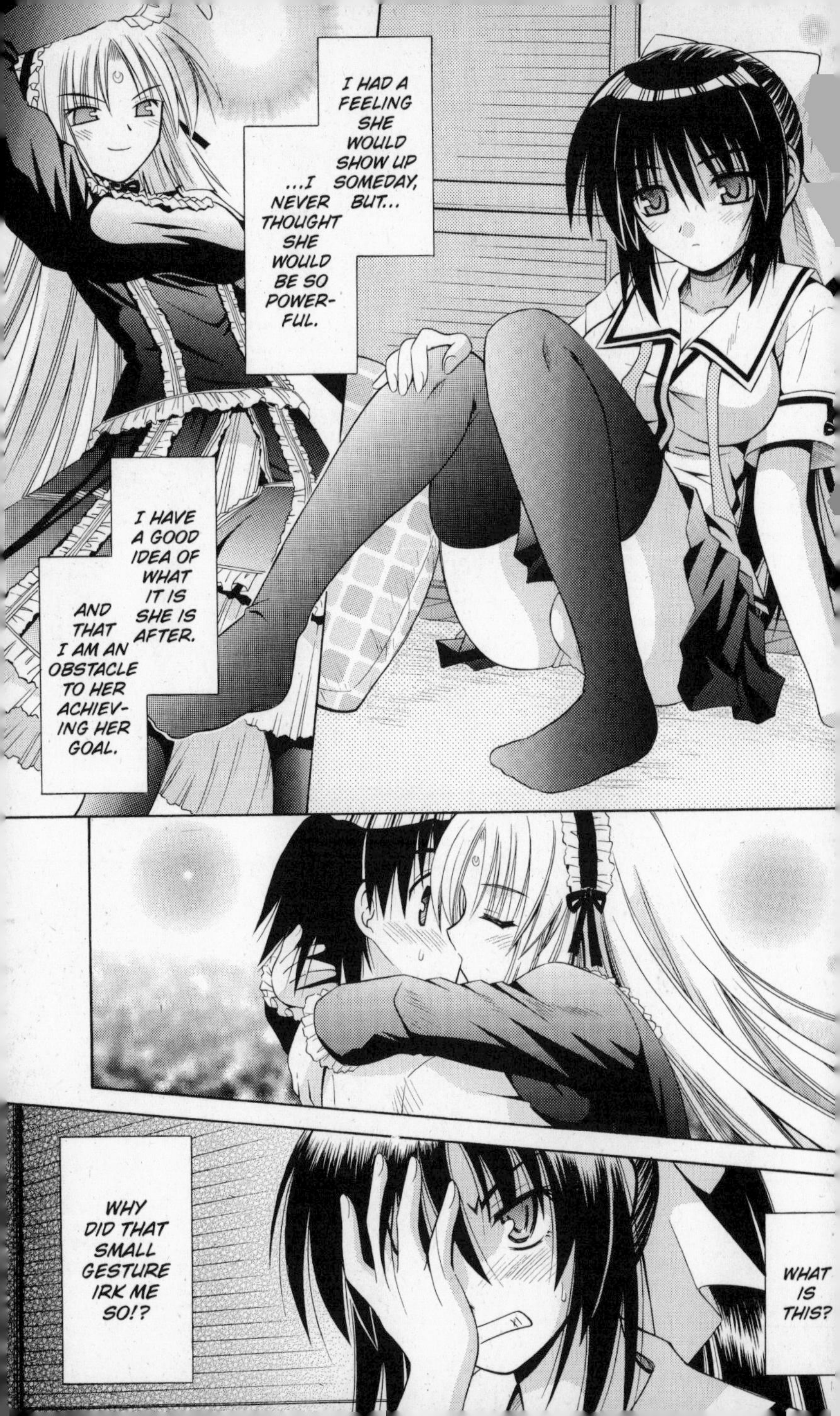
I HAD A FEELING SHE WOULD SHOW UP SOMEDAY, BUT...
...I NEVER THOUGHT SHE WOULD BE SO POWER-FUL.
I HAVE A GOOD IDEA OF WHAT IT IS SHE IS AFTER.
AND THAT I AM AN OBSTACLE TO HER ACHIEV-ING HER GOAL.
WHAT IS THIS?
WHY DID THAT SMALL GESTURE IRK ME SO!?

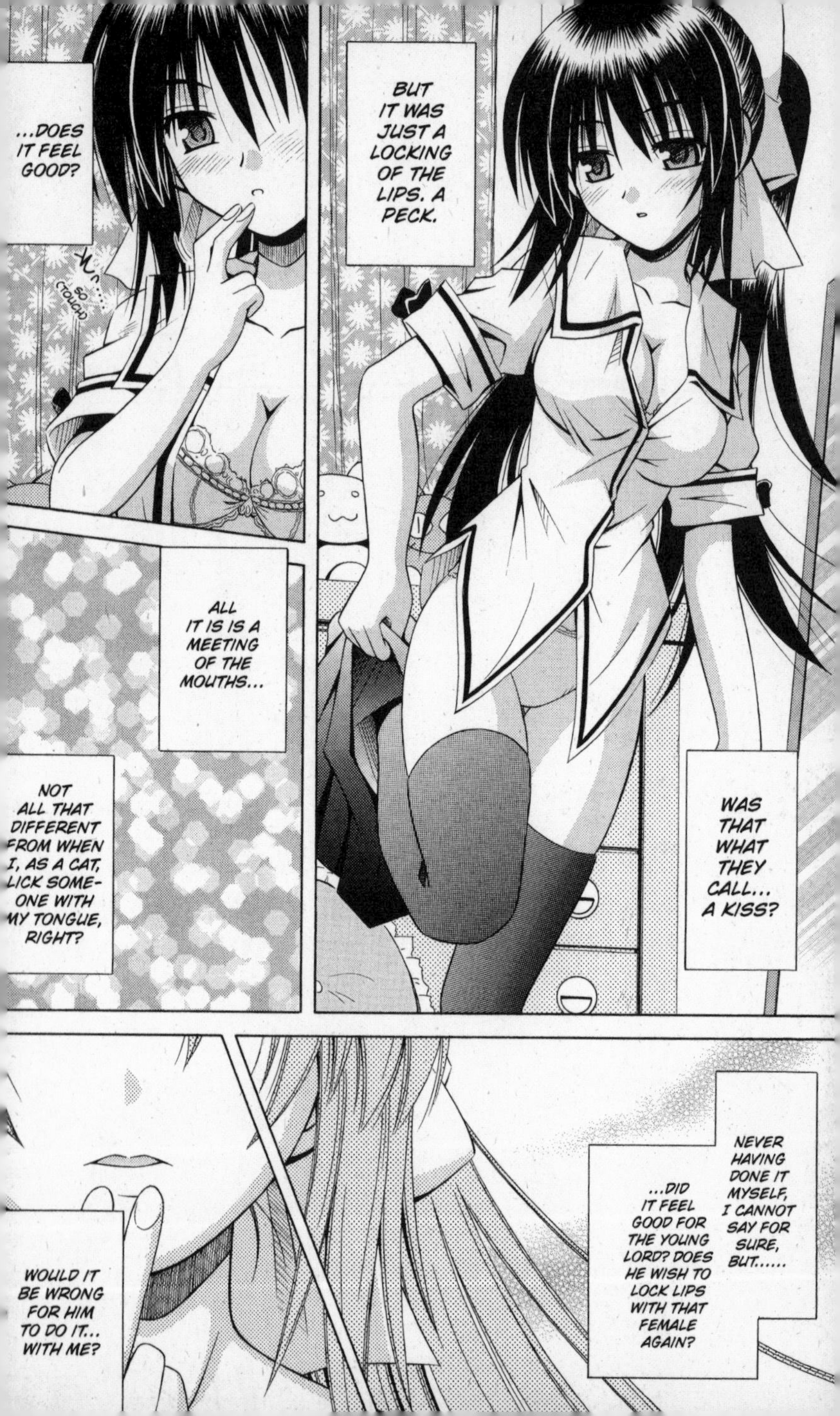
BUT IT WAS JUST A LOCKING OF THE LIPS. A PECK.
WAS THAT WHAT THEY CALL... A KISS?
...DOES IT FEEL GOOD?
SO (TOUCH)
ALL IT IS IS A MEETING OF THE MOUTHS...
NOT ALL THAT DIFFERENT FROM WHEN I, AS A CAT, LICK SOME-ONE WITH MY TONGUE, RIGHT?
NEVER HAVING DONE IT MYSELF, I CANNOT SAY FOR SURE, BUT......
...DID IT FEEL GOOD FOR THE YOUNG LORD? DOES HE WISH TO LOCK LIPS WITH THAT FEMALE AGAIN?
WOULD IT BE WRONG FOR HIM TO DO IT... WITH ME?

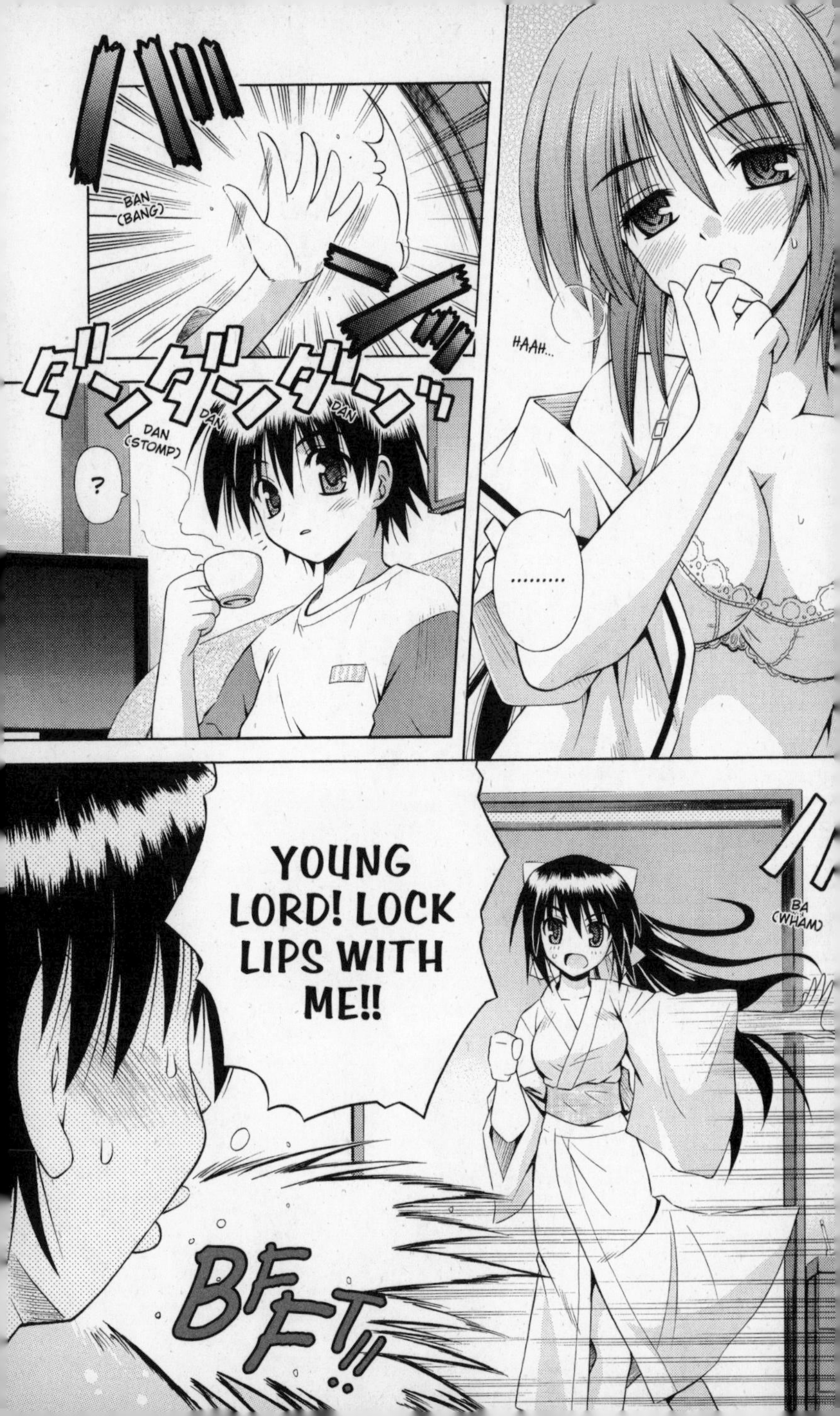
HAAH...
....
BAN (BANG)
DAN
DAN
DAN (STOMP)
?
BA (WHAM)
YOUNG LORD! LOCK LIPS WITH ME!!
BFFT!!

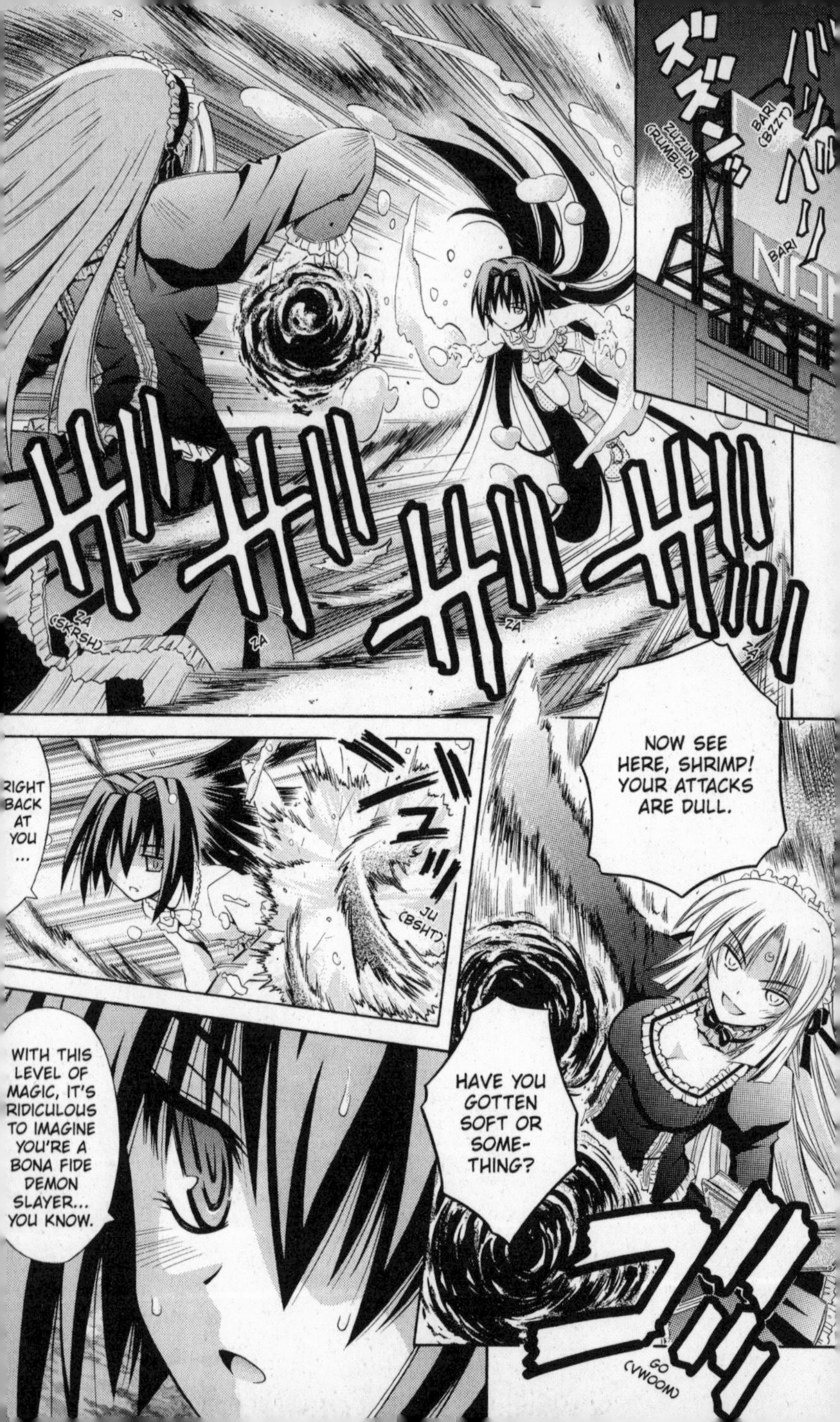
BARI (BZZT)
BARI
ZUZUN (RUMBLE)
ZA (SKRSH)
ZA
ZA
ZA
NOW SEE HERE, SHRIMP! YOUR ATTACKS ARE DULL.
HAVE YOU GOTTEN SOFT OR SOME-THING?
GO (VWOOM)
RIGHT BACK AT YOU ...
JU (BSHT)
WITH THIS LEVEL OF MAGIC, IT'S RIDICULOUS TO IMAGINE YOU'RE A BONA FIDE DEMON SLAYER... YOU KNOW.

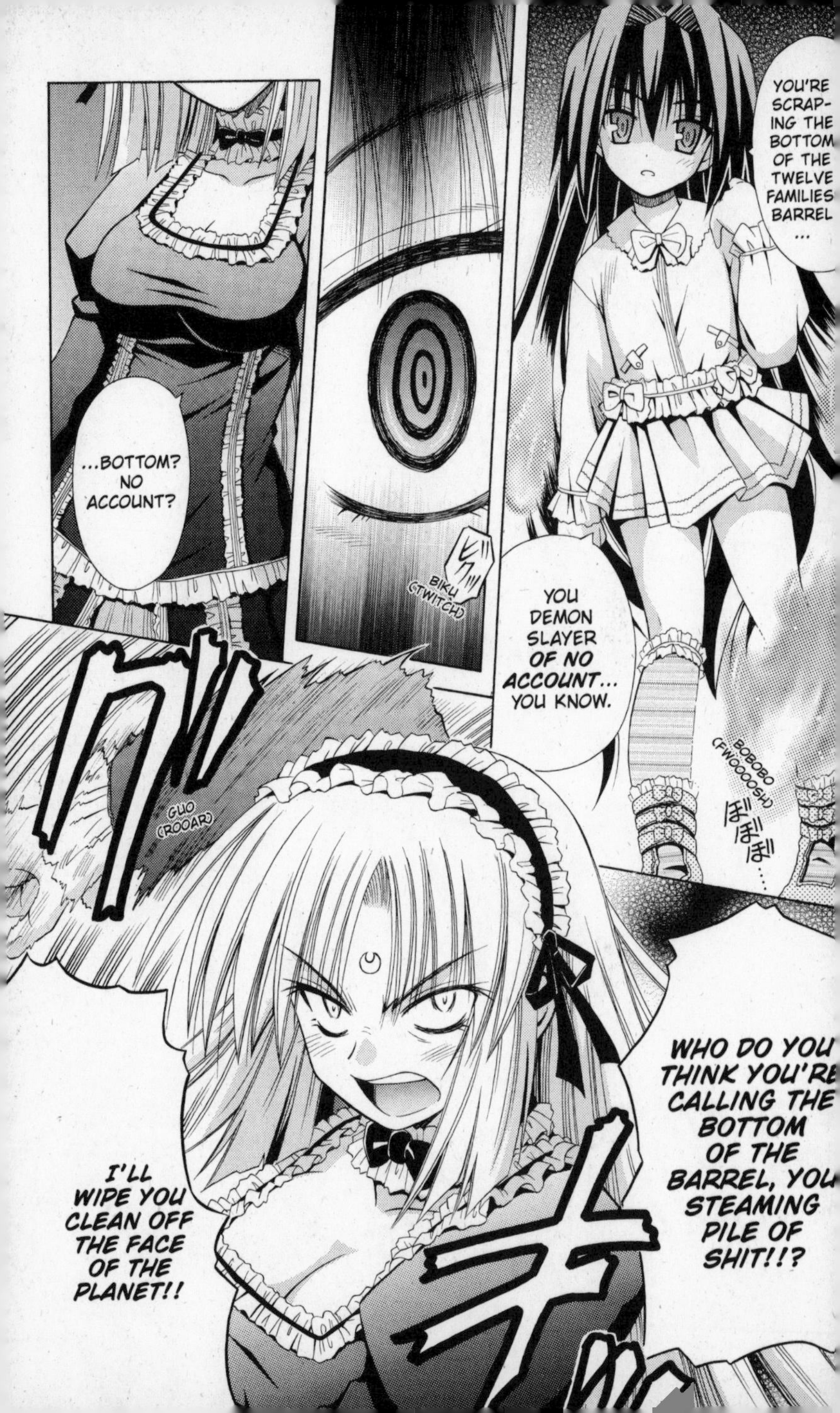

YOU'RE SCRAPING THE BOTTOM OF THE TWELVE FAMILIES BARREL...
YOU DEMON SLAYER OF NO ACCOUNT... YOU KNOW.
BIKU (TWITCH)
...BOTTOM? NO ACCOUNT?
BOBOBO (FWOOOOSH)
ぼぼぼ
WHO DO YOU THINK YOU'RE CALLING THE BOTTOM OF THE BARREL, YOU STEAMING PILE OF SHIT!!?
GUO (ROOAR)
I'LL WIPE YOU CLEAN OFF THE FACE OF THE PLANET!!

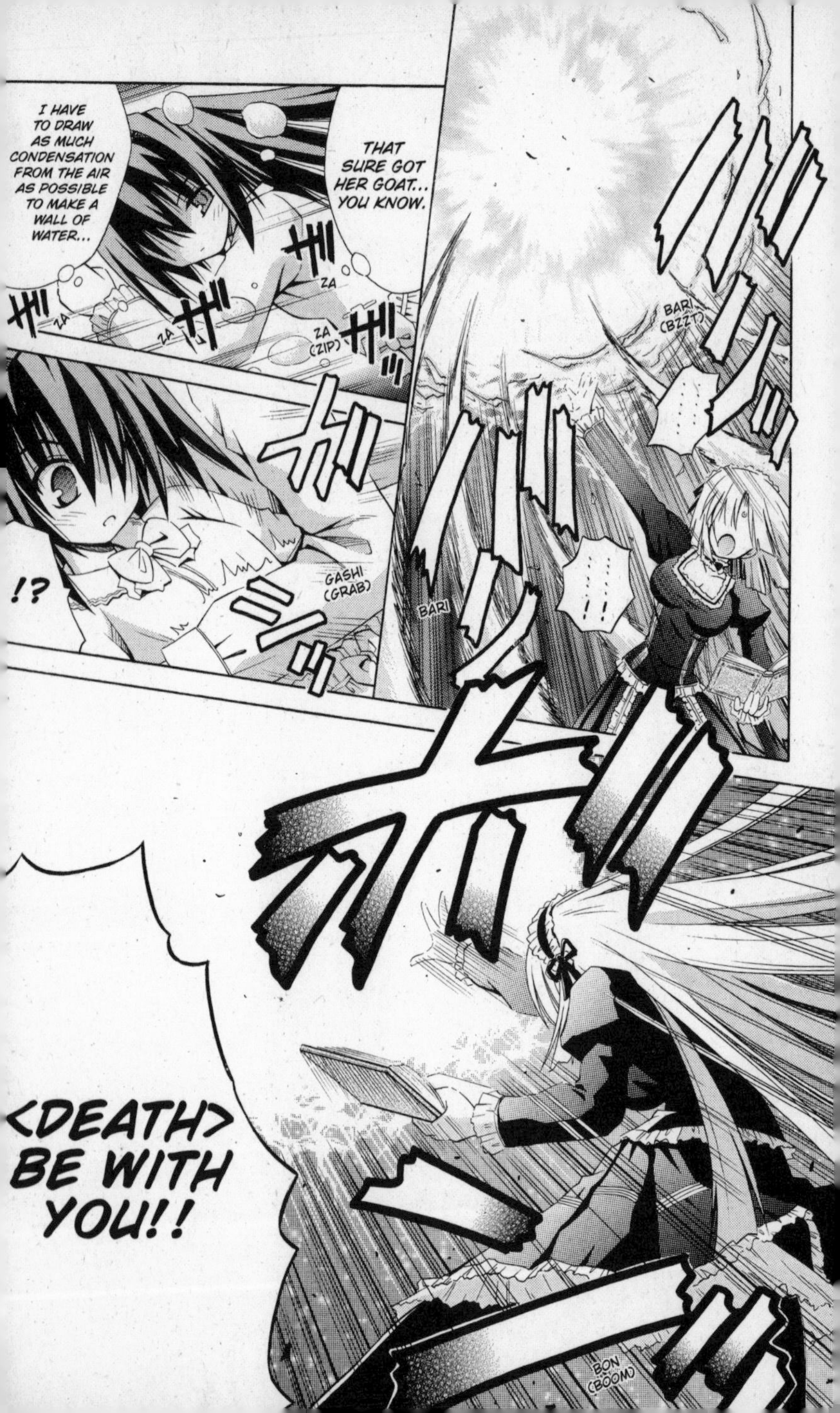
BARI (BZZT)
...!!
BARI
THAT SURE GOT HER GOAT... YOU KNOW.
I HAVE TO DRAW AS MUCH CONDENSATION FROM THE AIR AS POSSIBLE TO MAKE A WALL OF WATER...
ZA
ZA
ZA
ZA (ZIP)
GASHI (GRAB)
!?
<DEATH> BE WITH YOU!!
BON (BOOM)

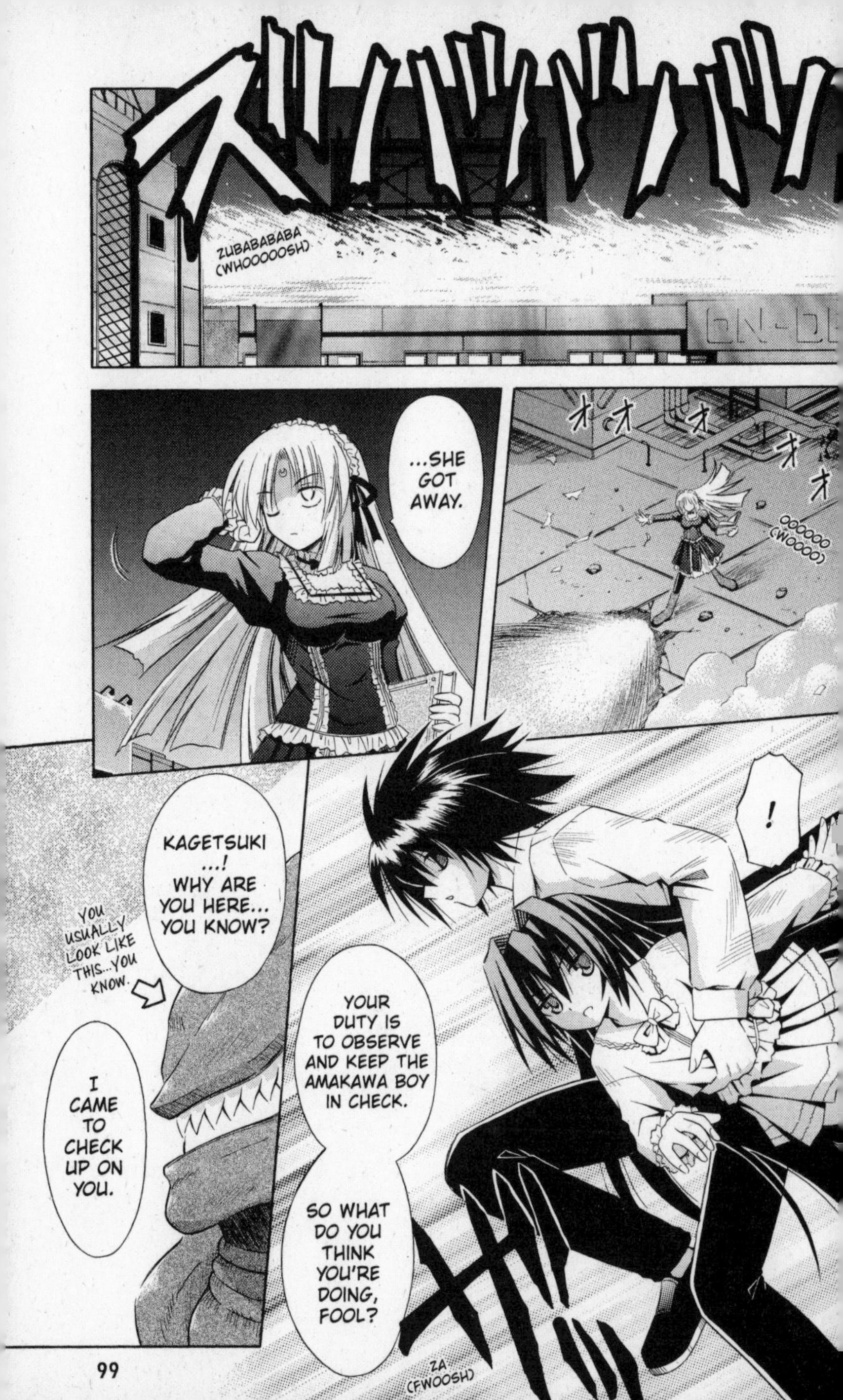
ZUBABABABA (WHOOOOOSH)
OOOOOO (WOOOOO)
...SHE GOT AWAY.
!
YOUR DUTY IS TO OBSERVE AND KEEP THE AMAKAWA BOY IN CHECK.
SO WHAT DO YOU THINK YOU'RE DOING, FOOL?
ZA (F.WOOSH)
KAGETSUKI ...! WHY ARE YOU HERE... YOU KNOW?
YOU USUALLY LOOK LIKE THIS...YOU KNOW.
I CAME TO CHECK UP ON YOU.

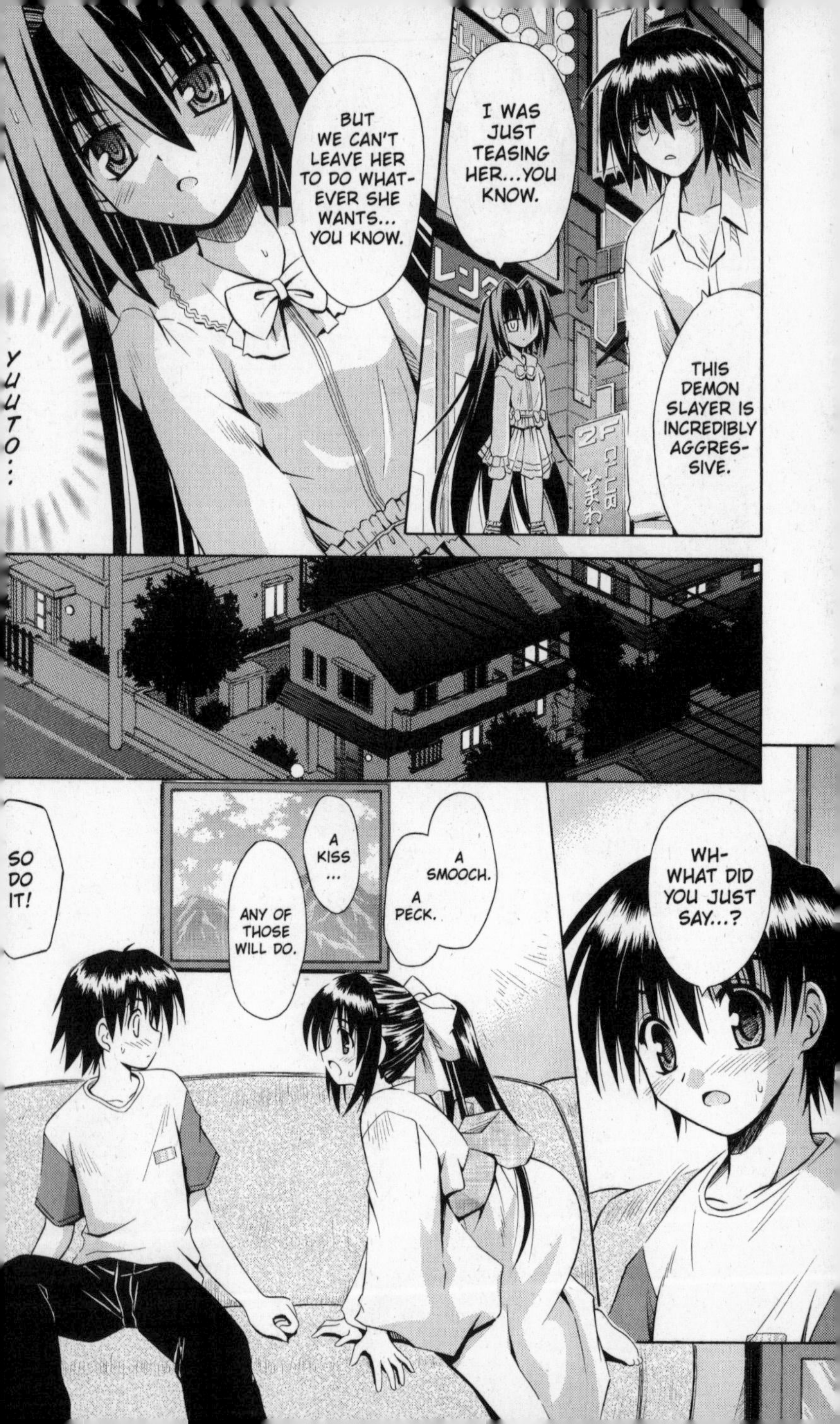
THIS DEMON SLAYER IS INCREDIBLY AGGRES-SIVE.
I WAS JUST TEASING HER...YOU KNOW.
BUT WE CAN'T LEAVE HER TO DO WHAT-EVER SHE WANTS... YOU KNOW.
YUUTO...
WH-WHAT DID YOU JUST SAY...?
A SMOOCH.
A PECK.
A KISS...
ANY OF THOSE WILL DO.
SO DO IT!

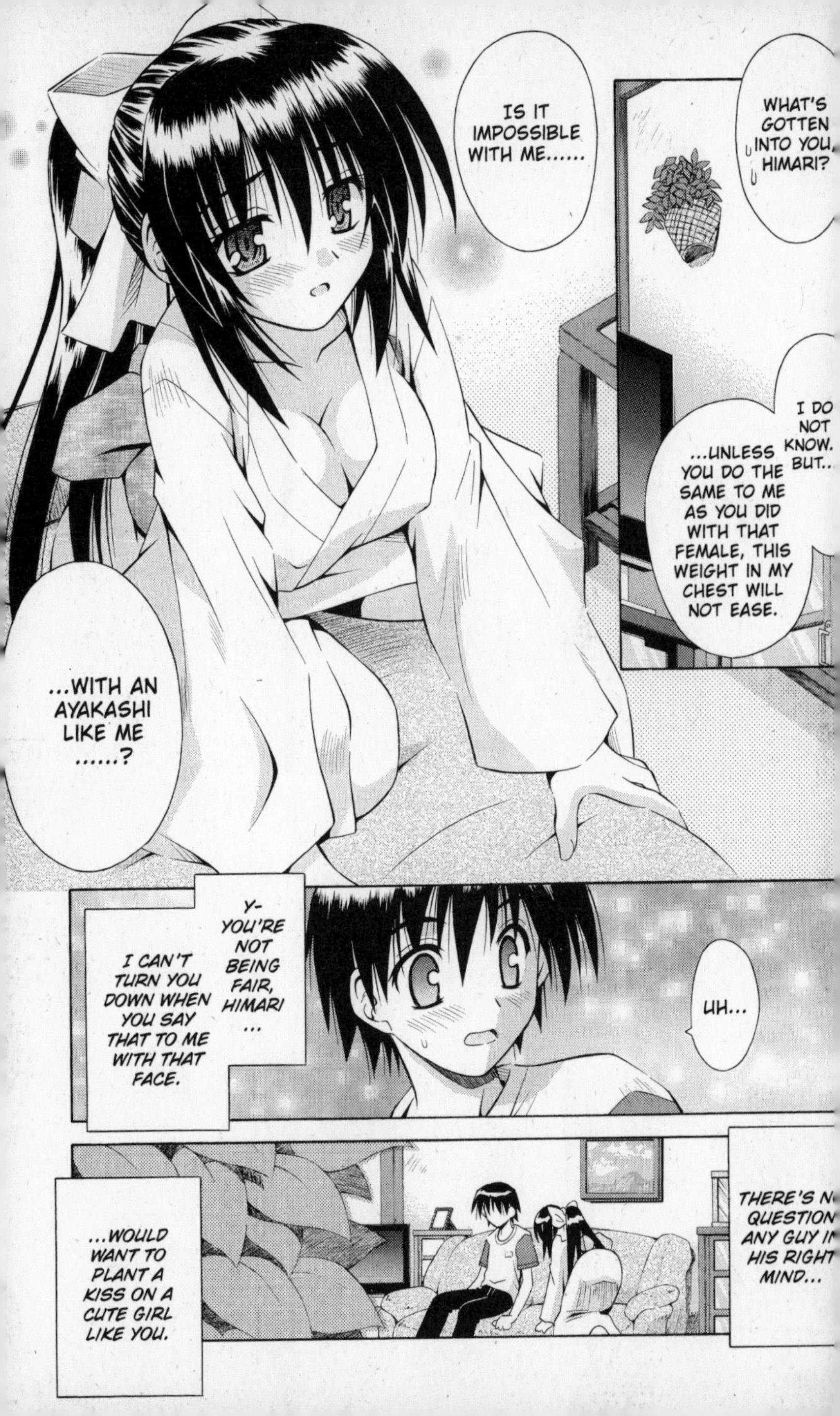
WHAT'S GOTTEN INTO YOU, HIMARI?
I DO NOT KNOW. BUT...
...UNLESS YOU DO THE SAME TO ME AS YOU DID WITH THAT FEMALE, THIS WEIGHT IN MY CHEST WILL NOT EASE.
IS IT IMPOSSIBLE WITH ME......
...WITH AN AYAKASHI LIKE ME ......?
UH...
Y-YOU'RE NOT BEING FAIR, HIMARI ...
I CAN'T TURN YOU DOWN WHEN YOU SAY THAT TO ME WITH THAT FACE.
THERE'S N QUESTION ANY GUY I HIS RIGHT MIND...
...WOULD WANT TO PLANT A KISS ON A CUTE GIRL LIKE YOU.

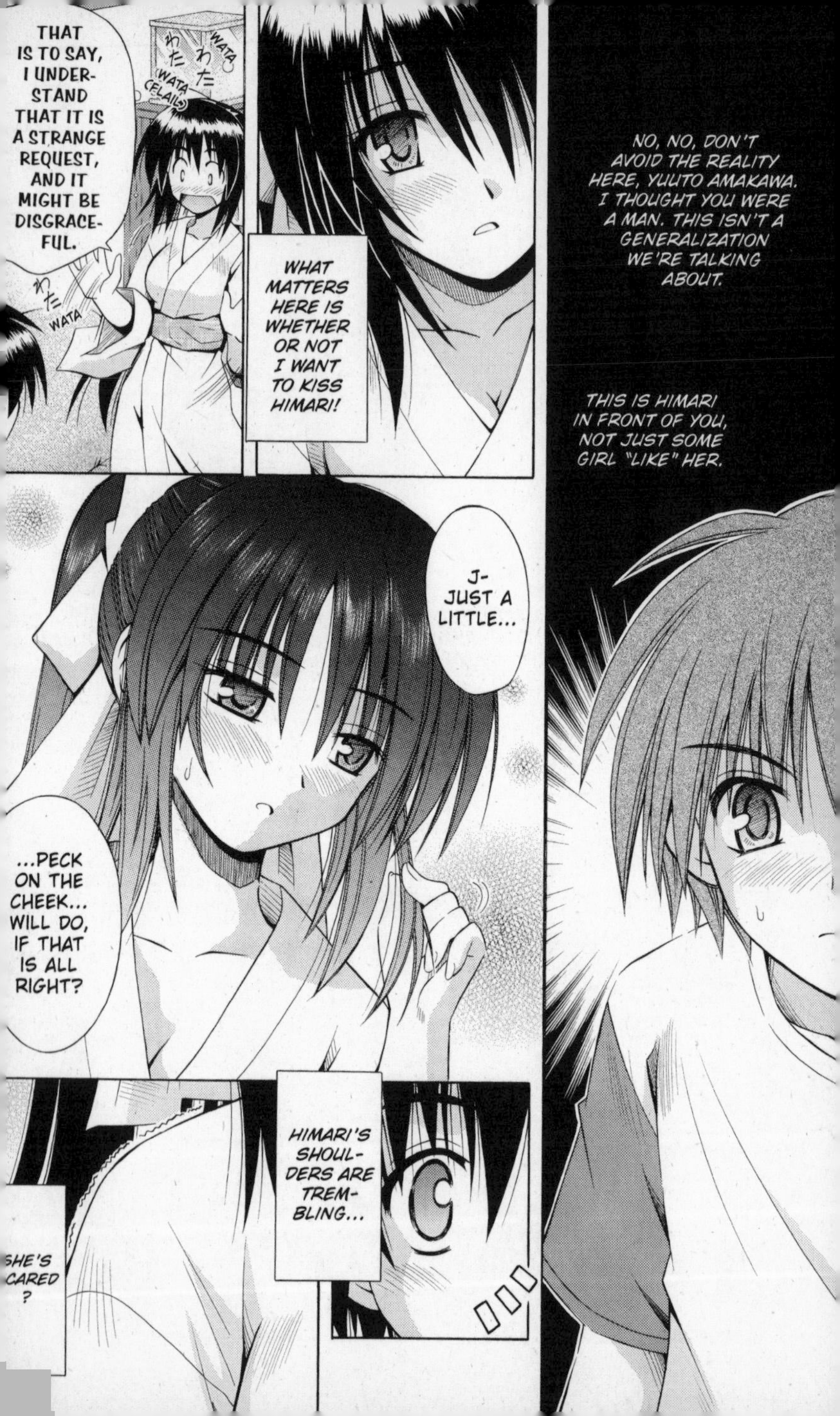

NO, NO, DON'T AVOID THE REALITY HERE, YUUTO AMAKAWA. I THOUGHT YOU WERE A MAN. THIS ISN'T A GENERALIZATION WE'RE TALKING ABOUT.
THIS IS HIMARI IN FRONT OF YOU, NOT JUST SOME GIRL "LIKE" HER.
WHAT MATTERS HERE IS WHETHER OR NOT I WANT TO KISS HIMARI!
THAT IS TO SAY, I UNDERSTAND THAT IT IS A STRANGE REQUEST, AND IT MIGHT BE DISGRACEFUL.
わた わた
WATA
(WATA (FLAIL))
わた
WATA
J- JUST A LITTLE...
...PECK ON THE CHEEK... WILL DO, IF THAT IS ALL RIGHT?
HIMARI'S SHOULDERS ARE TREMBLING...
HE'S CARED ?

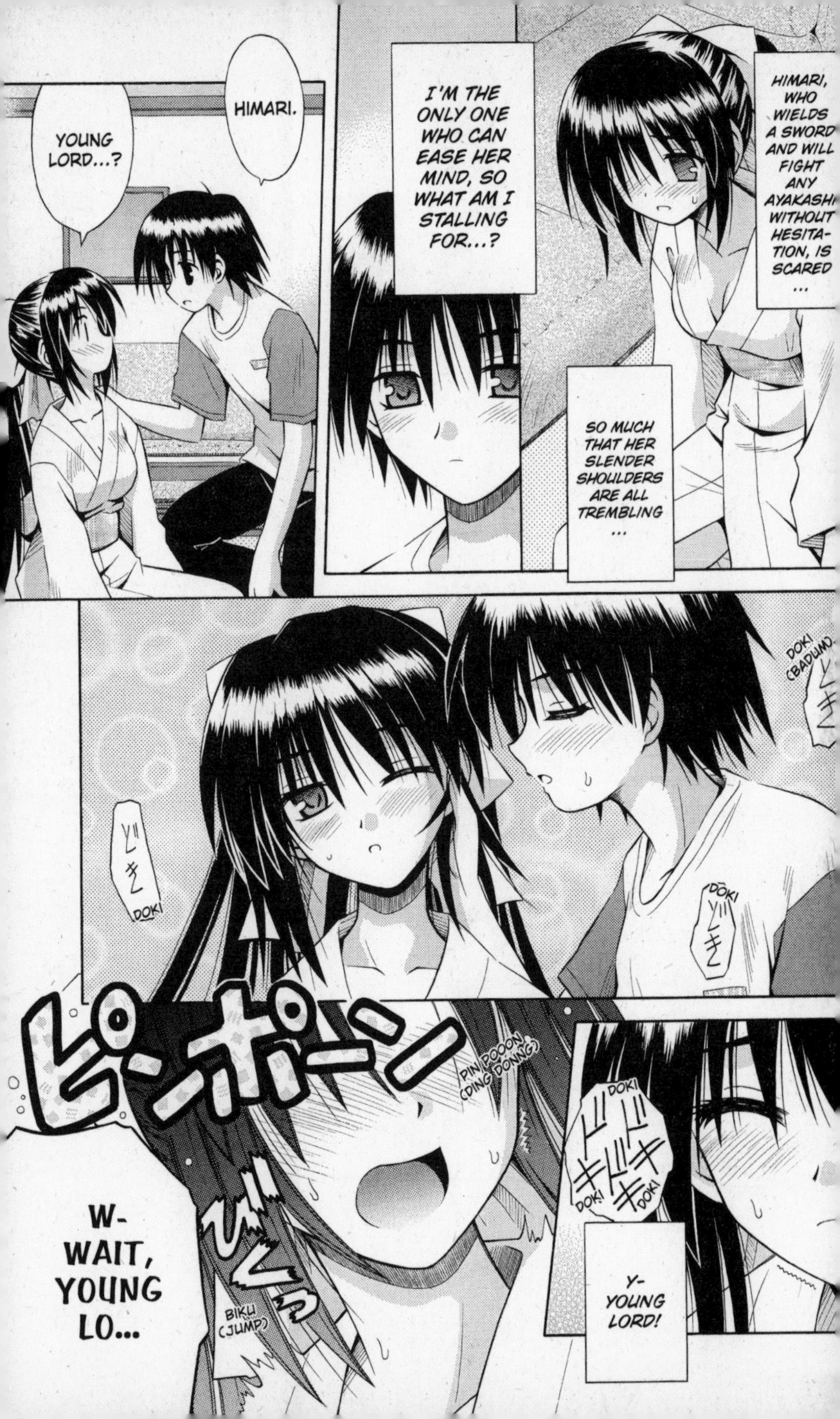
HIMARI, WHO WIELDS A SWORD AND WILL FIGHT ANY AYAKASHI WITHOUT HESITATION, IS SCARED ...
SO MUCH THAT HER SLENDER SHOULDERS ARE ALL TREMBLING ...
I'M THE ONLY ONE WHO CAN EASE HER MIND, SO WHAT AM I STALLING FOR...?
HIMARI.
YOUNG LORD...?
DOKI (BADUM)
DOKI
DOKI
DOKI DOKI DOKI
Y- YOUNG LORD!
PIN POOON (DING DONNG)
BIKU (JUMP)
W- WAIT, YOUNG LO...

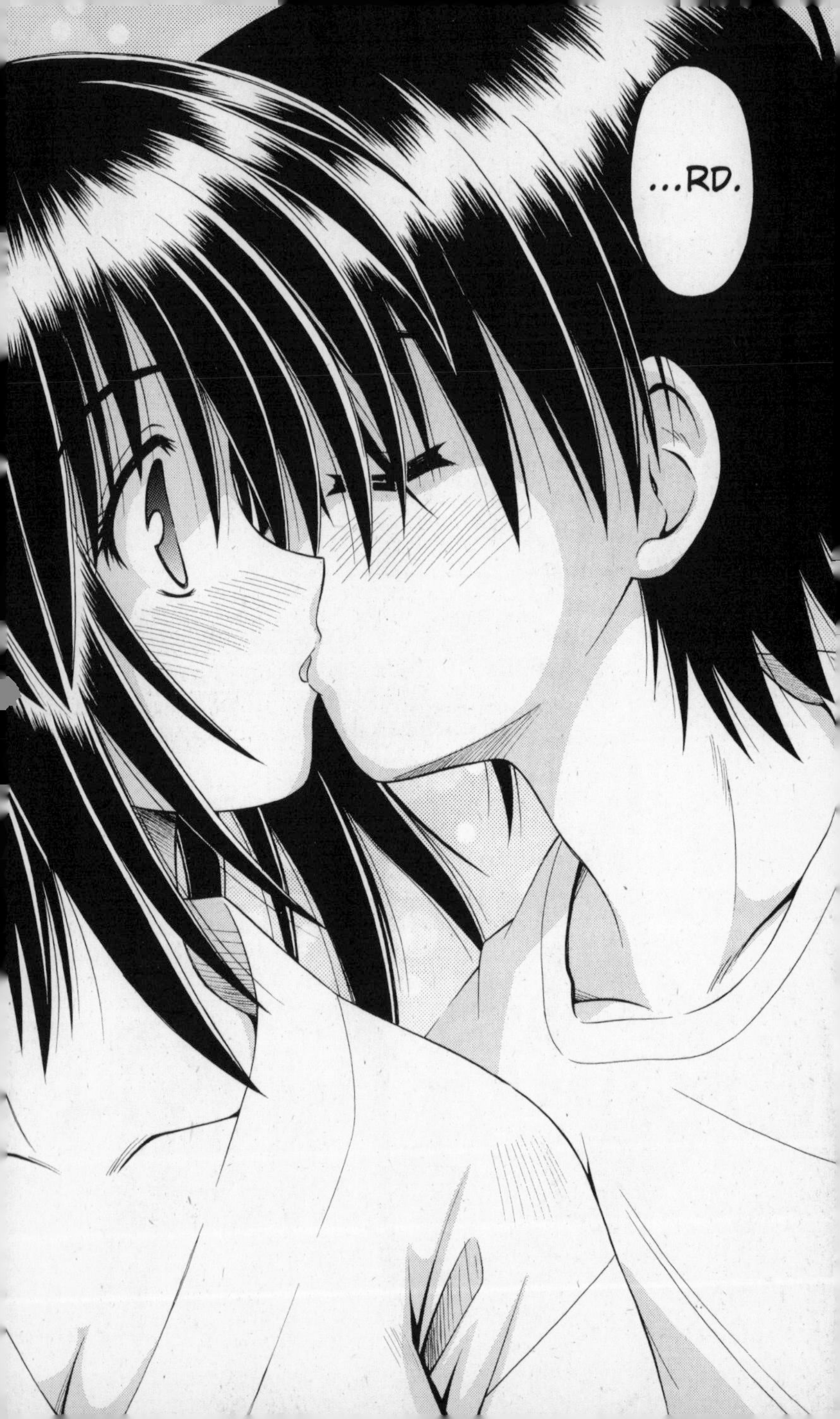
...RD.

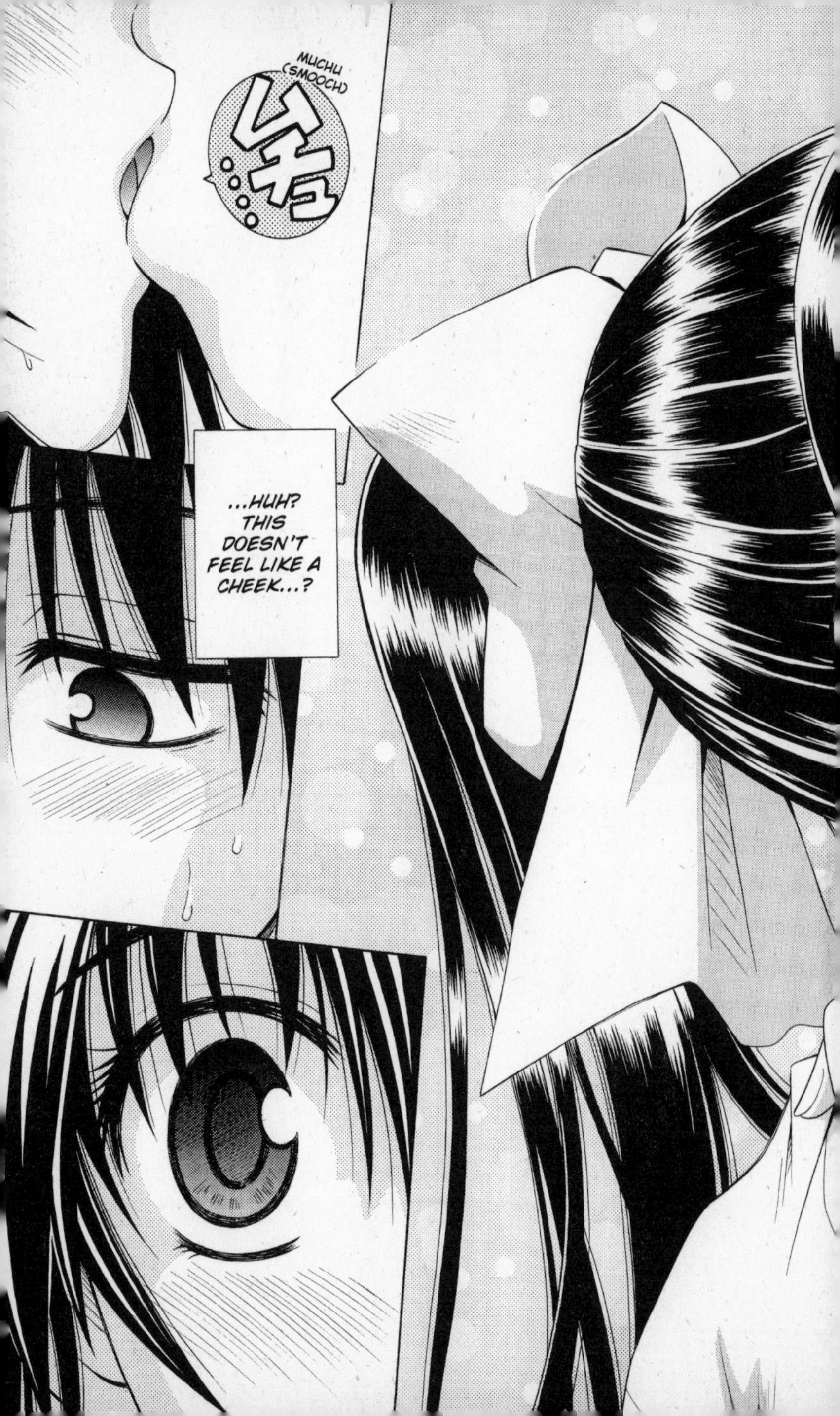
MUCHU (SMOOCH)
...HUH? THIS DOESN'T FEEL LIKE A CHEEK...?

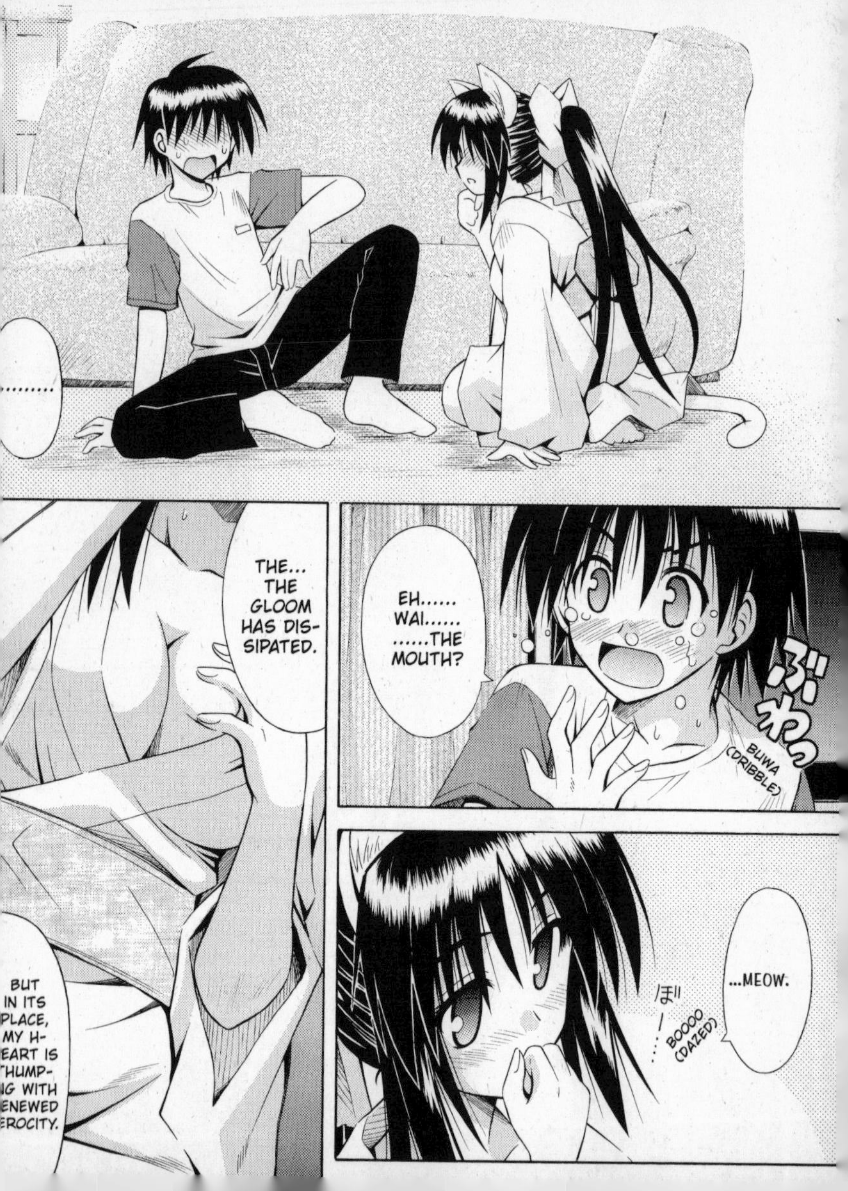
....
EH...... WAI...... ......THE MOUTH?
ぶわっ
BUWA (DRIBBLE)
...MEOW.
ぽ!
BOOOO (DAZED)
THE... THE GLOOM HAS DIS-SIPATED.
BUT IN ITS PLACE, MY H-EART IS HUMP-NG WITH ENEWED EROCITY.

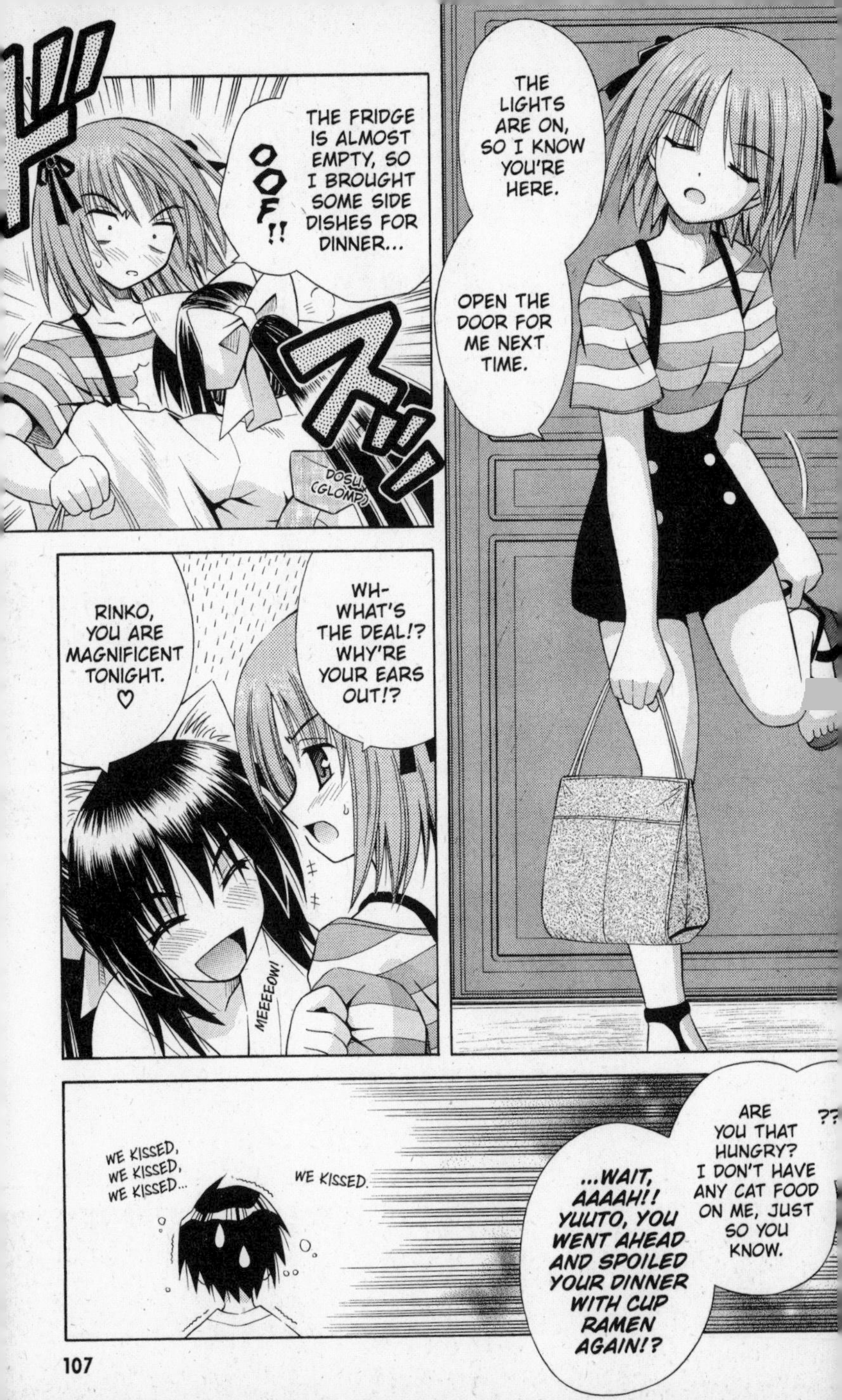
THE LIGHTS ARE ON, SO I KNOW YOU'RE HERE.
OPEN THE DOOR FOR ME NEXT TIME.
THE FRIDGE IS ALMOST EMPTY, SO I BROUGHT SOME SIDE DISHES FOR DINNER...
OOF!!
DOSU (GLOMP)
WH- WHAT'S THE DEAL!? WHY'RE YOUR EARS OUT!?
RINKO, YOU ARE MAGNIFICENT TONIGHT. ♡
MEEEEOW!
??
ARE YOU THAT HUNGRY? I DON'T HAVE ANY CAT FOOD ON ME, JUST SO YOU KNOW.
...WAIT, AAAAH!! YUUTO, YOU WENT AHEAD AND SPOILED YOUR DINNER WITH CUP RAMEN AGAIN!?
WE KISSED.
WE KISSED, WE KISSED, WE KISSED...

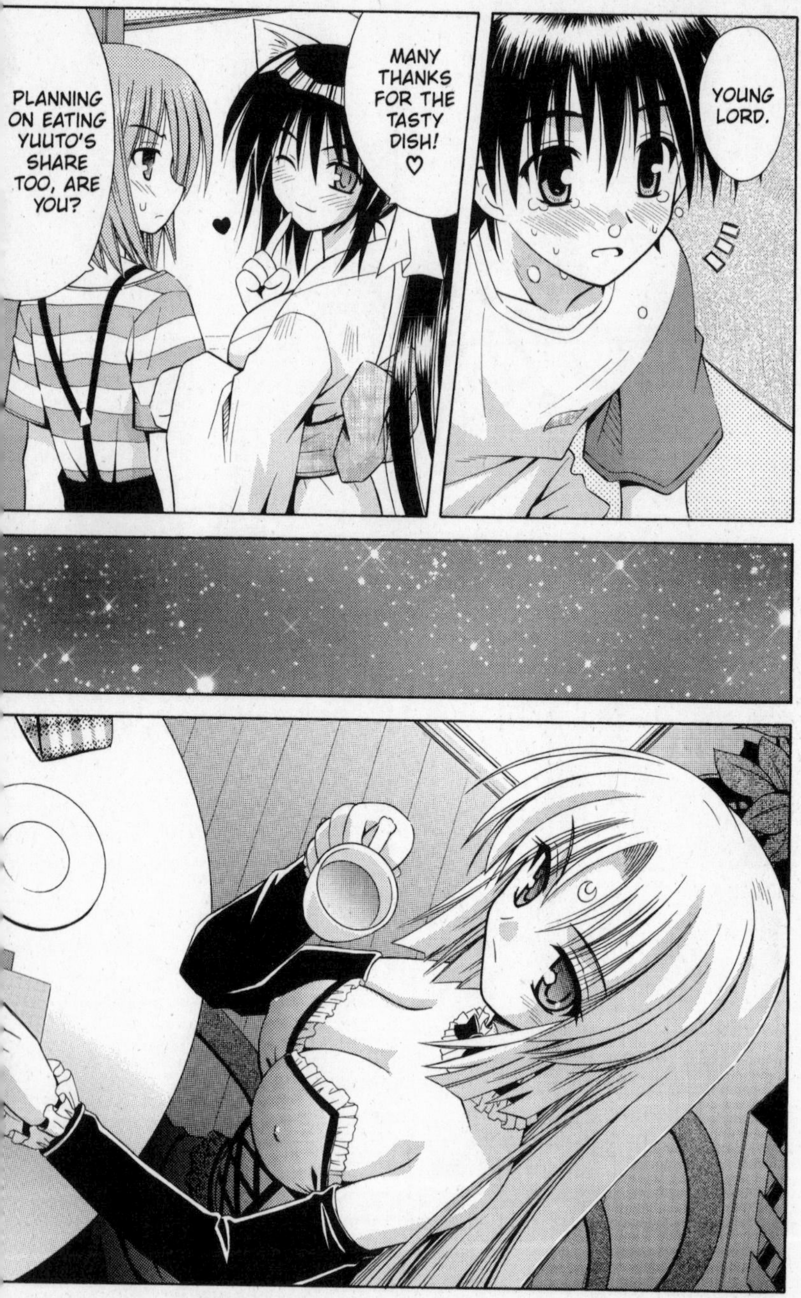
YOUNG LORD.
MANY THANKS FOR THE TASTY DISH! ♡
PLANNING ON EATING YUUTO'S SHARE TOO, ARE YOU?

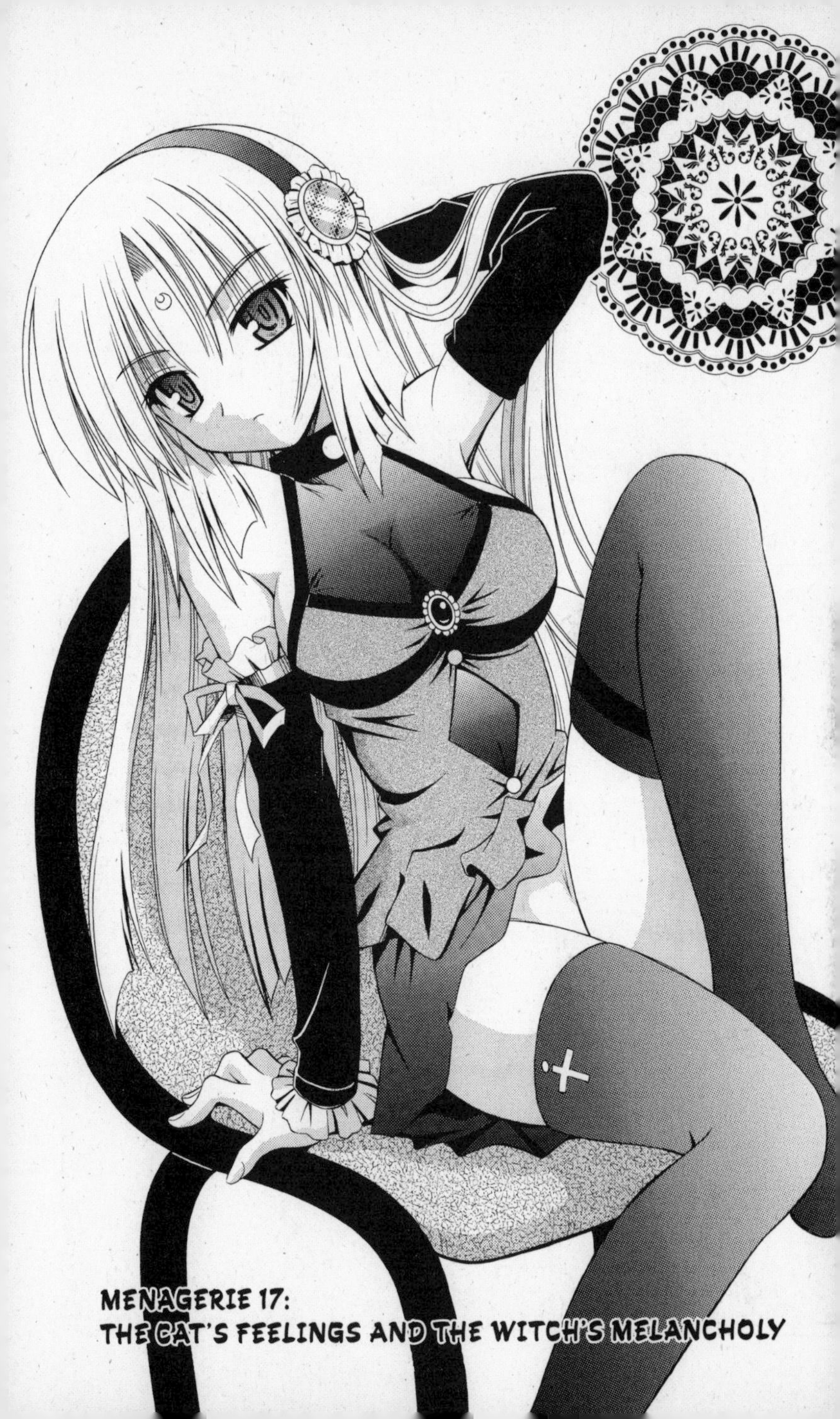

MENAGERIE 17:
THE CAT'S FEELINGS AND THE WITCH'S MELANCHOLY

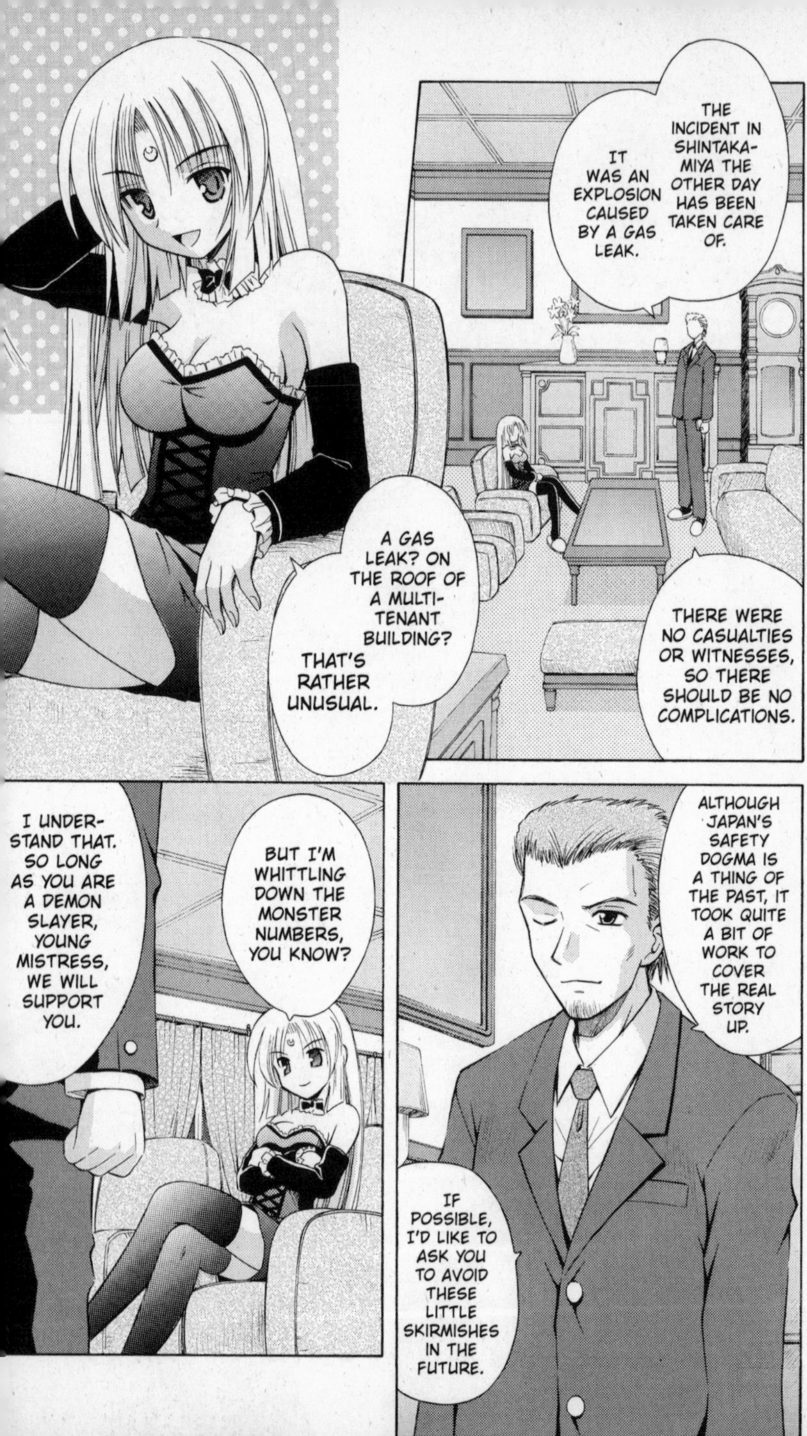
THE INCIDENT IN SHINTAKA-MIYA THE OTHER DAY HAS BEEN TAKEN CARE OF.
IT WAS AN EXPLOSION CAUSED BY A GAS LEAK.
THERE WERE NO CASUALTIES OR WITNESSES, SO THERE SHOULD BE NO COMPLICATIONS.
A GAS LEAK? ON THE ROOF OF A MULTI-TENANT BUILDING?
THAT'S RATHER UNUSUAL.
ALTHOUGH JAPAN'S SAFETY DOGMA IS A THING OF THE PAST, IT TOOK QUITE A BIT OF WORK TO COVER THE REAL STORY UP.
IF POSSIBLE, I'D LIKE TO ASK YOU TO AVOID THESE LITTLE SKIRMISHES IN THE FUTURE.
BUT I'M WHITTLING DOWN THE MONSTER NUMBERS, YOU KNOW?
I UNDER-STAND THAT. SO LONG AS YOU ARE A DEMON SLAYER, YOUNG MISTRESS, WE WILL SUPPORT YOU.

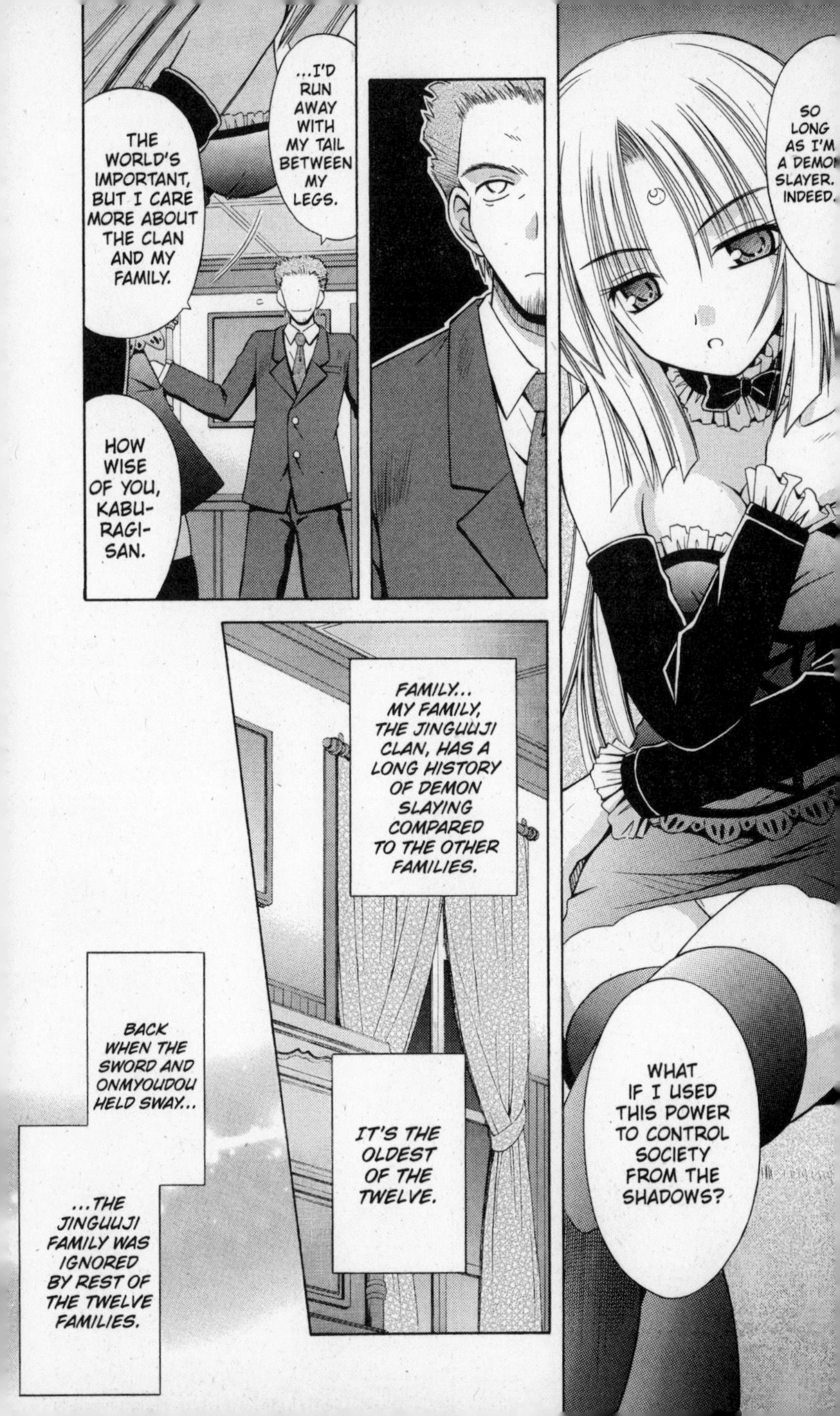
SO LONG AS I'M A DEMON SLAYER. INDEED.
WHAT IF I USED THIS POWER TO CONTROL SOCIETY FROM THE SHADOWS?
...I'D RUN AWAY WITH MY TAIL BETWEEN MY LEGS.
THE WORLD'S IMPORTANT, BUT I CARE MORE ABOUT THE CLAN AND MY FAMILY.
HOW WISE OF YOU, KABURAGI-SAN.
FAMILY... MY FAMILY, THE JINGUUJI CLAN, HAS A LONG HISTORY OF DEMON SLAYING COMPARED TO THE OTHER FAMILIES.
IT'S THE OLDEST OF THE TWELVE.
BACK WHEN THE SWORD AND ONMYOUDOU HELD SWAY...
...THE JINGUUJI FAMILY WAS IGNORED BY REST OF THE TWELVE FAMILIES.

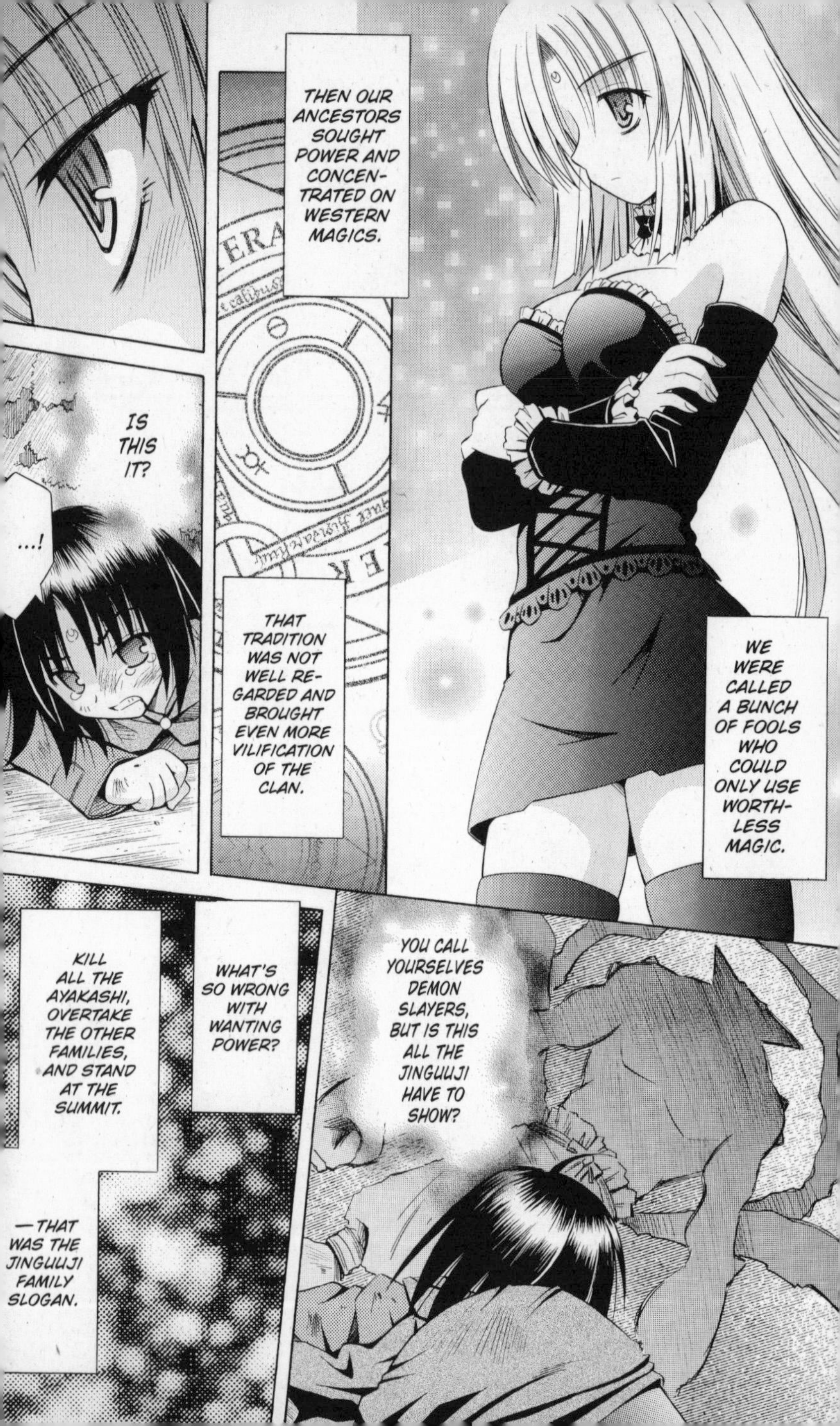
THEN OUR ANCESTORS SOUGHT POWER AND CONCEN-TRATED ON WESTERN MAGICS.
THAT TRADITION WAS NOT WELL RE-GARDED AND BROUGHT EVEN MORE VILIFICATION OF THE CLAN.
WE WERE CALLED A BUNCH OF FOOLS WHO COULD ONLY USE WORTH-LESS MAGIC.
IS THIS IT?
...!
YOU CALL YOURSELVES DEMON SLAYERS, BUT IS THIS ALL THE JINGUUJI HAVE TO SHOW?
WHAT'S SO WRONG WITH WANTING POWER?
KILL ALL THE AYAKASHI, OVERTAKE THE OTHER FAMILIES, AND STAND AT THE SUMMIT.
—THAT WAS THE JINGUUJI FAMILY SLOGAN.

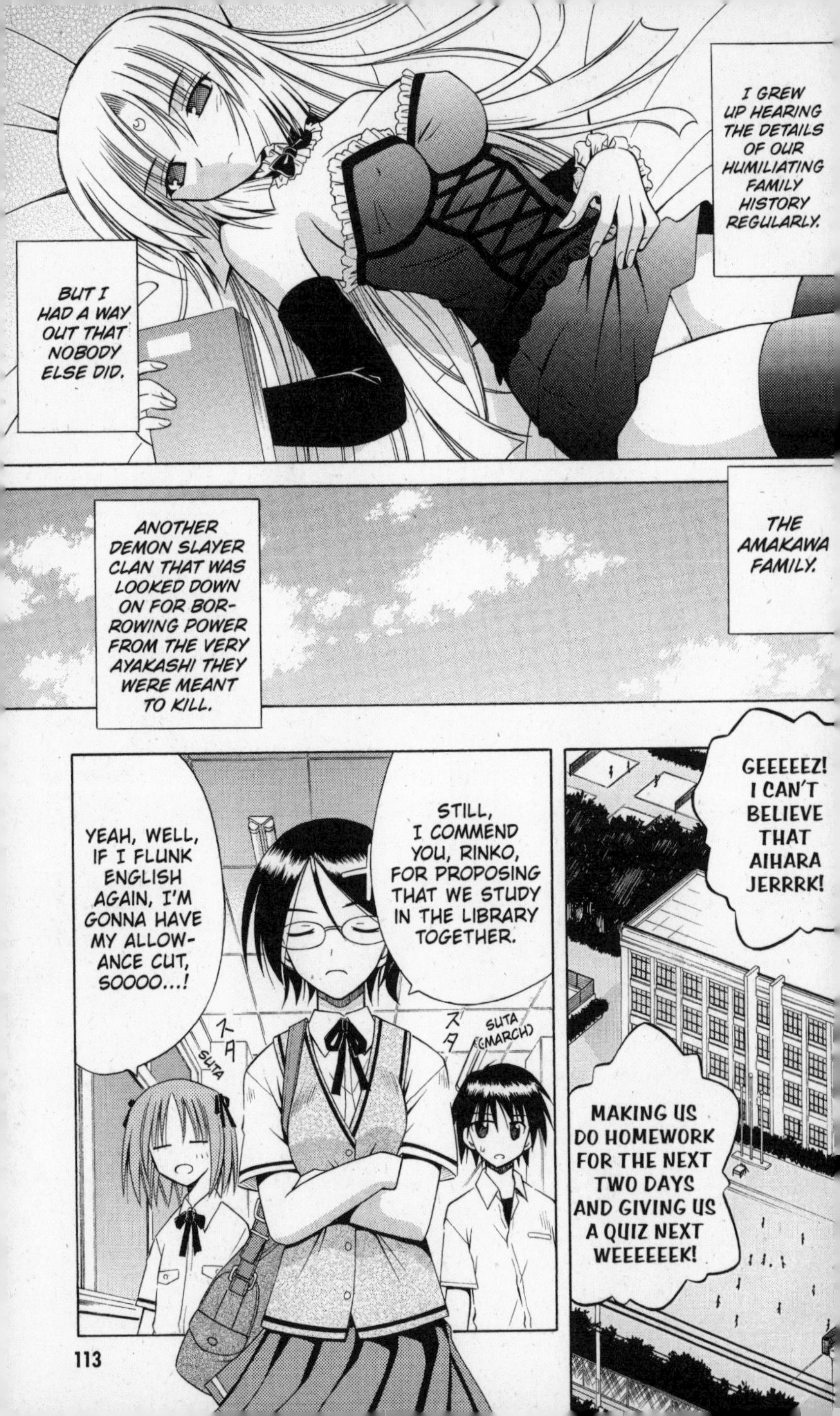
I GREW UP HEARING THE DETAILS OF OUR HUMILIATING FAMILY HISTORY REGULARLY.
BUT I HAD A WAY OUT THAT NOBODY ELSE DID.
THE AMAKAWA FAMILY.
ANOTHER DEMON SLAYER CLAN THAT WAS LOOKED DOWN ON FOR BOR-ROWING POWER FROM THE VERY AYAKASHI THEY WERE MEANT TO KILL.
GEEEEEZ! I CAN'T BELIEVE THAT AIHARA JERRRK!
MAKING US DO HOMEWORK FOR THE NEXT TWO DAYS AND GIVING US A QUIZ NEXT WEEEEEEK!
STILL, I COMMEND YOU, RINKO, FOR PROPOSING THAT WE STUDY IN THE LIBRARY TOGETHER.
スタ
SUTA (MARCH)
YEAH, WELL, IF I FLUNK ENGLISH AGAIN, I'M GONNA HAVE MY ALLOW-ANCE CUT, SOOOO...!
スタ
SUTA

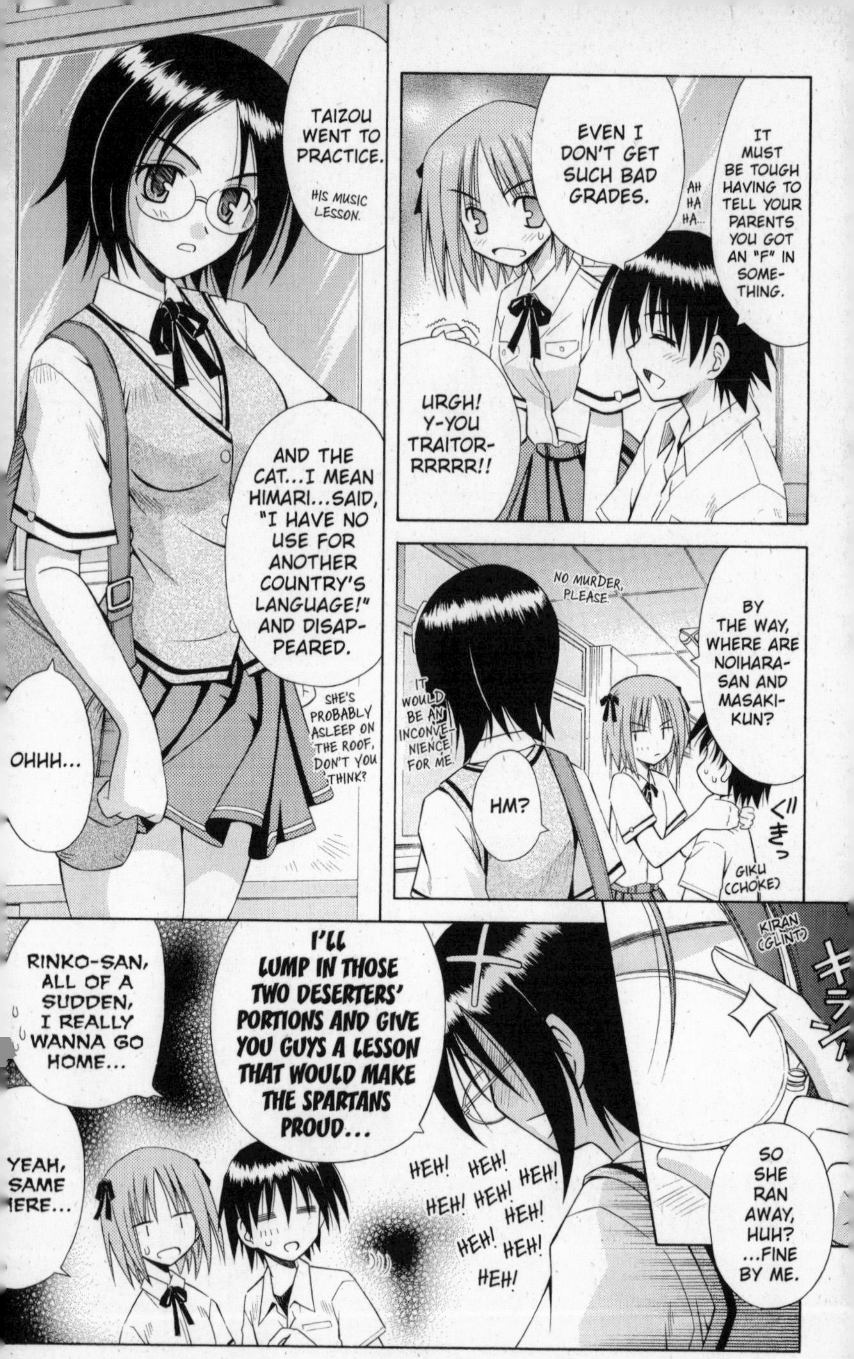
IT MUST BE TOUGH HAVING TO TELL YOUR PARENTS YOU GOT AN "F" IN SOME-THING.
AH HA HA...
EVEN I DON'T GET SUCH BAD GRADES.
URGH! Y-YOU TRAITOR-RRRRR!!
BY THE WAY, WHERE ARE NOIHARA-SAN AND MASAKI-KUN?
ぐきっ
GIKU (CHOKE)
NO MURDER, PLEASE.
IT WOULD BE AN INCONVE-NIENCE FOR ME.
HM?
TAIZOU WENT TO PRACTICE.
HIS MUSIC LESSON.
AND THE CAT...I MEAN HIMARI...SAID, "I HAVE NO USE FOR ANOTHER COUNTRY'S LANGUAGE!" AND DISAP-PEARED.
SHE'S PROBABLY ASLEEP ON THE ROOF, DON'T YOU THINK?
OHHH...
KIRAN (GLINT)
キラン
SO SHE RAN AWAY, HUH? ...FINE BY ME.
I'LL LUMP IN THOSE TWO DESERTERS' PORTIONS AND GIVE YOU GUYS A LESSON THAT WOULD MAKE THE SPARTANS PROUD...
HEH! HEH! HEH! HEH! HEH! HEH! HEH! HEH! HEH! HEH!
RINKO-SAN, ALL OF A SUDDEN, I REALLY WANNA GO HOME...
YEAH, SAME HERE...

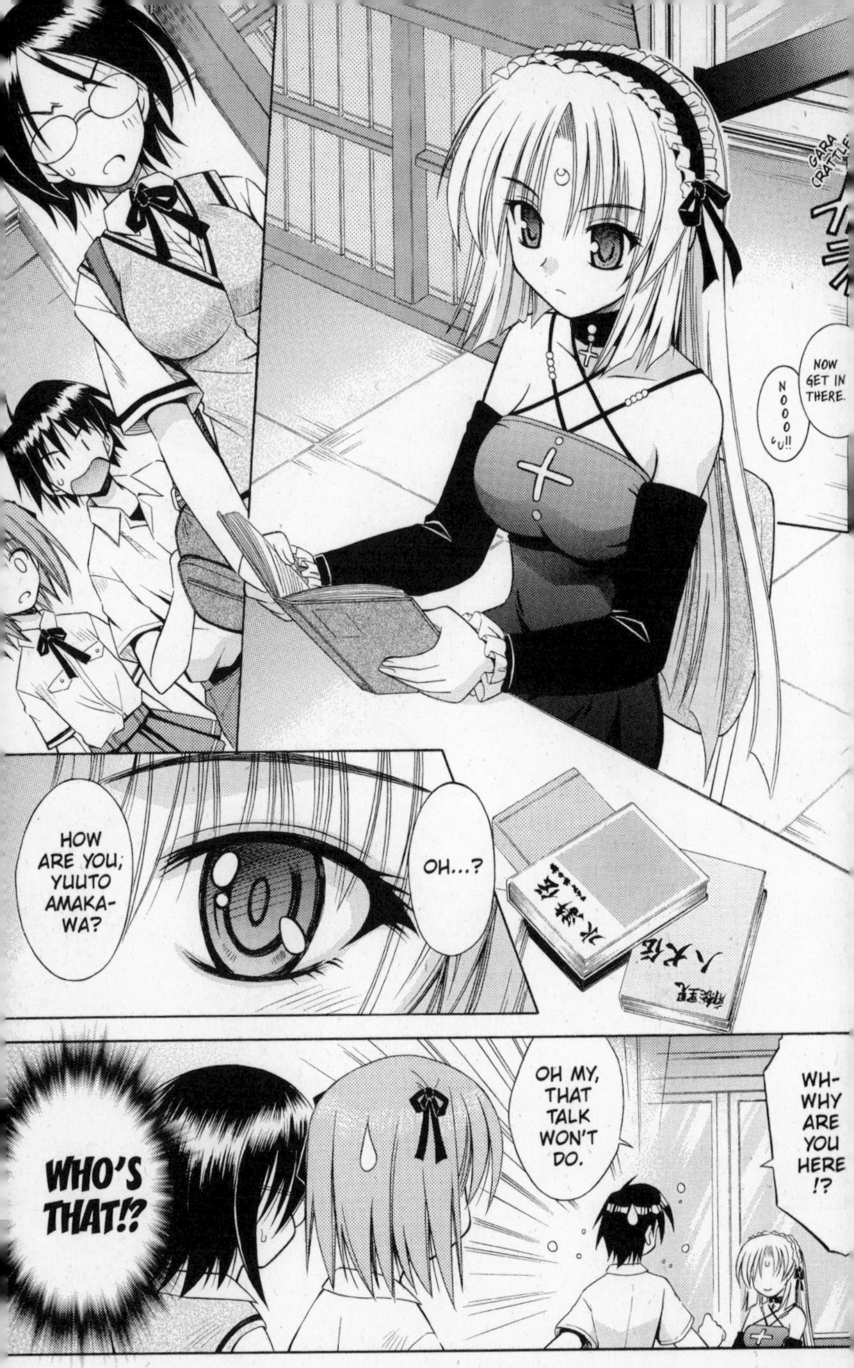
GARA (RATTLE)
NOW GET IN THERE.
NOOOOU!!
OH...?
HOW ARE YOU; YUUTO AMAKAWA?
WH-WHY ARE YOU HERE!?
OH MY, THAT TALK WON'T DO.
WHO'S THAT!?

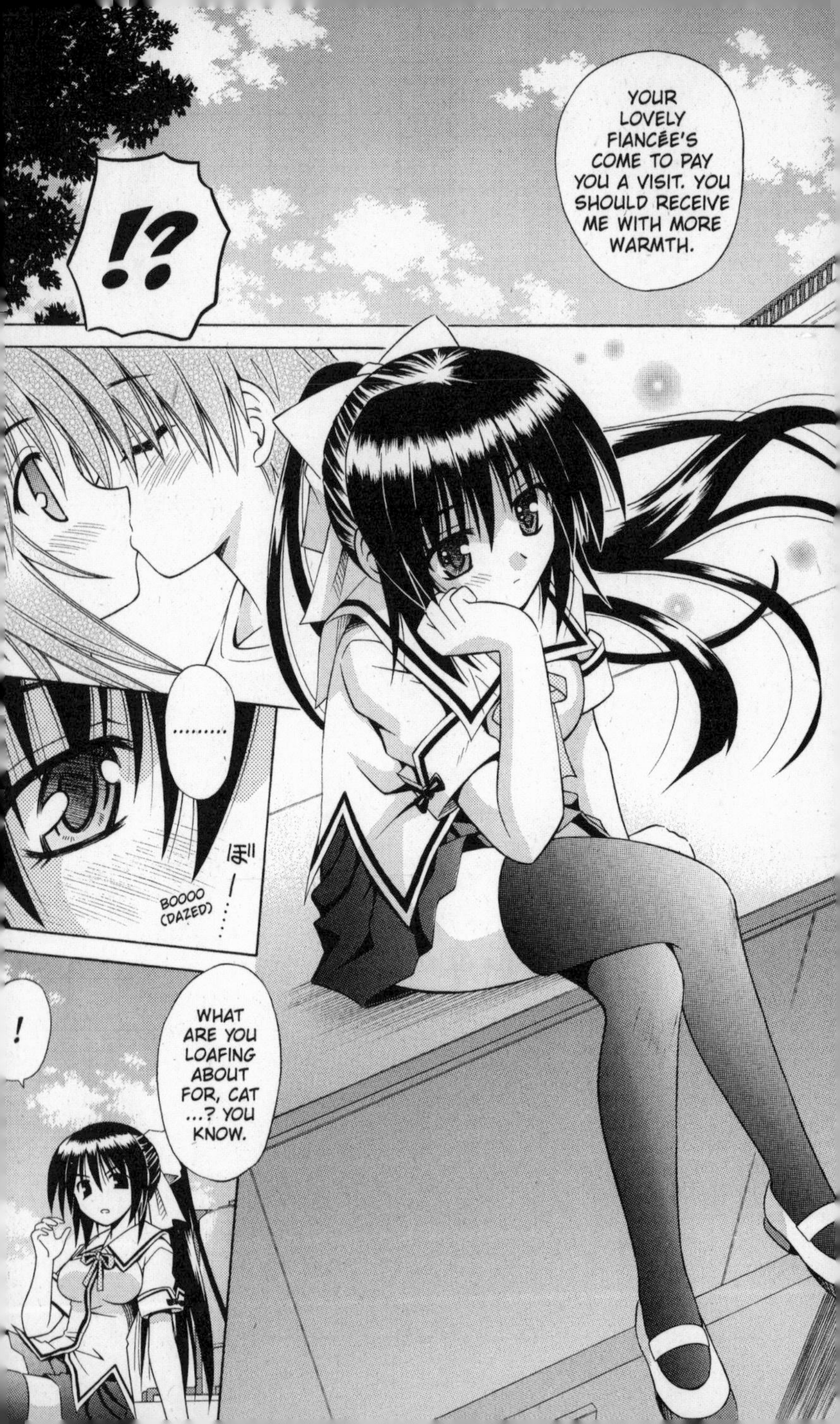
YOUR LOVELY FIANCÉE'S COME TO PAY YOU A VISIT. YOU SHOULD RECEIVE ME WITH MORE WARMTH.
!?
....
ぼー……
BOOOO (DAZED)
WHAT ARE YOU LOAFING ABOUT FOR, CAT ...? YOU KNOW.
!

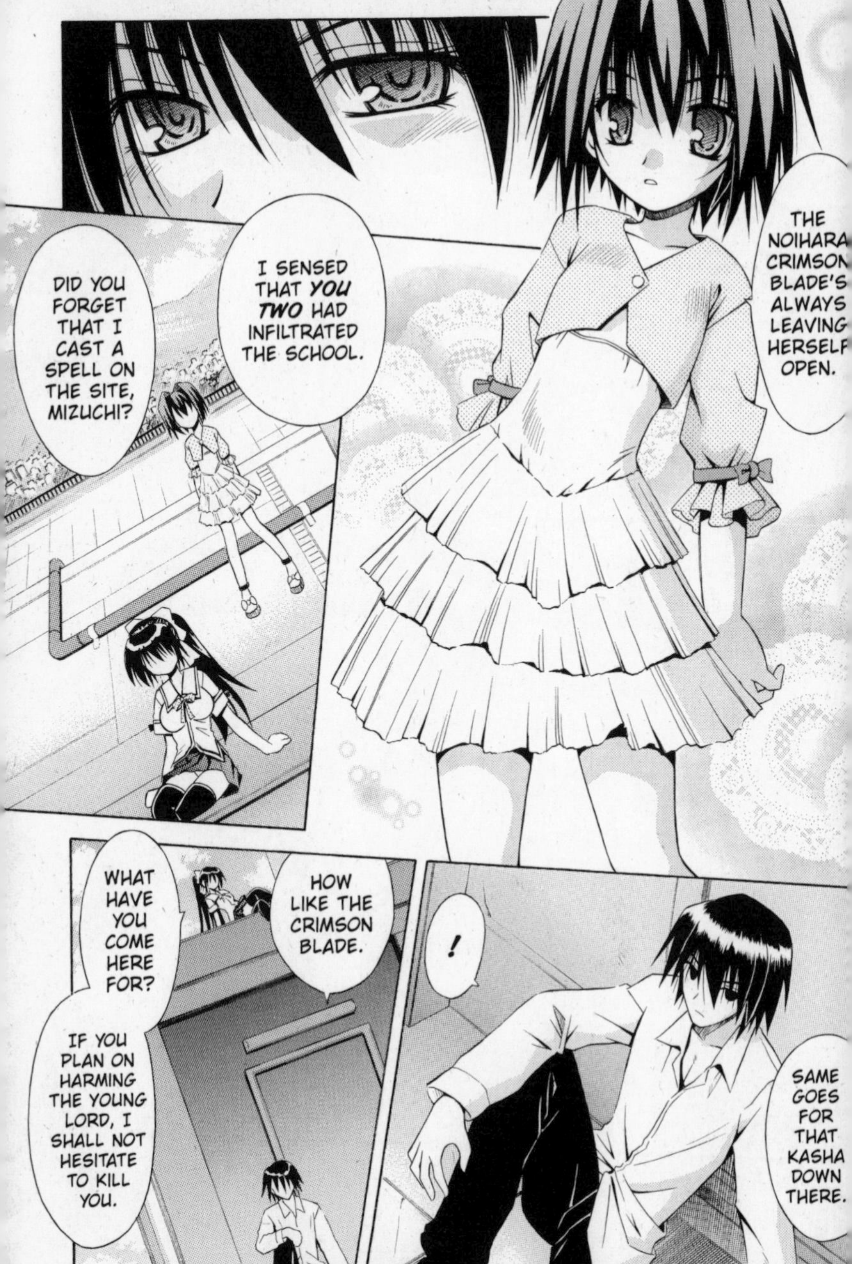
THE NOIHARA CRIMSON BLADE'S ALWAYS LEAVING HERSELF OPEN.
I SENSED THAT ***YOU TWO*** HAD INFILTRATED THE SCHOOL.
DID YOU FORGET THAT I CAST A SPELL ON THE SITE, MIZUCHI?
SAME GOES FOR THAT KASHA DOWN THERE.
!
HOW LIKE THE CRIMSON BLADE.
WHAT HAVE YOU COME HERE FOR?
IF YOU PLAN ON HARMING THE YOUNG LORD, I SHALL NOT HESITATE TO KILL YOU.

NOTE: A "KASHA" IS A KIND OF CAT-LIKE JAPANESE MONSTER KNOWN FOR STEALING CORPSES DURING FUNERALS.

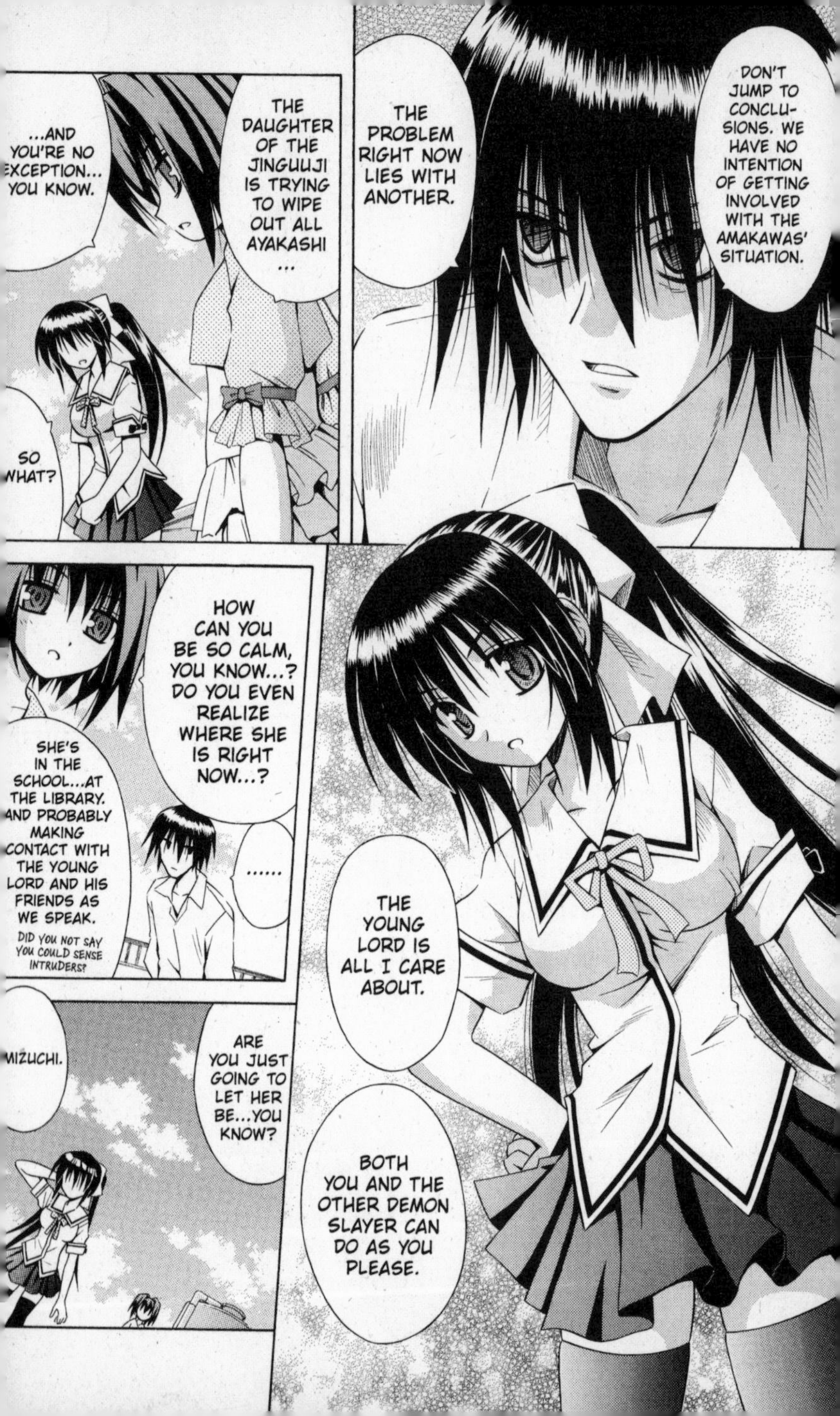
DON'T JUMP TO CONCLUSIONS. WE HAVE NO INTENTION OF GETTING INVOLVED WITH THE AMAKAWAS' SITUATION.
THE PROBLEM RIGHT NOW LIES WITH ANOTHER.
THE DAUGHTER OF THE JINGUUJI IS TRYING TO WIPE OUT ALL AYAKASHI ...
...AND YOU'RE NO XCEPTION... YOU KNOW.
SO HAT?
THE YOUNG LORD IS ALL I CARE ABOUT.
BOTH YOU AND THE OTHER DEMON SLAYER CAN DO AS YOU PLEASE.
HOW CAN YOU BE SO CALM, YOU KNOW...? DO YOU EVEN REALIZE WHERE SHE IS RIGHT NOW...?
SHE'S IN THE SCHOOL...AT THE LIBRARY. AND PROBABLY MAKING CONTACT WITH THE YOUNG LORD AND HIS FRIENDS AS WE SPEAK.
DID YOU NOT SAY YOU COULD SENSE INTRUDERS?
......
ARE YOU JUST GOING TO LET HER BE...YOU KNOW?
IIZUCHI.

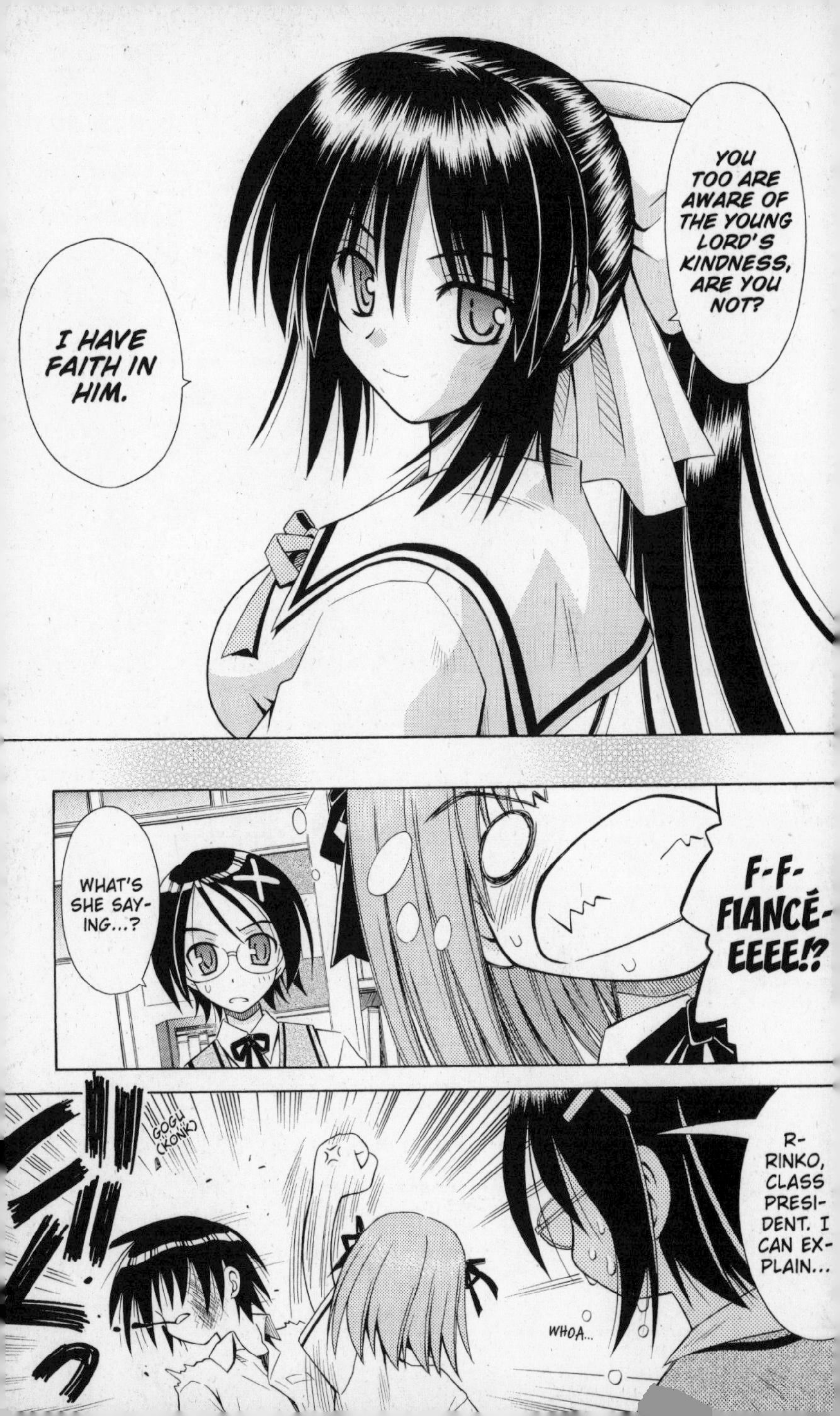
YOU TOO ARE AWARE OF THE YOUNG LORD'S KINDNESS, ARE YOU NOT?
I HAVE FAITH IN HIM.
F-F-FIANCÉ-EEEE!?
WHAT'S SHE SAY-ING...?
R-RINKO, CLASS PRESI-DENT. I CAN EX-PLAIN...
GOGU (KONK)
WHOA...

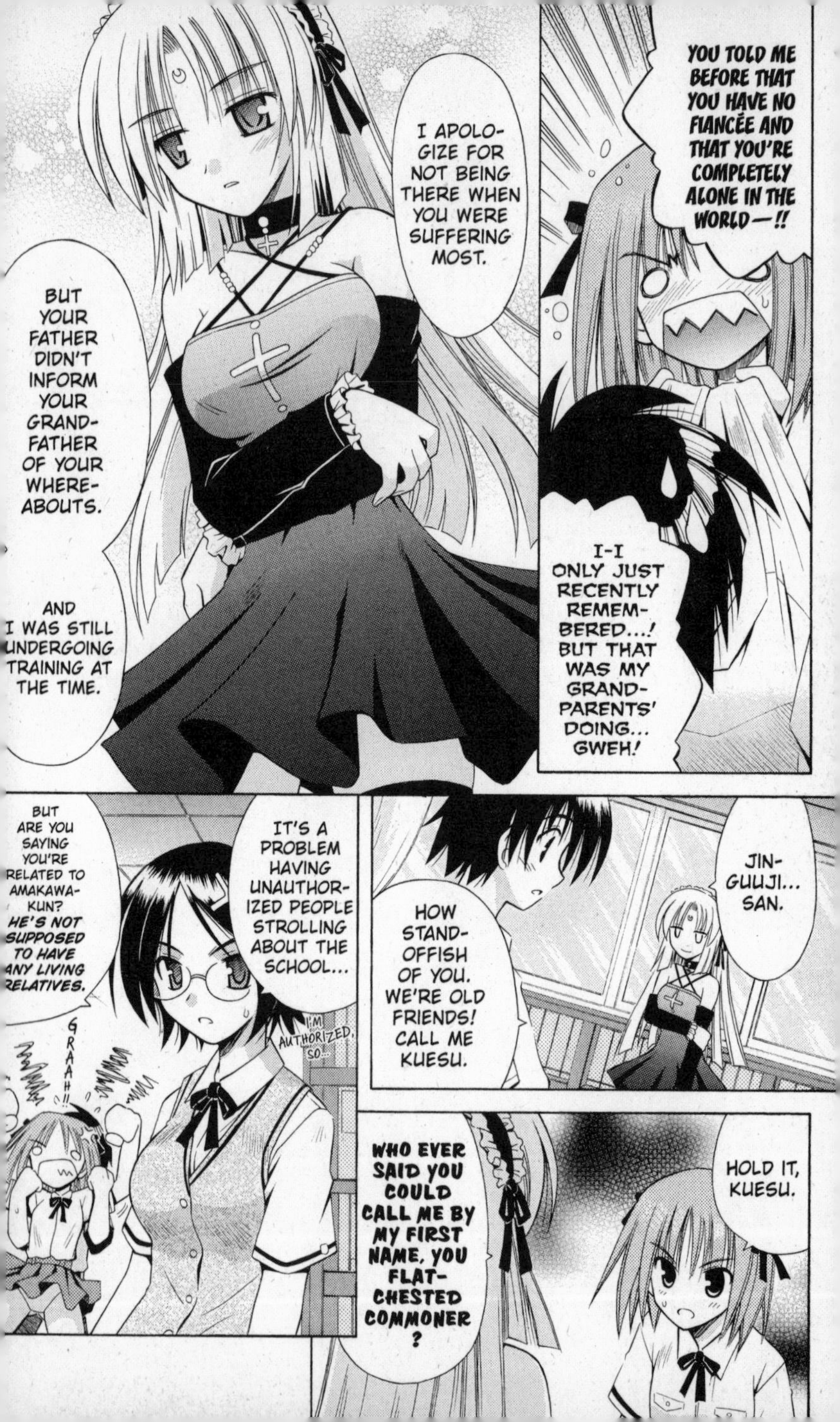
YOU TOLD ME BEFORE THAT YOU HAVE NO FIANCÉE AND THAT YOU'RE COMPLETELY ALONE IN THE WORLD—!!
I-I ONLY JUST RECENTLY REMEMBERED...! BUT THAT WAS MY GRANDPARENTS' DOING... GWEH!
I APOLOGIZE FOR NOT BEING THERE WHEN YOU WERE SUFFERING MOST.
BUT YOUR FATHER DIDN'T INFORM YOUR GRANDFATHER OF YOUR WHEREABOUTS.
AND I WAS STILL UNDERGOING TRAINING AT THE TIME.
JINGUUJI... SAN.
HOW STANDOFFISH OF YOU. WE'RE OLD FRIENDS! CALL ME KUESU.
HOLD IT, KUESU.
WHO EVER SAID YOU COULD CALL ME BY MY FIRST NAME, YOU FLAT-CHESTED COMMONER?
IT'S A PROBLEM HAVING UNAUTHORIZED PEOPLE STROLLING ABOUT THE SCHOOL...
BUT ARE YOU SAYING YOU'RE RELATED TO AMAKAWA-KUN? HE'S NOT SUPPOSED TO HAVE ANY LIVING RELATIVES.
I'M AUTHORIZED, SO...
GRAAH!!

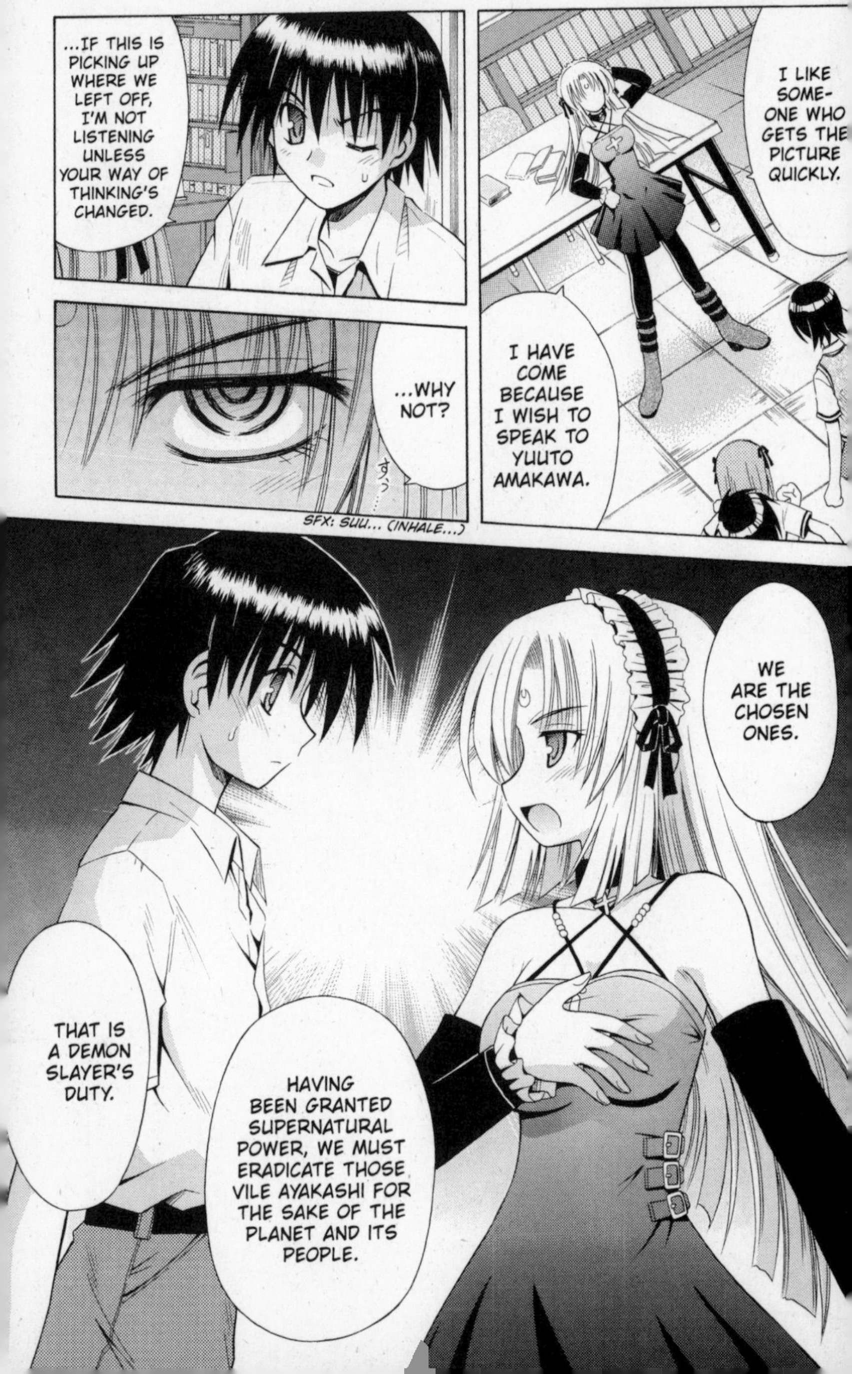
I LIKE SOMEONE WHO GETS THE PICTURE QUICKLY.
I HAVE COME BECAUSE I WISH TO SPEAK TO YUUTO AMAKAWA.
...IF THIS IS PICKING UP WHERE WE LEFT OFF, I'M NOT LISTENING UNLESS YOUR WAY OF THINKING'S CHANGED.
...WHY NOT?
すぅ…
SFX: SUU... (INHALE...)
WE ARE THE CHOSEN ONES.
HAVING BEEN GRANTED SUPERNATURAL POWER, WE MUST ERADICATE THOSE VILE AYAKASHI FOR THE SAKE OF THE PLANET AND ITS PEOPLE.
THAT IS A DEMON SLAYER'S DUTY.

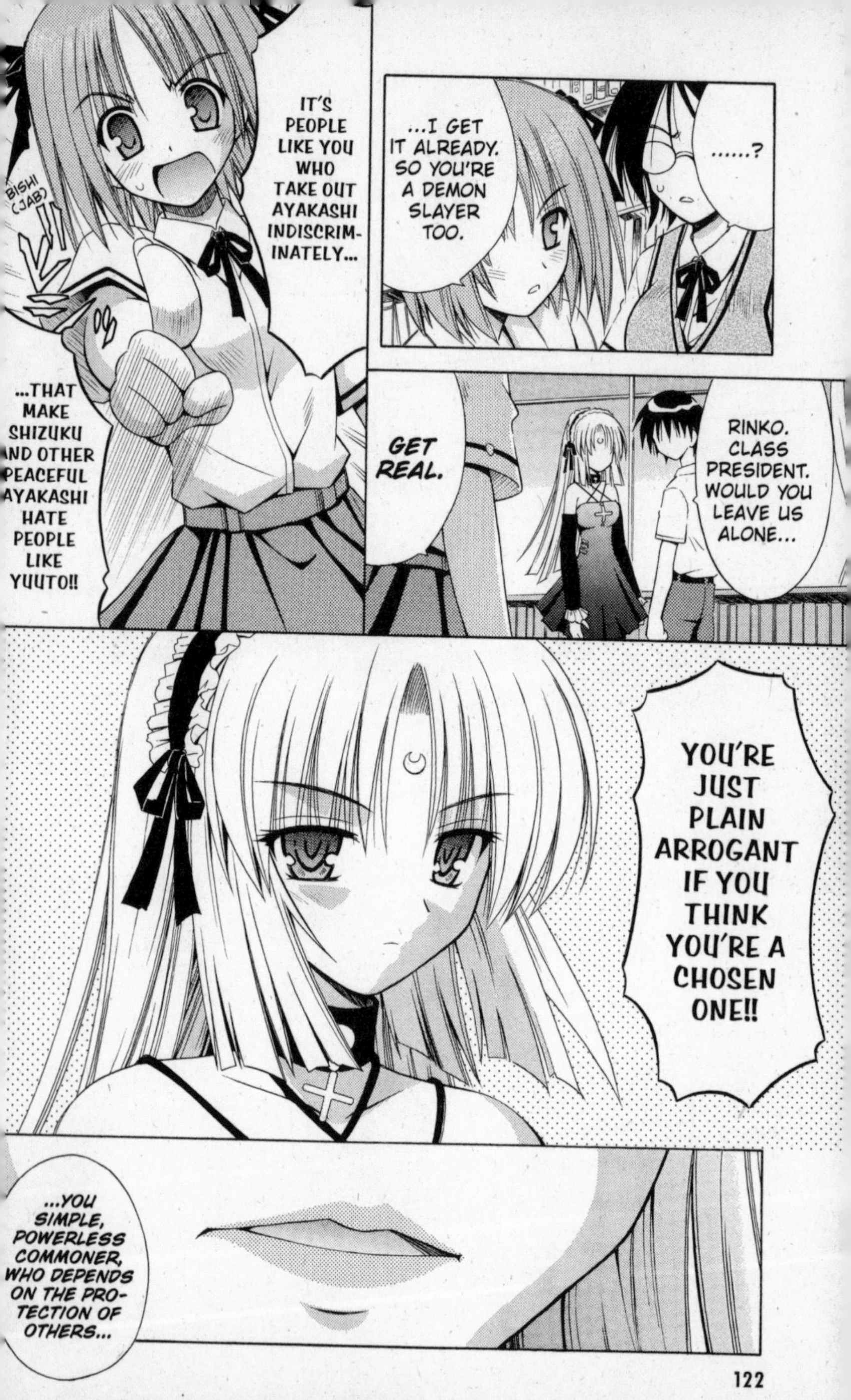
......?
...I GET IT ALREADY. SO YOU'RE A DEMON SLAYER TOO.
RINKO. CLASS PRESIDENT. WOULD YOU LEAVE US ALONE...
GET REAL.
IT'S PEOPLE LIKE YOU WHO TAKE OUT AYAKASHI INDISCRIM-INATELY...
BISHI (JAB)
...THAT MAKE SHIZUKU AND OTHER PEACEFUL AYAKASHI HATE PEOPLE LIKE YUUTO!!
YOU'RE JUST PLAIN ARROGANT IF YOU THINK YOU'RE A CHOSEN ONE!!
...YOU SIMPLE, POWERLESS COMMONER, WHO DEPENDS ON THE PRO-TECTION OF OTHERS...

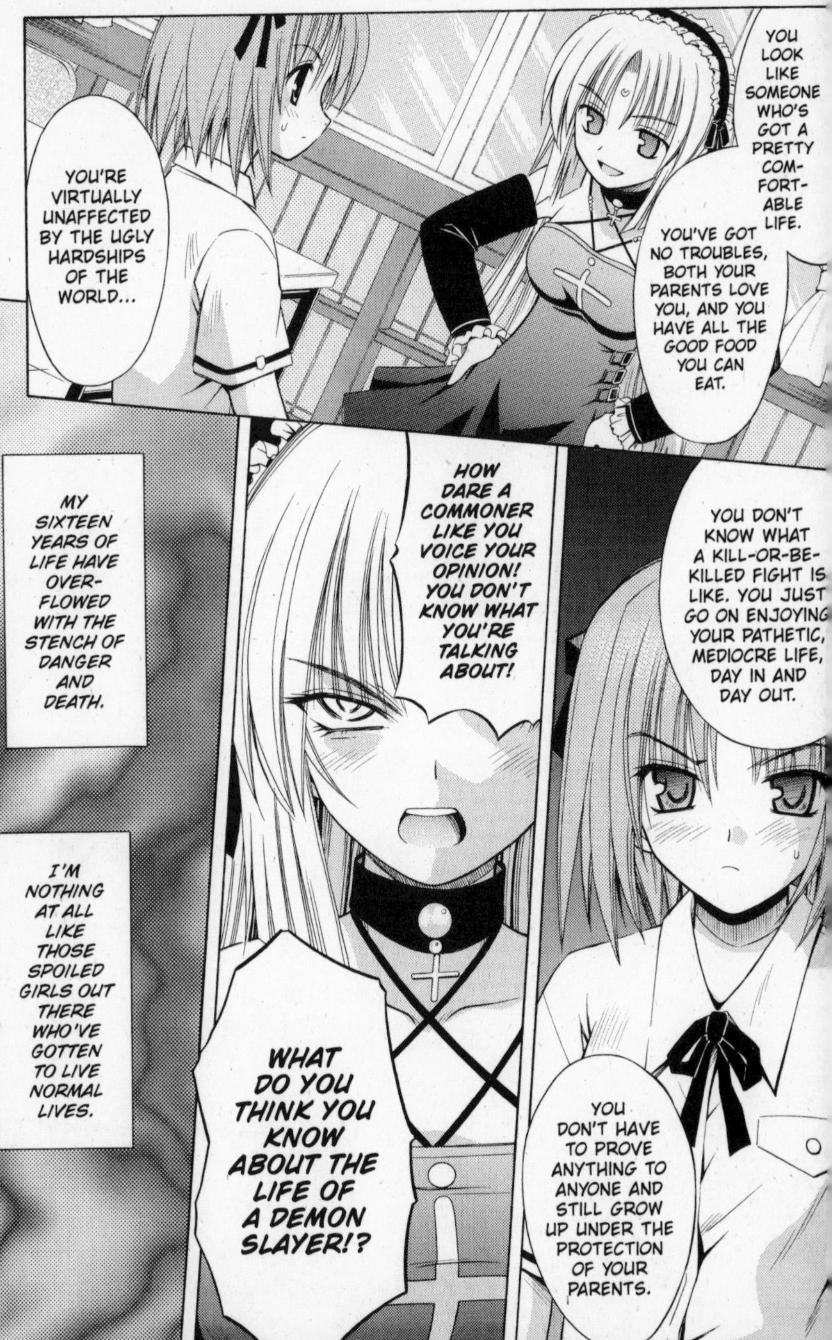
YOU LOOK LIKE SOMEONE WHO'S GOT A PRETTY COM-FORT-ABLE LIFE.
YOU'VE GOT NO TROUBLES, BOTH YOUR PARENTS LOVE YOU, AND YOU HAVE ALL THE GOOD FOOD YOU CAN EAT.
YOU'RE VIRTUALLY UNAFFECTED BY THE UGLY HARDSHIPS OF THE WORLD...
YOU DON'T KNOW WHAT A KILL-OR-BE-KILLED FIGHT IS LIKE. YOU JUST GO ON ENJOYING YOUR PATHETIC, MEDIOCRE LIFE, DAY IN AND DAY OUT.
YOU DON'T HAVE TO PROVE ANYTHING TO ANYONE AND STILL GROW UP UNDER THE PROTECTION OF YOUR PARENTS.
HOW DARE A COMMONER LIKE YOU VOICE YOUR OPINION! YOU DON'T KNOW WHAT YOU'RE TALKING ABOUT!
WHAT DO YOU THINK YOU KNOW ABOUT THE LIFE OF A DEMON SLAYER!?
MY SIXTEEN YEARS OF LIFE HAVE OVER-FLOWED WITH THE STENCH OF DANGER AND DEATH.
I'M NOTHING AT ALL LIKE THOSE SPOILED GIRLS OUT THERE WHO'VE GOTTEN TO LIVE NORMAL LIVES.

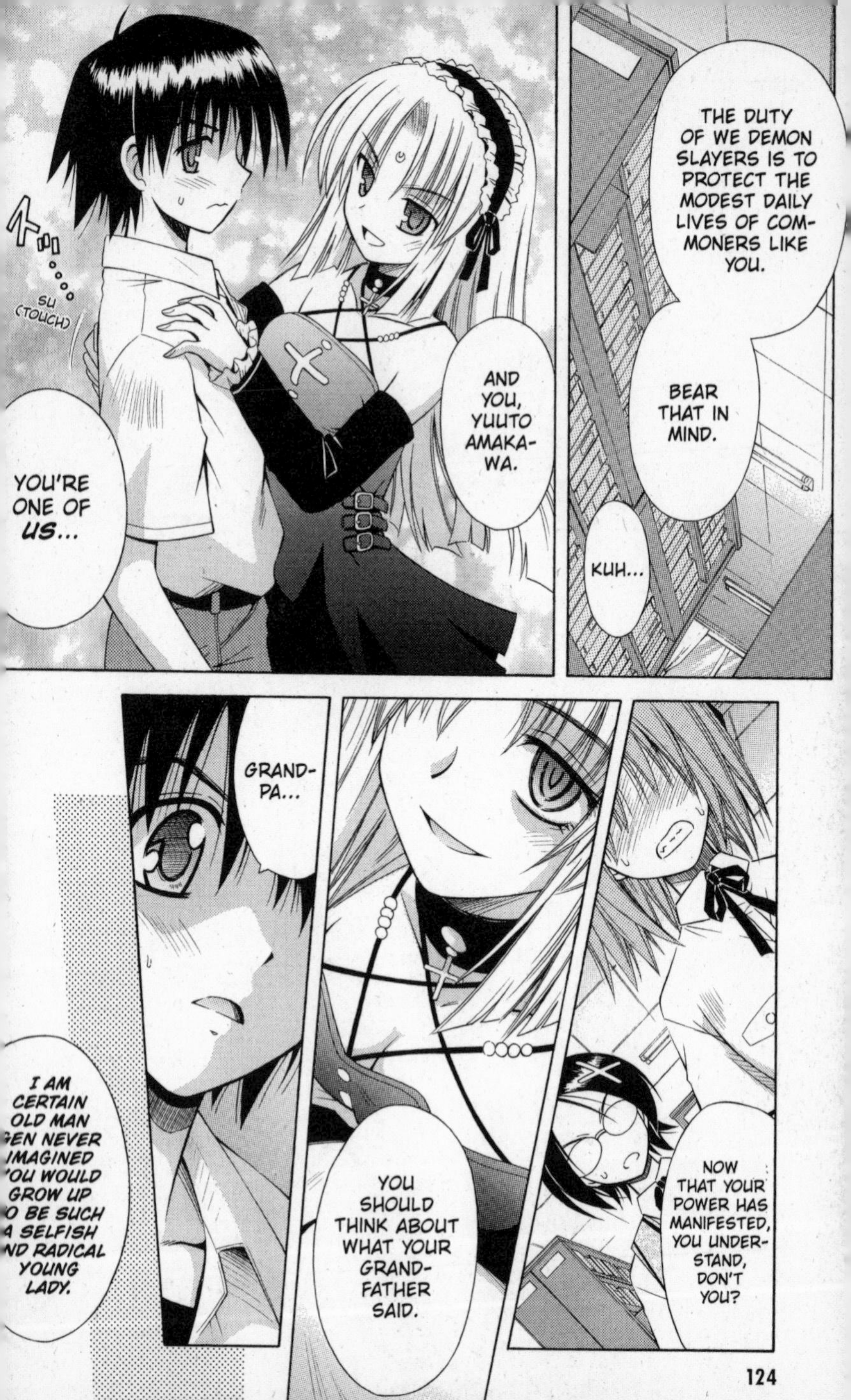
THE DUTY OF WE DEMON SLAYERS IS TO PROTECT THE MODEST DAILY LIVES OF COMMONERS LIKE YOU.
BEAR THAT IN MIND.
KUH...
AND YOU, YUUTO AMAKAWA.
SU (TOUCH)
YOU'RE ONE OF US...
NOW THAT YOUR POWER HAS MANIFESTED, YOU UNDERSTAND, DON'T YOU?
YOU SHOULD THINK ABOUT WHAT YOUR GRANDFATHER SAID.
GRANDPA...
I AM CERTAIN OLD MAN GEN NEVER IMAGINED OU WOULD GROW UP O BE SUCH A SELFISH ND RADICAL YOUNG LADY.

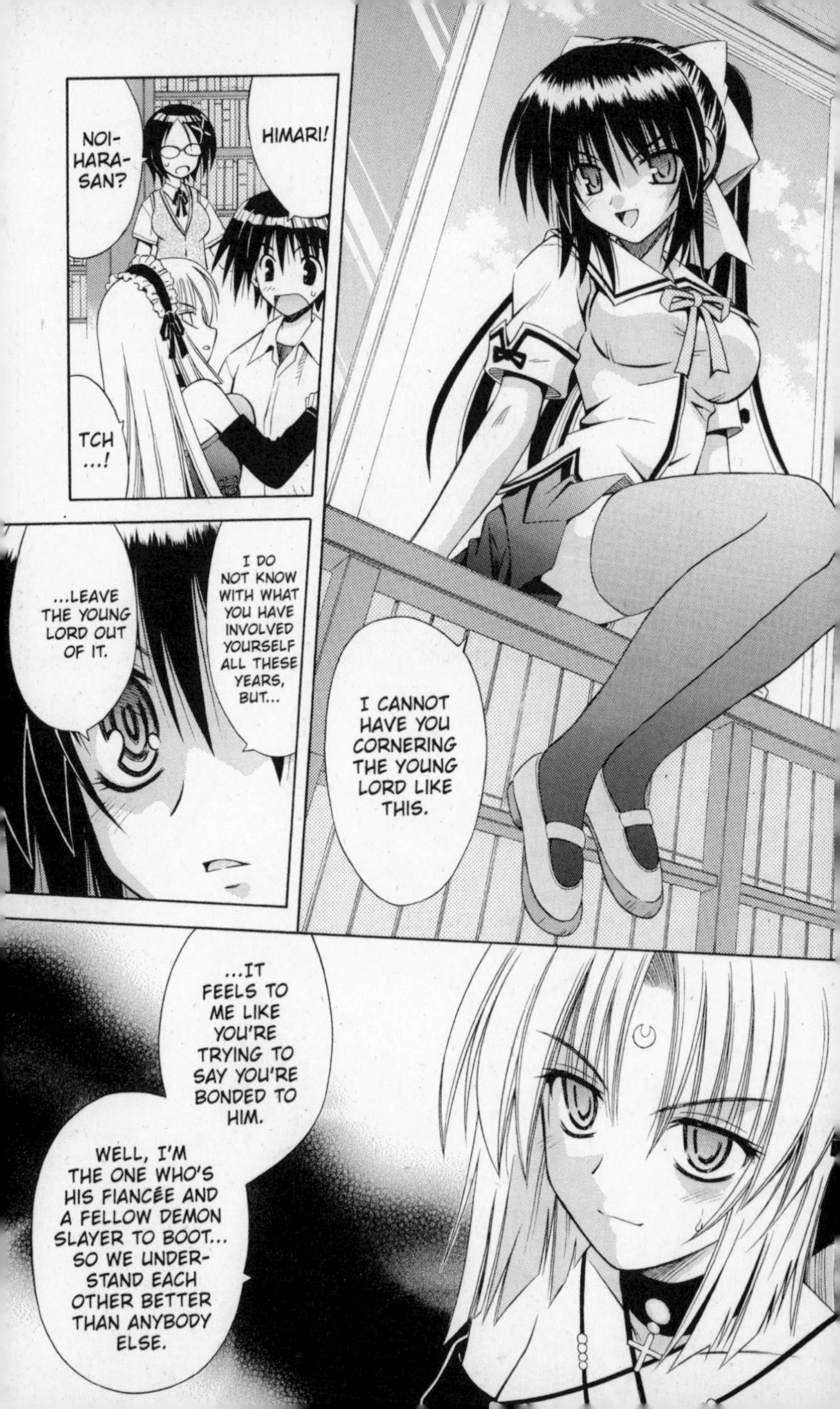
I CANNOT HAVE YOU CORNERING THE YOUNG LORD LIKE THIS.
HIMARI!
NOI-HARA-SAN?
TCH ...!
I DO NOT KNOW WITH WHAT YOU HAVE INVOLVED YOURSELF ALL THESE YEARS, BUT...
...LEAVE THE YOUNG LORD OUT OF IT.
...IT FEELS TO ME LIKE YOU'RE TRYING TO SAY YOU'RE BONDED TO HIM.
WELL, I'M THE ONE WHO'S HIS FIANCÉE AND A FELLOW DEMON SLAYER TO BOOT... SO WE UNDER-STAND EACH OTHER BETTER THAN ANYBODY ELSE.

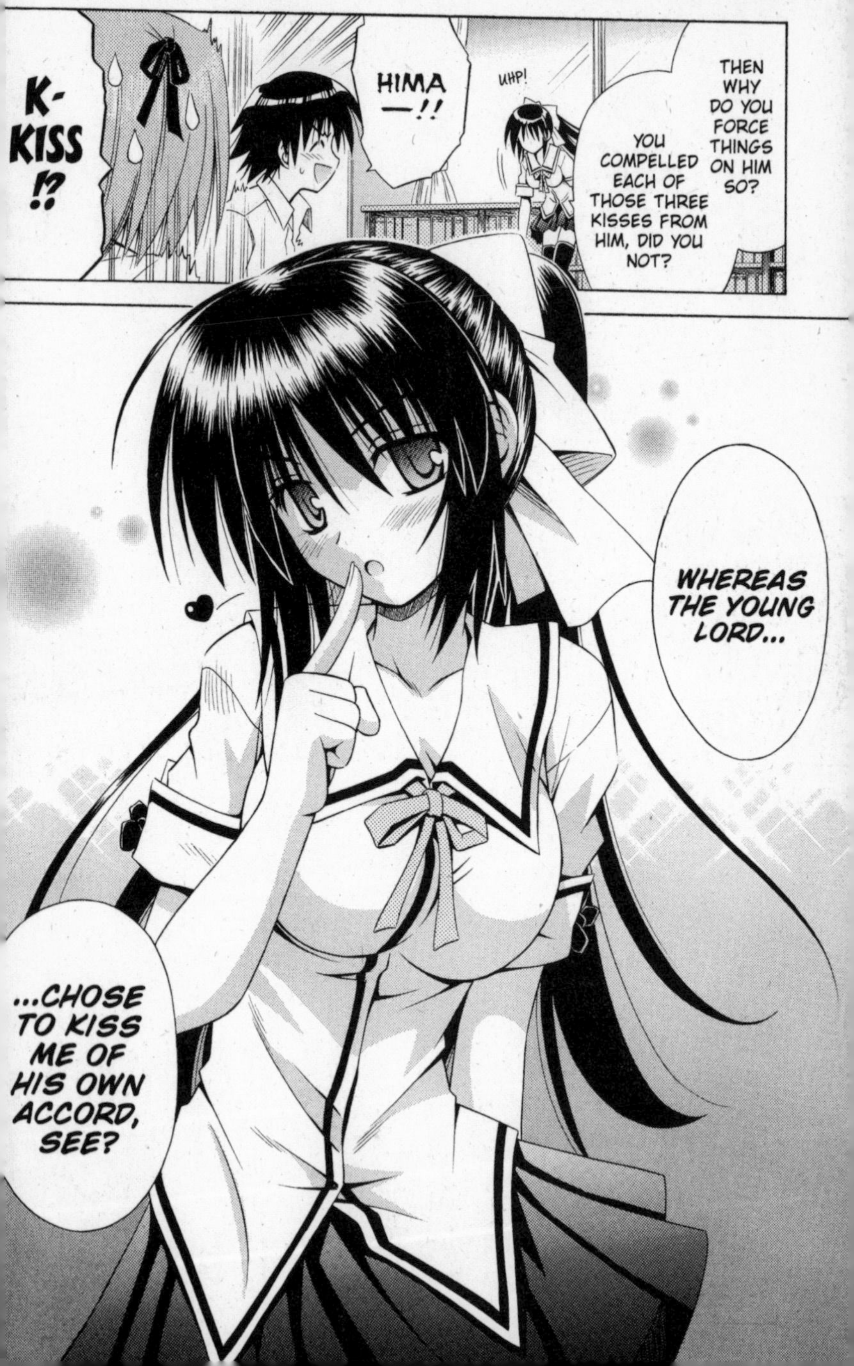
THEN WHY DO YOU FORCE THINGS ON HIM SO?
YOU COMPELLED EACH OF THOSE THREE KISSES FROM HIM, DID YOU NOT?
UHP!
HIMA—!!
K-KISS!?
WHEREAS THE YOUNG LORD...
...CHOSE TO KISS ME OF HIS OWN ACCORD, SEE?

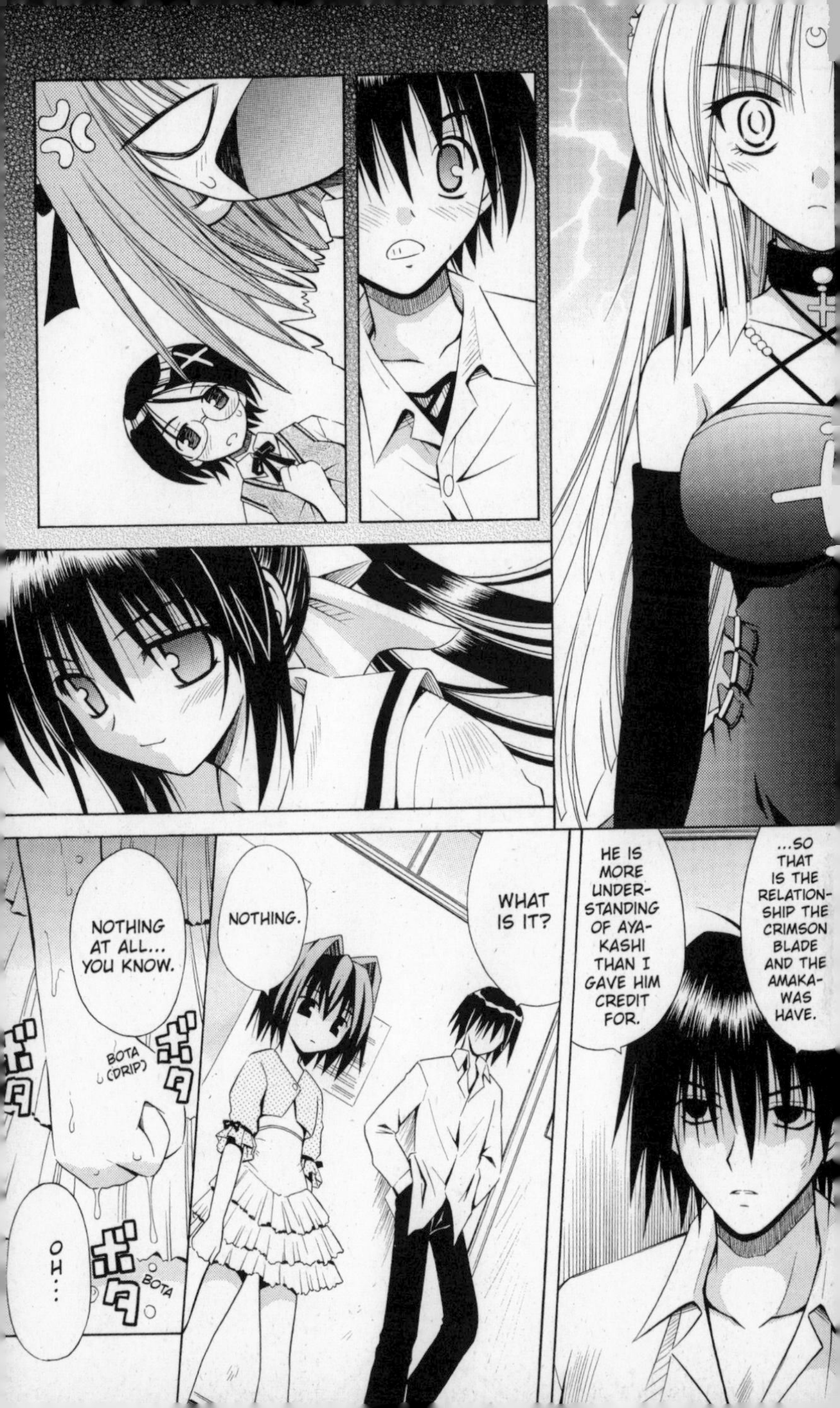
...SO THAT IS THE RELATIONSHIP THE CRIMSON BLADE AND THE AMAKAWAS HAVE.
HE IS MORE UNDERSTANDING OF AYAKASHI THAN I GAVE HIM CREDIT FOR.
WHAT IS IT?
NOTHING.
NOTHING AT ALL... YOU KNOW.
ボタ
BOTA (DRIP)
ボタ
ボタ
BOTA
OH...

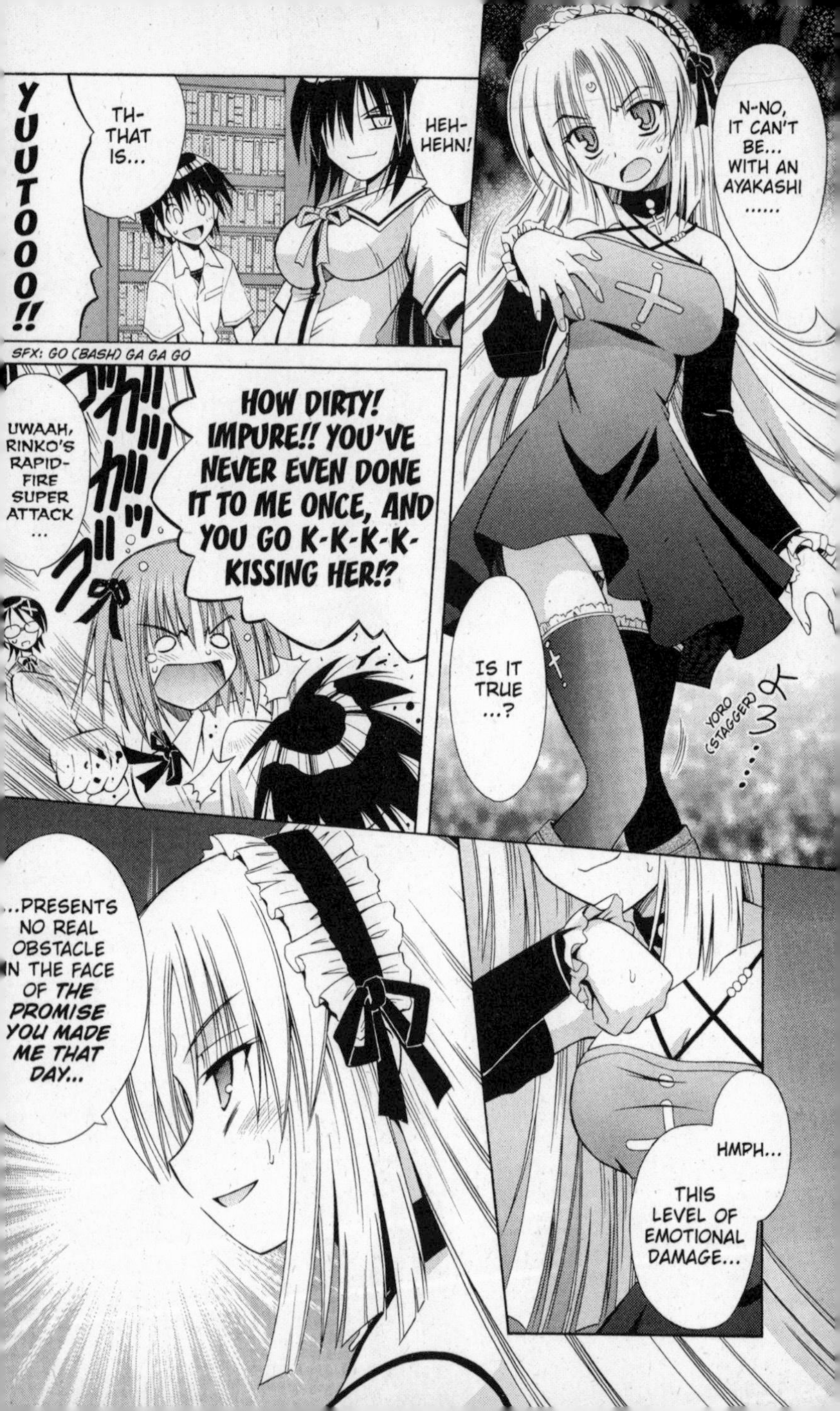
N-NO, IT CAN'T BE... WITH AN AYAKASHI ......
IS IT TRUE ...?
YORO (STAGGER)
HEH-HEHN!
TH-THAT IS...
YUUTOOOO!!
SFX: GO (BASH) GA GA GO
HOW DIRTY! IMPURE!! YOU'VE NEVER EVEN DONE IT TO ME ONCE, AND YOU GO K-K-K-K-KISSING HER!?
UWAAH, RINKO'S RAPID-FIRE SUPER ATTACK ...
HMPH...
THIS LEVEL OF EMOTIONAL DAMAGE...
...PRESENTS NO REAL OBSTACLE IN THE FACE OF THE PROMISE YOU MADE ME THAT DAY...

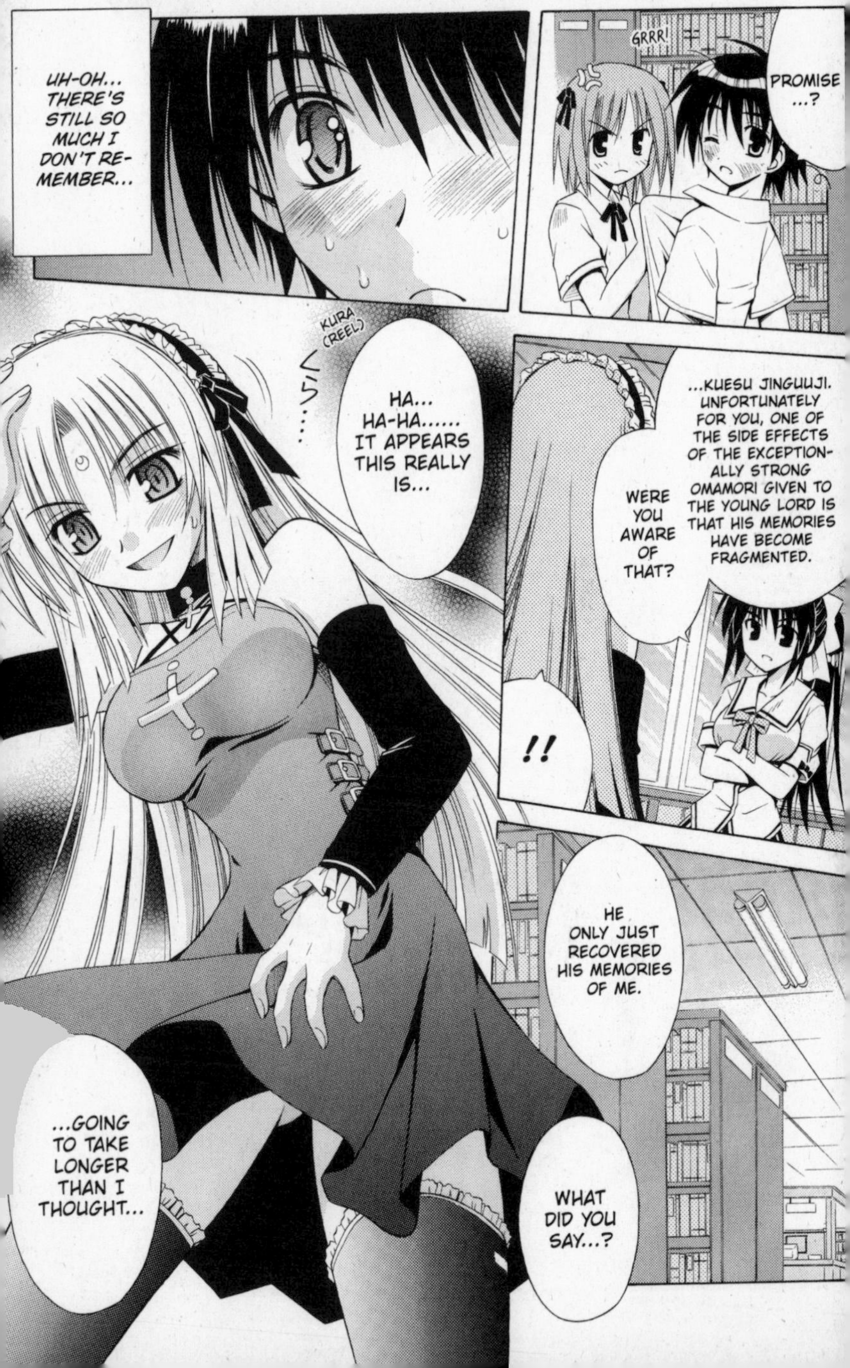
GRRR!
PROMISE ...?
UH-OH... THERE'S STILL SO MUCH I DON'T RE-MEMBER...
...KUESU JINGUUJI. UNFORTUNATELY FOR YOU, ONE OF THE SIDE EFFECTS OF THE EXCEPTION-ALLY STRONG OMAMORI GIVEN TO THE YOUNG LORD IS THAT HIS MEMORIES HAVE BECOME FRAGMENTED.
WERE YOU AWARE OF THAT?
!!
HE ONLY JUST RECOVERED HIS MEMORIES OF ME.
WHAT DID YOU SAY...?
KURA (REEL)
HA... HA-HA...... IT APPEARS THIS REALLY IS...
...GOING TO TAKE LONGER THAN I THOUGHT...

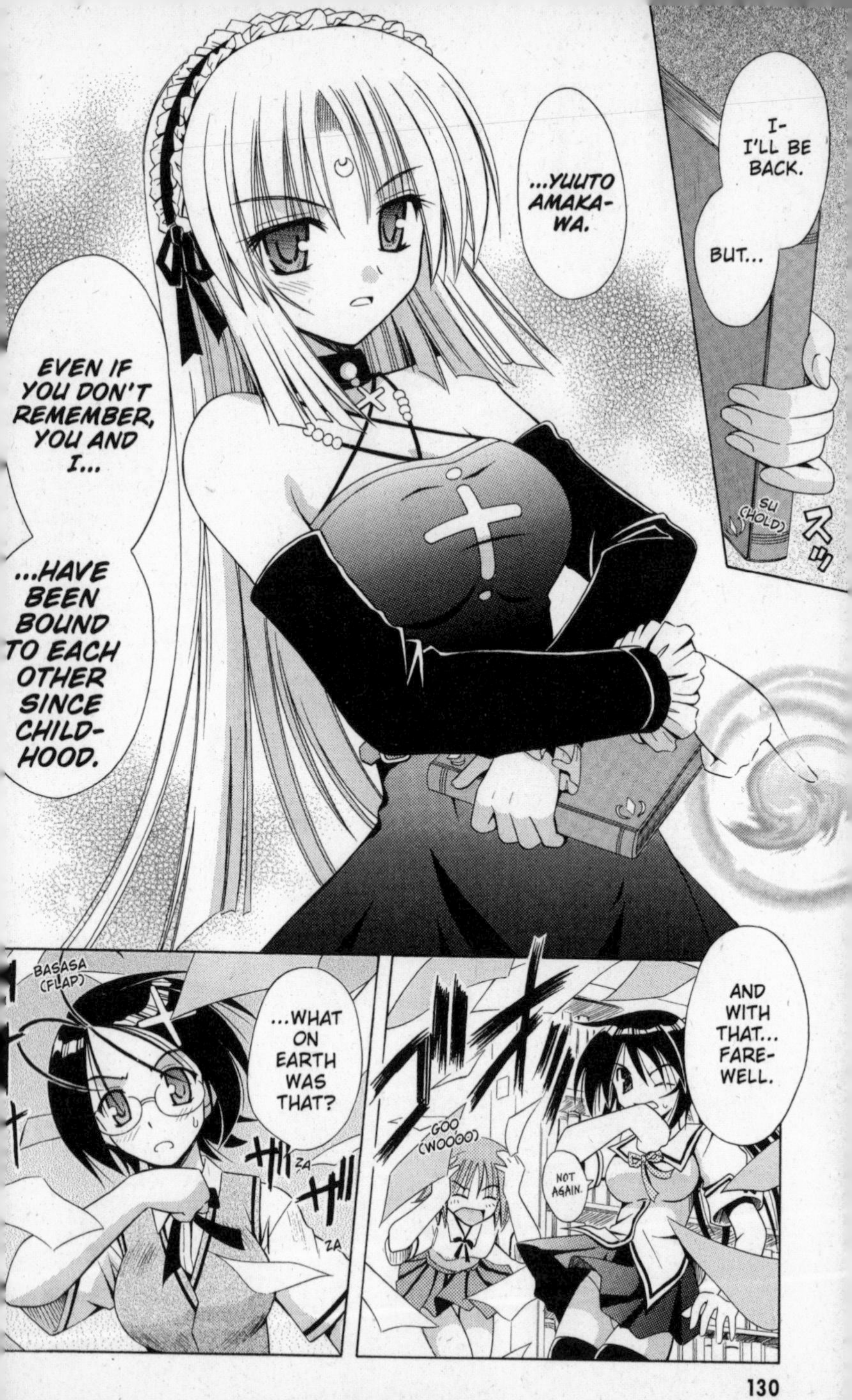
I- I'LL BE BACK.
BUT...
SU (HOLD)
...YUUTO AMAKA-WA.
EVEN IF YOU DON'T REMEMBER, YOU AND I...
...HAVE BEEN BOUND TO EACH OTHER SINCE CHILDHOOD.
AND WITH THAT... FARE-WELL.
GOO (WOOOO)
NOT AGAIN.
BASASA (FLAP)
...WHAT ON EARTH WAS THAT?
ZA
ZA

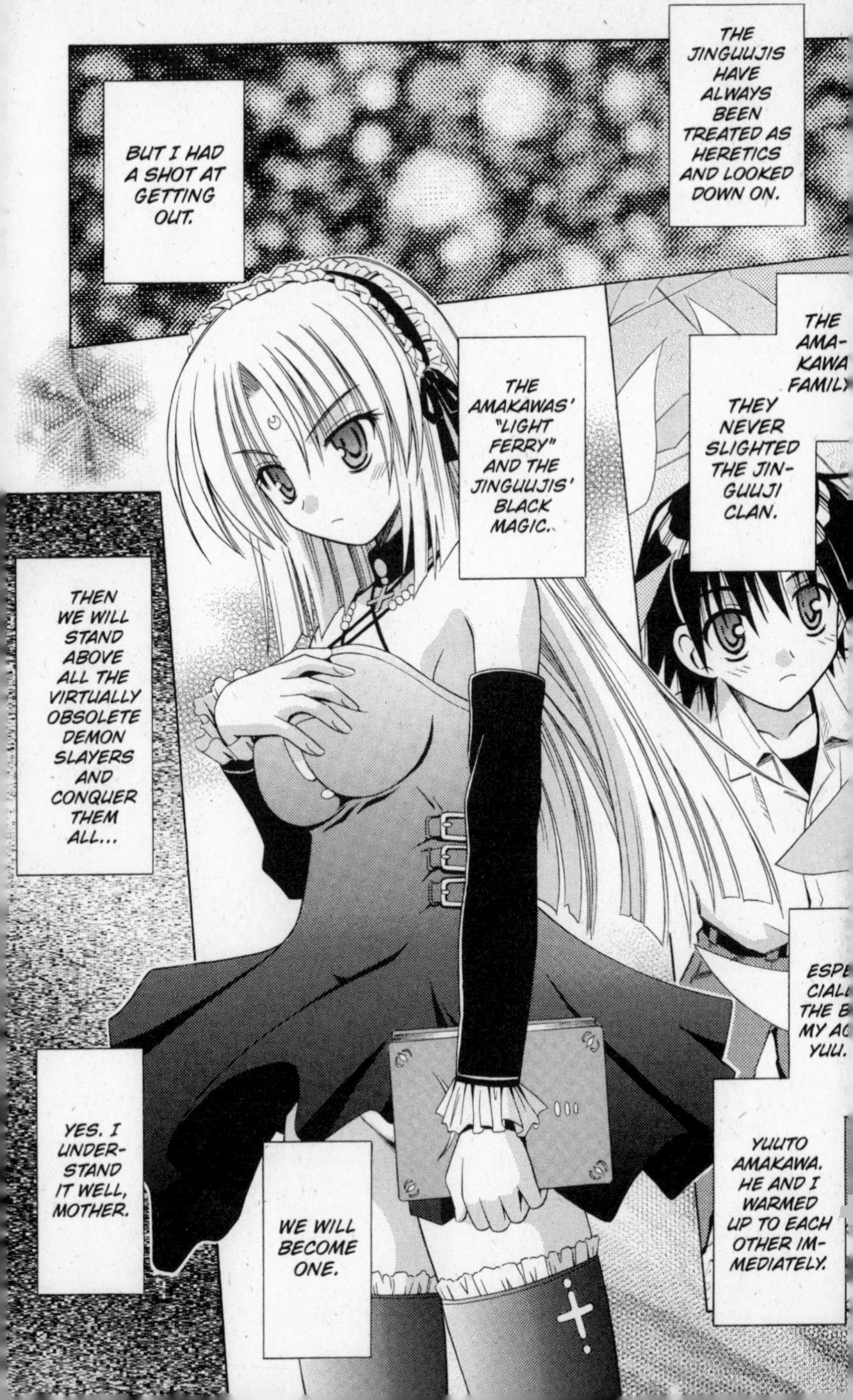
THE JINGUUJIS HAVE ALWAYS BEEN TREATED AS HERETICS AND LOOKED DOWN ON.
BUT I HAD A SHOT AT GETTING OUT.
THE AMA-KAWA FAMIL
THEY NEVER SLIGHTED THE JIN-GUUJI CLAN.
ESPE CIAL THE B MY A YUU.
YUUTO AMAKAWA. HE AND I WARMED UP TO EACH OTHER IM-MEDIATELY.
THE AMAKAWAS' "LIGHT FERRY" AND THE JINGUUJIS' BLACK MAGIC.
THEN WE WILL STAND ABOVE ALL THE VIRTUALLY OBSOLETE DEMON SLAYERS AND CONQUER THEM ALL...
WE WILL BECOME ONE.
YES. I UNDER-STAND IT WELL, MOTHER.

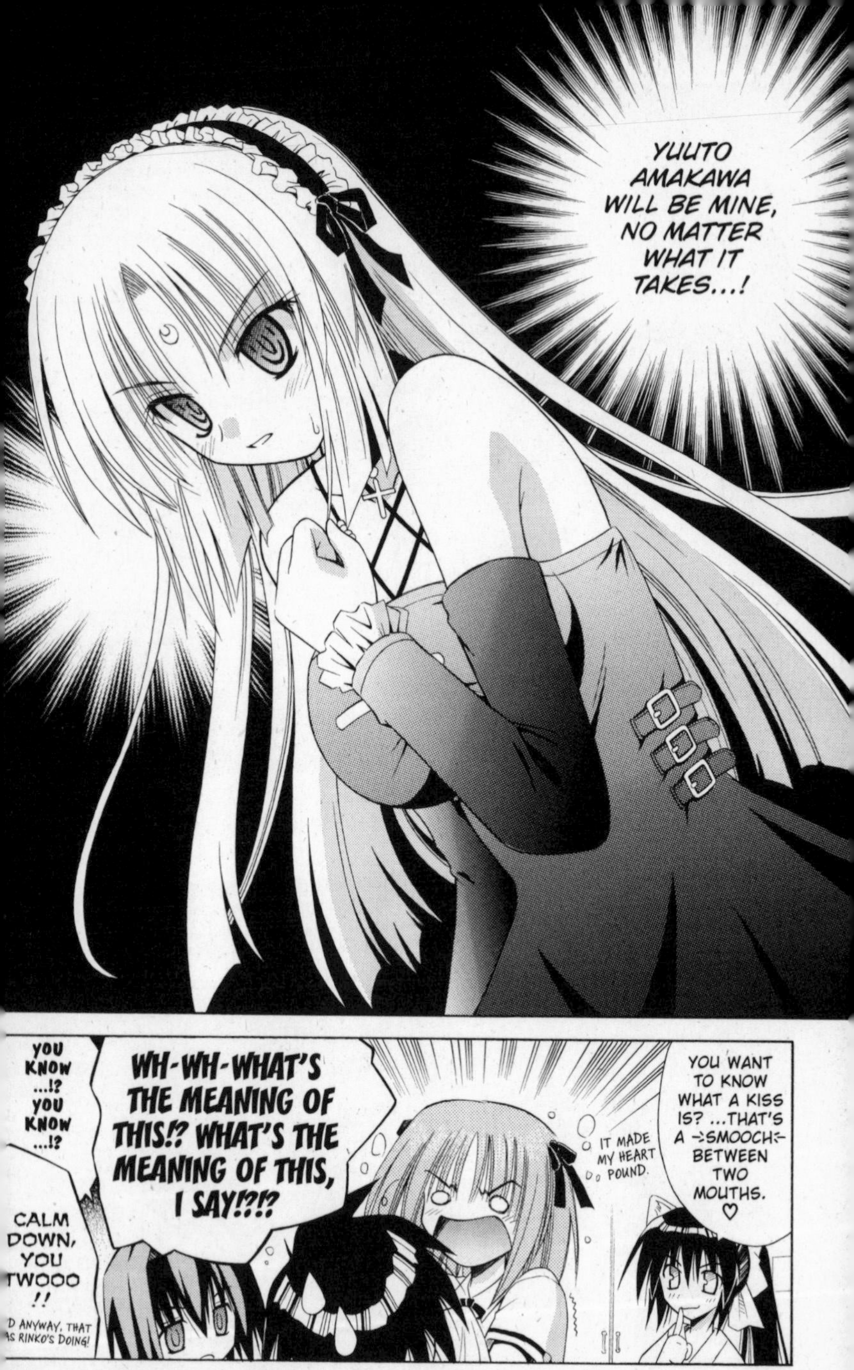
YUUTO AMAKAWA WILL BE MINE, NO MATTER WHAT IT TAKES...!
YOU WANT TO KNOW WHAT A KISS IS? ...THAT'S A ->SMOOCH<- BETWEEN TWO MOUTHS. ♡
IT MADE MY HEART POUND.
WH-WH-WHAT'S THE MEANING OF THIS!? WHAT'S THE MEANING OF THIS, I SAY!?!?
YOU KNOW ...!? YOU KNOW ...!?
CALM DOWN, YOU TWOOO !!
D ANYWAY, THAT AS RINKO'S DOING!

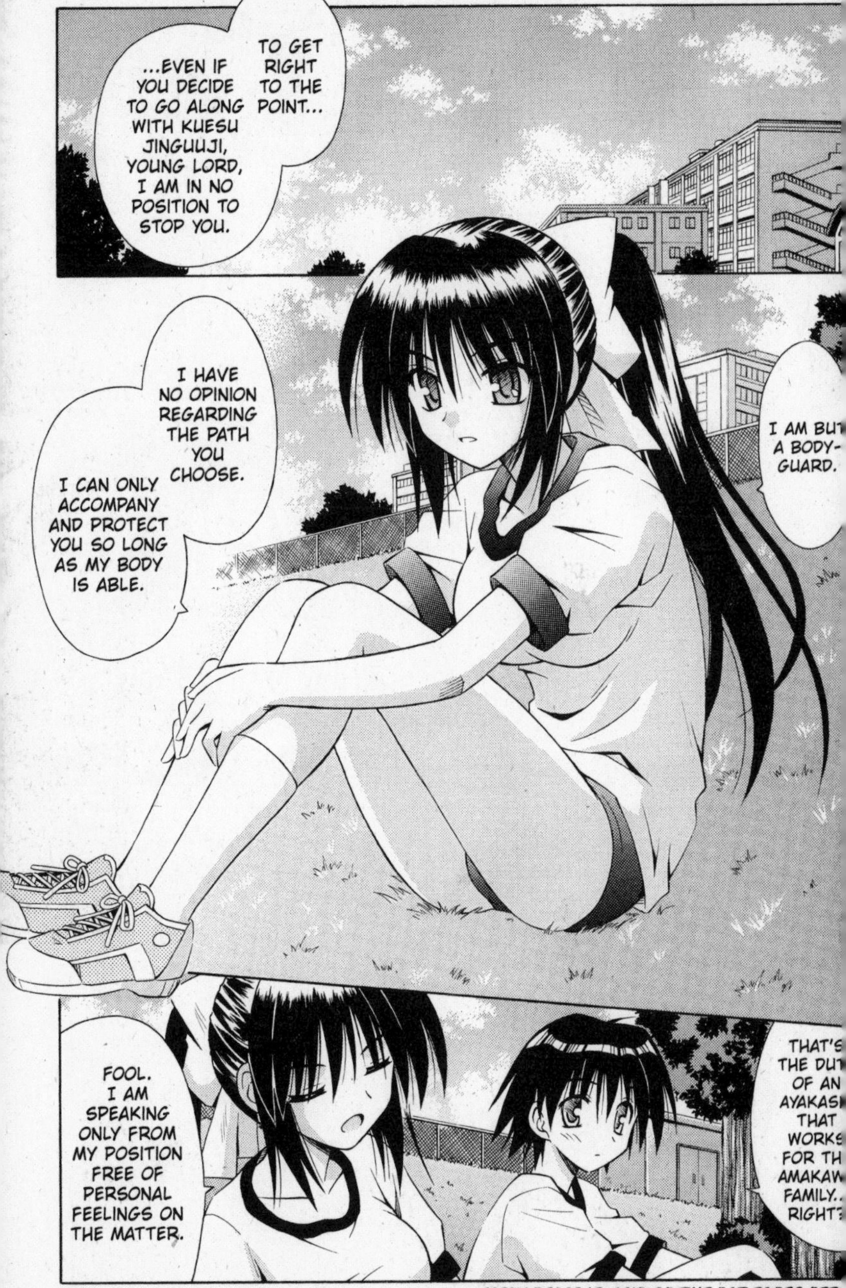
TO GET RIGHT TO THE POINT...
...EVEN IF YOU DECIDE TO GO ALONG WITH KUESU JINGUUJI, YOUNG LORD, I AM IN NO POSITION TO STOP YOU.
I AM BUT A BODY-GUARD.
I HAVE NO OPINION REGARDING THE PATH YOU CHOOSE.
I CAN ONLY ACCOMPANY AND PROTECT YOU SO LONG AS MY BODY IS ABLE.
THAT'S THE DUT OF AN AYAKAS THAT WORKS FOR TH AMAKAW FAMILY.. RIGHT?
FOOL. I AM SPEAKING ONLY FROM MY POSITION FREE OF PERSONAL FEELINGS ON THE MATTER.

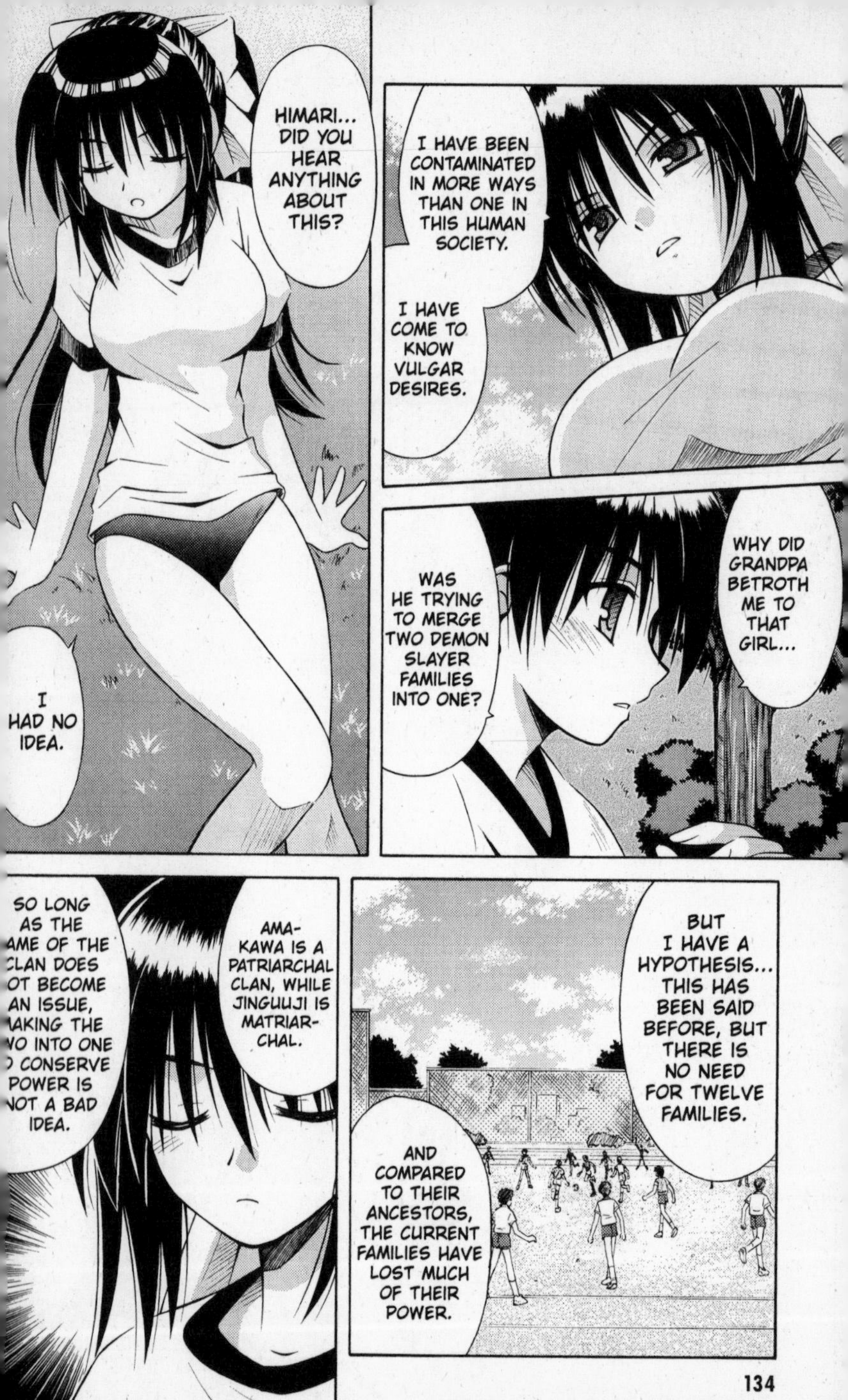
I HAVE BEEN CONTAMINATED IN MORE WAYS THAN ONE IN THIS HUMAN SOCIETY.
I HAVE COME TO KNOW VULGAR DESIRES.
WHY DID GRANDPA BETROTH ME TO THAT GIRL...
WAS HE TRYING TO MERGE TWO DEMON SLAYER FAMILIES INTO ONE?
HIMARI... DID YOU HEAR ANYTHING ABOUT THIS?
I HAD NO IDEA.
BUT I HAVE A HYPOTHESIS... THIS HAS BEEN SAID BEFORE, BUT THERE IS NO NEED FOR TWELVE FAMILIES.
AND COMPARED TO THEIR ANCESTORS, THE CURRENT FAMILIES HAVE LOST MUCH OF THEIR POWER.
AMA-KAWA IS A PATRIARCHAL CLAN, WHILE JINGUUJI IS MATRIAR-CHAL.
SO LONG AS THE AME OF THE CLAN DOES OT BECOME AN ISSUE, AKING THE VO INTO ONE CONSERVE POWER IS NOT A BAD IDEA.

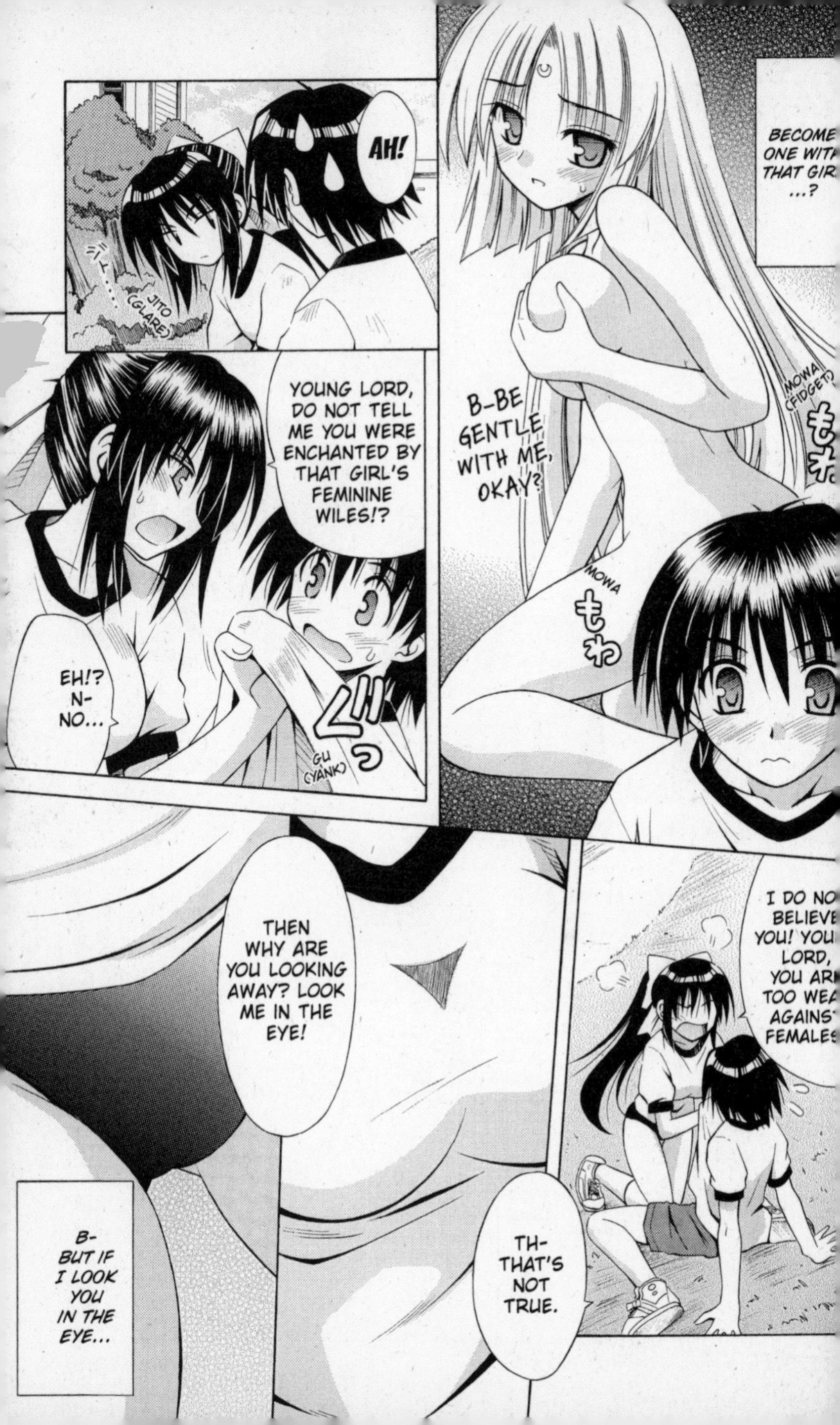
BECOME ONE WIT THAT GIR ...?
MOWA (FIDGET)
B-BE GENTLE WITH ME, OKAY?
MOWA
AH!
JITO (GLARE)
YOUNG LORD, DO NOT TELL ME YOU WERE ENCHANTED BY THAT GIRL'S FEMININE WILES!?
EH!? N-NO...
GU (YANK)
I DO NO BELIEVE YOU! YOU LORD, YOU AR TOO WEA AGAINS FEMALES
TH-THAT'S NOT TRUE.
THEN WHY ARE YOU LOOKING AWAY? LOOK ME IN THE EYE!
B-BUT IF I LOOK YOU IN THE EYE...

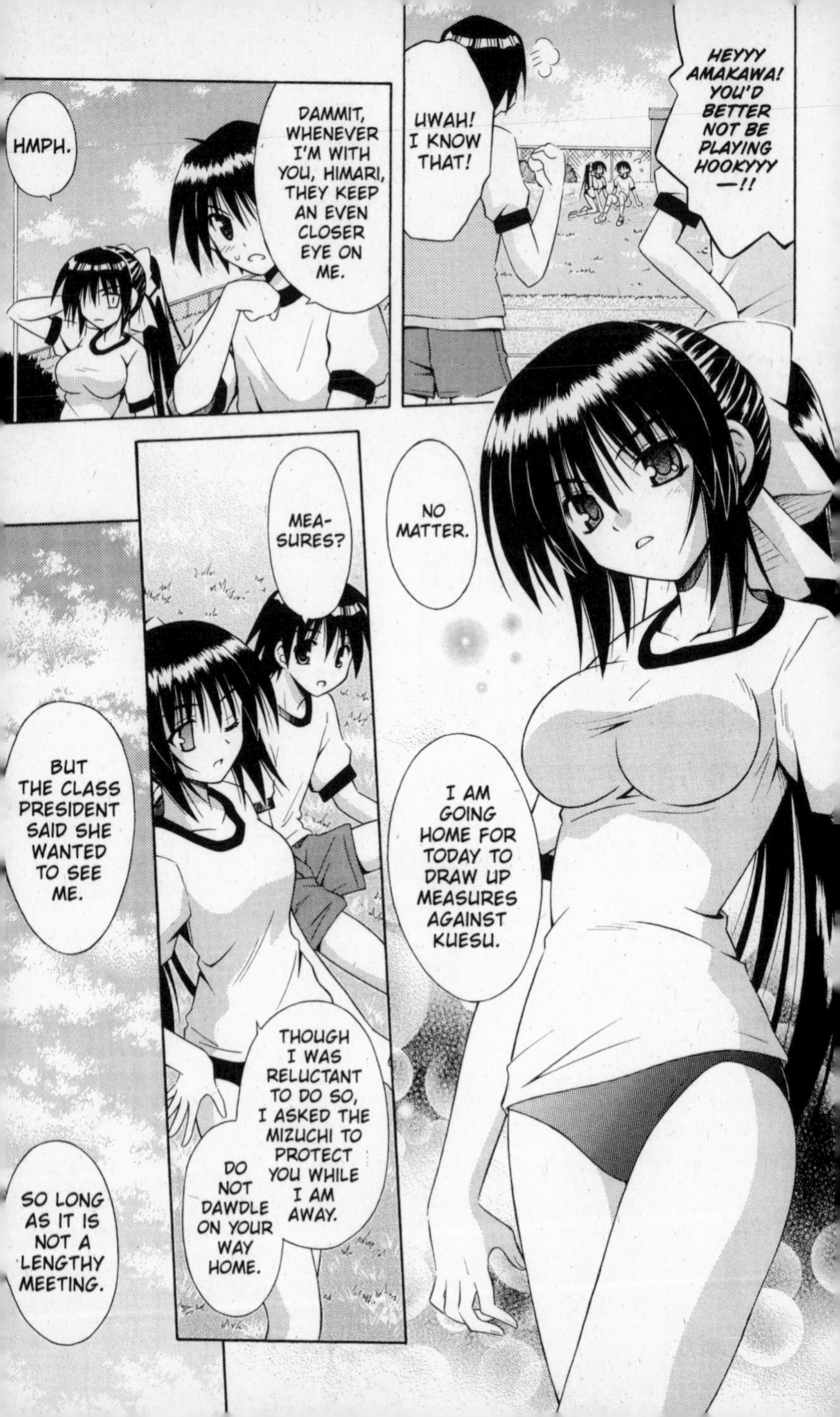
HEYYY AMAKAWA! YOU'D BETTER NOT BE PLAYING HOOKYYY—!!
UWAH! I KNOW THAT!
DAMMIT, WHENEVER I'M WITH YOU, HIMARI, THEY KEEP AN EVEN CLOSER EYE ON ME.
HMPH.
NO MATTER.
I AM GOING HOME FOR TODAY TO DRAW UP MEASURES AGAINST KUESU.
MEA-SURES?
THOUGH I WAS RELUCTANT TO DO SO, I ASKED THE MIZUCHI TO PROTECT YOU WHILE I AM AWAY.
DO NOT DAWDLE ON YOUR WAY HOME.
BUT THE CLASS PRESIDENT SAID SHE WANTED TO SEE ME.
SO LONG AS IT IS NOT A LENGTHY MEETING.

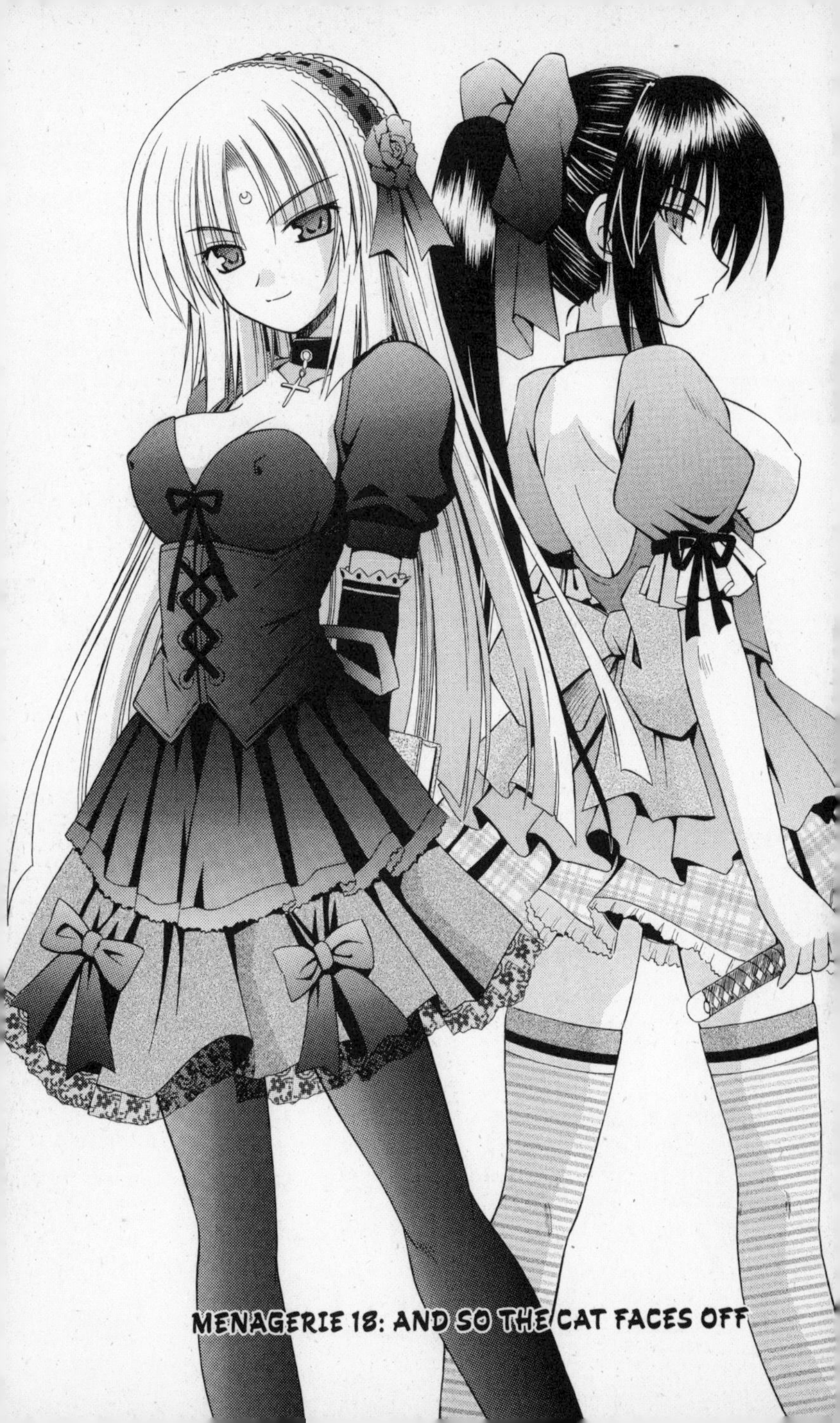
MENAGERIE 18: AND SO THE CAT FACES OFF

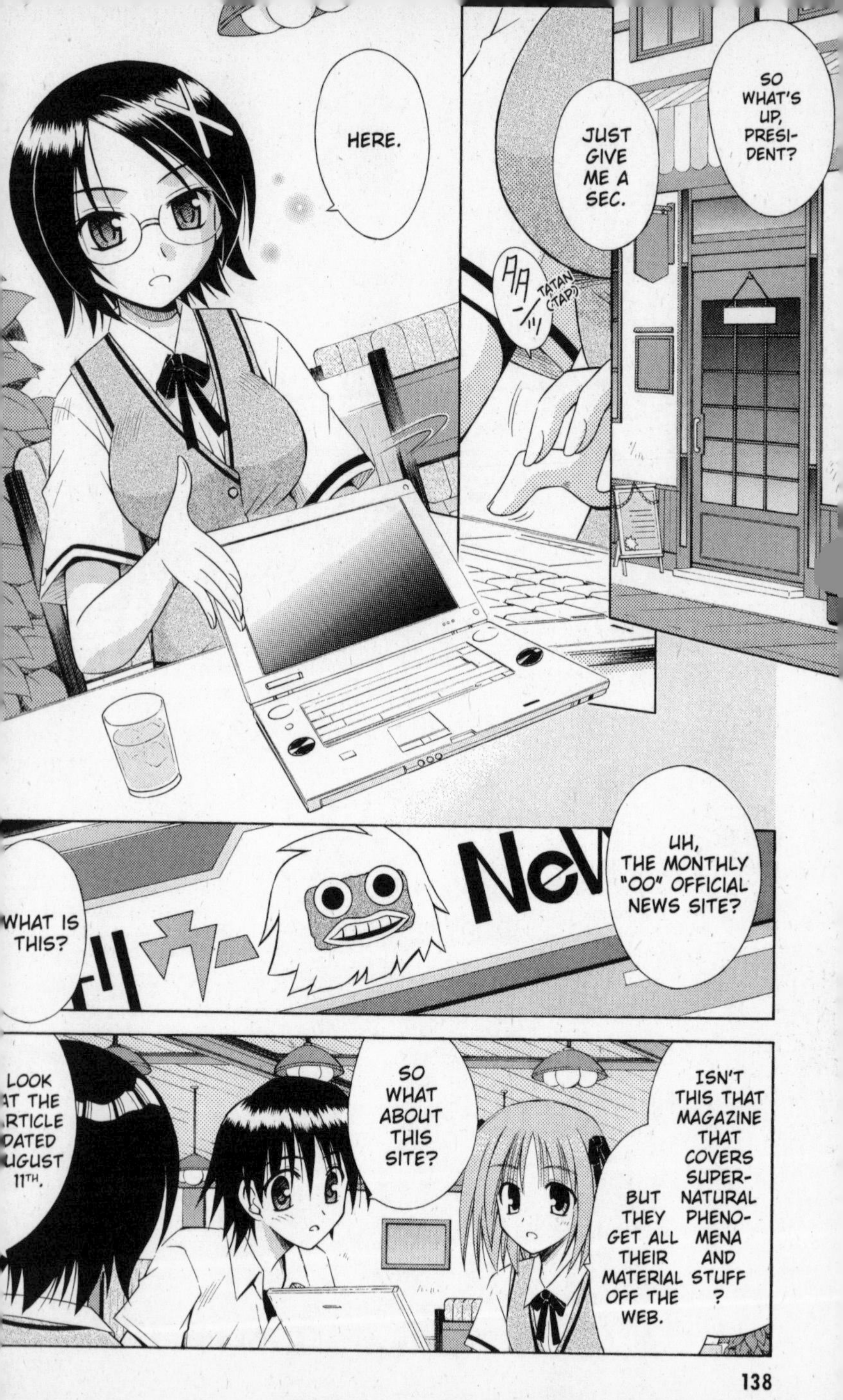
SO WHAT'S UP, PRESIDENT?
JUST GIVE ME A SEC.
TATAN (TAP)
HERE.
UH, THE MONTHLY "OO" OFFICIAL NEWS SITE?
WHAT IS THIS?
ISN'T THIS THAT MAGAZINE THAT COVERS SUPER-NATURAL PHENOMENA AND STUFF?
BUT THEY GET ALL THEIR MATERIAL OFF THE WEB.
SO WHAT ABOUT THIS SITE?
LOOK AT THE RTICLE DATED UGUST 11TH.

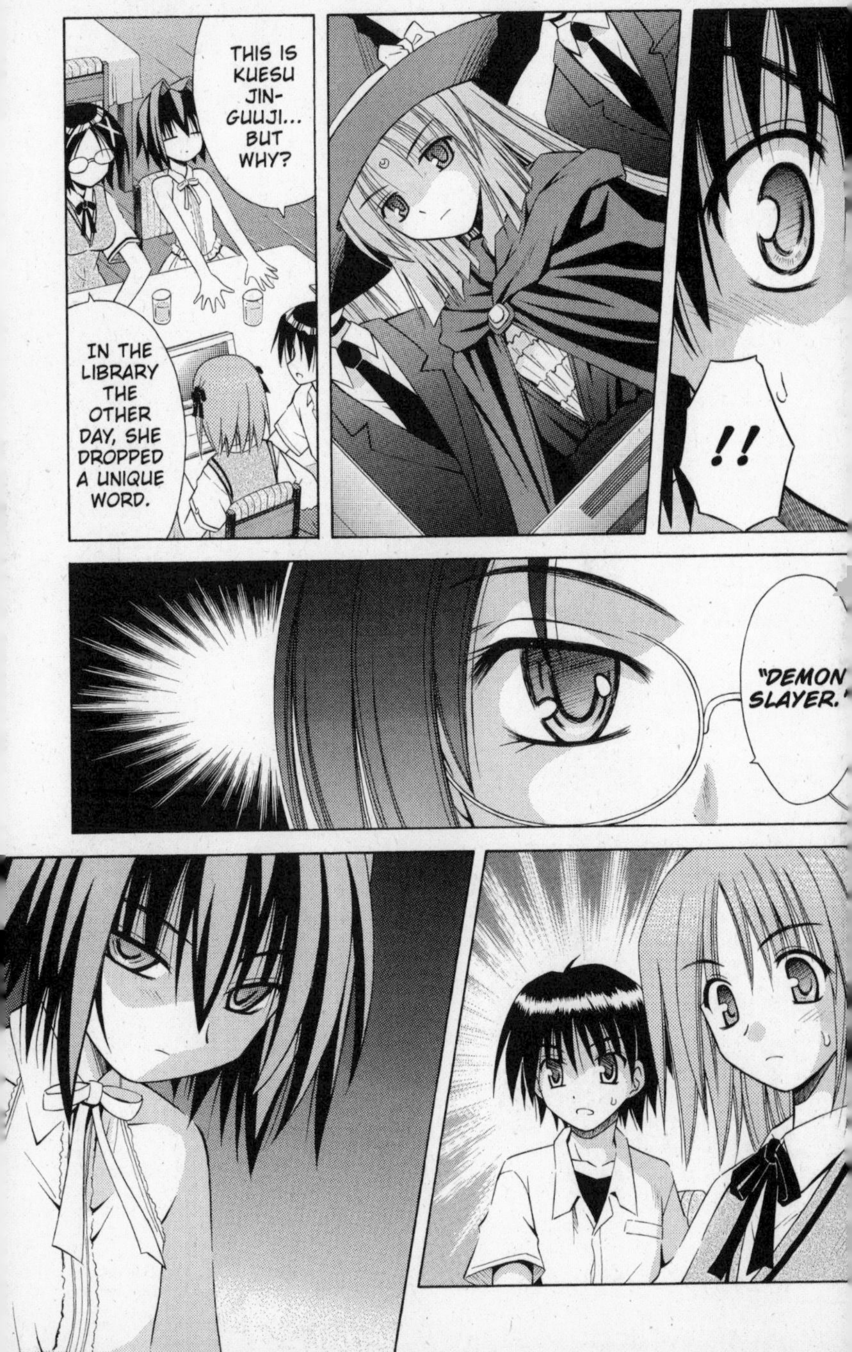
!!
THIS IS KUESU JIN-GUUJI... BUT WHY?
IN THE LIBRARY THE OTHER DAY, SHE DROPPED A UNIQUE WORD.
"DEMON SLAYER."

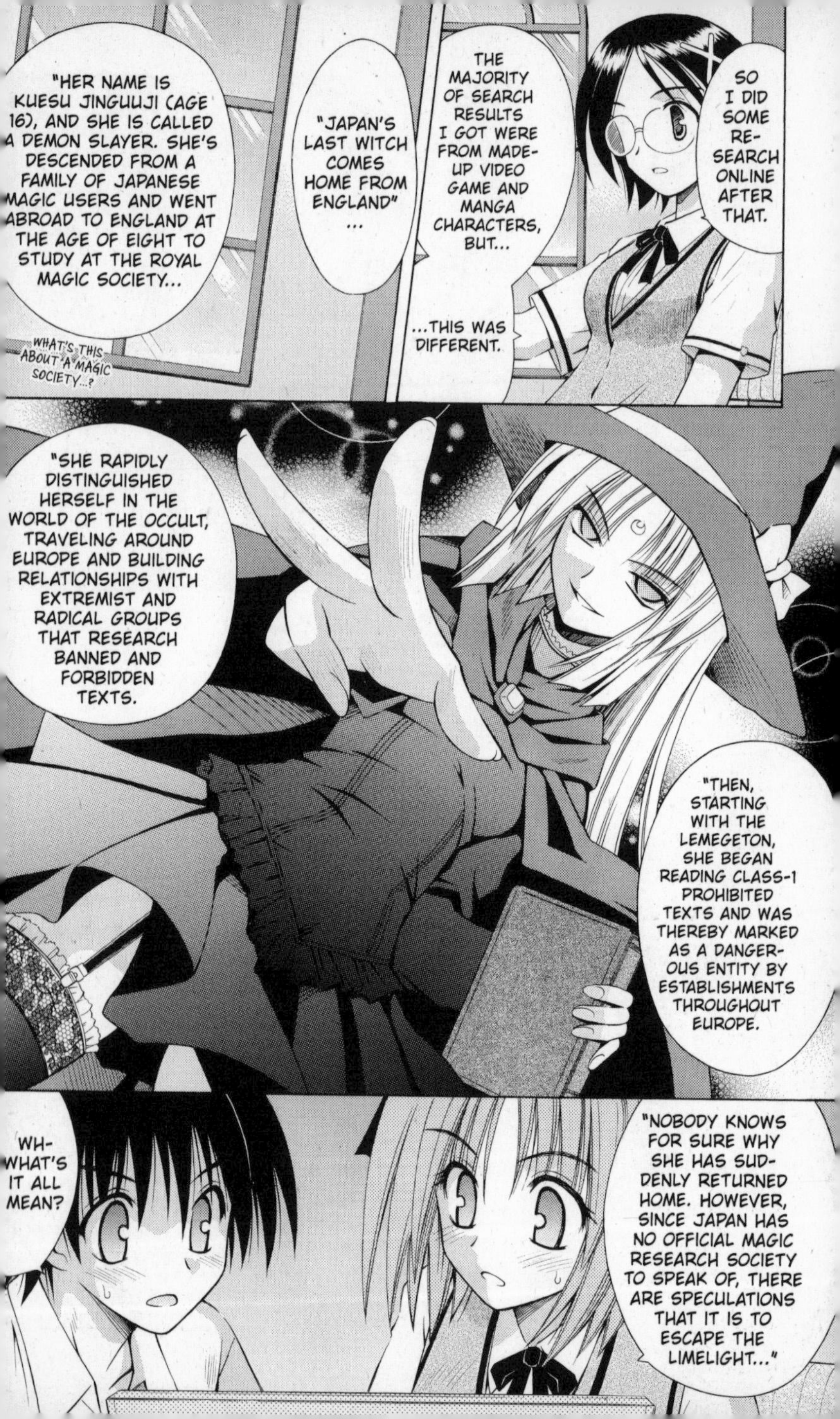
SO I DID SOME RE-SEARCH ONLINE AFTER THAT.
THE MAJORITY OF SEARCH RESULTS I GOT WERE FROM MADE-UP VIDEO GAME AND MANGA CHARACTERS, BUT...
...THIS WAS DIFFERENT.
"JAPAN'S LAST WITCH COMES HOME FROM ENGLAND" ...
"HER NAME IS KUESU JINGUUJI (AGE 16), AND SHE IS CALLED A DEMON SLAYER. SHE'S DESCENDED FROM A FAMILY OF JAPANESE MAGIC USERS AND WENT ABROAD TO ENGLAND AT THE AGE OF EIGHT TO STUDY AT THE ROYAL MAGIC SOCIETY...
WHAT'S THIS ABOUT A MAGIC SOCIETY...?
"SHE RAPIDLY DISTINGUISHED HERSELF IN THE WORLD OF THE OCCULT, TRAVELING AROUND EUROPE AND BUILDING RELATIONSHIPS WITH EXTREMIST AND RADICAL GROUPS THAT RESEARCH BANNED AND FORBIDDEN TEXTS.
"THEN, STARTING WITH THE LEMEGETON, SHE BEGAN READING CLASS-1 PROHIBITED TEXTS AND WAS THEREBY MARKED AS A DANGER-OUS ENTITY BY ESTABLISHMENTS THROUGHOUT EUROPE.
"NOBODY KNOWS FOR SURE WHY SHE HAS SUD-DENLY RETURNED HOME. HOWEVER, SINCE JAPAN HAS NO OFFICIAL MAGIC RESEARCH SOCIETY TO SPEAK OF, THERE ARE SPECULATIONS THAT IT IS TO ESCAPE THE LIMELIGHT..."
WH-WHAT'S IT ALL MEAN?

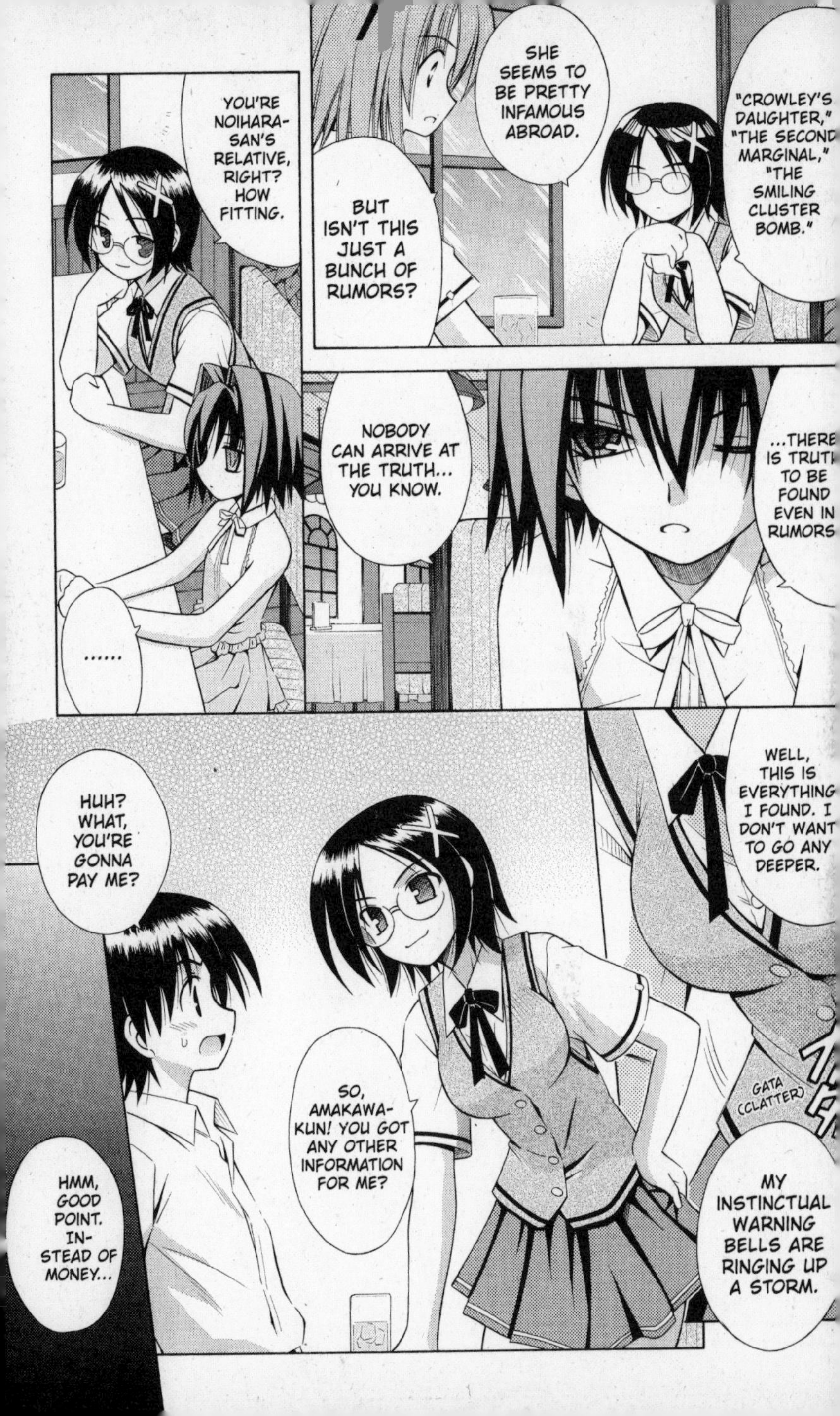
"CROWLEY'S DAUGHTER," "THE SECOND MARGINAL," "THE SMILING CLUSTER BOMB."
SHE SEEMS TO BE PRETTY INFAMOUS ABROAD.
BUT ISN'T THIS JUST A BUNCH OF RUMORS?
...THERE IS TRUTH TO BE FOUND EVEN IN RUMORS
NOBODY CAN ARRIVE AT THE TRUTH... YOU KNOW.
YOU'RE NOIHARA-SAN'S RELATIVE, RIGHT? HOW FITTING.
......
WELL, THIS IS EVERYTHING I FOUND. I DON'T WANT TO GO ANY DEEPER.
HUH? WHAT, YOU'RE GONNA PAY ME?
GATA (CLATTER)
SO, AMAKAWA-KUN! YOU GOT ANY OTHER INFORMATION FOR ME?
MY INSTINCTUAL WARNING BELLS ARE RINGING UP A STORM.
HMM, GOOD POINT. IN-STEAD OF MONEY...

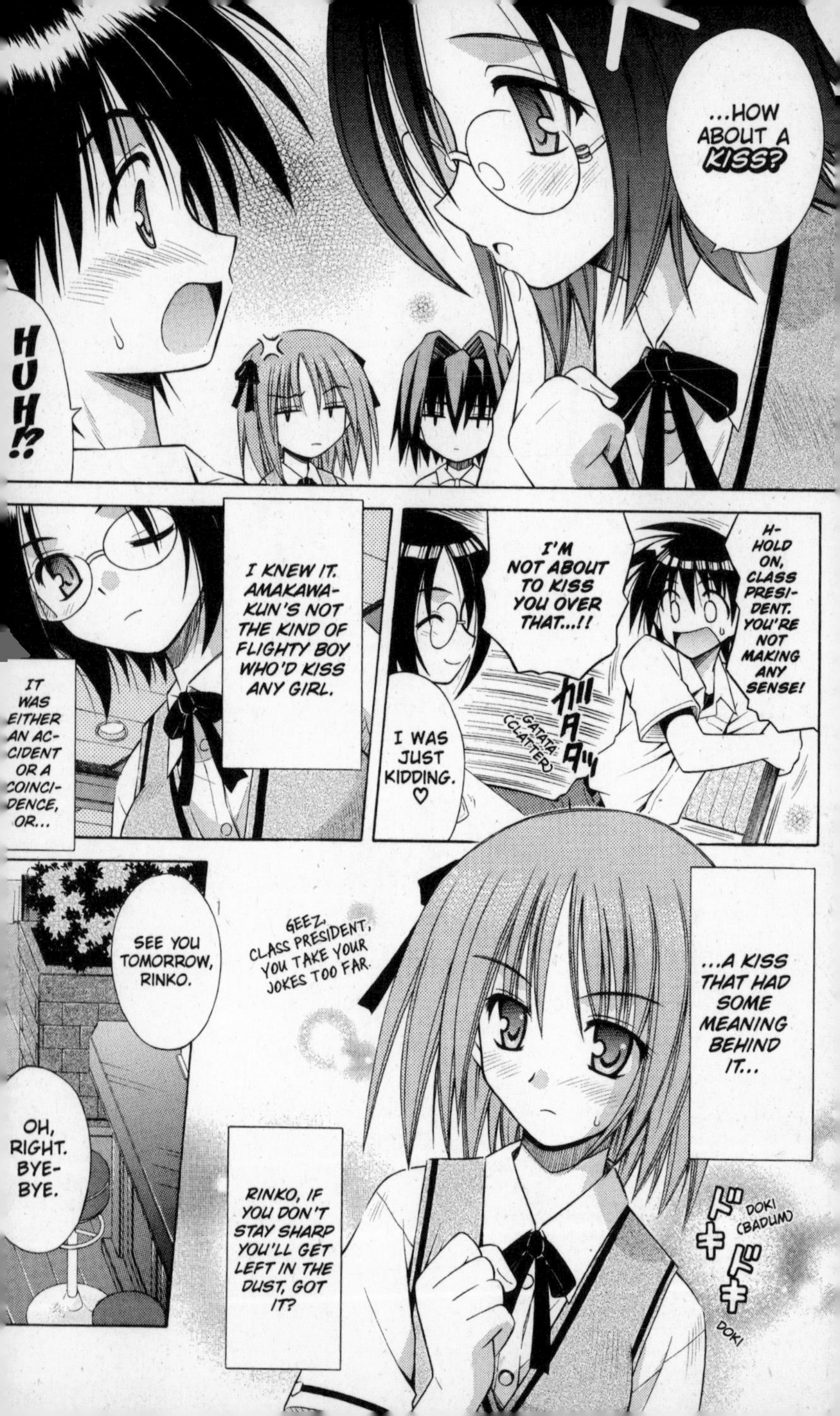
...HOW ABOUT A KISS?
HUH!?
H-HOLD ON, CLASS PRESIDENT. YOU'RE NOT MAKING ANY SENSE!
I'M NOT ABOUT TO KISS YOU OVER THAT...!!
GATATA (CLATTER)
I WAS JUST KIDDING. ♡
I KNEW IT. AMAKAWA-KUN'S NOT THE KIND OF FLIGHTY BOY WHO'D KISS ANY GIRL.
IT WAS EITHER AN ACCIDENT OR A COINCIDENCE, OR...
...A KISS THAT HAD SOME MEANING BEHIND IT...
DOKI (BADUM)
DOKI
RINKO, IF YOU DON'T STAY SHARP YOU'LL GET LEFT IN THE DUST, GOT IT?
SEE YOU TOMORROW, RINKO.
GEEZ, CLASS PRESIDENT, YOU TAKE YOUR JOKES TOO FAR.
OH, RIGHT. BYE-BYE.

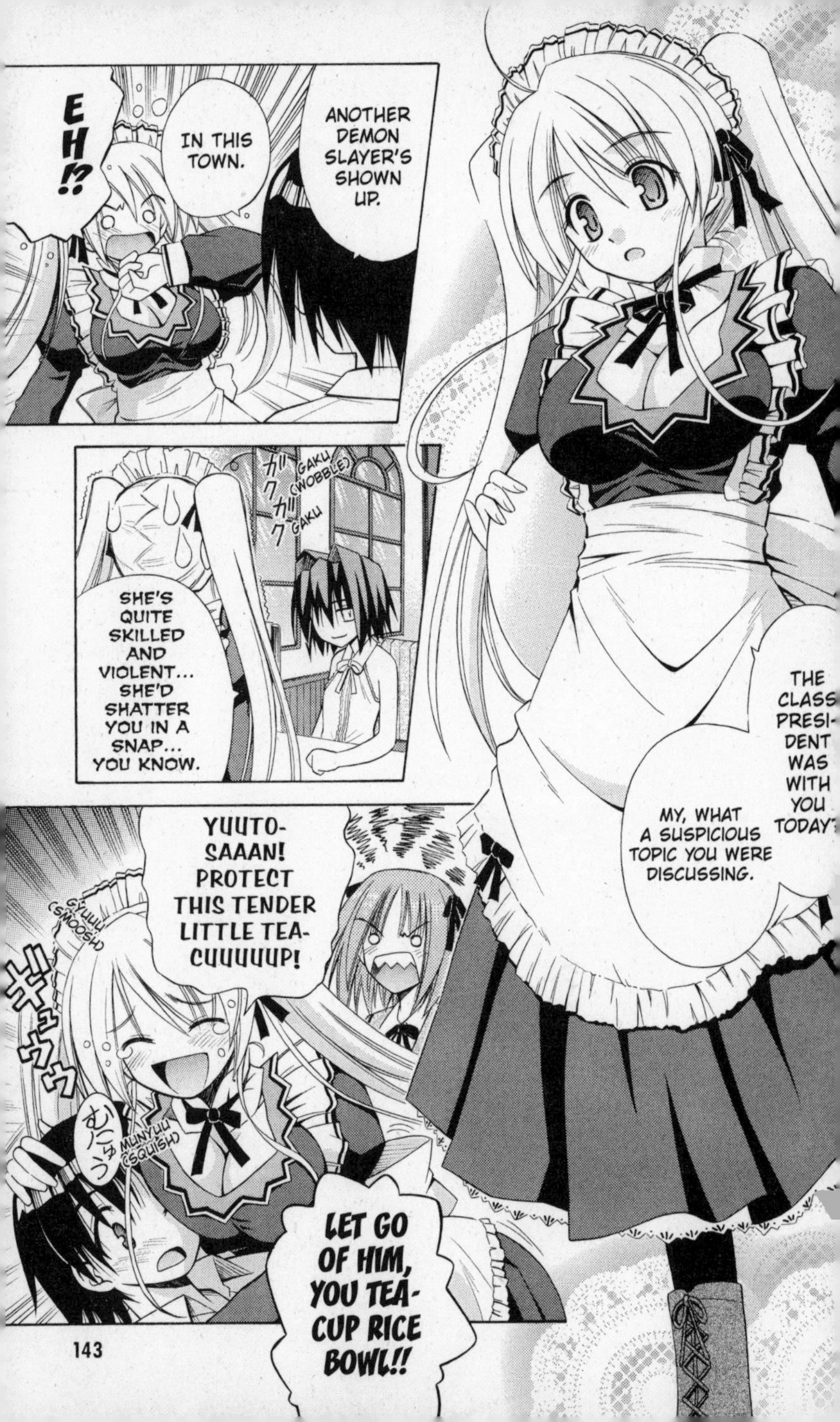
THE CLASS PRESIDENT WAS WITH YOU TODAY?
MY, WHAT A SUSPICIOUS TOPIC YOU WERE DISCUSSING.
ANOTHER DEMON SLAYER'S SHOWN UP.
IN THIS TOWN.
EH!?
GAKU (WOBBLE)
GAKU
SHE'S QUITE SKILLED AND VIOLENT... SHE'D SHATTER YOU IN A SNAP... YOU KNOW.
YUUTO-SAAAN! PROTECT THIS TENDER LITTLE TEA-CUUUUUP!
GYUUU (SMOOSH)
MUNYUU (SQUISH)
LET GO OF HIM, YOU TEA-CUP RICE BOWL!!

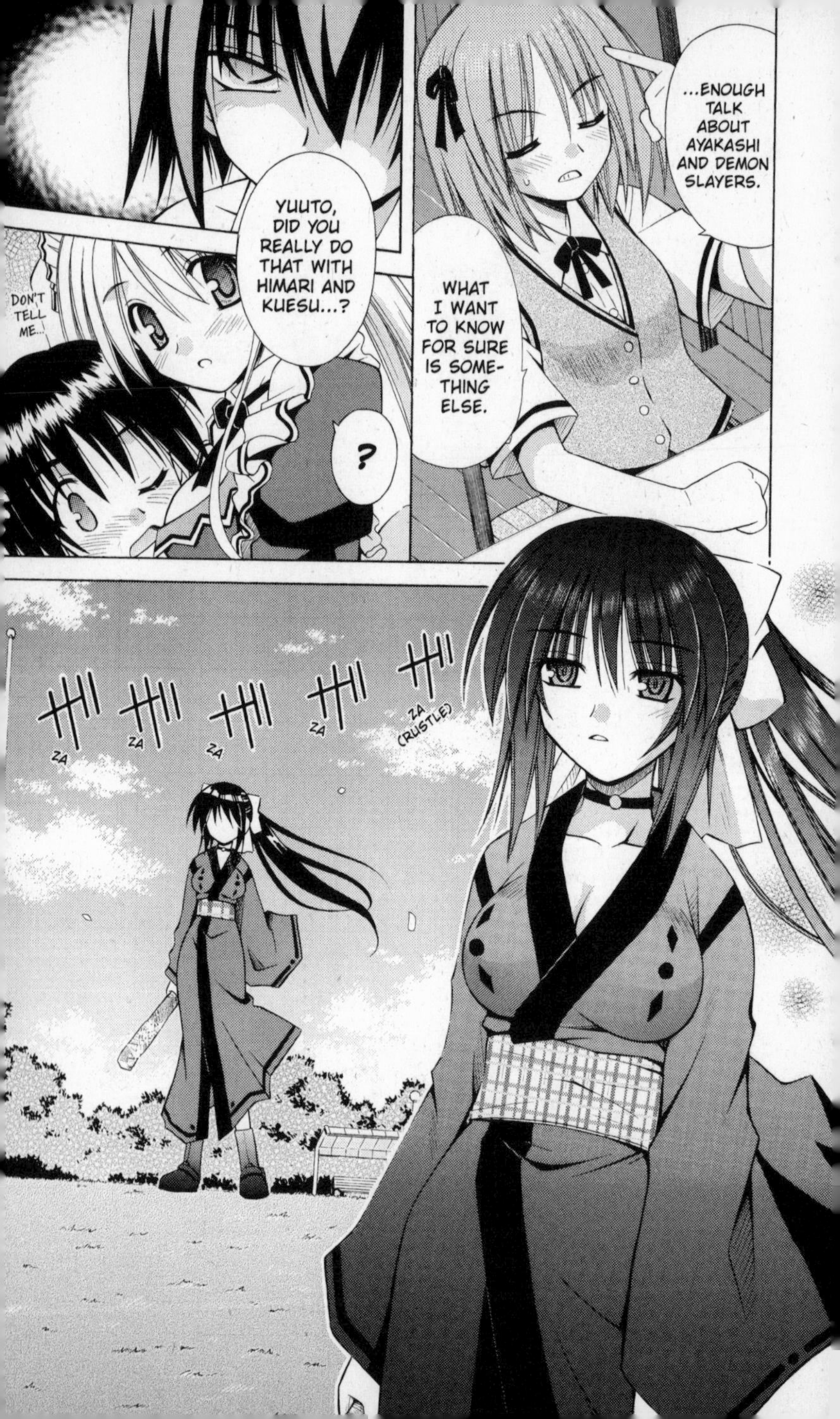
...ENOUGH TALK ABOUT AYAKASHI AND DEMON SLAYERS.
WHAT I WANT TO KNOW FOR SURE IS SOMETHING ELSE.
YUUTO, DID YOU REALLY DO THAT WITH HIMARI AND KUESU...?
?
DON'T TELL ME...
ZA (RUSTLE)
ZA
ZA
ZA
ZA

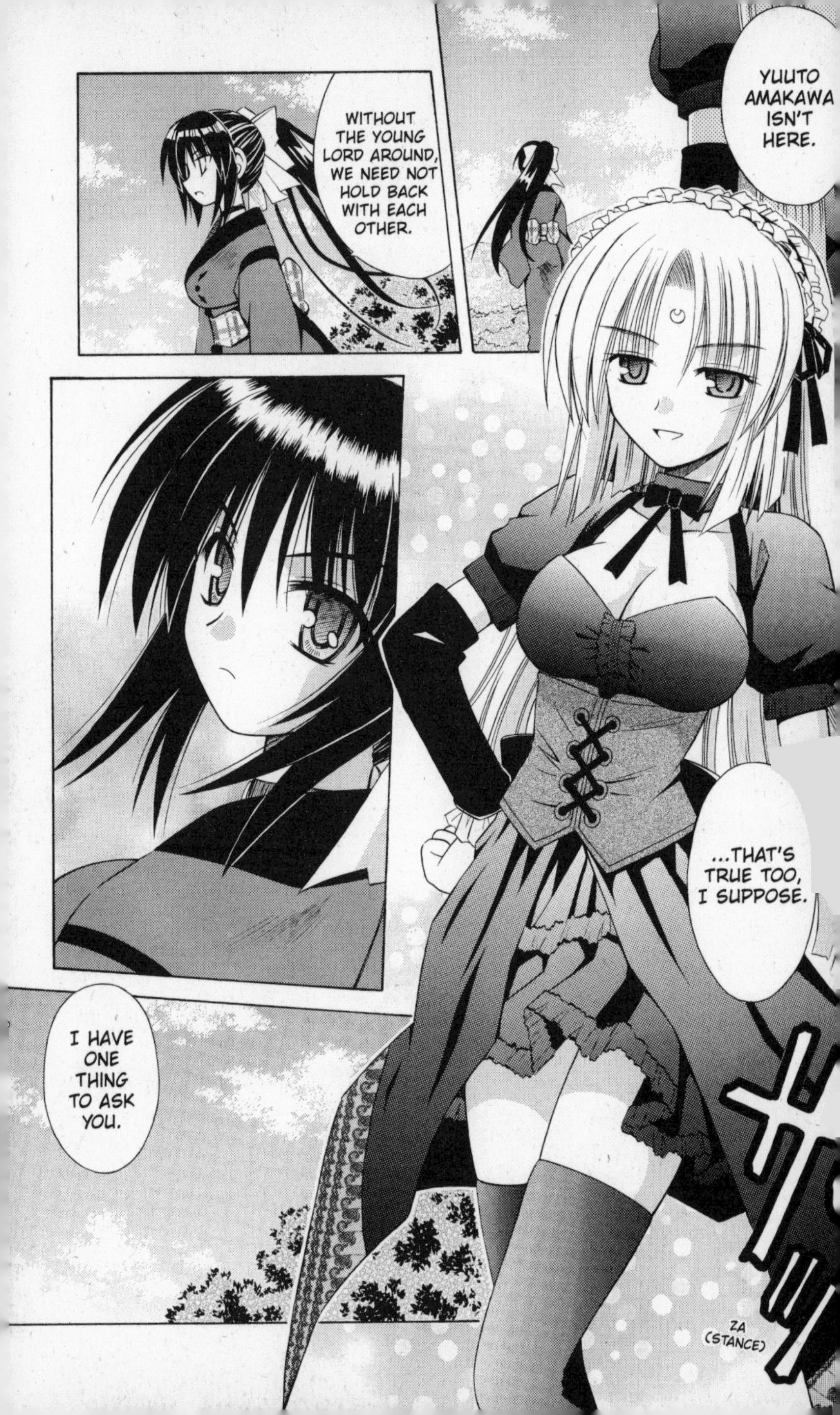
YUUTO AMAKAWA ISN'T HERE.
WITHOUT THE YOUNG LORD AROUND, WE NEED NOT HOLD BACK WITH EACH OTHER.
...THAT'S TRUE TOO, I SUPPOSE.
I HAVE ONE THING TO ASK YOU.
ZA (STANCE)

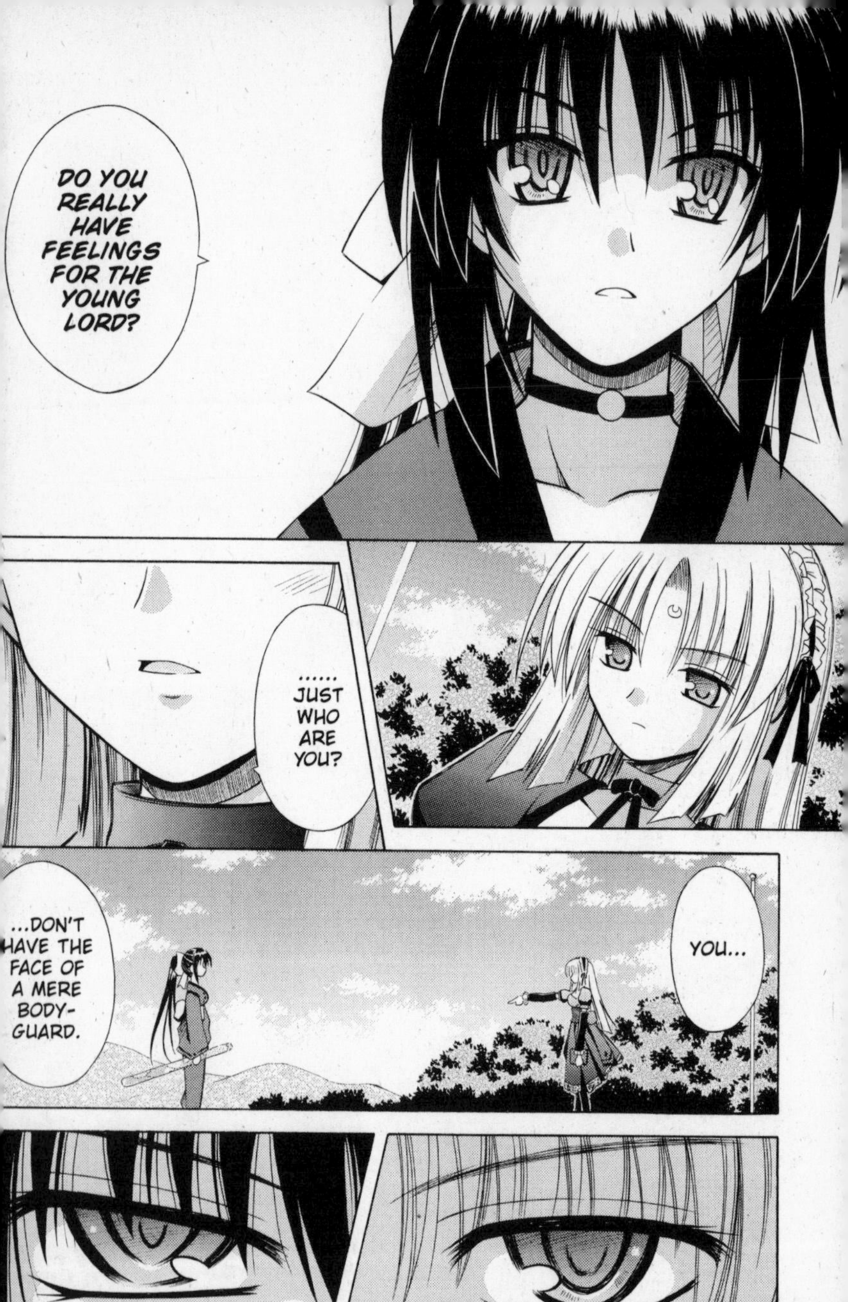
DO YOU REALLY HAVE FEELINGS FOR THE YOUNG LORD?
......JUST WHO ARE YOU?
YOU...
...DON'T HAVE THE FACE OF A MERE BODY-GUARD.

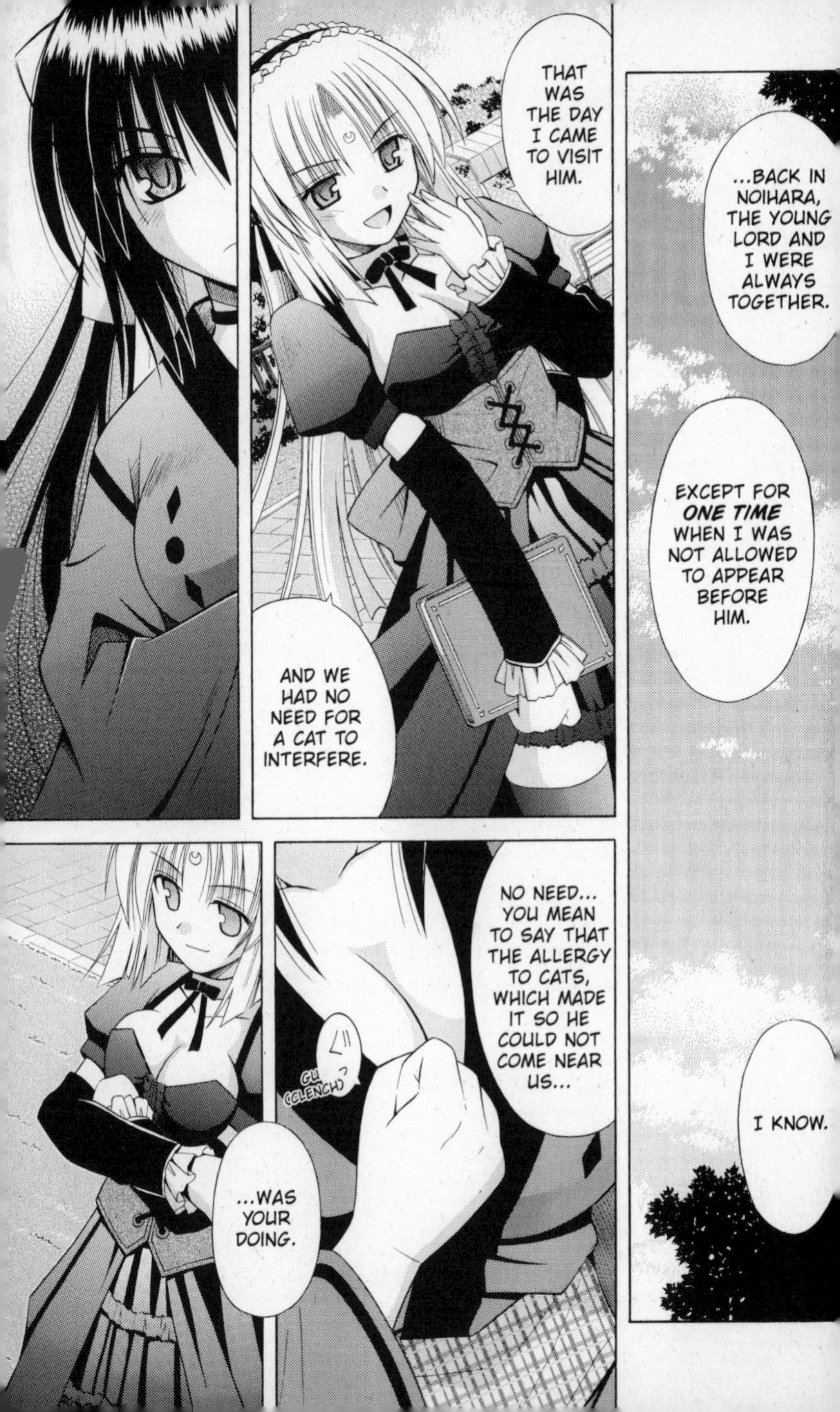
...BACK IN NOIHARA, THE YOUNG LORD AND I WERE ALWAYS TOGETHER.
EXCEPT FOR *ONE TIME* WHEN I WAS NOT ALLOWED TO APPEAR BEFORE HIM.
I KNOW.
THAT WAS THE DAY I CAME TO VISIT HIM.
AND WE HAD NO NEED FOR A CAT TO INTERFERE.
NO NEED... YOU MEAN TO SAY THAT THE ALLERGY TO CATS, WHICH MADE IT SO HE COULD NOT COME NEAR US...
GU (CLENCH)
...WAS YOUR DOING.

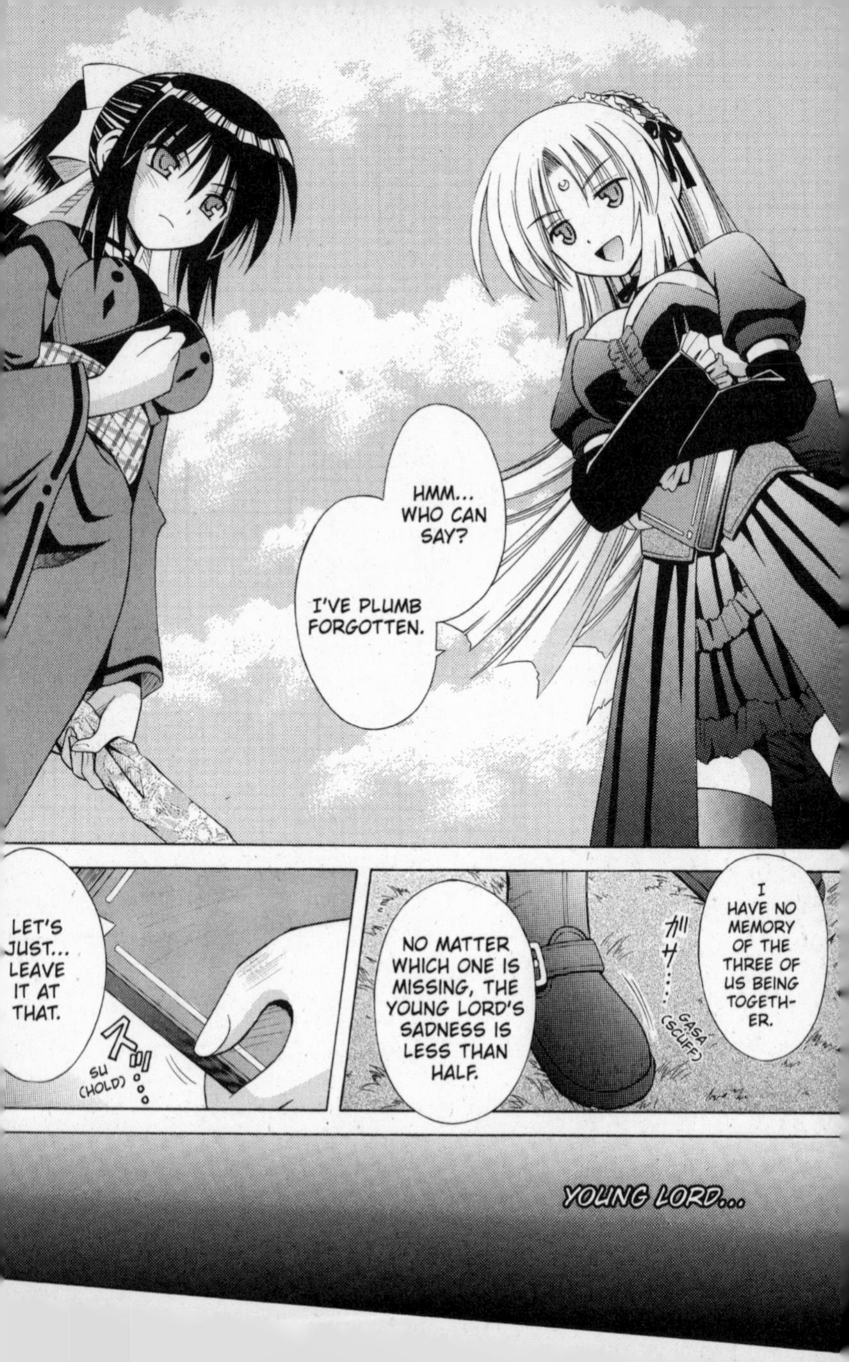
HMM... WHO CAN SAY?
I'VE PLUMB FORGOTTEN.
I HAVE NO MEMORY OF THE THREE OF US BEING TOGETH-ER.
ガサ...
GASA (SCUFF)
NO MATTER WHICH ONE IS MISSING, THE YOUNG LORD'S SADNESS IS LESS THAN HALF.
LET'S JUST... LEAVE IT AT THAT.
スッ...
SU (HOLD)
YOUNG LORD...

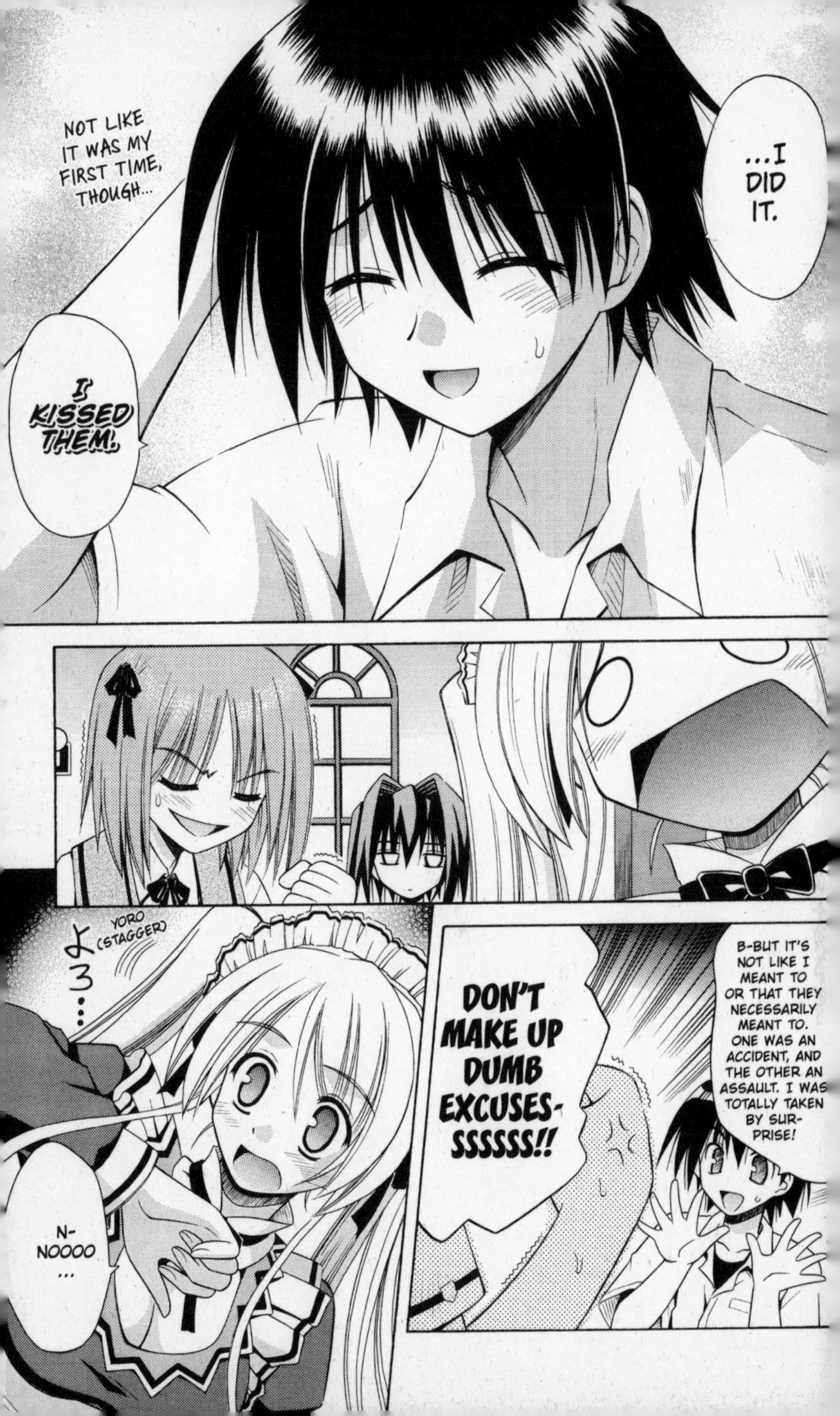
...I DID IT.
NOT LIKE IT WAS MY FIRST TIME, THOUGH...
I KISSED THEM.
B-BUT IT'S NOT LIKE I MEANT TO OR THAT THEY NECESSARILY MEANT TO. ONE WAS AN ACCIDENT, AND THE OTHER AN ASSAULT. I WAS TOTALLY TAKEN BY SUR-PRISE!
DON'T MAKE UP DUMB EXCUSES-SSSSSS!!
よろ...
YORO (STAGGER)
N-NOOOO ...

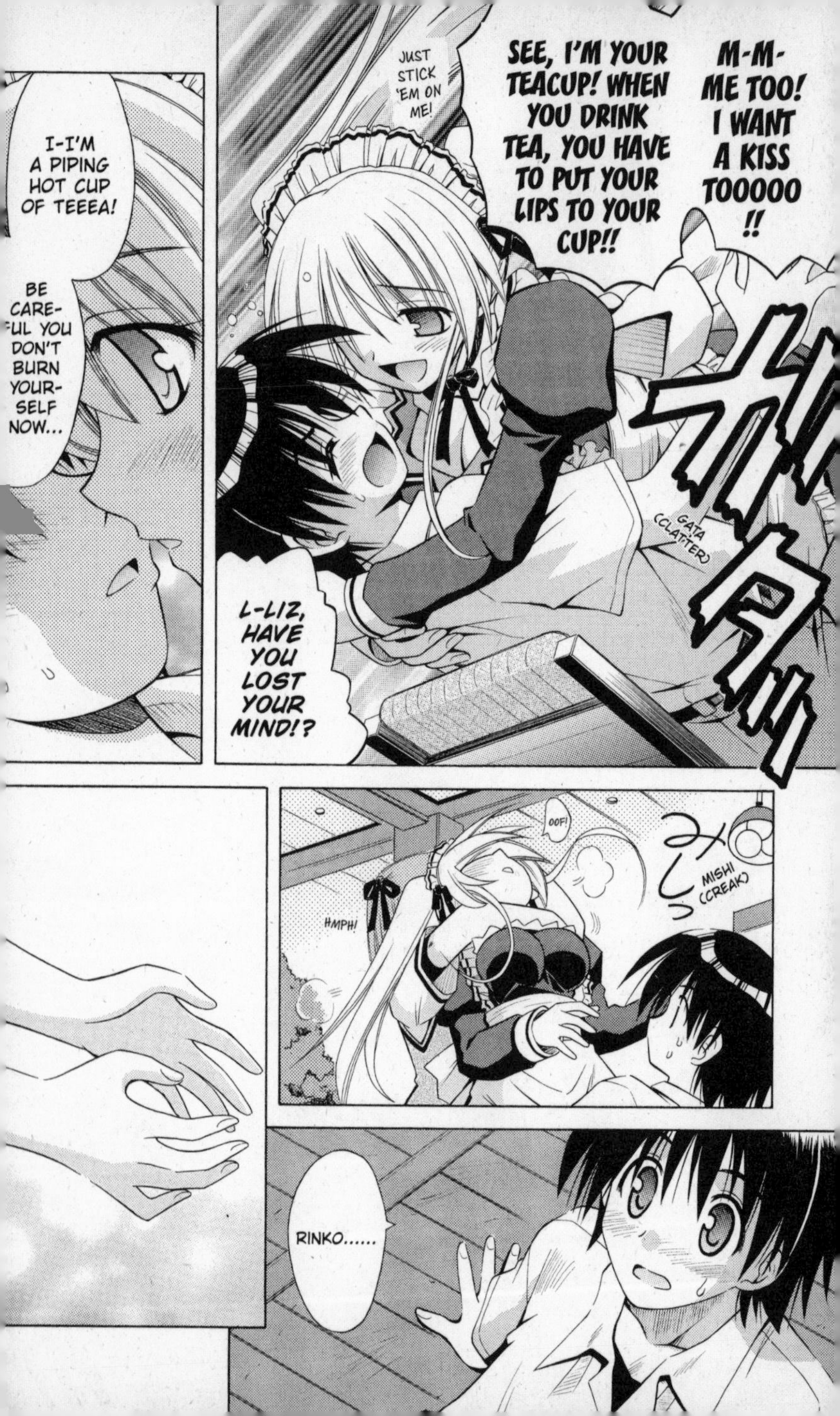
M-M-ME TOO! I WANT A KISS TOOOOO!!
SEE, I'M YOUR TEACUP! WHEN YOU DRINK TEA, YOU HAVE TO PUT YOUR LIPS TO YOUR CUP!!
JUST STICK 'EM ON ME!
GATA (CLATTER)
L-LIZ, HAVE YOU LOST YOUR MIND!?
I-I'M A PIPING HOT CUP OF TEEEA!
BE CAREFUL YOU DON'T BURN YOURSELF NOW...
MISHI (CREAK)
OOF!
HMPH!
RINKO......

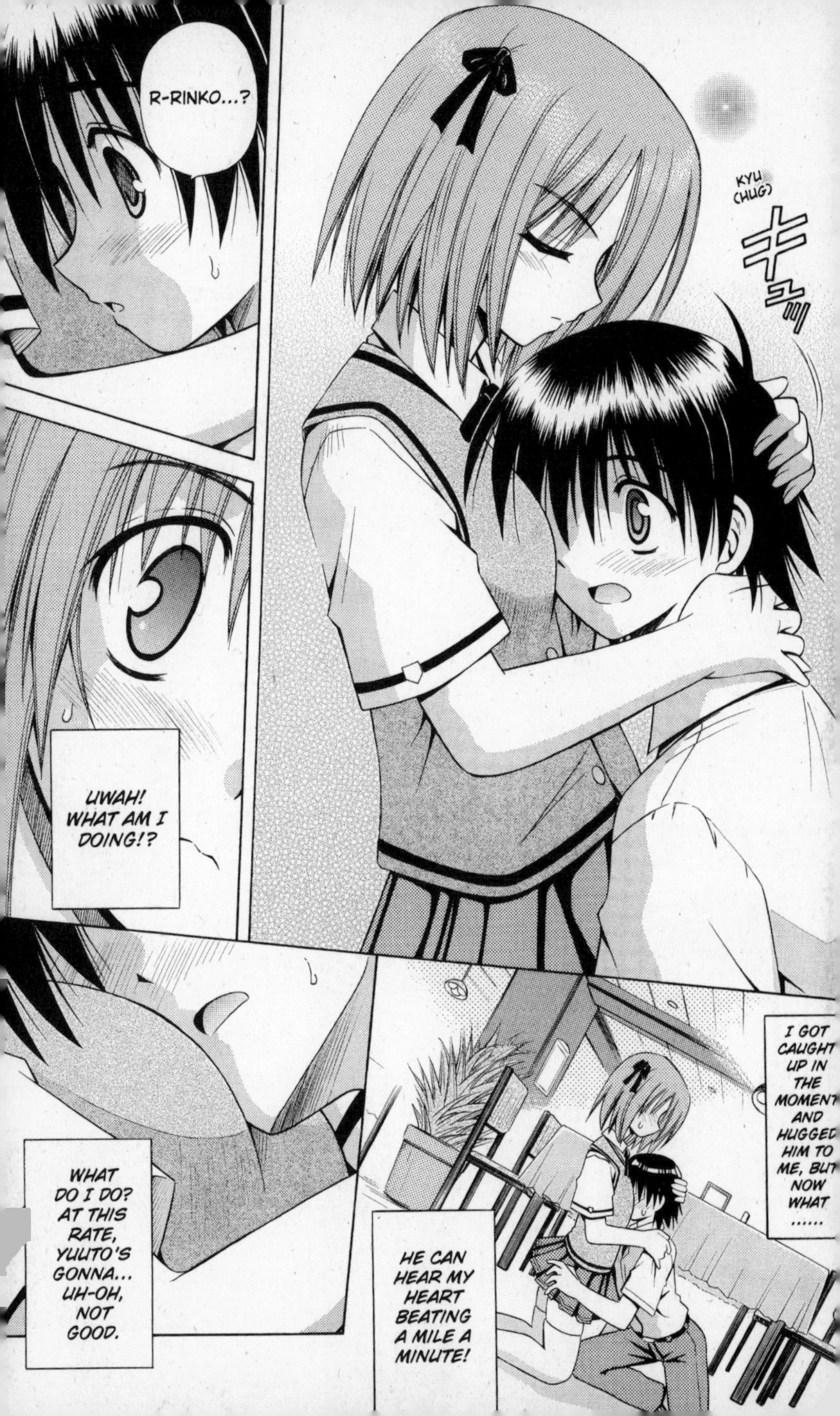
KYU (HUG)
キュッ
R-RINKO...?
UWAH! WHAT AM I DOING!?
I GOT CAUGHT UP IN THE MOMENT AND HUGGED HIM TO ME, BUT NOW WHAT ......
HE CAN HEAR MY HEART BEATING A MILE A MINUTE!
WHAT DO I DO? AT THIS RATE, YUUTO'S GONNA... UH-OH, NOT GOOD.

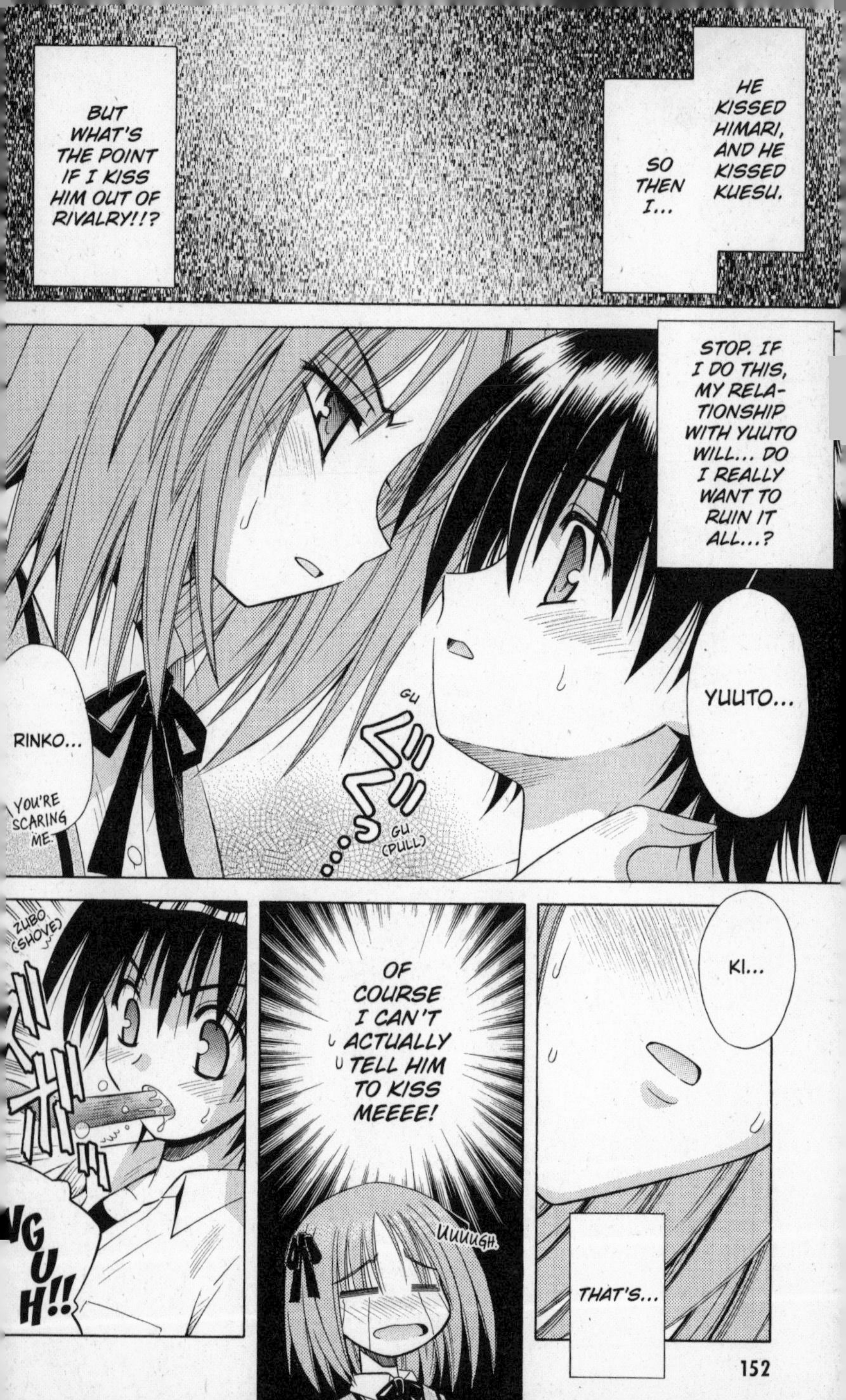
HE KISSED HIMARI, AND HE KISSED KUESU.
SO THEN I...
BUT WHAT'S THE POINT IF I KISS HIM OUT OF RIVALRY!!?
STOP. IF I DO THIS, MY RELATIONSHIP WITH YUUTO WILL... DO I REALLY WANT TO RUIN IT ALL...?
YUUTO...
GU
GU (PULL)
RINKO...
YOU'RE SCARING ME.
KI...
THAT'S...
OF COURSE I CAN'T ACTUALLY TELL HIM TO KISS MEEEE!
UUUUGH.
ZUBO (SHOVE)
NGUH!!

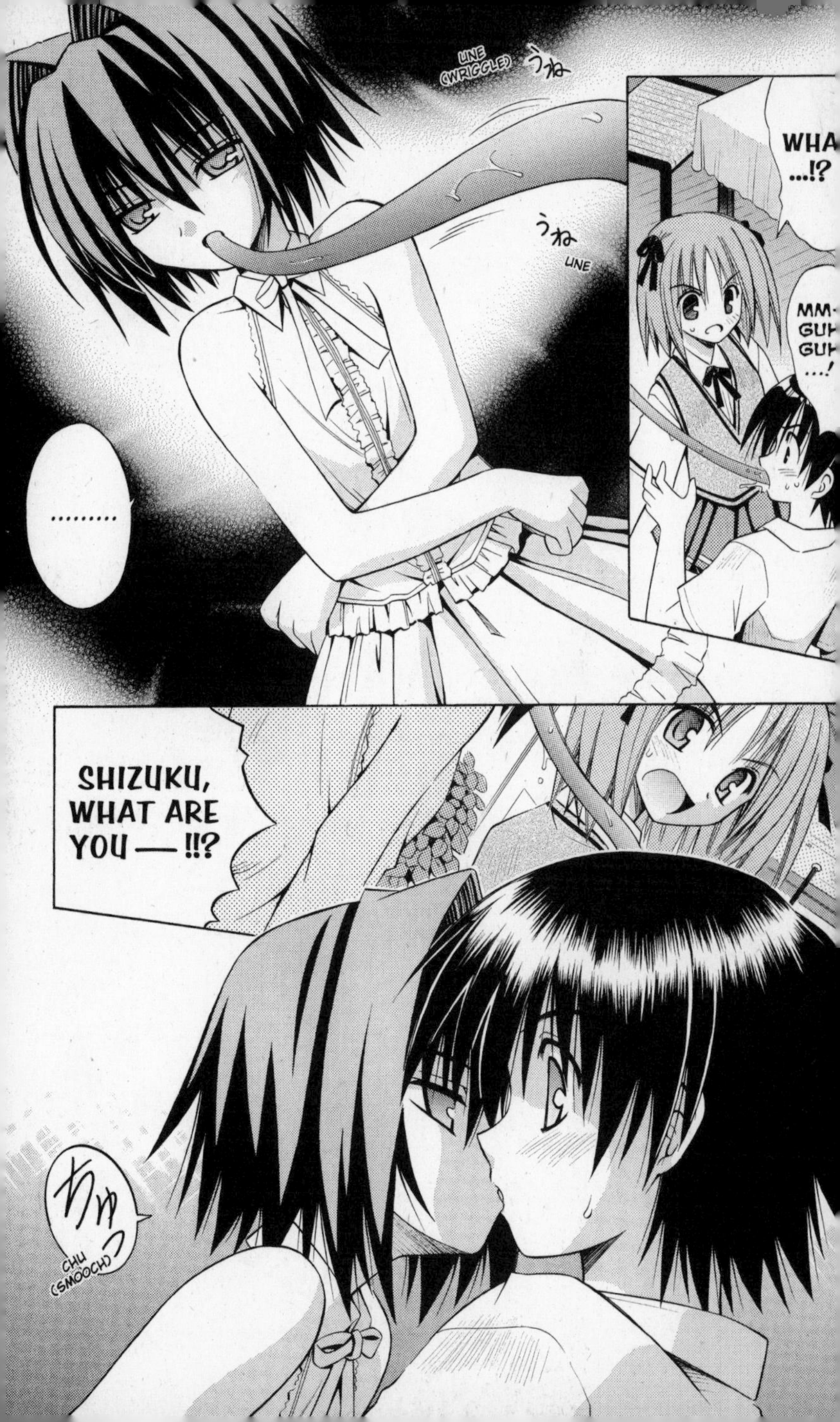
WHA ...!?
MM-GUH GUH ...!
うね
UNE (WRIGGLE)
うね
UNE
....
SHIZUKU, WHAT ARE YOU — !!?
ちゅっ
CHU (SMOOCH)

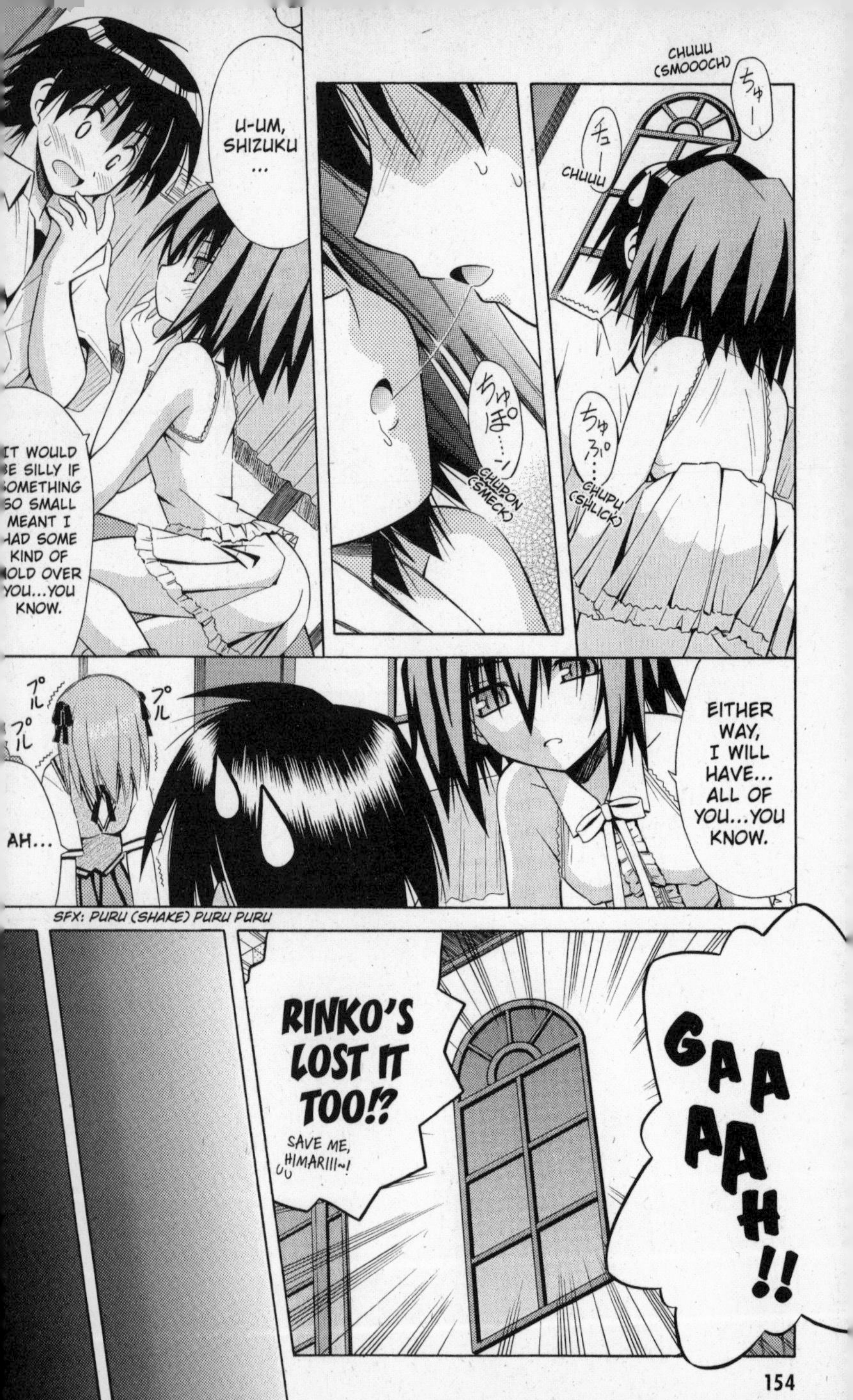
CHUUU (SMOOOCH)
ちゅー
チュー
CHUUU
ちゅぷ…
CHUPU (SHLICK)
ちゅぽ…ン
CHUPON (SMECK)
U-UM, SHIZUKU ...
IT WOULD BE SILLY IF SOMETHING SO SMALL MEANT I HAD SOME KIND OF HOLD OVER YOU...YOU KNOW.
EITHER WAY, I WILL HAVE... ALL OF YOU...YOU KNOW.
プル
プル
プル
AH...
SFX: PURU (SHAKE) PURU PURU
GAAAAH!!
RINKO'S LOST IT TOO!?
SAVE ME, HIMARIII~!

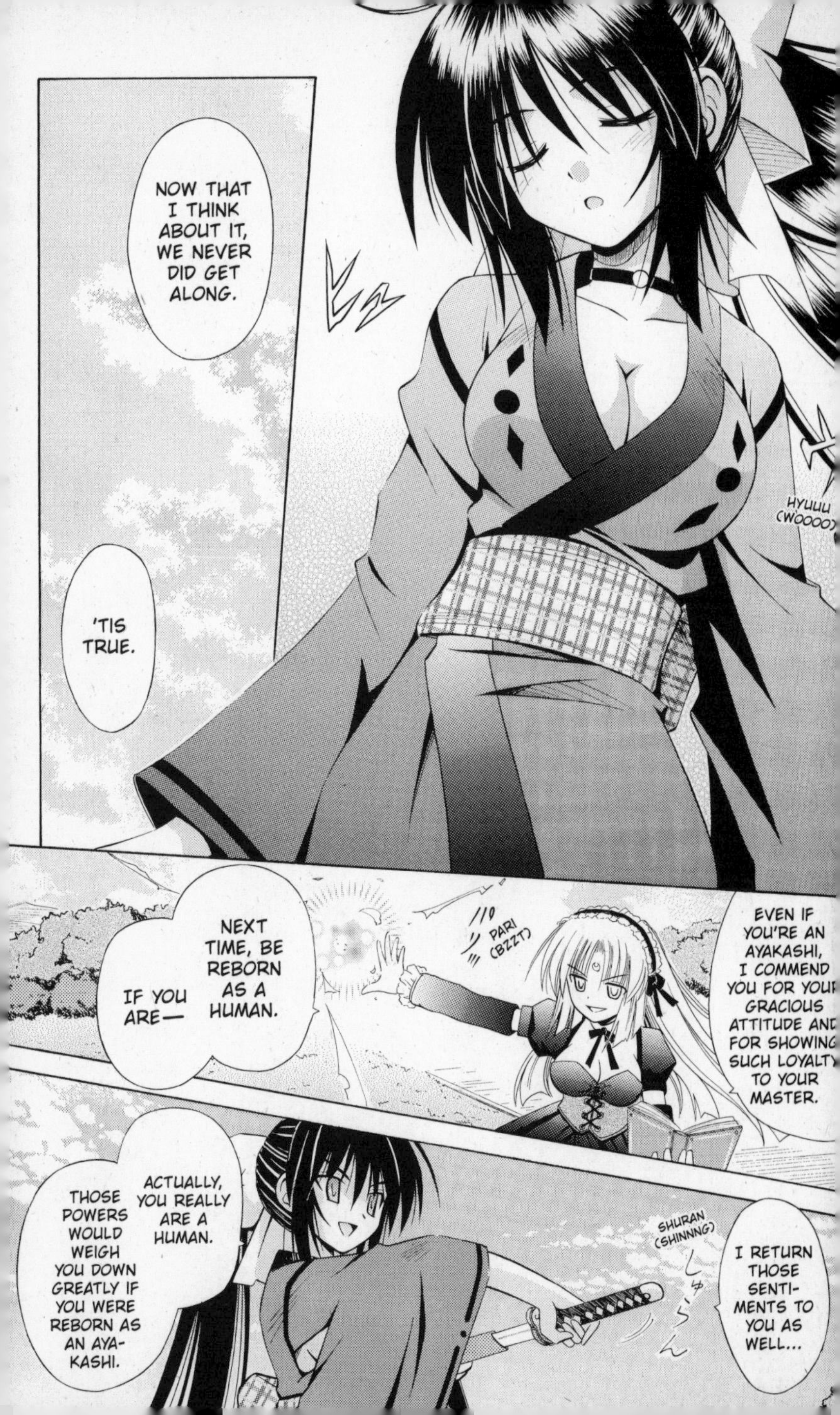
NOW THAT I THINK ABOUT IT, WE NEVER DID GET ALONG.
HYUUU (WOOOO)
'TIS TRUE.
EVEN IF YOU'RE AN AYAKASHI, I COMMEND YOU FOR YOUR GRACIOUS ATTITUDE AND FOR SHOWING SUCH LOYALTY TO YOUR MASTER.
PARI (BZZT)
NEXT TIME, BE REBORN AS A HUMAN.
IF YOU ARE—
I RETURN THOSE SENTIMENTS TO YOU AS WELL...
SHURAN (SHINNNG)
しゅらん
ACTUALLY, YOU REALLY ARE A HUMAN.
THOSE POWERS WOULD WEIGH YOU DOWN GREATLY IF YOU WERE REBORN AS AN AYAKASHI.

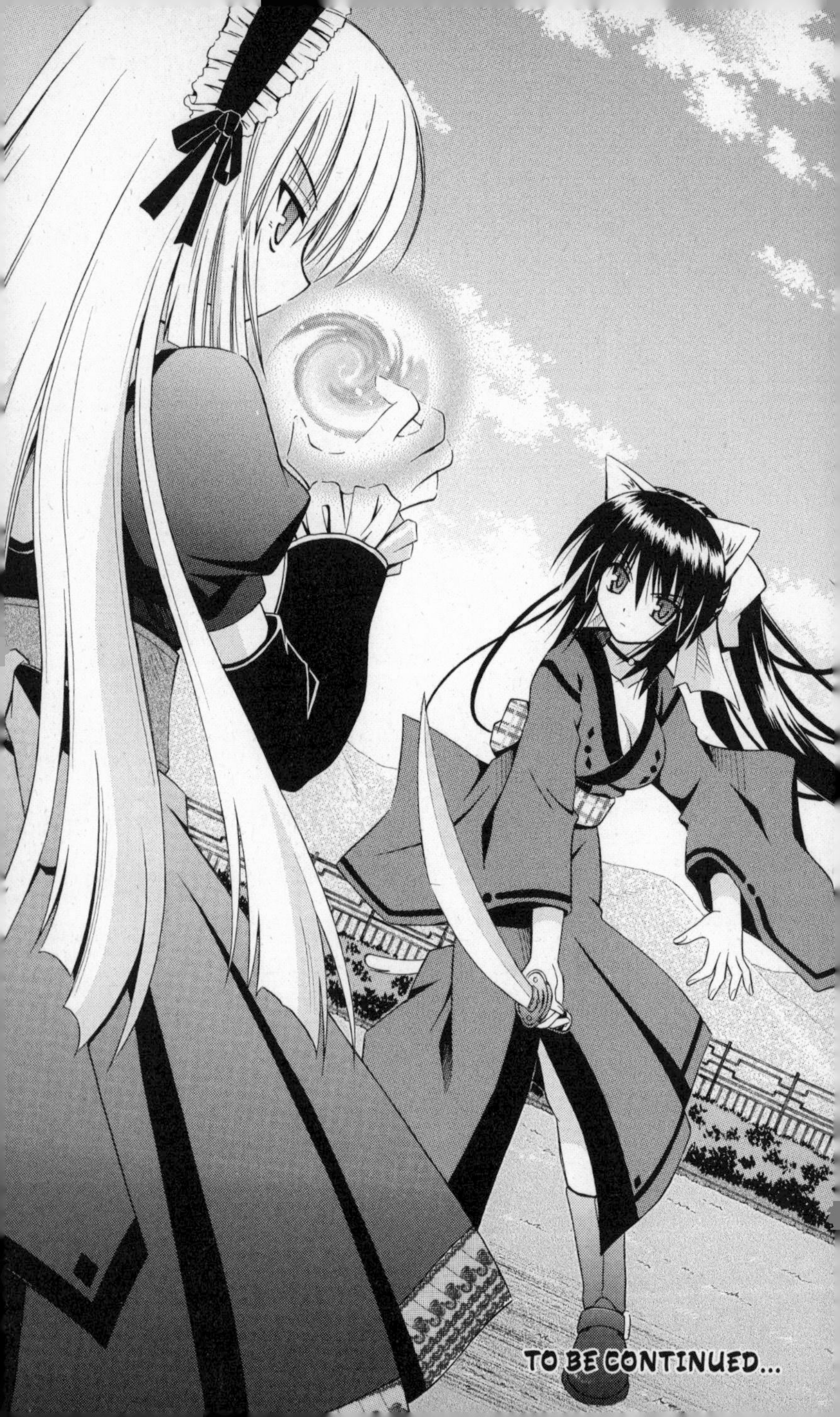
TO BE CONTINUED...

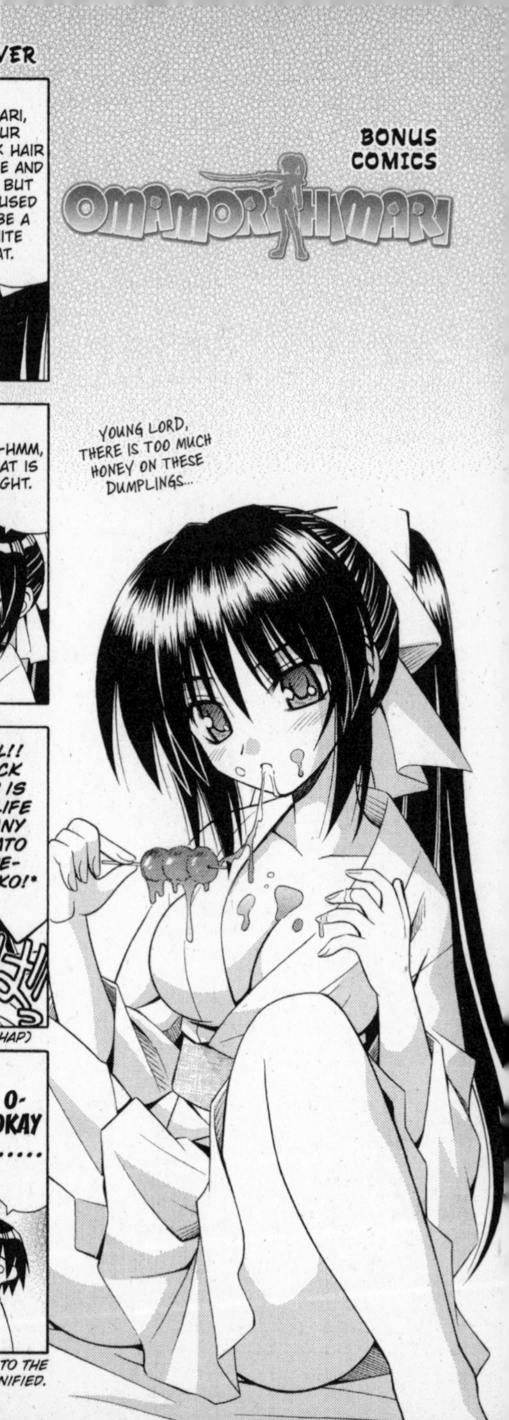
BONUS COMICS
OMAMORI HIMARI
YOUNG LORD, THERE IS TOO MUCH HONEY ON THESE DUMPLINGS...

BLACK, WHITE & BLACK ALL OVER

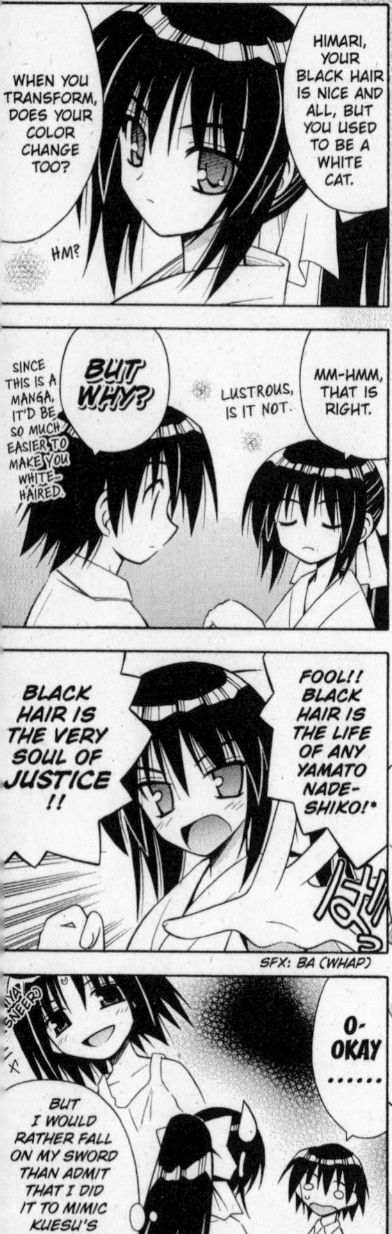
HIMARI, YOUR BLACK HAIR IS NICE AND ALL, BUT YOU USED TO BE A WHITE CAT.
WHEN YOU TRANSFORM, DOES YOUR COLOR CHANGE TOO?
HM?
MM-HMM, THAT IS RIGHT.
LUSTROUS, IS IT NOT.
BUT WHY?
SINCE THIS IS A MANGA, IT'D BE SO MUCH EASIER TO MAKE YOU WHITE-HAIRED.
FOOL!! BLACK HAIR IS THE LIFE OF ANY YAMATO NADE-SHIKO!*
BLACK HAIR IS THE VERY SOUL OF JUSTICE !!
O-OKAY ......
NIYA (SNEER)
BUT I WOULD RATHER FALL ON MY SWORD THAN ADMIT THAT I DID IT TO MIMIC KUESU'S APPEARANCE AS A CHILD...
SFX: BA (WHAP)

*YAMATO NADESHIKO IS THE NAME GIVEN TO THE TRADITIONALLY IDEAL JAPANESE WOMAN PERSONIFIED.

MODEST RINKO

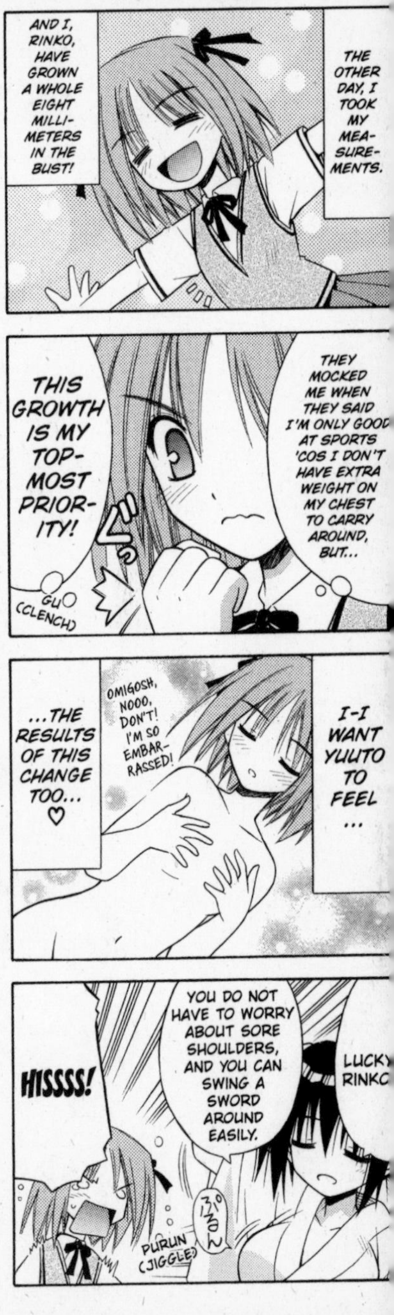

THE OTHER DAY, I TOOK MY MEASUREMENTS.
AND I, RINKO, HAVE GROWN A WHOLE EIGHT MILLIMETERS IN THE BUST!
THEY MOCKED ME WHEN THEY SAID I'M ONLY GOOD AT SPORTS 'COS I DON'T HAVE EXTRA WEIGHT ON MY CHEST TO CARRY AROUND, BUT...
THIS GROWTH IS MY TOP-MOST PRIORITY!
GU (CLENCH)
I-I WANT YUUTO TO FEEL...
OMIGOSH, NOOO, DON'T! I'M SO EMBARRASSED!
...THE RESULTS OF THIS CHANGE TOO... ♡
YOU DO NOT HAVE TO WORRY ABOUT SORE SHOULDERS, AND YOU CAN SWING A SWORD AROUND EASILY.
HISSSS!
PURUN (JIGGLE)

BUT HER AGE IS UNKNOWN

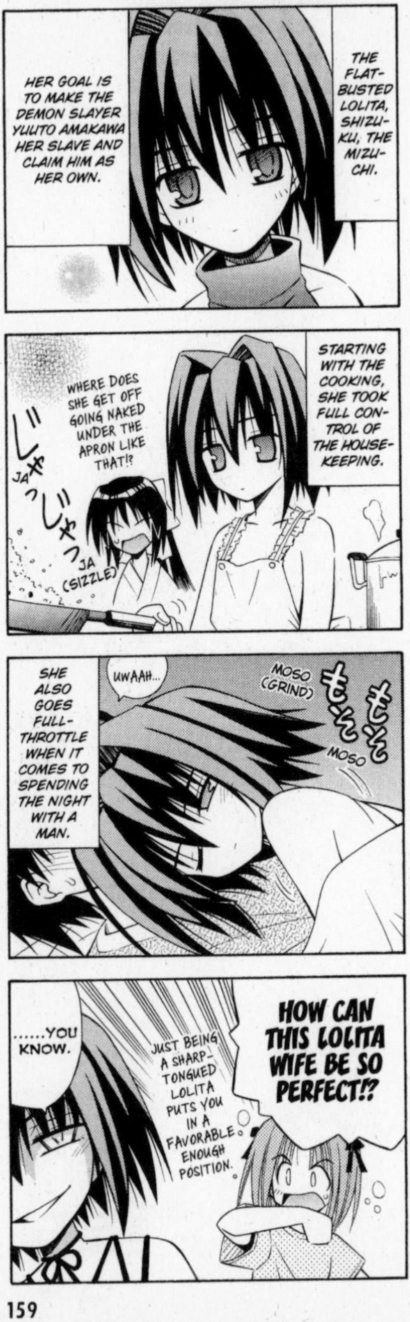

THE FLAT-BUSTED LOLITA, SHIZUKU, THE MIZUCHI.
HER GOAL IS TO MAKE THE DEMON SLAYER YUUTO AMAKAWA HER SLAVE AND CLAIM HIM AS HER OWN.
STARTING WITH THE COOKING, SHE TOOK FULL CONTROL OF THE HOUSEKEEPING.
WHERE DOES SHE GET OFF GOING NAKED UNDER THE APRON LIKE THAT!?
JA JA (SIZZLE)
MOSO (GRIND) MOSO
UWAAH...
SHE ALSO GOES FULL-THROTTLE WHEN IT COMES TO SPENDING THE NIGHT WITH A MAN.
HOW CAN THIS LOLITA WIFE BE SO PERFECT!?
JUST BEING A SHARP-TONGUED LOLITA PUTS YOU IN A FAVORABLE ENOUGH POSITION.
......YOU KNOW.

OMAMORI HIMARI

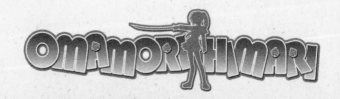

AFTERWORD

WOW, IT'S VOLUME THREE. VOLUME THREE!

THE FARTHEST MY SERIES HAVE EVER GOTTEN IS ONLY TWO VOLUMES, SO I FEEL I'VE ENTERED FOREIGN TERRITORY. USUALLY, WHEN I'M GIVEN THIS MUCH TO WORK WITH, I GET USED TO THE CHARACTERS AND STORY-WRITING AND REALLY NAIL DOWN MY WORK PROCESS INTO AN EFFICIENT SYSTEM, BUT...IT TAKES A WHOLE LOT MORE TIME NOW THAN IT DID THE FIRST TIME AROUND!! ONE REASON MIGHT BE BECAUSE I TOOK TOO LONG SEARCHING FOR THE PERFECT CROTCH SHOT REFERENCE...(HEH).

MATRA MILAN

2008.1 的良みらん

THANKS TO STUDIO HIBARI
NAGU-CHAN & MOGAMI-KUN & YOU

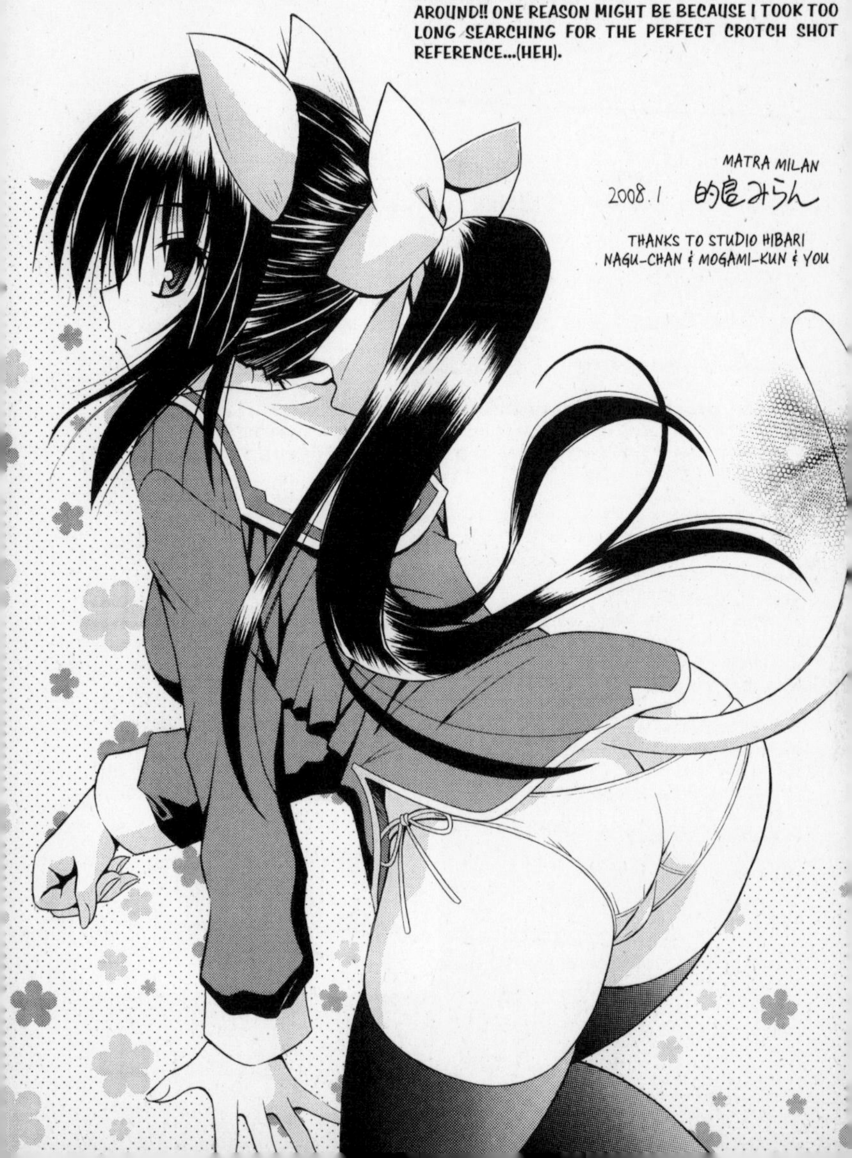

OMAMORI HIMARI ❸

MILAN MATRA

Translation: Christine Dashiell　•　Lettering: Hope Donovan

OMAMORI HIMARI Volume 3 © MATRA MILAN 2008. First published in Japan in 2008 by FUJIMISHOBO CO., LTD., Tokyo. English translation rights arranged with KADOKAWA SHOTEN Co., Ltd., Tokyo through TUTTLE-MORI AGENCY, INC., Tokyo.

Translation © 2011 by Hachette Book Group, Inc.

Yen Press
Hachette Book Group
237 Park Avenue, New York, NY 10017

www.HachetteBookGroup.com
www.YenPress.com

Yen Press is an imprint of Hachette Book Group, Inc. The Yen Press name and logo are trademarks of Hachette Book Group, Inc.

First Yen Press Edition: April 2011

ISBN: 978-0-7595-3181-9

10 9 8 7 6 5 4 3 2 1

BVG

Printed in the United States of America